Road to Montevideo

A diary by

Helen Richardson Coyle

PowerPress

Published by
Power Press
2617 East Randolph Avenue
Alexandria, Virginia 22301

ISBN: 984-31-1253-9

Dedicated to my grandchildren:

Sunshine, Brendan, Ali, Megan,
Scott, Ben, Ty, and Drew

"My country is the world, and my religion is to do good."

--Thomas Paine

While preparing our childhood home for sale in 1997, my brother, Rich, and I discovered a set of our mother's journals, kept during her bicycle trips in the late 1930's and early 1940's. As children, we were raised on tales of her extraordinary bicycle adventures and now we had in hand a complete record of these trips, including her most ambitious one: a one-year South American trip in 1941-42.

Her South American trip was contained in four volumes. She made entries almost every day. The tiny, fading pencil print and the brittle paper made it imperative to transcribe her writings into a more lasting and readable form. I have done my best to transfer her words into this book. Italics indicate place names and Spanish phrases, their accuracy checked by dictionary, atlas or other sources. Some proper names were illegible and are therefore guesses.

Overwhelmingly, her journal is a window on a wonderfully adventurous woman and her love of the many simple and joyous pleasures of life.

The introduction provides some genealogical and other background information. I have included an article, "Ahead of Her Time," from the 2001 winter issue of SPOKES magazine (www.spokesmag.com). It was written by Patrick Gilsenen who did a magnificent job of interviewing my mother and summarizing her South American adventure. It is reprinted with the permission of the author and SPOKES editor, Neil Sandler. Thanks to Joseph Yacinski of Yacinski Design for his beautiful cover design and to my wife, Jean Albright, for her careful editing of the text.

This is the second edition of Road to Montevideo. In response to the SPOKES article and a review by Michael McCoy in the August 2002 issue of Adventure Cyclist (www.adventurecycling.org), we sold out the first printing.

William T. Coyle
13 W. Windsor Ave.
Alexandria, Virginia 22301
wtcoyle@hotmail.com
May 2003

Road to Montevideo

A Single Woman's One-Year Bicycle Adventure in South America, 1941-42

Helen Richardson, a single woman of 27, embarked on a very unique adventure on November 21, 1941. With war raging in Europe and about to begin in the Pacific, she set sail from San Francisco, California, in a banana boat for South America, where she would spend a year cycling on her own. First a short trip through Panama and then on to Valparaiso, Chile, where she began a much longer journey that would take her over the Andes, across the Argentine *Pampas* to Buenos Aires and finally to Uruguay. Her trip was abruptly cut short in Uruguay, where she was detained for two weeks in Sept. 1942 on suspicion of being a Nazi spy. After 6,000 miles of cycling, she was ordered to return to the United States by the U.S. State Department, thus ending a year early her planned two-year adventure. This is the story of a fiercely independent woman, undertaking the adventure of her life, a journey rarely heard of even today.

Helen was born in California in 1914 to Martha and Walter Richardson. Both of her parents were of prominent lineage: her mother was a Bebb, daughter of a noted botanist and the granddaughter of William Bebb, the Governor of Ohio in 1846-49 and an appointee in the Lincoln Administration. A first cousin on her mother's side, Norman Mason, was Administrator of the Housing and Home Finance Agency during the Eisenhower Administration. Her father was an eastern transplant whose uncle, John Pierce, was a founder of the American Radiator and Standard Sanitary Co. (now American Standard Co.). Pierce had no children and willed part of his fortune to his stepsister, Helen's grandmother

Richardson. This legacy was a source of family wealth that helped support Helen's travels at a time when others were struggling to make ends meet.

Helen grew up on a citrus ranch outside the small town of Porterville, on the eastern edge of the San Joaquin Valley and in the foothills of the Sierra Nevada.

She got the travel bug from her family, particularly her father and two brothers. Her father traveled extensively in California and the Sierras and worked as an engineer for several years in the gold mines of South Africa, circling the globe going to and coming from South Africa in 1897-1903. One of her brothers, William, was a member of the Archbold Expedition to New Guinea in 1938-39. Her older brother, Hilton, traveled extensively in Central America and Africa and encouraged his younger sister to join the boys on camping trips in the Sierras. Helen herself had already cycled in Europe (July-Dec.1939) and in Japan and China (June-Aug.1940) before her trip to South America.

Her father gave her encouragement and financial support. When she was considering a choice between work and a South American jaunt, her father advised…

Get your South American trip first. That is my advice. For why? Because you can always get a job, but you can't always go to South America. For why? —One look at your brothers and sister tell the tale. They can't travel now because of jobs, family, etc., etc., etc. Sabe? Some people better stay home than travel, but not you. You will be a better teacher or anything you may want to do for having had it. You will learn better how to live and enjoy what you have by seeing how others do it.

In preparation for her trip, she gathered together a variety of documents to assure a successful trip, including a passport, membership cards with the American Bicycle League and the Pacific Northwest Cycling Assn. (Seattle Chapter), a 1941 pass for the American Youth Hostels, documents of good health, and a certificate of inoculation against cholera. She also carried letters from the Bank of America, vouching for her financial responsibility as "the daughter of one of the most substantial local citrus growers," and from the City of Porterville, certifying that she was "a person of good moral character and principle" and had never violated any laws or ordinances. She also meticulously planned what clothing and other effects to carry with her since she was seriously constrained by a small set of saddlebags and a diminutive overnight case that fit on the back of her bicycle. It was surprising what she was able to pack in those two small pieces: mechanic's equipment for a bicycle, a first

Timeline

Nov. 21, 1941--Departs from San Francisco
Nov. 29—Arrives in Puerto Armeulles, Panama
Dec. 7—Japan bombs Pearl Harbor
Dec. 22—Departs Colon, Panama
Jan. 1, 1942—Arrives in Valparaiso, Chile
Jan. 9—Arrives in Santiago; takes courses in summer school at University of Chile
Feb. 2—Departs Santiago for Puerto Montt and cycling in lake country
March 27-May 7—Returns to Santiago; stays in Santiago, making short side trips to areas around Santiago
May 7—Leaves Santiago
May 9-13—Crosses the Andes en route to Argentina
May 13—Arrives in Mendoza, Argentina
June 24—Arrives in Buenos Aires
June 24-Aug. 19—Stays in Buenos Aires with cousin's family
Aug. 19—Leaves Buenos Aires and enters Uruguay
Sept. 3—Arrested outside Minas, Uruguay, and spends night in jail
Sept. 4—U.S. Embassy official interviews Helen; takes papers
Sept. 5-17—Helen remains in Montevideo until "verdict" from U.S. State Department
Sept. 17—State Department gives Helen two months to return home
Sept. 27—Leaves Buenos Aires by air making stops in Bolivia, Peru, Colombia, Panama, Guatemala, and Mexico
Dec. 7, 1942—Arrives home in Porterville, California

aid kit, and a lady's wardrobe for all climates and social occasions. She also embarked with a small amount of cash (15 one dollar bills) and $800 in traveler's checks, which was supplemented later in her trip by an additional $1000. Her bicycle was a Raleigh three-speed, which she named "Chester", after the English town where she bought it two years before.

Ahead of Her Time

By Patrick Gilsenan
2001 winter issue of SPOKES Magazine

Sitting comfortably in her wheel chair in an Arlington nursing home, you'd have no idea Helen Richardson Coyle was once kicked out of Latin America on suspicion of being a spy.

She wasn't a spy, of course, but the year was 1942 and the authorities didn't know what else to make of a fiercely independent 27-year-old woman pedaling alone through the backwoods of Uruguay. They'd never seen such a woman before.

Women didn't often travel alone in 1942 and they certainly didn't travel on bicycles along back roads of developing counties.

But Coyle was not like most women. She had inherited her family's lust for travel and exploration which included a father who spent six years at the turn of the century circling the globe and a brother who was among the first white men to visit the native tribes of New Guinea in a late 1930's expedition.

She wasn't going to let the fact that she was a woman stop her from having her own adventures.

So in 1941, she grabbed her Raleigh three-speed and decided to spend two years pedaling the gravel and dirt roads of South America.

"I didn't plan on anything. I just had my idea of seeing the country and pedaling my bike," Coyle, now 89, recently told SPOKES.

Though she didn't consider herself or her trip a feminist statement, a single woman traveling alone by bicycle in a foreign-speaking country was undeniably radical for the time.

"They thought I was a little off track...they didn't think (such a trip) was anything anybody wanted to do," she remembered of friends' reactions. "They couldn't understand how my mother and father could allow such a thing."

But Coyle had previously spent summers cycling in Japan and Europe and, with an adventurous spirit of their own, her parents supported her idea.

So she left her family's ranch in Porterville, Calif., in mid-November 1941 and jumped aboard a banana boat bound for Panama as the only passenger on a nine-day voyage.

With war raging in Europe and soon to reach the Pacific, Coyle arrived in Panama to high-powered searchlights scouring the sea and military aircraft buzzing overhead.

Coyle spent three weeks exploring Panama's Pacific coastal areas from Puerto Armuelles to Panama City before cycling to the Atlantic city of Colón where she began her trip in earnest aboard a second ship bound for Valparaiso, Chile.

It was on that 12-day journey that Coyle first encountered a trend that remained throughout her trip: men happy to, shall we say, assist a single woman traveling alone.

"They were ... persistent," Coyle jokes. "(But) there was nobody that was very intrusive. I didn't have any experiences like that...I just said 'good bye' and rode on."

Coyle arrived in Valparaiso, Chile, Jan., 2, 1942 and pedaled down the coast before heading back inland for Santiago where she joined protests denouncing the Nazi regime and enrolled in a two-week program at the University of Chile in an effort to learn Spanish.

For her trip, Coyle brought only what she could fit in two saddlebags and a briefcase-size piece of luggage that fit on the back of her bike.

She also had a basic set of tools and patch kits that she used regularly along bumpy, unpaved roads. When something broke, she said, she simply taught herself to fix it.

Promising her mother she would sleep in secure locations, Coyle choose not to camp and planned her days along routes that would lead to the next town by nightfall. Coyle's family back home in California's San Joaquin Valley had become wealthy through a relative who was a founder of what is now the American Standard Company. The money helped support Coyle's travels. Between towns, however, Coyle ventured off the beaten path as often as possible.

"(The back roads) took me out into country that wasn't so spoiled with humanity," she said. And each new town brought out curious folks happy to talk and share with the North American woman on the bicycle.

After Santiago, she began a five-day ride over the Andes Mountains headed for Mendoza, Argentina. Her journey over the Andes was an odyssey including bread and tea with an isolated telegraph operator high in the mountains, and an evening in the grand Hotel Portillo and another at the Puente del Inca army barracks.

She rode for 300 miles, even pushing her bike uphill to a peak of 12,000 feet.

After leaving the Andes she headed for Cordoba, Argentina, where she encountered another trend of her trip: police asking lots of questions. As war had now moved to the Pacific, authorities had grown more suspicious.

"Two new officers questioned me," she wrote in her diary at the time. "Why was I in Argentina? Why was I alone? (they asked)...And my simple answer that I travel only because I love to travel seemed entirely too simple for the grave implications of their questions. They told me frankly they suspected me of having an interest in the politics of their country."

After only one afternoon's delay in Cordoba, however, police agreed to allow Coyle to continue en route to Buenos Aires and a two-month stay with her female cousin and her cousin's well-connected Argentine family.

As Coyle was the great granddaughter of former Ohio Governor William Bebb, she was not intimidated by her time among Argentine's high society.

After more than two months--July and August 1942--in Buenos Aires, Coyle left Argentina planning to travel to Montevideo and then on to Rio de Janeiro.

The political climate changed quickly, however, as she cycled into Uruguay. She was questioned twice by police during her first three days in the country and on September 3 she was stopped by local authorities, questioned and taken to the local police station where she was further questioned repeatedly the rest of the day. She was then escorted to a second police station were the questioning continued.

Though she didn't know it yet, her trip was about to come to an end.

"A man with keys was waiting. Tired from a lack of food and an afternoon of grilling, I lost control and gave up to tears, which came in spite of me. Why was I being held? What had I done?" she wrote in her journal at the time. "Down a long hall of barred rooms I was led, then a door was opened and (my bike) and I were ushered inside. A clanking of steel, a turning of a key in a lock, and for the first time in my life I knew the meaning of the loss of liberty. And I felt utterly hopeless and alone."

Before dawn, police roused her from her sleep and transported her back to Montevideo where a crowd of reporters and photographers awaited her arrival.

A second day of questioning followed, including inquiries from a representative from the U.S. embassy. Authorities confiscated her papers to prevent her from leaving the city while they decided her fate.

By the next morning the bicycling "North American spy" was on the front page of all of the city's newspapers. Coyle spent the next 10 days dodging photographers as she fought to be allowed to continue on her journey.

On September 17, 1942, however, she was informed that the U.S. State Department had requested her immediate return.

"It made me mad, because they cut short the things I wanted to do...(but) there was nothing I could do," she said.

Though she had planned to spend a second year in South America, she spent her remaining money on a plane ticket home with short, sightseeing stops in Peru, Colombia and Mexico. She arrived back in California two months later.

Despite the abrupt end to the trip, the journey was one of the highlights of Coyle's young traveling days.

"For a whole year I lived a happy, irresponsible life, pedaling from one country to another and living with the constant joy of activity, the beauty of an ever changing landscape, the warmth of strangers' hospitality. And I loved it all," she concludes her diary.

After returning to the states, Coyle joined the Red Cross and was shipped to New Caledonia to run a donut factory for locally stationed U.S. troops. She met her future husband, William E. Coyle, a navy officer, while in New Caledonia.

The two moved to Washington in 1945 where he worked for the Washington Star and later for the Washington NBC affiliate as director of advertising and public relations. Helen Coyle settled down to life as a full-time mom to six children.

And now, living a quiet life, the bike and travel long gone, she still smiles when she thinks of her love of far off places.

"Just the freedom of going out on the road, no destination no obligations, just rolling...I don't think (that desire) ever goes out."

Helen Richardson Coyle in 1999 Fairfax, Virginia, and at age 26 in December 1940, a year before her South American adventure

The Copiapó, the ship that carried Helen from Panama to Valparaiso, Chile, Dec. 22, 1941 to Jan. 1, 1942

Helen and "Chester" in Curicó in the Summer of 1942

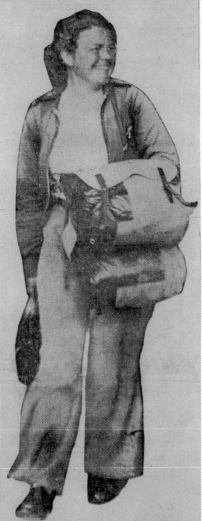

La Razón

MONTEVIDEO, VIERNES 4 DE SETIEMBRE DE 1942

CREEN QUE ES ESPIA ☆ HELEN RICHARDSON, estudiante de la Universidad de California, que fué detenida por la policía de Lavalleja, sospechada de actividades de espionaje. Su documentación está en regla, habiendo viajado hasta ahora sin dificultades por Panamá, con una estadía relativamente larga en Chile; en su poder se encontraron mapas y una copiosa correspondencia. Recorría nuestro país en bicicleta y sus movimientos llamaron la atención de las autoridades que procedieron a su detención. — (Amplia nota en la página 3)

Helen Richardson, student at the University of California, was detained by the Lavalleja police, on suspicion of espionage. Her documents were in order, having travelled until now without difficulty via Panama, with a relatively long stay in Chile. In her possession were maps and much correspondence. She traveled by bicycle through our country, drawing the attention of authorities which led to her detention.

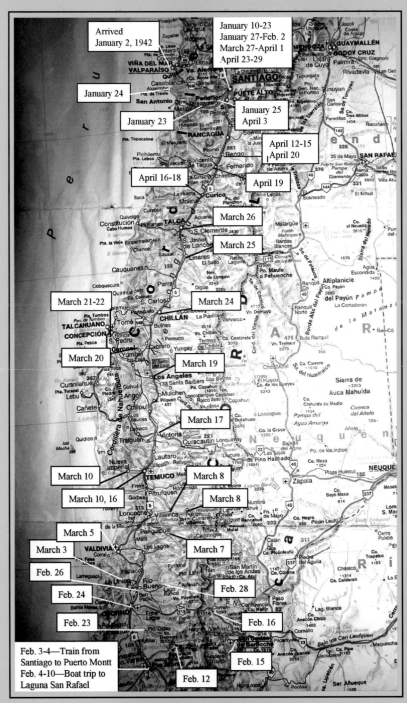

Itinerary in Chile

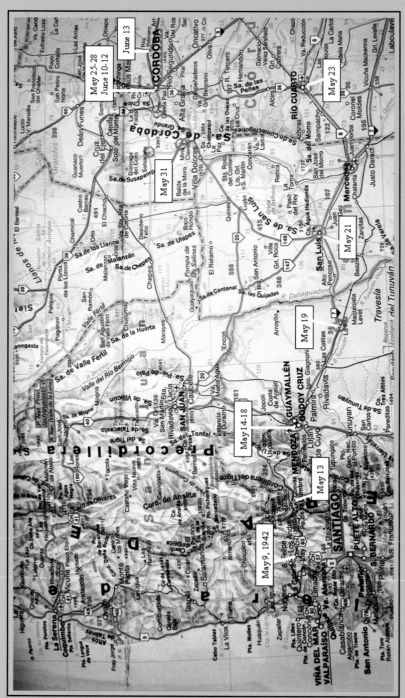

Itinerary from Santiago, Chile, to Cordoba, Argentina

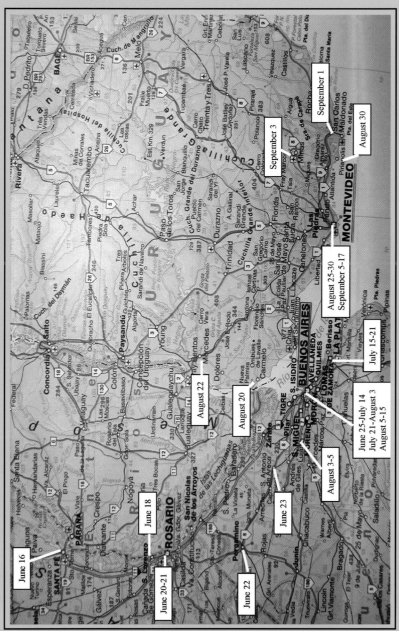

Itinerary from Santa Fe, Argentina, to Minas, Uruguay

SALUDOS

The Diary

November 22, 1941—S.S. Toltec—10:00 AM

Once again I'm out on the briny deep, and as the little Toltec rolls along laying back a white froth on the calm Pacific, this life at sea seems very familiar, very much as part of my life. And once again, as I start on my 3rd great adventure, the past and the future seem remote, unimportant, and the present looms as a tremendous, vital thing—an all absorbing reality. The knawing restlessness of past months has gone; in its place is supreme contentment: contentment in the white rails and stacks of the Toltec, in the endless expanse of blue on every side, in the gulls that fly beside us, in the masts and ropes which sway endlessly against the clouds in the sky and the quiet, distant horizon. Life is good.

Yesterday was too filled with excitement to leave any ounce of energy even for writing. For yesterday was the day the Toltec sailed. From our hotel in San Francisco, Mother and Dad took me, Chester, and my skimpy luggage down to the United Fruit Company's dock and put me aboard my boat. And I count mine a send-off *par excellance.* For I go with my family's trust and best wishes. They seem to understand the spirit which leads me far afield, the joy I feel in knowing new peoples and new places.

We were all convulsed to discover that I was the only passenger—just "me an' the crew", and it still seems very strange to rattle around the stateroom, the deck, the sitting room, and the dining room quite alone!   I eat dinner with the officers, sitting at the captain's right and across from the chief engineer, but I feel quite demure in the presence of so many uniforms!

As the Toltec pulled away from the dock, just Mother and Dad and a handful of others made up "the cheering crowds." There were no bands, no confetti, no flags. But the moment was none the less significant to me. And I was trembling with excitement as the tug moved us out of the slip and down the bay. Under San Francisco's two giant bridges and out the Golden Gate we went, and as I looked back at the city, I wondered, mildly, when and where I would again look upon the States. Out of the harbor a small sail boat came alongside to pick up our pilot, and thereafter I knew I was really on my way to South America.

But in days like these no traveler can be "really" sure of anything. With Europe embroiled in war and with war threatening in the Pacific, many things can happen to change the plans of individuals as well as the destinies of nations. Fortunately I am not a slave of plans. I make them always but am ready to change them anytime, anywhere.

Last night after dinner I went up to the captain's cabin to listen to the radio. He is a strange man, a hard weatherbeaten Dane, a man with the look and decisive manner of a man who has long handled men. And from his cynical remarks, I gather that he is a man with little patience for the foibles of his fellowmen.

November 23, 1941—S.S.Toltec—10:00 AM

Time flows by so easily, so painlessly, that the hours of the day lose all meaning. Even the ship's bells, which mark the passing of time, become a meaningless succession of sounds. There is only the sea, the Toltec and I.

Yesterday I spent by myself except for the evening hours in the captain's cabin. Walking the deck, watching the sea, reading, writing, and sleeping—yes even sleeping—have become my life.

I wakened early this morning, and hurried out to the windswept decks to watch the sunrise beyond the bow of the ship. The day is so clear and fresh and the sea so blue that I love to be outside. But hunger drew me down to the dining room where I had my breakfast in solitary splendor, and I came back to the deck only after that faint feeling was chased away with ham n' eggs.

November 24, 1941—S.S. Toltec—11:00 PM

Yesterday morning we passed land—islands rising stiff and barren above the sea and seeming very near in the clear air. And yesterday evening the sun went down in a blaze of glory. The whole day was idyllic.

This morning I stepped out into a warmer world where a blazing sun and impotent breeze gave promise of the tropical days ahead. And again we sighted land—the rugged silhouette of Lower California which revealed its desert hills and sandy coasts as we sailed nearer. But by mid-afternoon we had passed the tip of the peninsula, and once again the limitless sea closed in about us.

November 25, 1941—S.S. Toltec

Stifling, sticky, heat today brought out canvasses to provide welcome shade on the decks of the Toltec. And my energy gradually dwindled to a bare minimum. Two games of shuffleboard with the captain brought me up dripping with perspiration, and the rest of the day I was content to just sit and watch the coast of Mexico slide by. Another ship and a myriad of dolphins added interest to the day's routine.

Although the passengers are amongst the missing on the voyage, there is no shortage of human interest. Indeed the few I know have become absorbing studies. At the dinner table, it seems to be a case of "the chief speaks only to the captain, and the captain speaks only to God!" --For the captain is a straight-forward man who is accustomed to the role of king-pin, and the chief is an arrogant fellow swelled up with the importance of his position. Dwarfed to insignificance are the purser, a little old man who sits at my right and whose contributions to the conversation are ignored; and the first mate, a tremendous Dane who tucks his napkin under his chin and eats without saying a word. But removed from the domination of their superiors, these men become personalities in their own right. The purser, in spite of eyes which belie heavy drink, can tell a good story, and I like the British-accented "Isn't it" with which he concludes every statement. Moller, the mate, has a naïve way about him which is quite delightful, and today he provided us with much merriment as he sat straining paint, clad in a white floppy hat, an undershirt, and a pair of breeches which were split up the back and unbuttoned in front to accommodate his bulk. It is difficult to reconcile the spotless white uniforms of the dinner table with the sloppy, half-naked beings one meets on deck!

The chief steward, another well-fed Dane showed me through the kitchen, laundry, and storerooms this morning, and I enjoyed seeing the great stoves and cauldrons where food for all the ships personnel is prepared. Efficient, courteous "China boys" do the work here, but I know only the one who keeps my rooms in spotless conditions, turns back the bed at night, folds the blankets into fascinating forms, and keeps me always supplied with fruit.

Another personality on the ship is the radio operator, a pleasant, red-headed Englishman who always has a cheery smile and a volume of conversation for the passer by. I stop often on my rounds about the decks to talk with him, and little by little he gives out the gossip of the small world where pettiness is bound to play its part.

November 27, 1941—S.S. Toltec

All day yesterday we sailed along within sight of the Mexican coast, and nothing occurred to stand out in contrast against the day's routine. I lost myself in a book, experiencing the intensity and the futility of Mademoiselle D. in *All This and Heaven Too*. And was conscious of nothing else except the beautiful blue of the Pacific, the click of the games of shuffleboard between the captain and the chief, and the interruptions for meals in the salon below.

This morning I wakened to the roar of wind and the dark of waves against the ship's side, and I knew we were in the Gulf of Tehuantepec where a "blow" is the role of the day. Until noon the ship tossed, and the usual calm of the sea was broken with a host of dancing white caps. Then all was peaceful again.

After breakfast I lingered at the table to hear the first mate tell in glowing terms of his wife "who can do anything." Quite a contrast, I thought, with the pursers tale of a gin marriage and the wife who cost him $22,500!

And after lunch I followed the chief through the maze of the engine room and listened to his incomprehensible description shouted into my ear in broken English. Down there I met "Blondy", the grinning black boy who tends the boilers. And several Danes whom I had never seen before, even though I had been on the same boat with them for a week.

The beauty on the sea tonight is painful in its intensity. I like to stand in darkness on the forward deck and watch the masts rising and falling, watch the lights which tell of warmth in the crew's quarters, and revel in the living, silvery glint of the waves turned back from the prow in the moonlight.

November 29, 1941—S.S. Toltec

Nothing of yesterday stands out in my mind to mark it with special significance. –Just another day at sea, a day of blue sea and warm winds, but a fine day for all that. The sunset was lovely with the sun a ball of molten gold dropping out of banks of orange clouds and with none of the encumbering objects of land to crowd in on its vast beauty.

Before dinner I found the cabins in darkness and the chief, Oleson, splintering the wall above the fuse box. Smoke and excitement told of a short circuit. And it was some little time before the trouble was remedied. The purser and I ate dinner alone by candlelight. –Christmas candles with holders wreathed in holly!

Rain this morning contradicted the captain's promise that the rainy season was over. But it was short-lived, leaving only the banks of clouds over the blue mountains of the Costa Rican coast to remind us of the shower.

Activity on deck gave promise of the approach to *Puerto Armuelles*. All was put in readiness to receive the cargo of fruit—the 60,000 stems of bananas destined for Los Angeles and San Francisco.

Early in the afternoon we passed an island—a bit of land clothed in tropical green and wearing ruffles of white surf at its feet. Again I felt the old excitement which surged through me when I first saw Ireland's shores and first passed by the skerries of Bergenfjord. Land lying ready to explore always draws the same eager response from my adventurous soul. And that green I know is jungle—jungle which I have never seen before! And now its past midnight, but I'm too full of the presence of this new land to feel any tinge of weariness. Just after dinner we sighted the lights of Puerto Armuelles, and slowly, slowly we drew into the harbor. Presently we were tied up to the dock and had become the center of activity with new life all about us. Cranes moved into position, and endless conveyors began to carry a continuous stream of banana stems into the hold. Great jugs of acid were unloaded and sacks of onions too. And I looked on fascinated. But most interesting of all are the people. –Shapeless hats, tattered shirts, bare feet, brown skins glistening with sweat, lean shoulders stooped under bunches of bananas, and always a happy babble of Spanish. One sat on a rail and directed the winch operator with sweeping signals; another lay with a bell rope in his charge; another counted the stems going into the hatch; but most were carrying bananas, human links in that procession from box car to hold. Some few were merely lookers-on, and several were stretched out on the dock, oblivious to all the industry about them. Such a deluge of life after days of isolation at sea is almost overpowering!

November 30, 1941—Puerto Armuelles

A day so full that it's difficult to write of it! But most of the "fullness" has come from the surge of excitement inside rather than from genuine activity. At 5:00 I wakened to the rattle of conveyor and looking out saw the bananas still going their endless way into the hold. Men were still carrying bunches on padded shoulders, but the activity of the previous evening had dwindled to a minimum, and life appeared geared to a very slow tempo. All morning I waited for the promised car to take me up to the plantation beyond the port, but when 11:00 AM came I gave up hope, for siesta hour had arrived, and all the men were resting from their work, waiting for their women who trudged down to the dock with trays of rice and spaghetti on their heads. But at this point the general supervisor took action, and presently his private yellow "buda" manned by a neat little brown man arrived to take me on the tour. In solitary splendor I rode, smiling to myself at the spectacle of a lone girl going off in this fashion. Immediately beyond town we entered the jungle, and I was thrilled beyond measure to find myself engulfed by it. Its lush greenness was overpowering, and I was conscious of leaves of a thousand forms. There were broad ones and fingered ones, fine lacy ones and small pointed ones, and they formed a solid impenetrable wall. Soon we left this jungle and entered the banana plantation, acres of lush plants with fruit in all stages of ripeness. And my thrifty nature was shocked by the odoriferous dumps of rejected stems. Extremely interesting were the houses built on stilts and sheltering families under their high floors. Their children swung in hammocks, women washed, and men ate. And there too were meek dogs and sleepy mules. One's progress up and back the track was hampered by frequent switchings and phone calls, and a blatant horn urged all pedestrians to clear the way. I arrived back just in time for a belated lunch, swallowed while the rest lingered over their coffee.

Afternoon came with a blanket of humid heat, but in spite of it, I went with the radio operator up to the radio station where a large man entertained us with records and stories told with lusty laughter. Afterwards we walked to "the club" and I had a coke just as an excuse to go inside and look at the view and watch those who amused themselves with drink and dancing. Walking back toward the ship, the company agent informed me that my baggage was ashore and that he would take me to collect the all important passport. Relieved, I settled myself here at the girl's bachelor quarters and left duly grateful for the hospitality of the United Fruit Co.

This evening, the radio operator called again, and we went out to see a bit of the town. Stopping in at the village hotel for another coke proved a gala occasion, and I felt that here I gained more of a feel of Panama than I could possibly get at "the club." There in a dingy littered room filled with blatant music a little, black, intoxicated man waited on us with great flourishes of service, while we watched a few couples dancing to the endless blare. Later the second engineer and the third mate from the Toltec drifted in and we became a party. That third mate was the Norwegian whom I had never met, but in whom I was very much interested. The old sentimentalism for every thing Norwegian, I guess! When he left to stand watch, the party lost its verve, and I was ready to come home for a good night's rest.

December 1, 1941—Boquette—Pop Wright's

The "good night's rest" was interrupted at 3:30 this morning by a couple of drunks and a hilarious girl in the front room just next to mine. When they commenced to meddle with Chester I was wide awake in a minute, and I rushed out in a flurry of red robe to rescue my charge and bring him into the security of my own room. Thereafter I could not sleep, and at 6:00 I was quite ready to load up and pedal to the station in the rainy and reluctant dawn. Chester was tied to the back of the last car, while I was piloted to the first one to ride in state in *"primera clase."* Up through the jungle and into the plantations we traveled once again, and again I was struck with the beauty of the banana-like plant with the red angular flower stalk, a plant seen everywhere along the tracks. Dipping barrels and the gray and sprayed banana fronds were familiar sights now. But the rain, which lasted all morning, brought a new sight—a rider carrying banana leaves across the pommel of his saddle and over his head for protection. As a train climbed higher the vegetation became less dense with much open pasture, but the terrain continued to be flat. And then *David.*

During the three-hour ride I had company, for a couple of Americans sitting behind me made themselves known and were glad to tell of their two month's experiences in Panama. The one from Louisiana had only the worst to say for it, and in glowing terms he told of his greatest desire--t-bone steaks and fried potatoes, New Orlean's style! The one from Wisconsin seemed to be hankering' for a little snow! Along the way they bought oranges which they shared with me, and I found the fruit sweet and juicy in spite of green skin.

In *David* (as per Charlie, the radio operator in *Puerto Armuelles*) I looked up *"Señor* Handle-bar" at the station, and through him found Leo Machonski who knows Panama and speaks fluent English. Leo told me much about my proposed trip and banished all uncertainties, and he was kind enough to help me in getting permission to cycle in Panama. His store was my headquarters during my hours in *David.* And how I enjoyed those hours! For I was free to just poke around without the compulsion of sightseeing "musts." Up and down the streets I pedaled looking for all that was novel and picturesque, and I found much. Little white houses with hoary tile roofs and with floors flush with the sidewalk, colorful gardens, crumbling walls, cobblestone streets, sleek deliberate oxen pulling great carts, tall superbly graceful women walking bare footed and carrying loaded trays on their heads. In the Plaza I loitered to look into the old church with its garish figures and paper flowers and to just sit where I could feel the tempo of Panamanian life. A motorcycle policeman came to take me to the station and make out for me the necessary cycling permit, and there I had much fun trying to speak Spanish. At midday, I cycled out to the river, and there in the shade I rested and made my lunch on bananas, oranges, and pears. A plantain, my first, was discarded because of its starchiness. Across the river a man washed a white horse, and just in front of me several brown boys swam in the cool water. An iguana looked on from the grass beside me. And across the bridge came groups of horseback riders--always interesting to me.

Back in town again I left my bike with Leo and took the late afternoon train for *Boquette.* Much to my disappointment, darkness soon blotted out the green landscape with its picturesque thatch-roofed huts of bamboo poles. But again I found interest within the train, for the neat, dark gentleman in front was obviously interested in the funny foreigners, and after adjusting his tie, clearing his throat, and looking intently out the window, he turned and opened a conversation which was laughable because of its general incomprehensibility. But fun! And I appreciated the hospitality in the offer of cigarettes and cookies. With an *"hasta la vista"* we parted at *Boquette* station, but somehow he turned up to put me into a taxi and tipped the boy who carried my bags.

Tonight I am at the Wright's where hominess reins supreme, where Pop and Mrs. Wright accept their guests into the family circle. And I feel a glowing contentment.

December 2, 1941—Boquette--Pop Wright's

Up early this morning to look at *Boquette* with its mists and lush greens. After breakfast I hiked far up the river and into hills. Many riders and pack animals passing by. Saw first coffee plantation. Shown one plantation by *José Manuel Miranda.* Slithered down mountains and obscure trails. After lunch went to see *Boquette* and met companion from the train trip. He became my guide, and we wound up at his poor little home where in the backyard he served me an orange with all the attendant Latin courtesy. The navels here in *Boquette* are the finest I've ever eaten. Profitable afternoon because of Spanish learned. After supper and another lesson with a Spanish guest here at Wright's. These lessons with folks who speak no English are *"muy bueno."* Poinsettias, cape jasmine, and roses in my room tonight--picked by gallant *Cesár* with his little black mustache. Impressed by wild lantana and great jimpson weed, trees hanging full of clusters of dead white bells. Also by beauty of leaves and berries of coffee-and their sweetness. Never have I seen such rich gardens--a profusion of palms, oranges, sugar cane, bananas and a host of unknown plants.

December 3, 1941—Boquette—Pop Wright's

I am so in love with *Boquette* that I do not want to leave, but I must push on tomorrow in the direction of Panama City. The hotel here is unique in itself, operated as it is by an old couple from Texas. They are very kind, and one feels more at home than if he were in an ordinary hotel. Accommodations are primitive, but the hospitality is genuine, and I like eating my meals with the Wright's and sitting downstairs with them in the evening. Also I like the privilege which I have of helping myself to all the bananas and oranges which I can eat!

This morning I had a "date" to ride with my friend, *Cesár Candanedo*. But when I arrived no horses were to be had, and I gathered from his voluble Spanish that I had come too late. Nothing daunted, I just decided to walk with him to his *"finca"*. And this in spite of Pop Wright's rough admonition that it was a mistake "to go out with these birds." I went because I was curious about these folks and their ways, and because I know of no better way to understand them than to mingle with them. So off I went up the mountain with *Señor Candanedo*, a bit skeptical of what might be in store. The most impressive thing about *Cesár* was his gallantry--the spreading of his coat for me to sit on, the flourish with which he provided me with a handkerchief to wipe my heated brow, the readiness with which he carried my jacket and bundle, and the bow with which he presented me flowers from his garden. He showed me everything at his *finca*: his mill where he started a water wheel which turned iron wheels to crush cane to provide me with a sweet drink, the chicken coop where he fed the chickens and gathered the eggs, the pigs in their pen, and last of all his house, another poor structure made the poorer with its leaking roof. Here he showed me wet books and magazines and played a victrola for my benefit, and before we left he spread out a bunch of buns, sausage, ham, prunes, crackers, canned apricots, and oranges. If *Cesár* erred in suggesting I spend the night with him or in asking to kiss me goodbye, I charged his mistake up to the "Latin temperament" and accepted his hospitality with good grace, for after all, he remained a gentleman. And so I enjoyed my morning climbing up into the cool lush woods of the hills and down into the pretty valley which held *Cesár* farm. After lunch I set off again, this time with *Antonio Moles*, the Spanish gentlemen here at the Wright's. We walked the loop, about six miles, and I had another excellent lesson in Spanish. It was a pretty walk through the woods which seem more and more familiar. Once we had to run for shelter in a sugar factory, but the rain gave a filmy quality to the landscape which was truly beautiful.

December 5, 1941—Santiago—Hotel Companol

Yesterday was an endless day which merged into today without a break. Leaving *Boquette* early, the train soon brought me to David, and within an hour I had packed up Chester, said goodbye to Leo Marchosky and Mr. Dike, an American gentleman who came down from Wrights on the same train as I, and was pedaling off toward Panama. The thrill of the open road once again! It is irresistible! And as the green hills and lush woods of Panama unrolled before me I was content with the beauty and the interest of the country and the activity which Chester incorporated in it. As the day wore on, the heat became oppressive, and perspiration flooded over my body and soaked my clothing. But still there were the lovely tropical rivers and occasional flowering trees. Famished I stopped at a *cantina* for a Coke and was surprised to find there an English-speaking man--a Pole so he said--who assured me he was my friend. But one drink was never enough; I wanted gallons of liquid! And I doled my oranges out to myself on the basis of mileage. On a hill top, a dark Panamanian with black mustachio cheerfully dipped water from his *olla* and filled my empty bottle. Nectar of the gods! Though heaven only knows what germs it may have contained.

And then the sun waned, and suddenly, without warning, it was dark. *Remedios*, according to my cyclometer, was about 13 miles away, but it seemed very, very far along that road which was often so rocky that I had to push downhill as well as up. And the weariness which settled in my bones warned me that it would be several hours before I could reach town. To buoy up my spirits, I decided to have supper, and leaving Chester sprawled on the side of the road, I settled myself on the rain soaked grass and spread out the crackers and puree which *Cesár* had given. Life soon looked better, and the fire flies lent a cheery note. And then an angel arrived in the form of *Ricardo Tener* who hoisted Chester onto his truck and drove me to *Remedios*! En route he pointed out the difficulties of the road between *Remedios* and *Sona*, and I was persuaded to ride on after we had had dinner in *Remedios*. It was a fine ride too--one I shall never forget. The moon came up in great splendor, and I was conscious of a landscape of hills and rivers and patches of dense jungle where hardwood giants dwarfed all other growing things. And all the while I chattered to *Ricardo* in broken Spanish, for he knew enough English to make a fine teacher. I liked him too, for he was never forward, and he wore his big hat in a way which bespoke much self-confidence. Mile after mile we rode thus-- just *Ricardo* and I, Chester, a load of coffee, and the moon! In *Sona* we stopped, and *Ricardo* tried to raise someone at the hotel. "*Señora, tiene Ud. una cama?* No answer. Someone asleep at the front door sat up and looked at us, but that was all the response we got from that sleepy town! Nothing to do but to ride onto *Santiago*, and this we did, but conversation died and eyes grew heavy. And at *Santiago* we were still unable to secure a bed (for me!), so *Ricardo* parked his truck and found a place for himself on top of the coffee, while I curled up in the front seat. What a night! And what a tremendous amount of time seemed to separate me from *Boquete*!

December 6, 1941—Aguadulce—El Rancho

In the gray dawn of that morning, the hotel open, and *Ricardo* saw me settled before saying adios. Only one thing could I think of--a bath and clean clothing! And my bare, dark room with its dingy curtains and five beds (!) looks like a house of refuge! Cleaned up, I sallied out to find *Bernardo Fabriga* whom Mr. Dike had referred me to. And *Bernardo* not only answered all my questions in good English, but ordered a car and showed me about the town. First we went to the normal school, the largest in Central America and I passed through the imposing rococo entrance and along the arcades which connected various parts of the institution. Here was a building, conceived on a grandiose scale and yet somehow falling short of its pretense. But within its walls were all the familiar classes--art, physics, social science, etc. The students all rose when I paused at the doors, although I did not feel my slacks bedecked self so deserving of respect! From the school we drove to *Bernardo's finca*, a pretty country place where rolling pasture lands accommodated 200 head of milk cattle. And from there to "*Mi rancho*", an atmospheric *cantina* with guinea pigs and houses for "monkey business" in back. Pepsi Cola, my usual order. I shall be bogged down with the stuff 'ere long, but I have to have an excuse of some sort to go into these places which contained so much local color!

In the afternoon I rode out on Chester, thinking to see a bit of the road covered the previous night, and also in search of a spot to settle myself for an hour or two of writing. I found the spot beneath a tree with a view of distant hills, but I gave up all idea of writing when the natives commenced to stop and visit. A little girl explained to me that she had oranges, *muy fresco y muy dulce*, at her house and that she would get me some. Presently she returned with a bag and a great machete with which she peeled the oranges for me. We talked for a very long time in spite of language difficulties, and I found her a good teacher. As I walked back by her house with her, she asked me to stop, and stop I did to receive a king's hospitality in that humble shack with its thatched roof, cane walls, and mud floor. *Señorita Gonzalez* seated me on a low stool and fanned the embers of the fire on the floor to brew me a cup of coffee. And all the while I was the center of a circle of naked brown children who stared with unbelieving eyes. Mother *Gonzalez* also sat there, a wizened little woman with a great goiter. And I gave thanks to Allah for the fate which had thrown this experience my way.

In the evening as I sat at the front counter of my hotel, an American accosted me, and soon we were good enough friends to go look at the town together. At *"el Rancho"* we ordered drinks and exhausted the Nickelodeon and then walked back up town, stopping for ice cream, and eventually arriving at the *Plaza*. This was a fine place to "feel" Panama with its soft moonlight, its old rambling, tile-roofed buildings, and its myriad noises emanating from lighted rooms and groups of passersby in the streets. At 11:00 we turned back to my hotel which seemed to have grown dingier during the day. And as my companion urged me for one kiss I couldn't help but note the setting for romance at my front door: a water tower, a clothes line, a chicken pen, and a bottle dump all bathed in moonlight! There were sounds of drunkenness from the *cantina* in the hotel; I went to bed with a table across the door and open knife at my head.

This morning found me back on my bike again and headed for *Aguadulce*, rolling along through more open country where many of the tall, sleek, wide-horned cattle were feeding. Wildflowers everywhere! The road today has been excellent--black top, no less--and all my troubles of the first day are gone. No more upsets because of rocky roads. And no more broken carriers--thanks to the kindness of the mechanic in *Santiago*. I am freer now to enjoy the rolling panoramas and to note the many natives with their poor little horses, their great high oxcarts, or their burdened heads.

In *Aguadulce* while struggling to find a hotel, I bumped into *Tomás* Fogarty to whom Mr. Dike had referred me. Half Irish and hearty and sustained by a few drinks, he offered to do anything and everything for me, and to prove his point he showed me about town in his "76" truck. Past the road commission and the hospital we went and into quiet little *Pocri* where everything was snuggled in greenery and at peace with the world. Then passed the army post and back to the Main Street of town. With us, went a kid of 22 to claim to be an "intelligence man" and who talked in the grandiose terms of an adolescent!

Now I'm settled in the hotel where rooms are bare and where I anticipate a stormy night--Saturday night with army men in town!

December 7, 1941—Santa Clara

Last night was everything I feared it would be. The noise of *El Rancho* was a din which defied sleep. Hour after hour I lay awake listening to the blare of the music box, the loud thick voices of drunken men, the high pitched laughter of women, footsteps going and coming in the halls, and the sounds of Yankee soldiers closeted with their *señoritas* in the rooms about me! An endless night! But dawn brought a cessation of noise in a world of freshness and light to my tawdry surroundings, and after *dos huevos* and a cup of coffee I pedaled out into a world which seemed to have lost its tarnish.

More happy miles through the broad green plains of Panama with mountains rising in the distance. The country folk grow darker and more Negroid as I approached the zone, but they still have a cheery *"bueno dia"* for the passerby. Stopped at *Nata* to see the old church. In *Penonome* an army man stopped me and with a broad grin asked, "what's all this?" Presently I was introduced all around and was ushered into a nearby doorway to have a drink with the governor of the province. The cool glass was refreshing in spite of its alcoholic content, and I enjoyed this interruption, but I was very conscious of my weather-beaten face and the perspiration which dripped from my arms and legs! Afterward I was driven to *Dr. Hector Conte's* house where I had in opportunity to look through a great book devoted to Panama's *huacos.*

Tonight I'm settled in a cottage where silence reigns supreme, and the sounds of wind and insects are welcome relief from those of the *cantina* to which I have become accustomed.

December 9, 1941—Panama—Hotel Colón

Never before in my life have events and experiences crowded in on my consciousness so fast as they have during the past few days! Yesterday morning I vowed to start early, but during breakfast *Mr. Nelson Rounsevell*, the proprietor of *Santa Clara* casino, sat and talked to me, and I found his confidence in humanity so refreshing that I lingered long before making my departure. He reiterated the same thought which I have heard before and I have felt myself: the Panamanian people are as fine as any in the world.

Making the numerous detours around unfinished bridges was not as formidable as it had been painted, but the frequent steep stretches kept me in a lather of heat and perspiration. At one point where I rested, a man on horse back stopped to offer me a drink. In a gunny sack behind his saddle be carried a bit of raw meat, a bottle of soda, and a bottle of hard liquor. He gave me my choice of either of the latter, and when I took the soda, he bit the cap off with his teeth and presented it to me with a happy smile. Such is the kindness of those I meet on the road.

The rivers I crossed were gems of tropical beauty-- murky waters, great shade trees, and a riot of creepers, many of them with bright flowers. Sometimes the gorges were deep, and far below I could see native women washing on the spits of gravel. Then, presently, my road left the plains and was in the hills again when I looked out across a rolling sea of greenery where palms and white flowering trees made themselves conspicuous with their unique form and color. As I pedaled slowly up a long, high hill, one Westly Hartswell stopped and with careful maneuvering, packed both Chester and me into his car. Thence I rode clear into Panama City, but in spite of this interlude of rest, I was so disreputable when I reached the hotel that the man in charge would have refused me a room had I not mentioned the name of *Señor Moles*, my Castillan friend from *Boquette*. A bath and clean clothes helped no end and prepared me to sally out and see a bit of this new city whose narrow streets, overhanging balconies, and hoards of diverse humanity had caught and held my interest from the moment I entered. Such a cauldron of life and activity after the quiet *pueblos* of the back country! And such a host of divergent features! Negroid, Oriental, and Nordic in an infinite variety of combinations! Cars with harsh horns, people looking down from balconies, lottery salesman, all manner of shops, people, people, people--this is Panama. And yesterday little girls dressed in white and carrying flowers told of some special celebration in the city.

Rumors of war had crowded through the language barrier before I reached Panama, and an extra bought in the streets confirmed the grim news. The United States at war with Japan! Incredible! A sense of futility swept over me, and I wondered how I could go home to a teaching job which could have no significance in a world of chaos. All things creative lose meaning at times like these. And I fervently hoped that I might not be turned back but might at least be permitted to remain in Panama.

I felt more at home when *Señor Moles* came in with a warm greeting, and I was glad to wait for him to come home from a dinner engagement before going out to look at the city again. He gave me my first taste of night life in Panama and I had a glorious time. First to *El Rancho* for drink and dancing. A rum cooler for me! --Perhaps I'll get a taste for this tropical sport yet! And then to the Balboa Club for more drinks and more dancing! And before coming home, a stop at a little fruit parlor for my first taste of papaya. I crawled into bed very tired and very happy.

This morning I rolled out to walk the streets in search of a post office, a bookstore, and a tourist bureau. I went by trial and error and eventually found the things for which I sought, seeing also a good deal of city life en route. Stopping at the hotel before going on again, *Señor Moles* took me in hand and helped me to find the Grace Line and Chilean Line agencies where I tried to arrange a delay in taking passage for South America. As we walked back we stopped for papaya and pineapple juice at another fruit parlor, and I found these new drinks truly delicious. After dinner we visited long up stairs with a group of *Señor Mole*'s friends, and I strained my ears to catch a few words but my comprehension is very limited.

Mid afternoon brought that sleepy feeling which slides so easily into *siesta* time, and I find myself following the example of the rest of the *Latinos*.

December 11, 1941—Panama City—Hotel Colón

And the evening of the 9th, I went to a movie with the professor, a movie in a very modern, air-cooled theater, and afterwards we walked out along the sea where on one hand were the reflected lights of the city and on the other was a mellow tropical moon. We walked also through the consular district with its beautiful homes, and back at our hotel we climbed to the roof to look at the lights of the city.

Yesterday morning I went with the professor to Old Panama. We rode in a *chiva*, one of the conveyances so characteristic of Panama. Ours *"La amor de las amores"* had the usual gaudy decorations up front and the usual non chalant driver who hustled us through traffic with great unconcern.

Old Panama is just a few crumbling walls--a handful of ruins left from Morgan's depredations. But they stand out in the country near a palm-lined beach, and there is majesty in the calm that surrounds them as well as in the simple solidity of their construction. Today they are lost in sleep, and it is

difficult to visualize their stormy past--the gold and blood of
the days of the Spanish Main. But their age is attested to by
the great Panamanian trees growing from the walls.

We stopped again for *dos piñas* on our return, and it
was dinner time when we reached our hotel. I passed the
afternoon between a *siesta* and shopping for Christmas cards.
But in the evening I went to another movie with the professor.
The night was given over to a black-out, but some lights were
burning when we left the show. Cokes, and then home again
where we climbed to the rooftop to look at the darkened city.
--An indiscretion on my part, for I found myself in the
professor's arms and had to beat a hasty retreat with a
mumbled, *"No, Señor, por favor. No está bien."*

Today I have walked far in an effort to get better
acquainted with Panama. This morning around and about the
city. Down to the sea with glimpses of the harbor beyond the
sea wall. Past impressive public buildings. Along narrow
streets where the balconies seem to meet overhead. Into
Caledonia where washings made a veritable forest in the open
spaces along the shore, and where house fronts made a gay
pattern of yellow and green and blue and red and gray along
the streets. Here sordid little rooms opened directly into the
street, and scores of children tumbled out to play in the
broader space the streets provided. Balconies above were
festooned with plants and peopled with idle folks who
watched the life below. A fruit vendor with a long wheel
barrow shouted *"pa-pai-ya"* so that all might hear.

This afternoon I wandered up into *Ancón* and around
the hills where ample houses and gardens told of Yankee
influence. Here trees and shrubs were strange, but the pattern
of life was very familiar.

Another movie with the professor ended this day.
And afterwards the usual walk coupled with fruity drinks.
Pears and mangoes this time also.

December 13, 1941—On board the Dolphin in the Sambu River of Darien

Yesterday morning I went with the professor to the National Museum where the *huaco* collection was of very great interest to me. The ceramics with their hollow legs, their lovely shapes, and their black and red designs were different from anything I had ever seen before.

In back of the Museum a black mass of ashes was all that remained of the papers of the Italian consulate. Just another reminder of the war torn outer world.

In mid afternoon I packed up my belongings, and leaving Chester at the hotel set out on an excursion to *Darien*. Four of us assembled at the tourist bureau, and presently we were all aboard "Jungle Jim" Price's launch outward bound. After an informal evening on deck, I went to my bunk for a night of hanging on while our little boat pitched and tossed.

This morning I wakened to find myself off the shores of *Darien* in the mouth of the *Sambu*. On the shore a thatched-roofed village, *Garachine* and on the waters about the boat several long slim *cayucos*. When the tide came in we turned upstream, following this narrow jungle river with its high walls of greenery and all its myriad forms of life. Herons, egrets, orchids, creepers with yellow and purple flowers, *monaca* palms, *quipo* trees, and a thousand unknown things. Rain lent an almost mystical quality to the landscape. And occasional houses built on long legs told us that we were not alone in this vast wilderness.

At the forks of the *Sambu* and *Sabalo* Rivers we anchored and natives came out to our boat. Brown fellows they were with bobbed hair, red loin cloths, and bodies painted purple. And they traveled smoothly, swiftly in their *cayucos* and *piraguas*. After lunch we all went ashore, passed by the little trading post, and commenced a trek up into the jungle. Our trail led through deep, dark, damp bush with wet fronds and creepers hanging overhead, and we slithered and slipped through mud and water. Rain soaked us through and through, and my shoes caught in the mud and slipped from my feet.

Presently we came out of the rank vegetation into a banana grove and then to a group of primitive huts *(Chocó, the village of Sábalo).* Jim hustled us right into the largest of those and introduced us to his friend, Chief *Bigua.* And here we stayed for an hour or more looking curiously at the people and prying into their mode of life. Bodies were bare except for g-strings and wrap-around skirts, and both men and women were painted with some purple concoction. One small baby looked as if it had come straight from the ink well! The home was built on stilts with a split bamboo floor and no sides at all, and all the families' implements and supplies were scattered about the floor. A good many Indians were there in that large house--men, women, and children—and they all squatted on the floor and looked solemnly at us and at the photographs, candy, and balloons which we gave them. They showed their friendliness by offering us oranges. After satisfying our curiosity, Jim arranged for a *piragua* to take us down the river to our boat, and we all settled ourselves in the bottom of this dug-out while a boy and girl poled us downstream. The young man was one of the most elaborately dressed I had seen, and looked very handsome with his long ear rings, his broad bracelets, his many rings, and his purple dye--complete except for three bands above and below each knee and around each arm. He guided our boat with great dexterity, standing in the prow; and in the other end the girl with queer stripes of purple and red paint across her mouth and teeth and chin, kept the light little shell true in her course. Thus we traveled down that jungle river, sneaking through a great mass of dripping greenery and watching, and listening for all the strange sights and sounds of the bush. At one point a tree blocked our course, but our Indian boat man jumped out with an ax and cut it away so that we might pass. It was dark before we reached our own boat where we changed from our soaked clothing and sat down to a steak dinner!

December 15, 1941—Panama City—The Dolphin—7:00 AM

Yesterday morning I rolled out while the stars were still shining to look at the Southern Cross that Jim pointed out to me. And the river and the jungle were so beautiful in the early morning with dawn just breaking and I dressed and stayed up instead of going back to bed. Reflected jungle and soft morning colors. After breakfast we went ashore again and loitered around the trading post to watch the Indians come and go. Some sat on the front porch and cooked rice over a Primus stove! Two doors down a baby had just died, and we wandered by to see what went on. Men sat nonchalently by whittling a small coffin with a machete. When the bundle of rags with its blue cargo was placed in the box, the mother and grandmother of the child sobbed and chanted. The father, *José de la Nieve,* sat by expressionless. Jim officiated as priest at the Indian's request and sat with them praying and drinking their liquor. The lid of the coffin did not fit, and so much time was consumed adding small pieces that we had to have before the job was done. In a few minutes we were underway, sliding down the current, and only once did we run aground in the mud of a sharp bend.

At *Garachine* we dropped anchor and went ashore to see another village--this time a Negro one. By contrast this was very clean with sandy streets and neat bamboo pole houses with thatched roofs. The natives were fine looking too and were as delighted as children to have their pictures taken. Many of them were threshing rice by beating it with a wooden pestle and a great wooden mortar. Up the river we asked for coconuts, and a couple of small boys scampered up a tree to cut down the green fruit that was hacked open with a machete and presented to me. Back in our launch again we cruised along the coast for a way and admired the hills and *quipo* trees before starting back for Panama. Then we sat long by the rail watching *Darien* disappear behind and the Pearl Islands appear like black mounds ahead. Then sudden darkness. I sat up front with Jim until I feared our informality had gone beyond the point of discretion and then retreated to my bunk.

In the middle of the night I wakened to find a man standing by my bed--Jim, listening for trouble in the boat's mechanism!   And no sooner had I dozed off again than a crash and splintering of wood brought me suddenly to my senses. Bulloch, one of the passengers, suggested that it might be well to dress, so I jumped into my clothes and packed up my passport and checks in hopes that I might at least save the most necessary things! But nothing happened, and the boat moved on into port.

December 17, 1941—Panama City—Hotel Colón—7:00 AM

Leaving the Dolphin Monday morning, I returned to the *Hotel Colón*, glad of the chance for a bath and a change of clothes. Then out to steamship companies to try and settle the problem of passage to Chile. No luck. A midday downpour caught me, and I was grateful to a friend from the hotel who happened along and took me home under her umbrella. An afternoon of writing Christmas cards. And then evening at the *Teatro Nacional* to hear a program of chamber music. Afterwards the professor and I walked around *Las Bovedas*, the old city walls beside the sea, and it was beautiful there under the arbor of *bougainvillea* with a view out across the sea and into the starry night. Walking and sitting in the cool *plazas* have become our evening routine, and I sometimes fear that I may have gone a bit too far in my "acquaintance" with the professor. But I enjoy his company, and he has an endless amount of patience in teaching me Spanish. Therefore, I try to judge his attention by Latin rather than American standards.

Yesterday was a long, full day. After breakfast I went with the professor to see the churches of the city: *San José* with its famous golden altar preserved from the days of the pirate's plunderings. An elaborate altar, baroque and Arabic in design. The cathedral with its heavy stone façade and nondescript interior. And other churches of lesser import. I always move in awed silence with the professor's handkerchief tied over my head. And by the devotion of the others there-- the black and the brown who knelt to pray. After the churches, we took a bus to the outskirts of town and climbed to the top of a small hill for a view of the city. Panama, the sea, and busy civilization on one side, and on the other--lovely hills rolling to infinity. Impressed with the greenness of the tropical growth, I bubble over in Spanish "*Todo el mundo es verde aqui,*" and the professor's merriment over this burst out of bounds. He explained that my words referred to the licentiousness of the people rather than to the beauty of the landscape! Life down here is so difficult!

After lunch we hurried from the dining table to "*le Petite Paris*" where the professor ordered *helados con fruta* for our dessert. *Muy bien! Me gusto mucho!* Cold refreshing ice cream smothered in all kinds of fruits! Then more poking about the city--down by the waterfront with its market and its huddle of small sailboats, and passed the *Palacio del Presidente* with its flamingos in the patio. Back to the hotel for another afternoon of Christmas cards. And then another evening excursion! We returned again to the hill of the morning where the view of the city by night was equally beautiful. More *helados con fruta* after the warmth of climbing the hill. Then by foot back towards our hotel. At 11:00 the blackout engulfed us, and we resorted to a *chiva*.

December 18, 1941—Panama City—Hotel Colón

Early yesterday to the tourist commission and then to seek out the Flat Arch, said to be the reason why the present location was chosen for the canal. No earthquakes! This arch is part of an old church, and at present spans a garage--typical of Panama with its blend of old and new. Back to the hotel I went with the professor for a swim in the "olympic pool," a modern plant with clear, cool water, and it seemed good to dip into something besides murky heat. Another afternoon of writing. And another evening with *Señor Moles*. Back to the Lux Theater again for a movie, and afterwards another walk along the sea.

Today a whole morning of business--trying to arrange passage to Chile. Lack of definite word regarding a reservation on the boat sailing tomorrow sent me scurrying to a number of agencies only to be told eventually that no space was available. Discouraged I retreated to try to patch up my canceled Grace passage, but this afternoon the Chilean line discovered they had room for me! Definite word at last! And I dashed away from a Spanish lesson with the professor to buy my berth before the company had a change of heart!

I feel far removed from the war these days, and yet its evidence is on every side: the darkened city after 11:00 PM, the Japanese shops all locked and barred, the constant drone of bombers, the great search lights which send their fingers of light out across the sea, the headlines of each day's papers, the overtones of *"la guerra"* in the conversations of the street. All this and more.

December 19, 1941—Colón—Hotel Carleton

In *Colón* wishing I were back in Panama! --'Cause I miss the warmth of the place where I had friends, and I prefer my little cubbyhole on the Pacific side to this great barn of a room in a place so utterly strange. But it's best I lingered no longer in Panama, for each day I was growing more loath to say goodbye to *Señor*, the professor. And today I waited until the last possible moment before taking leave. I could have wept when the professor bent down and kissed me with tears in his eyes.

Last night we had a sort of farewell celebration: dinner at the Balboa Club--out under the stars with a fresh wind blowing. And I felt ever so much more elegant than a mere cyclist! Then a Mexican show with a comedy actor who amused even me who could not understand what he said. Fresh pears and *dos piñas* for refreshments. Followed by *El Club Nocturno* to watch the dancing and listen to the music. A Coke for me (I've consumed gallons since I arrived in Panama 'cause one has to drink something for sociability sake!') Then a long rest on a bench in a *plaza* followed by a slow reluctant walk back to the hotel. *"El último...,"* we were both thinking.

This morning to Grace Line for my refund, to the post office, to *Banco Nacional* to buy travelers checks, and then back to *Hotel Colón* to pack up Chester. Then out of the hotel in shorts on my bike with all looking curiously at *"la gringa."* Excitement over renewed activity sent me pedaling down the road to *Gamboa* at top speed, but midday heat combined with a feeling of "goneness" soon slackened my speed. The Zone seemed much less interesting then interior Panama, for it is a band of Yankeedom affixed to the isthmus, a place humming with the industry so characteristic of America and so familiar that it lacks the appeal of novelty. At *Gamboa* my road ended and I waited for a train to *Gatún*, so I thought this a fitting moment to consume *"la piña"* which the professor had given me. I ate until my mouth was too sore for more and then reluctantly abandoned the rest of that juicy, delicious fruit. It was evening when I reached *Gatún*, and the trip into *Cristobal* was made in the dusk with the palms and broad spreading trees of the tropics making lovely silhouettes against a darkening sky. By night *Cristobal* seemed hot, flat, cheap-- with its humanity pouring out into the streets to escape its sordid habitations. I found my hotel as quickly as possible, washed some clothes, and tumbled in the bed, overcome with weariness after a week of keyed up living.

December 21, 1941—S.S. Copiapó—Balboa

Yesterday morning I cruised about *Cristobal* and *Colón* on Chester--out along the windy, palm-lined coast, down the main shopping street with its substantial stores, past shanty town with its teeming black folks and thence to the docks to await my boat. At noon we went out to it by launch, and I went aboard with my usual curiosity--wondering who my companions were to be on this journey to Chile. Confusing at first, new surroundings soon become ordered, and people soon become personalities.

Passing through the canal became to me a momentous experience as I thought back to 1913 when men were digging there and dying like flies from the fever. Up through the three steps of *Gatún* Locks we went with our ship steadied by cables held by 6 chunky little rail cars that moved with us from compartment to compartment. And thence across vast *Gatún* Lake with its innumerable jungle clad islands. Darkness came with its usual suddenness, and we passed *Culebra Cut* and the Locks of *Pedro Miguel* and *Miraflores* with only the directing lights of the canal. In the distance the jungle was only a shadowy suggestion of hills and valleys. And we moved silently, almost ominously, in the darkness with our decks guarded by soldiers and more soldiers watching from the shores. One was never allowed to forget the military importance of the canal.

At *Balboa* we docked, and here we have been ever since--waiting, waiting, waiting for what no one seems to know. This morning more baggage and passengers came aboard. And I was amused to see a waiting Christmas tree being denuded by the black workmen, each of whom desired a sprig for his cap. A Christmas tree is a great curiosity in this torrid land.

In the afternoon I walked ashore to find a post office and have one last look at *Balboa*, the pleasant *Yanqui* settlement through which I made my first entry into Panama.

December 23, 1941—S.S. Copiapó

Early yesterday morning I looked out expectantly, but was disappointed to find the *Copiapó* still lying at the dock. How long would we be there? No one seemed to know. Strange are the ways of ships that sail in times of war! Presently four battle ships and an airplane carrier of the American fleet passed by us, and as if this were the signal we had been waiting for, our boat moved away from the dock shortly afterwards. Out past the islands, and into the open sea at last! --With a last glimpse of Panama City with its cathedral towers and its gray *Bovedas*.

Since land disappeared on the horizon, life once again has narrowed to the decks of our small boat. A limitless sea, days punctuated with four meals, the aimless going and coming of all the passengers. Spanish is spoken on all sides, but my comprehension is still zero; and I avoid my English speaking fellow travelers because so much of their conversations turn to what they don't like about the boat, the people, and the countries to the south. Hence I find myself rather alone, and I often climb to the forward deck and watch the sea--alone.

The sea has been amazingly calm, too. And the drone of the motors is the only reminder that the ship plows on. My quarters are comfortable enough, for there is only one other in my stateroom, and I find the food plenty good enough too. On one deck is a small improvised plunge [pool] which is an excellent place in which to spend one's time these hot days! All in all I'm comfortably settled, and I can overlook the dirt and the service which lacks the smartness of our American brand.

December 25, 1941—S.S. Copiapó --Guyas River

Christmas Day! --And not one wit of Christmas feeling! Instead the murky waters of the *Guyas* and the borders of greenery on its low lying shores. --With a warm, lazy feeling overall! My thoughts go home to family and friends, but there can be no pangs of homesickness on this day which has no semblance of those which have gone before.

Yesterday was the day of great celebration! In the early afternoon came Neptune's party to celebrate the crossing of the equator. The old man of the sea looked very fine in his rope costume and web shoes, and he was well attended with other be-costumed gentlemen, Hitler amongst them! Several persons were thoroughly baptized and treated with all the dangerous looking tools in Neptune's kit. Prepared for the worst, I waited in a bathing suit, but my lot was nothing more than a minor sprinkling. Later in the afternoon there were games on deck in a small square marked off by flags and graced by an honest-to-goodness Christmas tree. I found myself in the egg race, sucking the handle of the spoon that had been in any number of other mouths! But I lost the second heat. Balloons and noisemakers for the children added to the gaiety, but the din obscured the announcement of the games!

Dinner was a gala occasion with all the *señoritas* looking very lovely in their long dresses and with special hats and noisemakers for all. Toast followed toast on this *Buena Noche*, and we shouted hurrahs for *todos los paises de Sud America*. Latin merriment overflowed; the room rocked; everyone seemed to enjoy life. And then we adjourned to the deck for dancing, and it was fun to see the South Americans throw themselves into the rhythm of the music. All restrictions were down, and we even serpentined into the first-class dining room! At 12:00 we discovered the lights of *Guayaquil*, and presently the anchor rumbled down into the mud of this new land—Ecuador. A midnight supper of cold turkey. Embraces, hand shaking, wishes of *Feliz Navidad*! And then the launches disembarking passengers and carrying others to the nightlife in *Guayaquil*. Soon we were surrounded with broad boats bulging with bananas and pineapples, and the inevitable loading and unloading of cargo commenced. A Chilean, one *Guillermo Valdes*, walked me about the boat and would have gone further, but I begged off and retreated to my room at 2:30 AM.

Up this morning at 6:00 with hopes of going ashore, hopes that dwindled when no one else appeared. So instead I watched the activity about the ship: the loading of fruit; the arrival of kitchen cargo with its sides of beef, peppers, squash, milk, limes; the brown men whose muscles stood out with their effort and the brown men who slept sprawled out in any corner; the boy who fished tin cans from the river; the jaded passengers returning from the nights merriment. All morning the loading of fruit and unloading of cargo went on, and at high tide, the ships whistle sent the workmen scurrying to loosen their small craft from the sides of the *Copiapó*. As a parting gesture they tossed us ripe bananas that proved very delicious. Then we left *Guayaquil*, I with a feeling of having been cheated out of an anticipated excursion ashore. And now we're back in the old routine again: lunch, tea, dinner--with the intervening hours devoted to talking, writing, walking, watching the sea.

Nights on the boat prove diverting. Movies on deck under the stars. Banjo playing, singing, and dancing in true South American style. And always the endless hours of talking to other passengers. For true recreation I come to the forward deck by night and watch the sky and the sea alone.

Always there are other passengers to study. There is the large Swedish woman at my table who "believes in human nature" but who heartily dislikes the Latins whose customs do not conform to her own. There is the young American businessman filled with blustering braggadocio and judging all things in terms of Illinois. There is the tall, dark, attractive Chilean who used to talk to me but who now is enthralled by a pretty Colombian! There is the Swiss chap whose white hair and Spanish lingo seem incongruous. And there are many others--all interesting, all part of life here on the boat.

December 27th, 1941—S.S. Copiapó

All yesterday morning I sat on deck with *Señora Prat* and attempted to learn a little more Spanish. She is one of my new roommates, the vivacious wife of the commander of the Chilean navy. And she told me, with a pout, of her sadness over being unable to bring a new Cadillac back from New York! After lunch I talked with *Señor Valdes*, the handsome, blue-eyed (German??) Chilean who seems anxious to help me and also to hold my hand! And after tea I sat on the after deck and visited with *Joaquin Blaya* whose conversation is always amusing because of the art with which he supplies the English words he does not know. His discussion is always punctuated with *"What you call dis leettle animal?"* and *"How you say the name of dis man who come out of the sky?"*

The dinner hour brought another celebration with whoops of merriment. Even one who looks from the sidelines, as it were, and listens uncomprehendingly cannot escape the jovial spirit of these Latins. *Señor Blaya* (Neptune) acted as master of ceremonies while the loveliest lady and the ugliest man were chosen by popular ballot. The latter was a white Russian, the former an old maid who is not just right in her mind. Then *"Señor Quesos,"* the Swiss was crowned King. And when he embraced "Miss Copiapó," one friend, the Russian, dashed out in returned with knife and galdiator's cape (a tablecloth!) to threaten *Quesos* and carry away Miss Copiapó. The dining room was hysterical!!

The night was beautiful with the moon making a path of silver across the sea, and I spent the evening with *Valdes* whose pretty compliments are as constant as the drone of the engines. How fast these Latins work!

December 28th, 1941—S.S. Copiapó

Yesterday my first step on South American soil--with the old thrill of the unexplored still seething inside! We sighted land in the morning after the fog lifted: barren Peruvian shores and then *San Lorenzo* standing guard over *Callao.* The city stretching away to the hills was inviting. -- What people lived here and what mold had they poured their civilization into? But first there was the red tape of docking the boat, and it was not until after dinner that we went ashore. With my little Spanish roommate and my table companion I ventured into this new land and braved the buses rolling on to Lima. Beautiful tree-lined streets led to the capital. Flowering trees in yellow, pink, and violet; and broad spreading trees, too. In *Callao* were many signs of a recent disastrous earthquake--cracked walls and collapsed roofs--but these were lost in *Lima! Lima!* What drama had unfolded here! A city of tremendous memories. Narrow streets, balconies, busy people, lovely squares, impressive public buildings—all these seemed to belong to the present, but the past intruded itself on every side. *Pizarro's* shrunken body in the cathedral with its blue and rose ceiling. The lovely wooden balconies, tiled patio, and brocaded rooms of *Torre Tagle Palace.* The intricate wooden altars of *La Merced* Church. We devoted ourselves to the prosaic business of shopping first, and then turned to sightseeing, punctuated by tea at 4:00. And our last exploit was to seek out the congressional building and to stand in the parliamentary hall where President Roosevelt had stood before us! The policeman in their elegant uniforms were our guardian angel's wherever we went, always with patient explanations to our questions of *"a donde--."* And thanks to them we found what we sought and returned to the Copiapó in time for dinner. After dinner Mrs. Dufresne and I visited a Swedish boat lying next to the *Copiapó*. It was impossible to go aboard, but Mrs. Dufresne found a kindred Swedish soul with whom to talk, and I enjoyed myself talking to a little Peruvian officer with a red cape and a face wreathed in smiles.

All evening I talked with *Chilenos*, and it was 1:00 AM before I knew it. I find it easier and easier to do nothing but talk!

I'm still a little surprised at the Latin's way with women. For instance, there is *Comandante Prat* who stops to tell me I'm "a darling" and to assure me that the Chilean Navy is at my disposal!!

Dec. 29, 1941 –S.S. Copiapó

Great guns! A proposal already! I'm afraid *that' "yo no entiendo los costumbres de los Sud Americanos!"* Back on the after deck with *Valdes* last night, I was a bit startled to hear him say he loved me and wanted to marry me. After only three days of more or less casual acquaintance, I can't believe the man is serious, but I do not wish to hurt him, and I tried to explain the impossibility of his proposal. Speaking intangibles in a language I do not know! I was left without words! And half of what I said and of what he said went uncomprehended. A rather spectacular climax to a routine day--a day of talking, talking, talking. All its hours I devoted to visiting with the Chileans who want to learn to speak "nice English;" with the Swiss chap who spent some years in Japan and is sympathetic with the idea of cycling; with one of the football players from the Ecuadorian team; and of course with *Valdes*.

December 31, 1941--*S.S. Copiapó*

The day of the 29th was "just another day at sea" and now, a couple of days later I remember only that it passed quickly and pleasantly. More visiting with *"Queso"* and the rest. In the afternoon we came very close to land, and the desert hills of Peru, lovely in the orchid and purple of late afternoon, lay very near--just across a stretch of blue, blue sea. After dinner we saw a few dim lights in the distance, and at 11:00 PM we were in the harbor of *Arica* with a crescent of lights about us. I planned to go ashore with *Valdes*, but by the time all the formalities of arriving were past, it was very late, and my friend did not wish to go. So once again I stood on deck and watched the others depart feeling cheated yet unable to overcome the circumstances.

All day yesterday we followed the Chilean Coast, and I walked the decks under the spell of those barren, colorful hills which looked to be washed in pastel shades. And ever so slight haze softened their hard, lifeless reality, and gave them an indescribable beauty.

A considerable part of the day I visited with another Chilean, one I had not met before, but I found him interesting with his fondness for polo and racing. Then at dinner time came the diversion of another port, *Tocopilla*. Sparkling lights tucked between surf and sharply rising hills, and brilliant moonlight to give an ethereal feeling to that vast barren land. We all crowded into small boats and went ashore, landing by means of ropes and helping hands from our bouncing boats.

With *dos Americanos* I walked the streets and sat in the *Plaza* listening to radio music. But I had to build a wall and shut out my companions petty gossip and criticism in order to see the town with its poor little shops and the *Plaza* with its lacy trees and flooding moonlight. Some shops were open, even at that late hour, and many people were on the streets. Music blared from a small theater with a whole block of luring placards. And all the fruits of summer were displayed in the markets. The atmosphere in the town was rather tawdry, but the surrounding hills were magnificent in the moonlight. And there was life in the harbor with its numerous boats and dancing lights and its nitrate business.

January 1, 1942--S.S. Copiapó

Yesterday morning I wakened at 6:45 and dressed hurriedly to see *Tocopilla* by daylight. By day the town is no more than by night, but its mountains are a lovely quiet orchid in the dawn, and its breakers a froth of white on the rocky shores. I watched the unloading of heavy cargo until breakfast time, and when I came back to deck again, the Copiapó was continuing her way south.

Sun bathing during the middle of the day, and after tea a snatch of sleep to compensate for all that [was] lost. But after dinner, I needed to rouse out of my lethargy, for only then did the spirit of New Year's Eve take hold of the boat. At midnight we went into the dining room for *cena*, and such pandemonium I never have seen before! With the crazy hats and noise makers, the revelers surged around the tables, greeting each other with hearty embraces and wishing *Feliz Año Nuevo* to all. Supper was a succession of *"saludos"* and cheers from the Ecuadorian ball players with such a din of noise that all conversation was wiped out! But this spirit of good fellowship was contagious, and once again I marveled at the enthusiasm which these people pour into their celebration. After *cena* we sat in the salon to watch the revelers. The Ecuadorians with their hearty songs. And my fellow Californian who drank herself to a high pitch and held sway in a loud voice over a group of attentive *Chilenos*, *Valdes* included! I was content to sit by it with Mrs. Dufresne and the Swiss chap (who was handicapped with an injured foot). So content, in fact, that I sat thus until 4:00 AM! While the dozen left in the salon consumed a bottle of whiskey procured from first-class. As the Californian's laugh grew thicker, I grew more disgusted. -- And disgusted too with *Valdes* for I didn't want to believe what I know to be true of these impulsive Latins. One woman today -- -- another tomorrow. I guess I'm too serious minded to fit in with the South American scheme of things. And as I turned toward bed, the ship's doctor stopped me in the hall and asked if I'd like to drink a little whiskey with him!! Oh me!

January 2nd, 1942 – Valparaiso—Hotel Lebell

Yesterday was another eventful day in our lives at sea, for it brought another day in port. All morning I sat on the after-deck and visited with all my Chilean friends--a succession of them—*Comandante Prat*, the major, *Dr. Leoncio Andrade, Humberto Aranda*, and *Valdes* or Leidig as he is actually called. Just at dinnertime came the excitement of entry into another harbor, and from our decks, the town of *Coquimbo* with its dry hills and green farmlands looked *muy bonito*. Just after *almuerzo* we all tumbled into small boats and rowed away to shore. And many of us without stopping in *Coquimbo*, took the bus for *La Serena*. With Mrs. Dufresne I poked about this little town, so picturesque with its many church towers and cobbled streets, so like the South America I had anticipated. The buildings all crowded up close to the streets, and presented rather blank faces, but occasional open doors revealed glimpses of lonely patios with tile, greenery, and bright flowers. Best of always the principal *Plaza* with its brilliant flowering things—geraniums, broom, jacaranda, magnolia, canna--and with its fleeting subtle perfume. We rode back to town in a rattling gondola with some of the Ecuadorian ball players from the boat, and a bright moonlit night had settled over the world by the time we reached *Coquimbo*. Here we walked the principal street and the *Plaza*, and then returned to the *Copiapó* across a silvery bay. A visit with the Swiss chap and a turn about the deck with Leidig completed the day, and I turned in consumed with weariness.

And today *Valparaiso*--at long last, *Valparaiso*! This morning it seemed incredible that we should ever reach the end of our journey--that the easy, carefree life of the *Copiapó* should ever end--but end it did and here I am, embarked upon the trials and problems of a lone cyclist in a foreign land! A morning of packing in a helter-skelter state--full of trunks and femininity. And at 3:30 entrance into the bay with its semi-circle of hills carrying the city upward on its slopes. Great anticipation!--but first the dampening effects of passport inspection, transferring baggage from ship to shore, waiting helplessly and anxiously for Chester to come out of the hold, and finally waiting for inspection and the stamps which made everything official. And I went through the gates with a bicycle pump in one hand and a fur coat for Leidig in the other!! Then a few minutes of cruising through the streets and the help of a hospitable policeman, who shook my hand and wished me Happy New Year, brought me to this hotel where I'm relieved to have a room alone at last. And my 9:00 PM dinner tasted mighty good!

January 4th, 1942 – Valparaiso—Lebell Hotel

Yesterday I was out as early as possible to tend to tickets, money exchange, and general information, but Yankee-like I was too early for others and spent much of my time waiting! But business brought me familiarity with the financial district and with *Plaza Sotomayor*. I hurried back at noon to wait for my friend from the boat, the doctor, but he didn't appear until 5:30!! And then he had further business! So for two hours I poked about the city--getting its feel, as it were. Down Avenue *Pedro Montt* and along Avenue Argentina with its central parking devoted to a busy market. Great baskets and heaps of potatoes, tomatoes, peas, corn, beans, melons, and other products. And small boys selling handsful of garlic. Then back to sit a while in cool *Plaza O'Higgins* before wandering on through the central shopping district. This city is a modern one with a feel akin to our own cities, but it has different facets of life. There are the burdened horses and donkeys in the streets, carrying great baskets and bundles as well as their riders. There are the brown-uniformed policemen standing at attention and directing traffic elegantly with their wooden sticks. And there are the hordes of poor— so poor that they are clad in rags and in expressions of hopelessness. The rich are too rich, and the poor are too poor.

At seven I met my friend and drove to *Viña* and *Concon* in his new Chevrolet. This is a flowery way with brilliant reds and yellows and magentas. And the sea alternates between sandy coves and rocky headlands. *Viña* is all elegance with her palatial houses, casino, and hotel--a retreat for the wealthy. Evening came as we returned, and the night was lovely with brilliant stars and then a full moon over the sea. We stopped for Martinis at a little restaurant overlooking *La Salinas* cove, and then drove on around the crescent of *Vaparaiso* to a far point with a fine restaurant serving seafoods. Here we had our meal out on a porch overlooking the ocean and the city. Truly beautiful with the moon, the lap of the waves, and twinkling lights of the city. Chilean wine, Chilean consommé, and Chilean fish! All was fine, but once again I found myself warding off Chilean caresses and trying to give an answer to *"porque no?"*

January 6, 1942—Zapallar—Gran Hotel

Two days of comparative solitude with the life giving force of the country for good measure--just what I needed after the confusion of city life and the emotional strain of an overabundance of masculine attention. Tonight I feel recreated and deliciously tired.

Yesterday seems so very long ago that I can scarcely remember what took place. All morning I walked about the city. Starting by way of *Calle Condell* with its fine shops and well dressed women, I passed onto the old section of the city where life is meaner and the buildings more sordid. I stepped into old *"La Matriz"* church where people were coming for Sunday worship but here too was an atmosphere of resignation instead of one of release which one should expect of religion.

Choosing an *ascensor* at random I found myself up on a hill amidst the brightly colored hovels of the poor. Such poverty and dirt. Only a radio and a few potted plants to relieve the squalor of this jumble of houses clinging to the side of the hill. Back in the lower city again I took another ascensor and this time arrived at a pleasant terrace with fine views of the city and harbor. Past the stadium and the lighthouse and down a precipitous cliff to the promenade by the sea, and thence back to *Plaza Victoria* where people had gathered for the Sunday concert. After a hearty *almuerzo*, I packed my goods on Chester and took leave of *Valparaiso*. Back again to *Viña* and from here to *Parque Salitre*--a peaceful retreat in the hills, a place of woody walks, spacious gardens, quiet ponds. For an hour or two I drank in its calm, and then returned to *Viña* and passed on to *Concon*. This way is beautiful but one loses its grandeur in the masses of people and cars. I had to tend strictly to my pedaling! At *Concon* I stopped at *Hotel Mansilla* where I had dinner outside near this sea and where I could hear its roar from my room.

Today I left early--so early that a sleepy man in drawers delivered my bicycle to me! And shortly I had left the highway behind and was bumping along through the country en route to *Quintero*. Difficult—*peligroso*, I had been warned, but I wanted to see for myself. And I drew a deep breath of freedom. Along the river valley where vegetables were cultivated and then up into the hills where cattle predominated. The road was difficult all right, but I loved the broad vistas of purple mountains and dry hills with scattered trees. Life was there too in an occasional adobe house with its usual eucalyptus trees. And many wildflowers grew in the dry grass by the side of the road. All was hot and peaceful. In *Quintero* I made my way to *El Durazno* beach where I waited for *almuerzo*. Bright flowers and many vacationers here. A good meal sent powers surging through me, and I decided to push on to *Zapallar*. So I retraced my way to *Valle Alegre*, a *hacienda* where I secured a welcome drink of water. A fine saddle horse stood by the side of the road while his master lay stretched out, taking a *siesta*. And there were oxen yoked to lumbering carts. Up into the hills again in the afternoon heat. *Barancas* and scattered vegetation, and always the mountains. Just as I was wondering whether or not I'd be able to reach *Zapallar*, two men in a Ford stopped and added Chester and me to their cargo! Through *Puchuncavi* with its low, white buildings lining the streets--a typical native town--and back once more to the coast. A beautiful view of the beach at *Maitencillo* with the breakers rolling in. Thence along the rocky coast to *Zapallar*. *Zapallar!* Most beautiful of all the beaches! A small crescent of sand in a rocky bay where the sea swirls in foam and dashes high on the rocks. With elegant homes on the hillsides above--dignified, quiet, rich--set amidst eucalyptus trees, some straight and tall and some lacy and drooping, and many junipers. Glowing gardens on every side. Masses of petunias, white daisies, dahlias, geraniums, bougainvillea, hydrangeas, snapdragons, morning glory. Riotous, vivid color. And in the street--fine looking people who have known elegance, not poverty. Behind the town a background of hills to lend coziness to the beach and exclusiveness to the lives of the people. *Zapallar* is a place I should like to stay.

January 6, 1942—Zapallar—Gran Hotel

This morning I wakened in a happy mood after a luxurious night in the *"gran" hotel*. I like this place because it is all white--white walls, white furniture, white table covers, white crushed shell in the walks, white daisies in the garden. It's all so cheerful. And it gives extra brilliance to the bouquets of vivid flowers on the tables.

The breakfast was brought to my room—*café con leche y tostadas*—and I ate everything, including all the lumps of sugar, in order to fortify myself until noon! Then I rolled Chester out of my room and took off for *Papudo*. The road wound around the hills above the sea, and I had it all to myself in the gray of the early morning. Here the slopes were clothed only in low shrubbery, and there were broad views of the waves breaking on the rocks below. At one convenient point, I left the road, and making myself comfortable behind some bushes, I wrote for an hour--with only the waves and the mist to distract me. Then off once more, delighted with the great purple thistles, the white poppies, and the red lilies by the side of the road. In *Papudo* I only cruised and looked. Down the Main Street by the beach with its many hotels; past the station and toward the interior where the call of the open road, an unknown way, was hard to resist; back through town on the less pretentious streets where there was more of Chile and less of tourism. And then back once more to *Zapallar*. As I pedaled along, I made plans to leave after lunch, but as I rounded the point and saw the brilliance of *Zapallar's* sea and flowers in the midday sun, I decided to stay on another day. Irresistible!

After lunch I scrambled down to some lonely rocks and sunbathed for several hours. And then I came back to *Zapallar's* cove to watch the sun go down. A cypress silhouetted on a nearby point. A blaze of orange clouds across the sky. A faint evening star. And the sea, an iridescent mass of green and blue and violet, breaking in thundering white surf on the beach. In *Zapallar* a wisp of smoke and a light and a boat riding at anchor. Nature and humanity in harmony, at peace. And I, too, am at peace after my 9:00 PM dinner.

January 7, 1942—Maitencillo—Las Rocas Hotel

Another lazy day by Chile's coast. All morning I spent in strolling past *Zapallar's* bright gardens and in sitting on the rocks which flank her beach. Then after *almuerzo* I packed up and departed--happy to be back on the road again but sorry to leave *Zapallar's* quiet beauty. Retracing the way towards *Valparaiso*, the scenery seemed more brilliant now-- viewed from the seat of a bicycle instead of from that of a Ford! The blue of the sea, the white of the surf, the multicolors of the roadside flowers--all were intensified by the sheer joy of pedaling. --Even with an admixture of pushing through sand! Outside the bounds of *Zapallar*, life lost its elegance and became a common work-a-day thing. Low, white washed, adobe houses; farmlands lined with eucalyptus; deliberate oxen so broadly yoked that I could scarcely pass them; men on horseback--always men on horseback; children playing in the dust, devoid of the neat braids and clean skirts of *Zapallar*.

After a leisurely 10 miles, I stopped here at yet another beach, a broad expanse of gently sloping sand with breakers rolling in one after another in endless succession. *Maitencillo* is only a handful of houses, and the hotel looks as if it basked in the memory of past traffic, but the location is excellent, and once again I hear the roar of the ocean from my room. In the heat of the afternoon I lay in the sand on the beach, and in the cool of the evening I walked along the hard sand where I could see the sun sink behind a bank of clouds and turn the sea to gold and green. I even took Chester for a turn close to the lapping waves! Frustrated for lack of water and light earlier in the evening, I now have both. And also a bountiful meal to fill the eight hour gap since lunch!

January 8, 1942—Valparaiso—Hotel Adria

Phew, what a day! --So long that it's hard to believe I was eating *desayuno* in *Maitencillo*--and spilling coffee on the tablecloth and covering the spot with a plate! Out into a dull, gray world. Welcome coolness. Sometimes hauling Chester through sand, sometimes bumping over rough road, I made my way slowly back toward *Concon*. But I had a whole day, so what matters if I [was] slow. A handful of other cyclists made me feel less alone in my escapade. And Chilean cheese and Chilean hard bread eaten by the side of the road made everything look easy. Instead of following the coast, I took the long way via *Limache* and *Quilpue*. My map showed roads and I had the time, so I couldn't resist it! Up a river valley rich in farmlands, and then through hills with only scattered vegetation. Hot, hot, hot. Welcome the rows of tall eucalyptus which sometimes lined the road. And welcome the murky water which a *carbinero* dipped for me! In *Quilpue* I stopped for an *helado*, and one was so good that it called for two! An excuse, too, to talk Spanish with the man in charge. Instead of staying in *Quilpue* as I had planned, I came on into *Valparaiso*. A flat tire en route! --My first this trip. Rode with a couple of other cyclists from *Viña* to *Valparaiso*, and they escorted me clear to *Playa Victoria* and *Hotel Adria*. A new hotel this trip--one with better room and a lower price.

January 10, 1941—Santiago—Hotel Victoria

Another long day! Leaving *Valparaiso* about 8:00, I climbed up over the hills and away from the sea. Up, up, up to--and then down--rolling with the joy that comes of having pedaled up the hard way. Again through rolling land with scattered vegetation and a few farms tucked in the hollows. Groves of eucalyptus, weeping willows in the damp places, primroses by the side of the road, and little white adobe houses where the country folk lived. In *Casa Blanca* I stopped to buy more bread and cheese and to learn about the road ahead. Only two more hills they assured me! But sun had come out of hiding, and the first up was hot. It was dinner time too my knees told me. So I stopped in the scraggly shade of a mesquite bush and had my bread and cheese--a fine lunch for a hot day with a scarcity of water! My throat and tongue felt like breaded cutlets! --But just after starting up again I came upon a cold spring by the side of the road. Allah be praised! The rest of the climb seemed less tedious. Then I was whirling down again, this time into *Curacavi*, a pleasant little town in the hills. Here I stopped to buy fruits and consumed a dozen nectarines before going on. And as I rested I became the center of a curious crowd of young vendors. Another opportunity to practice Spanish! On the road again I was stopped by a gentleman in a green car who saw my club plate and wanted to ask about Seattle. He knew the state and spoke fluent English; and he offered to carry me over the next hill, but awkward Chester wouldn't fit in his car. So he gave me his card instead! It was truly hot now, and I stopped to wash the salt from my face in a roadside ditch. Then up again, the last hill. –With no breath of air, just overpowering heat. Not even a mesquite bush to take refuge under! Only cactus. The two boys in a truck stopped and I couldn't resist. On to *Santiago* by motor! As we topped the hill, we looked out on a spectacular panorama--below a green cultivated valley and in the distance beyond the snow-capped mountains of the Andes. A thrilling sight. My friends took great pains to deliver me to the office of the American Express where I hoped for mail, but it was the wrong department. So I stopped at this hotel and freshened up before sallying forth to look in earnest. Only two letters and not a single word from home. I was crushed! Salved my sorrow with a dozen apricots and then went out to look at the city. Walking, walking, walking--through the central section with its elegant shops and its hordes of people. The darkness came and things looked so different that I lost myself. Had to ask a policeman how to find my way home!

January 11, 1942—Santiago—Hotel Victoria

        Yesterday morning I devoted to business--American Express, Chilean Line, tourist agency, and the like--and this took much time for all the while I was learning my way about *Santiago*. First my own section and then neighboring ones, little by little it becomes familiar. In the afternoon I looked up the friend of *Señor Moles* of Panama, but since only his wife was there, I arranged to return today. In the evening as I wondered about the streets who should I bump into but Mrs. Dufresne! A familiar face seemed startling!
        All day I sampled Chile's fruits and *helados*. And I consumed dozens of peaches, pears, figs, etc.! Sort of a holiday from the quantities of meat I've been consuming! A typical Chilean meal consists of soup, often times a hearty one with great pieces of meat and potato in it, a fish and potato course, a vegetable course consisting of a stuffed vegetable or a vegetable omelet, and a meat and salad course, followed by fruit and coffee. Always there are two hard rolls without butter. Once I asked for *"un poco mantequilla"* and was charged extra!

January 12, 1940—Santiago—Hotel Claridge

Yesterday I slipped into my 29th year without celebration, but *almuerzo* of green corn, green beans, spring chicken, and peaches I counted a special birthday treat.

In the morning I packed and departed from *Hotel Victoria*. The place seemed good, and I liked the view of the mountains and also the animated room boy with his boundless interest in *mi viaje solita para bicicleta*, but the plaque of *"animales chicos"* was intolerable. Two blocks brought me to the Claridge where I have a great high-ceilinged room, a private bath, two beds, and *pensión*--better and cheaper than the *Victoria*. I went out and climbed to the top of *Santa Lucia* hill, a landscaped knoll with a grand view from the top. Quantities of trees and shrubs interspersed with statuary and benches make this a pleasant place to rest, and others were there too. Most of the seats were occupied by students deep in books, by men sleeping, by innumerable lovers. A fine place to while away a Sunday morning.

After lunch I returned to *Señor Tarrago's* house, and I found him very agreeable and quite ready to talk. I stayed for coffee with him and his wife, and I enjoyed speaking Spanish with them, for their's is a brand more readily understandable than the Chilean.

I walked slowly home by way of the *Mapocho* River and its woodsy park, and I felt thoroughly steeped in Sunday ease and leisure.

January 13, 1942—Santiago—Hotel Claridge

Yesterday again I tried to get the refund on the return portion of my Chilean Line ticket. No success. And here I stay until I'm able to collect those *pesos*! At 11:00 I hunted out *La Escuela de Verano* and slipped into *Señor Tarrago's* class on astronomy. He speaks clearly and I am able to understand a good deal of his Spanish. Perhaps I shall stay on and go to school to try and train my ear to good *Castellano*. In the afternoon a special errand to secure *tacos de goma* for my shoes then more walking. Across from *the Plaza de la Libertad* was a crowd of people, and curiosity led me into their midst. Someone was shouting over an amplifier and the people answered with applause. On every side were police, mounted and on foot, watching. Making my way toward the front, I was able to read the banners and placards. A Communist mass meeting, of all things! Complete with hammer and sickle and printed words to the effect that Russia, Britain, the United States, and China were defending the world against Nazism! The crowd was interesting. Tattered clothes and work-a-day faces interspersed with cynical, derisive, prosperous faces. That all were not Communist was attested to by the chorus of *"vote por Ibañez"* which at one time drowned out the speakers. Here was a typical bit in the life of a republic, and it was refreshing to find that not all popular demonstrations have been stamped out in the name of WAR. And amongst the crowd were fruit vendors and paperboys and men who had set up their portable "lunch counters" to sell hot meat tarts to the public! Life went on as usual.

The sun is bright this morning and the shadows of the grill work beyond my French doors make lacy patterns on the floor. I must go out and get better acquainted with this city.

January 14, 1942--Santiago--Hotel Claridge

Yesterday I walked and walked and walked. --Seeing *Santiago* on foot! Down *Avenida Bernardo O'Higgins*, weaving back and forth across the wide parkway to read the inscriptions on all the monuments. Then across and back to the *Escuela de Verano* to gather more details on summer courses. Just in time for the reception of *extranjeros* by the minister of education! And who should be there but two other passengers from the *Copiapó*!

After lunch I went in search of the reference Uncle Charlie had given me. The kind little German *dueño* here at the Claridge had taken great pains to try and locate the whereabouts of the elusive Petersons, and he suggested I go to *Barros Araña* and ask for them at various shops. Straight down *Augustinos* I went and out of the business section and into an older part where low houses stood shoulder to shoulder close to the street and guarded their inner loveliness with iron grills and large doors. Across the *Quinta Normal* with its shaded avenues and agricultural plots, and out amongst the collection of hovels where streets degenerated into dust. Here was the street I sought! Obviously some mistakes in directions! Back I trudged toward town, stopping in the *Quinta Normal* to watch the people and enjoy the gardens. And right there was the *Museo Nacional*, so in I went. Passing quickly by the plants and animals and fish and shells, I lingered long over the colorful bits of fabric and the small, perfect arrowheads from an early *Chileno* culture. Also interesting was the *Araucanian* room with its life-like representation of native Indian life.

Back to the sanctuary of the Claridge to read and write and dine. Then a short walk, more writing, and to bed. Above the usual noises of the street which stream in my open doors, came a chorus of *"vivas"* for some presidential candidate.

January 15, 1942--Santiago--Hotel Claridge

Yesterday morning to school again. Visited classes in *Castellano para Extranjeros* and philosophy, and resolved to stay on in *Santiago* to take advantage of summer school. Gathered in my refund from the *Compañia Sud America de Vapores*, and went to the *Banco de Chile* to cash my check. No luck! Identification demanded--that which I have not got! Upstairs an *Americano* scrutinized me carefully, perused my passport, and secured the necessary okay. Allah be praised! I walked out with *3000 pesos* in my purse!

Another long walk. First to the home of *Aranda*, a fellow passenger from the *Copiapó*. But he was not there.

Then to another *Barros Araña* Avenue to try and locate the Peterson family. Again--futility. Home and discouraged, I called up "the Doctor," and was repaid for braving the intricacies of a Spanish phone by an instant response. He came to the hotel, all smiles of welcome, and promised to return after supper if work permitted. And it did permit, so I went with him on two short calls, and then off to the top of *San Cristobal* with the lights of the city glittering all about us. Chicken sandwiches, Scotch, a bit of dancing on a terrace high above the city—a splendid vantage point.

A strange fellow, the doctor. I go back to him because he fascinates me, and yet all my evenings with him are devoted to parrying kisses and caresses. He believes in lusty living and calls me a child in the way of life. He believes that the moment is important and that love is important, and he laughs at what he calls my mystical concept of the relationship between man and woman. We talk freely and frankly of love and sex and marriage, but our differences are infinite. And I almost fear his sensuousness.

January 16, 1942--Santiago--Hotel Claridge

Yesterday morning to school again--a regular pupil now. My class in Spanish is very elementary, and even I can understand it! But the philosophy lectures are beyond my comprehension! I listen only for the pronunciation of familiar words, but often I lose myself in the music of the language and forget to listen for any meaning.

A letter from home, my first, sent my spirits soaring, and I read it excitedly in *the Plaza de Armas*, and then spent the early afternoon writing home. I felt almost as if I were having a real visit with the family!

Bumped into Gross of the *Copiapó* and fell into his arms in the middle of the street! He is the insufferable American who does nothing but rail against the Chileans, but the bond of casual acquaintance draws people together in a strange city, regardless.

In the late afternoon I went out on Chester, anxious to go farther afield then is possible on foot. Explored the section to the north and the road leading to *Colina*. Then returned to attend a lecture at the school. But this proved unintelligible, and I was too weary to try to understand, so I walked out. In the late afternoon the Andes were very clear, and their snowy tops caught the last rosy rays of the sun--a beautiful sight.

January 17th--Santiago--Hotel Claridge

More school yesterday, and at long last I know just what I want to take: astronomy from *Señor Tarragó*, *Castellano* from *Señora Iribarren* and philosophy from *Señor Ferrateri*. This program I think will give me all the Spanish I am able to absorb for the time being.

In the afternoon something inside of me stirred restlessly, and I couldn't sit in peace. I wrote a little, washed a little, started for a walk and turned back; called up *Aranda* who wasn't home. Then I resorted to Chester and found there what I wanted--physical activity in the peace of the fields beyond the city. Down the full-length of *the Avenida Bernardo O'Higgins,* and then off to the south, choosing streets at random. Ultimately a through street led me away from the confusion of town and out into the open where there were majestic views of the Andes. And what a thrilling sight they are to one who loves the mountains! Rising sheer and barren and snowy-crested so close beside the city! I pedaled recklessly for some time, reveling in their beauty, and when I returned home I was refreshed.

Unable to escape the fascination of those peaks, I climbed again to *Santa Lucia* hill and looked at them in the clear evening air--watched them change from the rich warm purples of the setting sun to the sharp cold blues of night. And their beauty was enhanced by the foreground of trees and shrubs which the hill provided. As I climbed down, the *Santiago* skyline was crystal clear against the sky--the spires of medieval devotion and the stacks of 20th-century industry.

But the love of the couples on all the benches of *Santa Lucia*, I presume is timeless!

January 18, 1942--Santiago—Hotel Claridge

Yesterday was a fuller one than I had anticipated, and I do love full days! Having contacted both *Andrade* and *Aranda* and having heard nothing from them, I decided that the Chileans were living up to their reputation for saying one thing and meaning another, and I went off by [myself], the best way, after all, if one wishes to accomplish anything. With Chester I left the city and made my way toward the beckoning Andes, along the *Mapocho* and then into the road to *Apoquindo*. Once off the pavement I felt more in the country and more content, even though the going was more difficult, and I loved the snatches of picturesque countryside which were mine at every turn--the white adobe walls with fruit trees showing over the top, the rows of stately poplars, the open gates revealing rich and flowery estates. But I was astonished to see men wetting down the dust of country roads with buckets filled from roadside ditches! No water wagons in Chile.

I loitered under the eucalyptus trees of *Apoquindo* Park for a while and then returned to *Santiago* by another road. And when I reached the hotel, I found that both *El Doctor* and *Aranda* had called! At 3:30 *Humberto* came and I was delighted to see him again. After talking at great length we sallied out to see *Parque Consiño*, stopping en route for a great glass of ice cream. I like *Humberto* because he is never forward and also because he has a twinkle in his eye and a ready wit. He called the donkey in the park "his brother in the gray suit!" He also makes the pretty speeches for which Latin men are famous and by which women are enthralled. Said he to me, "take care of your nylons because they cost $120 down here—without your beautiful legs!"

At 6:00 I rushed home for an appointment with *El Doctor*, fearing all the while that *Humberto* and I might come in at the same time as he. But all went smoothly, and when

Andrade called, I was ready. We went out in his car to see more of *Santiago*. *Parque Japonese, Tobalabla* where there are countless fine new homes, *Nueva Playa*, the Prince of Wales country club, the *Estadio Nacional*. And next weekend we would go to the *Cordillera* he said. I was all enthusiasm until I discovered that this involved spending a night out, and then I went into reverse because I feared *El Doctor* would expect more of me than I would be willing to give. And with this decision I think I ushered *Señor Andrade* out of my life, for I could not adequately explain why I did not have confidence in him. I shall be very much surprised if I ever hear from him again.

January 19, 1942--Santiago--Hotel Claridge

Yesterday morning I rode away on Chester at 7:00 AM, before *desayuno*. A fine Sunday morning with the usual freshness of the early hours. Taking a road to the South, I whirled along on pavement until I reached *Puente Alto* where I found a market in full swing--crowds of men and women buying produce for sale in the street. Turning almost instinctively toward the mountains, I found myself on a dirt road but one which forever led me on to the next corner to see what view was waiting there. For this road wound up into the hills beside the muddy, rushing *Maipo*, always ahead were the great hulks of the Andes, majestic, snow streaked. Clear to *El Canelo*, a quiet little village with lovely old trees, and beyond I pedaled, and *El Volcán* lay like a challenge ahead of me. But time was short and reluctantly I turned back, taking another road from *Las Viscachas*, a road leading through much picturesque countryside. Little adobe houses smothered in vines; masses of weeping willows; long lines of tall poplars; walls which hid their secrets from the public; and an occasional rich house with ample gardens. Beside the road were men and women taking their Sunday leisure, and passing by was the usual traffic of high-wheeled carts drawn by 1, 2, or 3 horses. Typical of these are the *panaderias* which bound along at great speed, their horses whipped into a gallop. On the road too were Chile's typical horsemen, mounted on good horses and riding strange padded saddles with carved wooden stirrups. Over their shoulders they wear a bright poncho split in the middle to accommodate their heads. Very colorful! Very intriguing to this girl who is steeped in the tradition of the West.

After *almuerzo*--rest from my 45-mile jaunt, rest interrupted by the *dueño* who apologetically asked me to change rooms. Certainly no problem for one with my small number of possessions! And thereafter a jaunt by bicycle with the *dueño*'s small son, *Carlos*. He on his little bicycle pounding along like a mosquito but having many troubles en route--soft tires, a loose steering head, etc.! A capital guide, *Carlos*. Took me out through *Tobalaba* to the *Canal San Carlos* and thence back to the center by way of the *Mapocho*, chattering all the while in Spanish which I only vaguely understood!

Attempting to walk after *comida*, I found myself too tired, and I used up my last bit of energy in crawling home to bed.

January 20, 1942--Santiago—Hotel Claridge

Mornings at school are routine now, but I feel a bit futile in my efforts to learn Spanish because I learn so very slowly.

Yesterday afternoon another excursion with young *Carlos Stuermer*. Off to *Parque Consiño* we went, he in the lead, darting through traffic and beckoning me on. Round and round and round the Park we rode, along all the trails, across all the bridges, through all the gullies. And I was interested to see the life there: men sleeping on the grass, old women selling ice cream, boys swimming naked in a dirty pond, boys exercising sleek race horses, and always lovers, oblivious to all but their love. For a long time we stopped to watch a derailed streetcar put back on its track with much official supervision. And in this crowd, as always, I found my PNCA plate the source of great curiosity. *"Por favor, señorita, que significa esto?"* Returning through afternoon traffic, I was frightened to see *Carlos* run into one pedestrian and another cyclist but he came through unscathed. And the cyclist, instead of taking offense, piloted us back to our hotel!

January 22, 1942--Santiago--Hotel Claridge

Tuesday afternoon I rode again toward the mountains, following the road to *Apoquindo* but turning left towards *Arrayan* and thence pedaling up the *Mapocho* on a narrow road overhanging the river. I was actually in the Andes here, actually on the slopes of those barren, precipitous mountains. And below, the *Mapocho* was a muddy, rushing stream. Few people lived in this narrow canyon--just an occasional hut clinging to the slope--and I felt far, far from the crowds of the city. Coasting back to *El Arrayan* with its wider cultivated valley, the vistas broadened, and soon I was out of the hills in typical rural country once again. Back another way through nice little *Barnechea* and along the road closer to the *Mapocho* where once again I thrilled to the sights of Chile's *campo*. Geraniums banked against low, dilapidated adobe walls, slim, prim poplars in long rows, horsemen jogging along in their colorful costumes. And behind me the Andes, which I needed to stop to look at. The only blight on the afternoon was the breaking of my gear cable, a very real tragedy. And as the wire snapped, I saw my dream of crossing the Andes by bicycle fade away into the realm of the impossible.

But yesterday young *Carlos* piloted me to a cycle shop where the damage was repaired and now I live in peace again! After 5:00 when the job was done, the two of us started for another ride, but *Carlitos* found himself with a flat tire, and by the time this was repaired there was only enough time left for a few turns about the streets of *Santiago* and a few mad dashes through the late afternoon traffic. My hair stands on end as *Carlito* winds in and out, straddling car tracks and riding on blithely on the wrong as on the right side! But perhaps he has a guardian angel!

Another letter from home yesterday called for a celebration. And I settled myself with a dozen nectarines! Chile's fruit is truly delicious, and I find myself loitering by every street vendor, unable to resist the fragrance of peaches and melons.

January 23, 1940--Santiago--Hotel Claridge

I enjoy school these days, for it has a great novelty for me. Since I cannot understand all of the content of the lectures, I find myself studying the professors—*Señor Ferrater* who sits quietly, looking from one to another of us with the brown eyes which we northerners find so fascinating and *Señor Tarragó* who lectures with much gusto, looping about the room to indicate the courses of the stars! But little by little, *poco a poco*, more and more words become meaningful, and what was only chaos at first, now has some significance.

Yesterday afternoon valve trouble sent me scurrying with *Carlos* to the nearest bike shop. And as we stood waiting for the iron doors to roll up (3:00 PM), a man stopped, inquired about my Seattle plate, and said he had been a consul in Seattle for three years! He gave me his card and invited me to drop into his office later in the afternoon. My PNCA insignia is bearing fruit! But first there was business to attend to: the steam ship company to find out the hour at which my boat leaves for *Laguna San Rafael, Expresso Villalonga* to arrange to ship by bicycle to *Puerto Montt*; a fruitless search in tourist agencies and the automobile club for a good map of Argentina, a fruitless search for a flag of Chile, and finally a fruitless search for a woman in the home economics department of the department of agriculture! But I didn't neglect to drop into see *Señor Nagel,* and he was most hospitable! Over tea and cookies we talked animatedly of America and Chile, and from him I gathered more valuable information. I can understand how he comes to hold his position as Executive Secretary of the Commission for Inter-American Cooperation!

At dinner I found that my sour Chilean companion had been replaced by a friendly Peruvian *señorita* who, like myself, is traveling alone. And she not only gave me a good lesson in Spanish but she came to my room and talked to me of her country and what to see there.

I've also made the acquaintance here of a Czech *señorita* who sings over the radio. She knows much of Europe and South America, and I find her humanistic philosophy very refreshing. Night before last I stayed till midnight in her room, looking at newspaper clippings and photographs and listening to her stories of contracts in London, Paris, Stockholm, Buenos Aires--!

January 23, 1942—Melipilla—Hotel 21 de Mayo

My mind wandered in *Castellano* and astronomy this morning, for I was full of the thought of my trip to *Cartagena*. Open roads unfolding before my tireless pedals! Wild, uncontrollable spirit of the vagabond! And immediately after lunch I packed, said goodbye to my Peruvian and Czech friends, and pedaled away. *Down Avenida O'Higgins* and through the commercial section of the city where there were myriad carts and trucks but where the activity seemed stagnated by the midday heat. Here I can always depend upon being the object of hisses and remarks from the workers--poor ragged fellows whose lives are barren--but I always ride with speed and sureness, looking neither to right nor left. Through green fields beyond the city, and then off the highway along shaded avenues to *Peñaflor*. A beautiful spot, *Peñaflor*, a garden *pueblo* with both houses and streets in deep shade. And a land of fruit trees too. I bought half a dozen nectarines for "*onces*" and sat and talked with the farmer's wife who sold them to me. Good practice, this! The country road to *Talangante* was delightful, lined on one side with weeping willows, and on the other permitting views of the Andes. Back on concrete again, I rolled easily intimate into *Melipilla*, stopping only once, in *Chinique*, where I asked for an *helado* and wound up with a tomato! Water from a dirty beer mug tasted like nectar of the gods, despite the strong flavor of beer, and I sat and talked a while with the proprietor of the ramshackle establishment. Thus I make the acquaintance of many kinds of people.

Here in *Melipilla* a *carabinero* directed me to *el mejor hotel*, and after washing and changing, I went out to see a bit of the town. A crowd moving out of the *Plaza* attracted me, and I fell in with them. Another Communist demonstration with hearty "*vivas*"! But this procession had more than marchers; it had *huasos*! And I walked beside the mounted section, looking at saddles, bridles, spurs, hats, and ponchos out of the corner of my eye. Chile's horsemen are certainly colorful. They lend atmosphere to demonstrations as well as to country lanes! I was so engrossed in horses that I saw little of the town, but there was very little to be seen in the dim streets--only an occasional meat shop with assorted carcasses hanging from the ceiling.

And now I am *muy contento* in my shabby room for I have had *comida* and half a melon, and I wait for tomorrow with its new sights, new people, new experiences.

January 24, 1942—Algarrabo—Residencial Buenos Aires

A cup of Chilean coffee, a mournful dog, and a confusion of voices kept me awake most of the night, and by 7:00 AM I was glad to take to the road again, fortified with the other half of my melon instead of *desayuno* which is always so late in arriving. At *Leyda* I turned off the highway, and then began the hard work by which this day shall be remembered. First the problem of keeping my balance on a road graveled with treacherous little round stones, then a head wind which necessitated peddling downhill as well as up, and finally sand so dry and soft that I could scarcely push Chester through it! The joys of cycling!

As I neared the coast I entered the realm of bleak windswept hills, and I met few people until I reached the beaches. Cruising leisurely through *Tejos Verdes, Llolleo, San Antonio, Cartagena, El Tabo,* and *El Quisco* gave me some idea of the crowds of people who flock to the coast. In *San Antonio* I bought a *tortilla* from one of the basket salesman who are a sure indicator of holiday crowds, and the little seaside restaurant in *Cartagena* where I had *almuerzo* was a hubbub of activity. Outside, the beaches fairly swarmed of people and with the rows of tents that are ever present. All these *pueblos* are more or less exposed, lying close beside the sea on low, barren hills, but they have fine beaches and an occasional rocky promontory to provide interest. Here I encountered my first difficulty in finding a place to stay, and the shades of Japan rose again to haunt me. I could go no further. But this residential took me in, and I was glad to stop, even though there is no *agua potable*.

January 25, 1942—Peñaflor—Residencial La Quinta

My weary body said, "Go back the way you came by a road you know is good," but my adventurous spirit said, "Nothing ventured, nothing gained. Perhaps some new experience lies over yonder unknown hill," and the latter won! So I took 4 lumps of sugar in my coffee and used up all the butter on my bread in anticipation of a long, hard day! What was in store I did not know, for it is impossible to get cycling information here in Chile. When I seek it, I come away with the admonition that it's impossible to go by bike, plus detailed information concerning busses and trains! My only recourse is to depend on maps, and today I laid my course accordingly, turning toward the interior and hoping to beat my way through to *Peñaflor*. Looking back over my shoulder for a final view of *Algarroba* Bay, I pedaled into rolling hills—hills that reminded me of home—dry, open hills. And after having the sands of the coast, the road was very good. It was fun to pedal swiftly and silently again after so many tedious, bumpy miles, and I waved merrily to the crowds of holiday-seekers driving to the coast. At the second fork in the road I had some misgivings, for my way looked a bit rough, and before going far I realized that Chester's wheels were turning where only bare feet, horse hooves, and the wheels of oxcarts had gone before. But I liked my valley with its mud houses and cultivated patches. And just when I thought my path was going to disappear in a creek bed, I found myself in another good road! And here too was a nice little village where a young Chilean cyclist joined me for a while. But he stopped in the shade of a eucalyptus when the road commenced to climb, and I pedaled on, streaming with perspiration and sucking plumb pits to alleviate the thirst which always plagued me. At the summit of this *cuesta* I stopped for bread and cheese. Welcome pause with a fresh breeze blowing. Then down again into cultivated lands where again I shared the road with *huasos* and oxcarts. At the next fork in *"el camino"* I asked about the way ahead and was discouraged from attempting it, but the day was still young. So off I went, pedaling easily through a beautiful, narrow, green valley where people loitered in Sunday ease and where the *huasos* wore their best Sunday trappings. Happy was I to have persisted in my route! Stopping at a *carbinero's* house to ask for water I received a smiling welcome and was urged to sit a while. Then I was provided with the equipment for washing and was served a great, delicious piece of watermelon! And after this I was sent with the children to see the animals at the dairy across the road. Here I met a young German Jew whose simple statement that here he could work was filled with pathos. Seeing my interest in the horses, he brought out a horse for me to ride, and at long last I had my chance to try out one of these strange padded Chilean saddles! How good to sit on a horse again! And to be there in the country with the cattle and the simple country folk! I lingered long here where I had stopped only for a drink of water, and when the shadows lengthened and I knew I must push on, a cup of tea was waiting for me. I could not repay the *señora* for all her kindness; the best I could do was to leave a *peso* with each of the 5 children. One *cuesta* remained to be climbed, and a steep one it was. Even pushing was a tedious task. But my reward was the view from the top. The chance to again look down on the garden lands of Chile's central valley. Then down into these garden lands and into *Peñaflor* with its shaded avenues. And now I live in one of *Peñaflor's quintas* where apples and grapes and flowers abound. And I love the green seclusion of my *residencial*.

January 27, 1942—Santiago—Hotel Claridge

Back again to baths and silk stockings after a "grand excursion"! Yesterday I was so close to *Santiago* and I could afford to be leisurely and so I was. Before breakfast I wandered about *Peñaflor*, enjoying the wealth of growing things and the shady coolness, and then I had a late *desayuno* under the arbors of my hotel. When I finally pedaled off, I chose roads at random, wandering first through *Peñaflor* and then crossing the highway in search of a country road by which to return to the city. But before leaving the land of fruit, I bought a dozen delicious nectarines to go with bread and cheese I carried for lunch. At midday I crawled through a fence and made myself at home behind a row of poplars beside a muddy ditch of water--a fine place for a picnic lunch and safe from the. stares of the country folk. In the afternoon I rode through *Maipú* to see the place where one of the battles of independence was fought, and I passed a while beside the monument dedicated to the heroes. Then a hot dash brought me back to the city, and I drew up to the Claridge all sunburned, steaming, and dirty. How welcome a bath at times like this!

In the late afternoon I walked towards the school to attend a *"conferencia" sobre "Cuzco"*--compensation for having skipped my morning classes. And who should I meet on the street but my old friend *Guillermo* of the *Copiapó*. We had tea together, and then he delivered me to school in his shiny red car. -- Very pleasant to bump into a friend in the street! He left me with promises to come to see me again, but I imagine they were promises of the Chilean variety--pretty sounding but devoid of intent! After the *conferencia*, which I did not understand, I hurried home to have an early *comida*, and then I dashed off in a *"micro"* to *San Cristobal* to join my astronomy class in a field trip to the summit of this most excellent vantage point. Very interesting! We saw the *Cruz del Sur* in all its glory, *Falses Cruces, Can Mayor, Gemelos,* the *Gran Nube de Magallanes, Orion* and the planets *Jupiter, Saturno,* and *Marte.* Also *Can Menor,* the *Nebulosa de Orion,* and *Aldebaran,* and the *Plezades.* Beautiful also were the lights of the city and the filmy boughs of pepper tree framing the views from the hill. I returned home with two students from Argentina, and they both have given me their addresses – *Cordoba and Tucuman.* Happy day! Little by little my way ahead becomes peopled with folks I know.

January 28, 1942 -- Santiago -- Hotel Claridge

Yesterday afternoon I rested and mended and wrote letters, but after a dozen nectarines had stirred up life in my system, I looked up *Carlito* and went for another afternoon's bicycle jaunt. To *Plaza Italia* and the foot of *San Cristobal* and thence in a loop which took me past the cemetery and back into the city on a main thoroughfare humming with traffic. *Carlito* is unpredictable. Sometimes we stop at corners to watch the life of the city, sometimes we run madly with the traffic, and sometimes we turn off on cobblestone streets which are scarcely navigable!

After a very early *comida* (8:00 PM!) my new Argentine friend, *Señor Cecilio,* called to show me the way to the *universidad* where the astronomy class had assembled for another field trip. By *micro* we rode to the south of the city where the observatory is located, and until midnight we looked at the heavens. Mars, Jupiter, Saturn with its rings, the craters of the moon, the nebula of Orion, *Cirio* glowing brilliantly in blue and yellow, and the multicolored cluster of *Centauro.* As instructive as the telescope was, my opportunity to speak Spanish, and *Señor Cecilio* proved to be an entertaining teacher. He obligingly explained to me that the joke in Coca-Cola was the fact that *cola* meant horse's tail in Spanish! We were all convulsed with laughter!

January 29th, 1942 -- Santiago -- Hotel Claridge

School's become quite a sociable place these days. We Americans gather in a small clique and talk in English, greeting our Chilean friends with a *"Buenos dias"* as they pass by.

In the afternoon I read, wrote, and consumed quantities of ice cream and nectarines, and walked restlessly through the streets. I bought a ticket to *Temuco* and then had a change of heart, only to find it is impossible to exchange railway tickets in Chile. The unsettled spirit inside of me kept me up past midnight, and rather frightens me. If I feel like this after only three weeks in the same spot, what will be my reaction when I settle down to teaching in the USA!!

After supper shouts in the street brought me out of the hotel at top speed to watch the processions of men, women, and children who were parading in the name of *Ibañez*. Such enthusiasm! Shouting, singing, flag waving, and scattering of hand bills! And quantities of solemn policemen following their horses and standing at attention in strategic positions. I felt almost as if something momentous might happen there in the crowded streets, but nothing did, and by midnight the city was again as usual. Chile's election will soon be over, and the contest between *Ibañez* and *Rios* settled.

January 30, 1942—Santiago—Hotel Claridge—8:00 AM

Yesterday was the last day of summer classes, and so it was *"Hasta luego"* to all our professors. I'm sorta sorry to see it end 'cause it has been great fun, but I look forward to more wandering on Chester.

In the afternoon I met again in the streets the couple from the *Copiapó* whom I had met in the streets of *Valparaiso*. We're old friends by now!

And then I donned my one and only dress, put on my gloves which are the only elegant touch of which I am capable, and went forth to take tea with American friends who have been in my class in *Castellano*. Miss Scott of *Santiago*

College was our hostess, and we had our tea and sandwiches and pastries under the trees in the beautiful grounds of that school. Later we saw the interiors too, fine rooms that are very American. But the charm of the institution is in its Spanish touches: the spacious, quiet patios, the arcades with their solid round arches, and in the tile and the grillwork. There within those walls I felt very far removed from the endless activity of Santiago's streets.

January 30, 1942—Chalet de "Las Vertientes"—midnight

Errands after breakfast—shopping for all the odds and ends I needed before leaving Santiago. Then at 11:15 to the *Salon de Honor* of the *Universidad* for a final "*acto*" of the *Esculea de Verano*—an *acto* with pretty speeches interspersed with musical numbers. Then back to the Claridge for *almuerzo* and packing. And finally—off again on Chester for a weekend excursion! *–y que linda mi viaje!* Working my way east on residential streets (*Tobalaba*) to avoid the eternal jarring of the cobbled thoroughfares, I eventually arrived at the banks of *Canal San Carlos*, and here I turned south, following the canal road through all its vicissitudes of dust and gravel! For the way was a pretty one with its banks of blackberries, its weeping willows, and its occasional views of the Andes framed by tall poplars. A shady avenue lured me to the east again, to *La Reina*, but I had to return for there was no crossroad. And then with purpose I rode to *Peñalolen,* but the way was steep and I was grateful to two small urchins who delightedly pushed me for a way. All seemed to be sleeping at *Peñalolen,* and after pushing through an unlocked gate and riding through a park with a great house in its center, I turned back down the hill, not quite sure whether or not I had trespassed on private property! Back at the canal again, I stopped at another *carabinero's* for water, and once more I was invited to wash myself and sit awhile. Welcome shade and a view across vineyards to the Andes. Then on once more until my canal road disappeared in the *Planta Electrica* and I had to cut back *to Av. La Florida* in order to make my way to

Las Viscachos and the road to *El Volcán*. Again I thrilled to the trip up the *Rio Maipo* with its beautiful views of the Andes—all so near in the clear air. And I couldn't resist a small chalet on the very brink of the river in the shadow of the mountains. So here I stopped—and spent a leisurely 2 hrs. before *comida* down by the river enjoying the beauty of the spot. A young chap on horseback made his way down to me and let me ride his horse, skirt, silk stockings, and all! After *comida* I talked with the four men who seemed to be taking charge of the chalet, and they were interested to know if all North Americans didn't think that there were nothing but Indians in Chile! Then with one of them I wandered out into the soft beauty of a moonlit night. Fatal mistake! Even that boy, a mere child, took me by the hand and said, "Wait a minute, I kiss"! I give up!!

January 31, 1942—San Alfonso—Residential Corrio

Long, long ago—this morning!—I left my nice little chalet and pedaled up the river in the cool of the early hours. Welcome the streams of good mountain water which poured down the mountain sides to quench my endless thirst! By one of them I stopped for a late breakfast of bread and cheese and lumps of sugar carefully saved from past *desayunos*. Then on and on and on up the narrow rocky road which followed all the twists and turns of the gorge of the *Maipo*—a majestic canyon with high rock walls which now and then permitted a view of more distant, snow-striated crests. But always the valley was broad enough for life, and there were green fields and an endless succession of adobe shacks. Where these joined forces to form *pueblos*, all was green and cool with trees and vines and wetted rocks. A dry yellow field dusted with pale blue flowers caught my eye, and I was interested to see a horse thrown in the road while several men nonchalantly shod its feet. As I pedaled on I climbed out of the region of trees and up into wild, rocky canyons. And here at last was *El Volcán* with its factory clothed in white dust and its nondescript collection of houses. All seemed poor and uninteresting in the midday heat, and I stopped only long enough to buy a melon for my lunch. Turning back I realized why I had worked so hard coming up: the way was truly steep. But I rolled on until at the joining of the *Volcán* and *Maipo* rivers I found a spot to lunch—complete with shack, grass, and a clear stream. Here I stayed for 2 hrs. resting, eating, reading. And only when the shadows had grown very long did I go back to the road. A beautiful time of day to travel—this. And I stopped after to look back at the sunlit peaks behind. Traveling in the cool of the shadows of the canyon walls was refreshing after hours of burning sun, and the lateness of the hour was unimportant for I knew I could easily find a place to stay before dark. And here I have stopped in a *residencial* of one of the *Maipo's* green *pueblos*.

All day there has been much traffic on the road. Men on horseback driving pack mules. And *micros* jammed with men going to *Santiago* to vote—men crowded into the aisles, hanging out the doors, and stacked on top! It's a case of do or die for *Ibañez* or *Rios*, I guess!

February 2, 1942—Santiago—Hotel Claridge

Yesterday morning an early start! No waiting for *desayuno* or for the unlocking of doors. And I welcomed my opportunity to pedal in the early morning freshness, to see the sun creep down the rocky walls, to watch the first stirrings of morning activity. Breakfast bread and cheese I took up on a bushy hillside, screened from the eyes of the curious but in full view of a grand peak of the *Cordillera*. Then leisurely down to *Puente Alto* over the old familiar road. Here I joined a scrambling crowd in a *panaderia* and came away with 2 rolls so fresh they fairly burned my hand. The day was yet young, so instead of turning toward *Santiago*, I pedaled south to *Pirque*, an old and comfortable looking community with great trees. Crowds of men had assembled here to vote, giving the *pueblo* a holiday air. Thence along the *Maipo* on pretty country roads with lunch on bread and cheese taken under a weeping willow beside a canal. Turning back towards "home" the heat of midday sent me pedaling top speed to the Claridge for a welcome bath and a long, long drink. But Chester's wheels were scarcely cold before I dismantled him and packed him (with *Ibañez* handbills gathered along the road to *Puente Alto*). Then I put all in readiness for my trip to the south and went out for a last *helado* and a last look at Santiago. The streets were full of police standing by for election disturbances, and on one corner I saw them neatly intercept a fight.

February 3, 1942—Hotel Fourcade—Temuco—8:00 AM

What a day! Wooo-eeee! Up early for last minute packing and in ample time to catch my train. Then off again into the unknown with a bag in one and my saddlebags in another! But gone was the confidence with which I travel on Chester, and I wondered if I'd reach the station in time, if I'd catch the right train, if I'd make the right change in *Temuco*, if I'd reach my boat in time!! Traveling on schedule is all so complicated!

Seated in the *"expreso,"* I felt more at ease, and I watched Chile unroll with great interest. Through rich agricultural lands we rumbled at first, but south of *Curicó* these gave way to a more pastoral landscape—drier and more expansive. And always we were in sight of the Andes—the magnificent crests and the unmistakable volcanic cones. In the train there was little life; each of us sat in his first class seat and spoke no word. A porter brought me a German magazine to read (!), and he also explained that the train had a *comedor*, but I continued to hop out at each station in order to lunch on the fruits and "poisonous pastries" which were always for sale. By evening I was tired of my hit and miss diet and decided in favor of the *comedor*, and there began another "adventure." For at my table sat a man bound for *Temuco*—one *Juan Espinosa de Rosa*! At first we only ate, but at last he ventured a question and soon we were friends. And when we arrived in *Temuco* he helped me to the hotel where he planned to stay. Since I was a stranger in *Temuco*, he suggested we go out and see the town, and far be it from me to turn down an opportunity to go places! –And so I walked the streets with my new friend, the plump middle-aged little businessman from *Concepción*. The hour was late and the town deserted with all the iron doors rolled down, but nothing daunted, we walked up and down through all the principal streets, through the *plaza*, into the two theaters to see the ends of 2 movies, and finally to the "*cafeteria principal*" for café. This was followed by sherry, and we loitered until the orchestra went home and the management was ready to close up shop. Then "*Juan*" suggested we go to a restaurant for a typical Chilean dish, and I decided I might as well make a night of it! It seemed incredible that any place could be open in the town at 2:00 am, but J*uan* knew all, and we found a little place where he ordered *cazuela de ave* and *criadillas* plus a bottle of wine! So here we had *cena* and danced to a succession of records! And I finally had to insist that we go home! As we walked back, *Juan's* romantic spirit warmed up—stirred by the moonlit night, I guess. And by the time we reached the hotel he was insisting on a kiss, and declaring his eternal love! Latin *amor* is always the same! I had to close my door by force, and it was 4:30 before I finally got to bed!

February 4—S.S. Trinidad

Fearing that the hotel management would put off waking me until "*manana*," I came to at 6:30 after only 2 hrs. of sleep! A step across the street brought me to the railway station, and I resolved to travel 3rd class for a change in order to see another class of people as well as to save a little money. Asking when *el tren ordinario* arrived, I received many different answers, and since I had to catch my boat in *Puerto Montt* at 9:00 pm, I almost weakened and took the expresso. Only after the conductor assured me that we arrived at 6:30 could I settle back and enjoy myself. And then I thoroughly enjoyed my plebeian ride! --For the coaches were packed with common folk carrying diverse bundles and bags, and there were many *huasos* with big hats, high-healed boots, and checkered pants. Some of 'em were fresh from the 'ole corral, and they came with manure on their shoes!! And with this motley crowd came salesman and beggars too. But I found people friendlier in 3rd than in 1st and I had an opportunity to talk a little with my fellow travelers. One young chap settled himself beside me and was soon talking of his love for me like the sighing of the wind in the trees! When I spoke to him in English, he translated my words into "*Yo te quiero*"! Not until *Puerto Montt* did I see the last of him.

South of *Temuco* the landscape changed, the dry hills giving way to wooded ones, and everything becoming more lush, more green. And in the evening we reached Lake *Llanquihúe*—a beautiful sight, with two snow-clad volcanoes rising in the background. Then in a few minutes we were back at the sea again in *Puerto Montt.*

From the station in *Puerto Montt* I hurried to the office of the *Servicio Maritimo*, and, Allah be praised, it was open and I was put aboard a bus and sent to my boat without further ado. How easy! First of all I was interested in cleaning up, getting rid of all the dirt accumulated in my 3rd class coach. And then there was the beautiful view of *Puerto Montt* and the snowy volcanoes to absorb my interest. Not until after our little boat was underway and the dinner gong had rung did I begin to get acquainted with the other passengers. First with the two pleasant German ladies at my table and then with *Julio Cesár* (!), an Argentine lawyer, who started to make love to me in the moonlight and who wanted to come to my cabin "to talk"!!

February 5, 1942--S.S. Trinidad—Aysen--Midnight

Yesterday morning I wakened to the familiar sounds of unloading cargo, and when I reached deck we were just leaving a small port. We were traveling in a maze of islands and on both sides were low hills cut up into agricultural patchwork. But views were not extensive because on every side were low clouds. And later, rain transformed everything into a vague suggestion of reality. Only once or twice in the whole day did we catch glimpses of the high mountains which encircled us. In the afternoon bad weather sent most of the passengers below; but strangely enough the bouncing of our little ship did not affect me, and I spent the afternoon talking with the *Capitán*, looking at his photographs and finally taking tea with him. After dinner *Julio Cesár* and his companion from Argentina joined me when I sat in the *comedor*, but *Julio* didn't feel very well, and he finally left in a great hurry, leaving his companion and me the only ones still aboard. We talked at great length and finally retired for want of anything better to do. The only diversion was my falling flat on the dark, plunging deck! Later when sound asleep in my cabin, I was roused by a voice saying, "You sleeping?" and *Cesár* Ghost! It was *Julio Cesár* in my cabin! I said, "Go, go, go" in my firmest English, but it was some little time before he ushered himself out the door. One never knows what to expect here in South America!!

Today has been a great day, for the clouds finally lifted and gave us magnificent vistas of Chile's southern splendor. Green and blue and purple mountains, bare peaks with patches of snow and green ice, innumerable cascades and green *"canales"* through which the Trinidad wound her way. Somber wooded mountains rising abruptly from the sea brought back memories of Norway, and I was completely happy in the solitude of this grand country. But there was no loneliness on the boat, for all morning I stood on the top deck talking and listening to American phonograph records! And when we were in sight of *Aysen*, I agreed to go ashore with Julio. We became a party instead of a couple, for which I was thankful, and our spokesman, a suave little Chilean, finally procured a car from the *carabineros*. We met first one and then another and then another of these police, and each time we shook hands all around and talked at great length, but finally the sought-after car was forthcoming and after *onces* in our boat, we drove off, five of us, with a chauffeur and a *carabinero*! Up the road to Argentina we went in a river canyon with high mountains rising on either side and with beautiful, bush woods beside the road. Wild fusias everywhere! And a lovely waterfall. More food in a little wayside restaurant--sandwiches and cheese with hot peppers-- and then we turned back towards our boat. But not before a bottle of whiskey had been procured and enough drink to put the crowd in a merrier spirit. Lusty Chilean songs graced the entire return trip. Great fun! And back in *Aysen* our *carabinero* friend procured a boat for us, and we rowed out on the river to enjoy the evening and to stop at another point to visit the cemetery! More Chilean songs, this time with a guitar accompaniment. But we had to be rescued from the current in the river by another chap who really knew how to row. After dinner the captain asked me in to meet some of his friends, and we all had a round of drinks in his cabin. Then we walked up town and had another round of drinks at the hotel. I came back alone with the captain, and afterwards visited with him on deck where we could see the moon rise over *Aysen*. But aside from a few pretty words, he made no advances, and this was a refreshing relief from some of the others I have known! For this, I like the captain.

February 7, 1942--S.S. Trinidad

Yesterday morning I rushed out to deck in anticipation of a bright day after the brilliant night in *Aysen*. Shattered hopes! A heavy fog and a drizzle of rain grayed all the landscape and blurred the mountains until their shapes were mere shadowy hulks in the mist. A day for writing instead of looking! But I chose the *comedor* with its windows as a place to sit just in case the weather might clear! Exasperating, this weather which closed out the grand view we had come so far to see. After lunch the weather was agreeable enough for deck, and we congregated topside to watch the ship slide down the narrow channel and to amuse ourselves with songs and guitar. As we neared *San Rafael*, we scrambled into the bow of the boat to better see the first icebergs--small bits of ice moving in solemn procession with the tide. And we gave a cheer of delight as we entered the lagoon and saw the great glacier which sent its myriads of *tempanos* across the surface of the water. What beauty! Murky green water; great and small icebergs each with a heart of ethereal blue revealed in its cracks and crevasses; mountains of diverse shades of purple rearing their heads into the clouds and thence into infinity in our imaginations. Incredible panorama! Four of us remained in the bow in spite of short squalls of rain, and to keep dry we disappeared periodically under the poncho of our Chilean friend who clucked with great glee as he spread his "wings"! We all went ashore in a small launch to see the few desolate houses, the beginning of a canal to the Pacific, the poor inhabitants with their braids and weather-beaten faces, and a baby seal kept in captivity. Then we moved on across the lagoon to a great hotel beside the glacier. Here, after dinner, we went ashore again to marvel at the spectacle of a luxurious resort in the wilderness--empty. A drink and a little radio music completed the evening's entertainment, and we returned to the Trinidad shivering in the cold night.

This morning a loud knock on my door brought me to at 5:30, and again I hurried to deck. Better luck this time, for the clouds were high enough to permit a fine view, and our last look at *Laguna San Rafael* was an impressive one. The captain obligingly took us up close to the glacier before he turned and took the Trinidad across the lagoon to the narrow exit hidden in the hills. The icebergs, still an unearthly blue, floated on a sea turned yellow-green in the morning light. Presently all my early morning companions had disappeared-- gone back to bed--and I had breakfast alone with the captain. I stayed a while with him on the bridge too, listening to him direct the man at the wheel. And it was not until later that I made my fatal mistake and accepted the captain's invitation to go into his cabin to escape the rain and cold on deck. He too wanted a kiss! And the strength of his arms plus the danger of being overheard by the other passengers made me quite helpless. Life these days seems to be nothing but a series of amorous men, and I find myself wondering why. Is it the fact that I am traveling alone? Am I being coquettish without knowing it? Or is this masculine aggressiveness just an old Spanish custom?

Most of the afternoon I stood glued to the smoke stack where there was welcome warmth and from where I could see at least a bit of the rain-blurred landscape with its canals and shadowy mountains. Once we stopped near a cluster of cabins on the shore from whence several boats came to sell us shellfish. And the fisher folks in their poor rags and bare feet made me ashamed to be shivering in my jacket and shoes. One woman in a huddle of black rags rushed up and down in her bare feet, busy exchanging her strings of shell-fish for a piece of beef.

A talk with two young Germans who speak English, a game of casino with a *Chileno*, and an hour with the little ponchoed man with the guitar completed the day, and I turned in with heavy eyes, glad to go back to my bunk once again.

February 10, 1942--Puerto Montt--Miramar Hotel

Sunday the weather was still wet, but there were delightful intervals of sun and breaking clouds and freshness. All day we ran close to low hills with patches of cultivated land--the great island of *Chiloe*. Writing, talking with the two young Germans who spoke English, watching the world of water and land beyond the boat, standing in the windy bow, loitering on the top deck in the shelter of the bridge, visiting with the captain--these things came to be the essence of my life on the Trinidad. Before dinner I went to the captain's cabin again, but I found he hadn't changed. Same old thing! But later I guess he repented because he called me up to the bridge and promised never again, *nunca*. In the course of the day we stopped at a little town on the shore to take on mail and passengers. A clean, gray, windswept town with no vestige of the character of the towns of the north. Tall houses without walks and without shrubbery. Houses all of wood. The towns of the southern region are all like this--changed through the pressure of a different environment. In the evening we sailed up to *Castro* through a narrow channel, and the hills so near on either side were beautiful in the saffron evening light which accentuated their agricultural patchwork.

I stood on the bridge with one of the mates who pointed out our course on his charts as we approached the lights of the city. And then with other passengers I went ashore to see the town, but the hour was late and the streets dark, and my memories of *Castro* are memories of a crowd of miserable little beggars, steep streets, lots left vacant by a fire of several years ago, a shadowy *plaza* with its church, and the "*Club Social*" where we stopped for drinks. After the visitors had filed down the gangplank and all of us had filed up, our little boat turned around and sailed back the same channel, losing the lights of *Castro* behind the bend. When the captain called to me from the bridge I went up to him, which was a sign of weakness on my part, I guess, but I found him very attractive and before the trip was over began to watch for him with anticipation. Later we visited in his cabin until the hour of 1:30 AM--this time "*sin abrazos*"! While lusty songs floated up from below where our little be-ponchoed *Chileno* was entertaining three new *señoritas* just come aboard!

But the hour of *comida* brought the most spectacular event of the day, for at this late moment the sun broke through the rain, and a vivid, perfect rainbow with a shadowy double arched itself across our channel, one foot on either shore. A brilliant, thrilling thing it was there in the gray and olive and gold of late evening. And this, plus the passing of the "*Tenglo*," completely disrupted the dinner hour.

Yesterday morning-more rain. And this added to a sore eye and the knowledge that I must leave the Trinidad reduced my spirits to low ebb. Packing, chattering disheartedly with other passengers and watching for the captain made up the morning, and before I was quite able to comprehend it I was passing with my two small bags through the *aduaña* and into the gondola which brought us to the office of *Servicio Maritimo de Ferrocarriles*. Thence a step across the street brought me to this hotel where I was glad to rest and unpack and play "*floja*" for a spell. After dinner I asked about *Expreso Villalonga* and my bicycle (with fingers crossed), and with the aid of an English gentleman here in the hotel, I was able to convey my wishes to the *dueño* who procured my bike for me without further ado. And happy I was to see Chester again, all intact, but I was less happy when it came time to inflate the tires. Holes, holes, holes! With the well-meant but bungling assistance of a host of "*secretarios*" from the hotel, I pried off tires and patched tubes and blew up tires until I was weary and worn. After two patches fore and two aft, I still had a flat, and I decided to give up the ghost until later. All afternoon I had watched for the captain who had said he would come to my hotel. Being skeptical of Chilean promises, I knew better than to set my heart on it, but I did hope. No *capitán*. Typical but disappointing. After a short walk and a hearty *comida*, I felt equal to another flat tire, and so I carried Chester up to my room and struggled with him for another couple of hours. No success. And I went to bed very tired and very discouraged.

But a good night's rest can change the world, and this morning all seemed right. After breakfast I pushed Chester off to a place where I was told a man could fix my tire, and so I left my bike, skeptical but hopeful. Later I came back to find it fixed, and when I asked "*Cuanto vale,*" the mechanic patted me on the shoulder and said, "Nothing. I too have ridden a bicycle many miles." The brotherhood inspired by cycling reaches clear to Chile. Free of the pressure of watching and waiting for another, I set out to see *Puerto Montt.* --Wandered up and down *Calle Varas*, around the *plaza* with its white daisies and red geraniums, along the shore where a sailing vessel lay at anchor, into a "back-alley" market where fish and seaweed and strings of *mariscos* were on display. Watched with interest the townsfolk and the many ox-carts moving deliberately through the mud. And then who should step out of the crowd to greet me but the captain! And my heart was all upset again just when I thought it had settled down to normal operation! We wandered up to the hospital on the hilltop to get a better view of the town and the harbor and then, in spite of threatening rain, we went off to the island of *Tenglo* via gondola and rowboat. There in the lovely garden of *Quinta* Hoffman we had *chicha de manzana* beneath a wet arbor surrounded by dewy flowers, and through the trees we could see the bay with its many little fishing boats. A beautiful spot, all damp and deserted. From the boat landing we walked back to town, and there "Al" took me to a little upstairs restaurant famous for its seafood. I went deliberately in spite of rain-streaked hair, parka, and bobby socks, and we both ignored the stares of the curious. Until 3:00 we loitered over *almuerzo* of oysters on the half shell (!!), cazuela de congrio, beefsteak con ensalada, and *postre* of grapes. And then *El Capitán* went off on an errand with the promise of returning to my hotel. And he did come back! But he was told I wasn't in, and it was late before I happened downstairs and found him there. All we had time to do was to go back to the Trinidad together and sit a while in his cabin before the time of sailing. He kissed me good-by, without any resistance on my part (!), but his kisses were interrupted by a succession of persons at his door, and it was funny to see how quickly he changed from lover to captain! Then 8:00 PM was there, and I left the boat, walking back home in the rain with heightened consciousness of the closing day, of the men in ponchos, of the well-stocked fruit shops, of the glistening water in the streets. But that the captain's going meant much to me was attested to by the fact that I stopped to watch the Trinidad sail out of the harbor and again to watch her dwindle to a mere dot in the bay. Fool that I am! I know that to take Latin *amor* seriously is to "play the sucker," but a personable man can easily pry his way into my loneliness. And the captain has a boyish way about him. Oh me. After a 9:00 dinner I sat and visited with another passenger from the boat and we topped off the evening with a walk and a bag of delicious Chilean grapes.

February 12, 1942--Petrohúe—"Restaurant"

Yesterday morning dawned gray and desolate, and since *Puerto Montt's* zest had gone with the Trinidad, I determined to push on. The hotel personnel watched me curiously as I packed up and took off in the rain, but after three years of cycling I'm very adept at ignoring others' curiosity! I wouldn't be the happy traveler if I weren't! Up over the hills behind the port and into rolling farmlands I traveled, and although the rain foreshortened every vista, I could see a great many cultivated plots with their substantial houses and barns--gray wooden buildings with picket fences--building which sheltered hardy animals and blond German heads. Spikes of range lilies, white flowering trees, and purple thistles were fresh and bright beside the road. And although the rain was filling my shoes and penetrating my pack, my spirits ever high, and I sang as I pedaled! Too, I felt a sort of camaraderie with all the other be-ponchoed folks on the road. And I was delighted with the bits of road that were arched with spreading trees--spots where the smell of eucalyptus and cypress were washed down to me with the rain. In *Puerto Varas* I stopped at *Hotel Bella Vista*, and who should I meet at the desk but the jolly German lady who had been my table mate on the Trinidad! I felt at home immediately, and was glad to have company at mealtime. After *almuerzo*, I stopped by *Expreso Villalonga* and hopefully waited for mail. One letter only and no word from home--So I salved my sorrow by walking about *Puerto Varas* in the rain, up and down the main *calles* and up to the fine, modern hotel on the hill. Then back to my room to wash and write. But just before the sun set, the stormy weather broke, and I ventured forth again, anxious to make the most of each bit of sunshine. Seeking always some high spot, I found a wooded hill behind a church where a broad path wound around to the top. Every little way there were religious images where others stopped to mumble but where I only looked. And from the top--a glorious view. Below, the town with its red roofs and pastel walls--all clean and neat and rain-washed. Several little boats in the lake making bright reflections on the water. Hills with plots of brown and green and gold. A bit of rainbow. I stood, just looking, for a very long time. And then as I went back into town, I stopped at a little saddle-maker's shop where I was invited to sit down and where the saddle-maker and his wife told me about their family and how they had built their house themselves. Just another fact in my *conocimientos* of Chile.

Supper, a visit with my German friend, and bed completed the evening.

This morning--the sun! And I packed and took to the road in great excitement. The rarity of sunshine makes it the more precious, and I reveled in its brilliance. My way took me to *Ensenada* along the shore of *Lago Llanquihué* where beauty unfolded on every side and where I felt that I was in a very new and different Chile. Rich farm lands. Plots of golden wheat. Very green pastures where good animals fed. Neat gray horses. Fruit trees. With the blue of the lake below and *Mount Osorno* rising in perfect symmetry to a cold blue point. *Precioso*! At *Ensenada* I left the comfortable farms and entered the woods with their almost tropical lushness. Creepers, fronds, cane, and great spreading trees--many with white blossoms. A narrow, woodsy way along the *Rio Petrohué* where once I stopped to seek out a wild cascade. Always beautiful. And on I pedaled. I played hide and seek with an auto which frequently stopped and whose passengers were soon my friends. Here in *Petrohué*, I really made their acquaintance--a *señora*, a number of children, a mild *señor*, and another very gay *señor* who invited me to join them in a drink, asked me all about my trip, and insisted on an *abrazo* before leaving! The balance of the afternoon I have spent out beside *Lago Todos Los Santos*, considered the most beautiful of the Chilean lakes. And beautiful it is with its surrounding mountains and woodsy shores. Sitting on a narrow beach to read and write, I watched the waters change from emerald green to steely blue as storm clouds drifted in, and I watched bits of rainbow come and go. Here I feel as if I were truly removed from toil and turmoil, for the handful of houses here are the only signs of life on the lake.

February 14, 1942--Casa Parque--the Carabineros

All yesterday morning I wandered alone about *Petrohué*--through the lush damp woods with their ferns and moss and lichens and fushias and up onto the slopes of *Mt. Osorno* where rivers of lava had destroyed all living things except a yellow moss which spread itself over the terrain like a rich Chinese carpet. I walked softly without a sound. Billowing clouds rolled about the summits of the mountains and wisps of thin clouds floated down into the canyons. Once or twice I caught fleeting glimpses of *Osorno's* snowy sides. But *Lago Todos Los Santos* was not so elusive, for it lay unveiled for all to see. Back at the restaurant I was confused by the throngs of people who had arrived by bus and boat. My solitary splendor was completely shattered! And I felt a bit self-conscious there amidst so many elegant tourists. After *almuerzo* Chester and I went aboard the little *"Esmeralda,"* and after a long wait on her decks, we steamed away across the lake toward *Peulla.* I found refuge from the mob up in the prow where I had the best vantage point in the boat. And I thrilled to the deep green of the lake's water, to the high mountain sides rising abruptly from the shores, to the many cascades, to the occasional houses clinging determinedly to bits of cultivated land, and to the clouds which lent a dark and wild note to all the landscape. In *Peulla* I sought a room in the great hotel, but not being a "regular" tourist and not having a book of assorted coupons, I wasn't welcome, and the *dueño* thought it "better for me" to continue on. So on I came in the late afternoon up the deep, dark canyon of the *Rio Peulla.* Dark masses of trees, a roaring river, innumerable falls, ragged snowy peaks, swirling clouds; but forms on the canyon floor in spite of the wild country. Shades of Norway! The beauty of the land and the lateness of the hour inspired me to ride fast and recklessly over the graveled road. But it was not until after dark that I arrived here at *Casa Parque* where I expected to find a room. No vacancies! Thanks to the kindness of one of the *carabineros,* I have been given a room, and the good *señora* has provided me with everything. Coffee with bread and cheese last night in her warm, candle-lit kitchen, and then a bed with a great down coverlet. In my room, too, slept one of the boys, but he came and went without a sound. I feel very grateful for all the little things--the candle, the chair, the pot under the bed--things provided especially for me. But I feel helpless to repay such hospitality.

Feb. 15, 1942--Bariloche--Pensión Rosa De Esperanza

A long day with much changing brought me through to Argentina yesterday. After breakfast of coffee, bread, and cheese, I said good-bye to my kind hostess and her small boys, and started the long push up over the *cumbre* toward *Laguna Frias*. Four miles of steep, rocky road put a kink in my back, but I could happily ignore it, because my way led up amongst the wild, misty heights where great trees and bamboo lined the road and where masses of pink and white foxglove, orange lilies, and white margaritas blossomed. A beautiful, damp morning without another person to be seen. And then suddenly I was at the top from whence a short coast down brought me to the hotel at *Laguna Frias* and into the midst of a horde of tourists. The Argentine customs official tried to dissuade me from taking my bike through, but when he saw I was intent on it, he kindly agreed to let it pass. I wanted to change money here, but I disliked the arrogant hotel manager and his low rate, so I decided to risk getting by without Argentine pesos. When I finally found time to look about me, I discovered that many of the curious tourists who gathered about my bike were folks from the boat of *Lago Todos Los Santos*, and at our second meeting we were old friends! Shortly I was putting across *Laguna Frias* in a small launch, a ride of only a few minutes across green water at the foot of abrupt mountains. Then 3 kilometers through lovely woods brought me to *Puerto Blest* on the shores of *Lago Nahuel Huapi*. Here my friends from B.A. asked me to join them at lunch, and I ate a tremendous meal without wincing!

After cycling I can eat nails! Then, since we were all amongst friends, we decided to make a side trip to *Los Cántaros* before going on to *Bahia Lopez*. A few minutes by boat and a walk through lush *bosque* brought us to the *cascada*, and we went a bit further to a lake shut in by sheer walls of rock. Then rain sent us scurrying back to our boat. The couple of hours on *Lago Nahuel Huapi* which followed passed quickly, for there were magnificent mountains to be seen when the clouds lifted, and when rain obscured this world of beauty. There were the other folks on the boat to talk to. The water was blue now instead of green, but the peaks were still wild and snow-streaked. A spot of sun brought us all to the prow where the young man with the [camera] snapped innumerable pictures. Then *Bahia Lopez* and good-byes, and I was off for *Bariloche--solita* once again. I went by way of the peninsula *Llao Llao* where the *bosque* was dark and deep with great spreading trees, and it was not until I came to the hotel and the paved road that I was really able to see the lake near which I pedaled. *Qué hermoso!* Blue rumpled waters with snowy mountains on one side and bare deserty hills on the other--and over all the patchy light of a gusty, rainy day. Pavement, *tambien!* I traveled at top speed, stimulated by the scenery and also by the remarks and shouts from the sidelines. *"Qué lastima que yo no tengo una bicicleta"!* --This from a young blade! In *Bariloche* I fell into the first *pensión* where I stopped to inquire for a room, and poor enough it was. A mere hole in the wall with a bed. But it was cheap, and this appealed 'cause it's rather a shock to find things in Argentina almost double the price of those in Chile.

February 16, 1942--Lago Correntoso--Hotel Ruca Malen

Yesterday morning my dark little room gave no hint of the glory of the sun without, and it was not until 9:00 that I ventured forth. Then I was thrilled beyond measure by the brilliance of the day. The lake blue, the mountains sharp and clear, and the orange daisies very bright. With Chester I made an excursion up through the scrubby growth which befitted these barren hills, so different from those through which I had passed in Chile. Then back to my *pensión* for *almuerzo*. -- And I ate as if I'd never eat again, for these days I truly wonder where I'll get the next meal! Thus fortified, I packed up and headed for *Correntoso*. Around the end of the lake and out into open grasslands I rolled, out where the wide open spaces lent joy to my pedals. But the road was worse and worse--covered with loose stone which forced me to push down hill as well as up! A man on horseback, who answered my questions about the road, suggested that I stop at the *casita* of an American lady. And by the time I had struggled the 15 minutes to her door (*Paso Coihue*), I was glad enough to stop! Then in her unkempt house she offered me the hospitality of a true pioneer, and I spent the rest of the afternoon and evening with her and her five Spanish children--climbing through the *bosque* with the oldest girl, sitting in the kitchen while supper was prepared, reveling in the taste of fresh milk and whipped cream, and watching the hilarious youngsters blow thistle down about the room.

This morning I had coffee with kind *Mrs. Lobos*, and she packed me a lunch before I went on my way around the lake in the frosty morning. The first mile was discouraging, and I nearly weakened and turned back, but then, without cause, the road improved, and I rolled merrily along with a song in my heart. The lake was near, the *bosque* was beautiful, and once an all-white peak stood like a ghost on the horizon. I had left the deserty hills of *Bariloche* and was back in bush woods again. At *Correntoso* I paused and who should be there but friends from the boat! The man with the camera too, lining me up for more pictures! But I soon rolled on, for I wanted to go much further. Lunch amidst the bamboo of a beautiful stretch of *bosque*. Then on past lovely *Lago Espejo* set amidst high peaks. Stopping to make an adjustment on my bike, I made the acquaintance of a young chap in the road. And when I broke a spoke shortly after, he pushed my bike all the way to the hotel here. Repairs for Chester, a bath for me, and just now a *comida* during which I have tried to eat enough to last me all day tomorrow! For tomorrow I expect to travel far from *pueblos* and hotels.

February 17, 1942--Lipela Grande--La Lipela

Things always seem to work out for the best, and here I am in a hotel when I fully expected to be sleeping in the *bosque*! --Not a "grand" hotel, but a nice little rambling one with white washed walls and rows of poplars. And for dinner a piece of mutton which tasted as if it had been roasted over coals! What matter if my room has no windows at all and only a candle for light. I'm quite content. This morning I wheeled away when the sun was just breaking over the lake and when the canyons and the *bosque* were so dark and chilled that I had to stop often to warm my hands. But I loved those deep dark woods, and then the sun finally filtered through, there was a feeling of spring in the air. Up and up and over and down and then--Lake *Traful.* Beautiful Lake *Traful* with its blue, blue waters and its guardian *cerros.* Up and down, up and down, sharp little back-breaking hills with so much rock in the road that going down was as difficult as going up. But there was always the lake to compensate for the labor, and I had the whole day ahead of me. --Then--*mal suerte*--I shifted into low and felt the loosening of my cable which I have come to recognize as a sure sign of trouble. No more change of speeds! But knocking about the world has given me a nonchalance which amazes even me; and I tied the cable to the frame, took up the slack with a strap, and ambled on in middle gear, confident that my good legs would carry me through. When I felt hungry and was ready to stop and beg some bread, I came upon a little *café* where I sat down to a good table and devoured a tremendous meal--sustenance for the rest of the day. A pleasant spot too--*Villa Traful*--with its many clear windows and its German hostess. The afternoon brought me to the valley of the *Rio Limay*, and here the landscape was totally different--another world. Gone the lush *bosque*, and in its place weird towers of rock and occasional pointed conifers. A green world this--yellow, green, blue green, gray green-- lovely soft greens enhanced by the evening light and the deep shadows. With the road following the river through its valley- -an easy road for which my weary legs were grateful. Curious motorists stopped to take my picture and to offer me candy. And a swish of air reminded me that my bicycle still had to be considered! An old patch gone bad! My heart sank. But I slapped on another with crossed fingers, and it held, Allah be praised!

February 19, 1942--Casa Parque--Señora Beuhla Richard's

Yesterday morning my ruddy-faced host served me *café con leche* at the unheard of hour of 7:30 AM! And I left the rows of poplars and the white-washed walls before the sun came to warm them. Up the *Limay* once again, thence over a hill and down a broad valley into the old familiar road at *Nahuel Huapi*--the circuit completed. A hot day this, and I arrived at *Bariloche* dripping with perspiration. Who should I meet in this street but my old friend the *administrador* of *Mrs. Lobo's estancia*, and also Mrs. *Lobo's* mother and children. How good to meet old friends! They dissipate any feeling of loneliness I might otherwise have. More difficulties in finding a room, and I had to take a cot in a private house. A bath, washing clothes, talking to the dapper Englishman in *Expreso Villalonga*, having my bike repaired, and knocking about *Bariloche* consumed the rest of the afternoon. And in the evening I wandered down to the *Barrio Civico* to watch the sun set over the lake and mountains. Here I met another friend from the boat, and after dinner we went together to *Hotel Italia* to see the "man with the camera," his wife, and cousin-- the three I have met twice before. But after a short interval of tea and photographs, I excused myself and crawled wearily home to bed, conscious of my three days of pedaling. This morning at 9:00 I went aboard the launch, *Modesta Victoria*, and cruised from *Bariloche* to *Puerto Blest* with stops at *Llao Llao* and the Island of *Victoria*. How different this trip on a clear day! Vivid mountains and waters with none of the mystery of masks of cloud. No tantalizing momentary vistas; no darkly impressive atmosphere. And all the way I visited with a young German chap who offered to help me when I was faltering in my conversation with the custom's official. At *Laguna Frias* I waited to pay for my launch ride, but the *dueño*, toward whom I felt antagonistic, made himself so difficult to see that I pushed on without paying--and without a guilty conscience. Over the hill and back into Chile--the old familiar road, but this time flooded with sunlight instead of rain. And here at *Casa Parque* I have found a room with a smiling, toothless *Señora* who served me a welcome tea when I arrived. I have had a good visit, too, with my old friends, the *carabineros*. And all afternoon I have sat here by the river at the foot of *Cerro Tronador* marveling at its wild, icy crests--a truly impressive mountain. A pathetic note in the day's trip was the man with 5 small children making his way on foot from Chile to Argentina in search of work. Poor, ragged, barefoot humanity.

February 21, 1942--Peulla

Yesterday was a lovely, lazy day idled away in *Casa Parque* under the spell *of Cerro Tronador*. Visiting with the *carabineros*, lying in the meadow grass amidst the dandelions and *margaritas*, wondering at the rivers of ice flowing down the sides of *Tronador*, looking at the *señora's* photographs, eating my meals in a regular fashion--those things made up my day, and I loved the solitude and peace of my mountain retreat. My quarters there were far from elegant: broken windows, a lumpy bed, creaking floors, a clothesline at the front door, and a tumbledown privy; but my hostess was generous in her kindliness and she tended to my every want, trotting about in worn shoes and ragged pink wrapper, and smiling benignly over me, her guest from the north who spoke the language of her dead husband. I walked with the young *carabinero, Alfonso Mendez,* in the late morning and again after *cena,* and he ran true to form, first showering me with compliments and finally suggesting that we marry!! These *Chilenos* are all alike, and by now I almost know what they will say before they say it! But *Alfonso* went a step farther and inquired into how much wealth I possessed! In the afternoon an open-air bus arrived at the station and amongst the passengers I spotted my teacher of *Castellano* from summer school in *Santiago*--the same *señora* I had met in the road between *P. Varas* and *Ensenada. Abrazos* from her and her husband and a host of questions attracted the other passengers, and soon I was the center of a curious crowd. Surprised exclamation of *"sola!"* and *"solita!"* emanated from all. And when they left, I shook hands all around! The quiet reigned again at the foot of *Tronador*.

February 22, 1942--Puerto Octay--Hotel Haase

Yesterday morning at 5:00 AM *Señora* Richards padded down creaky stairs on broad feet and wakened me that I might pack and be off by 6:00. She served me coffee by candlelight and fixed a sandwich for my lunch, and then saw me off in the faint morning light. Having allowed plenty of time to catch my boat, I ambled deliberately along the stony road, enjoying the grandeur of the canyon as it became more and more distinct in the morning light. When I prepared to wade a stream, 9 men, one with a lathered face and a shaving brush in hand, waved me back to a foot-log and obligingly helped me across with my bike. In *Peulla* I waited for the *Esmeralda*, and when she finally steamed away, I found a lot of friends (from the bus of the day before) aboard, amongst them the 4 English chaps from B.A. Hence I had a pleasant sociable journey across green waters surrounded by grayed mountains. No sun this day, high clouds instead. And *Osorno* was masked although we were able to see *Puntiagudo*. One stop in route at an elegant island home. At *Petrohué* I said good-bye and took to my bike, but I felt a tremendous ennui as the afternoon wore on, and I traveled without purpose, stopping by the *Rio Petrohué* to munch my thick sandwich of sour bread and salami, stopping to eat berries which grew in profusion by the shore of *Llanquihué*, pedaling slowly, and walking up most of the hills. Rolling through the lava rock and the woods at the foot of *Osorno* reminded me of Japan's lake district--the same horizontal feeling in the trees and the same lacy fineness in the greenery. And then--another broken gear cable! What luck! It was late now, and when I inquired the distance, I was shocked to discover I couldn't possibly reach *Puerto Octay* before dark. More speed. And a short cut which proved so bad that I had to turn back. But as the sun sank, I became resigned and pedaled steadily without fretfulness. After all, the sunset was lovely, and *Osorno* could be seen as a faint ghost in the distance. Sheer utter darkness and the discovery that my flashlight had burned out! Sliding over the loose rock and wondering about the dark figures passing in the road was an experience which added great enthusiasm to my approach to the lights of *Octay*. There they were--shining by the side of the lake--a refuge from the cold and hunger of the night. I came into this great wooden hotel with a sense of relief, and was completely content to find a hot supper, a hot bath, and a clean bed.

February 23--Puerto Octay—Hotel Haase

Yesterday another lovely, lazy day. For the ennui of the day before persisted, and I decided *Osorno* could wait until *mañana*. How Spanish I am becoming! After a late *desayuno* (with honey!), I walked up and down the hilly, unpaved streets of *Puerto Octay*, watching the Sunday loiterers, walking about the *plaza*, wondering what joys and sorrows went on behind the stark wooden fronts and the white curtained windows of the tall houses. A funny little town this, with many red roofs and a church of chartreuse, but it is beautifully situated in a hollow in the hills, and it runs down to an irregular bit of lakeshore. After *almuerzo* I decided to explore further afield and started with Chester in the direction of *Frutillar*. Up and down, up and down along the lakeshore--through opulent farmlands where large well-built houses told of prosperity and where ripened grain lent a richness to the landscape. Across the lake, *Osorno* stood up in perfect, snow-capped symmetry, and occasionally the clouds unveiled *Calbuco's* crest. A beautiful region where I wanted only to loiter, and I pedaled aimlessly, traveling but halfway to *Frutillar*. One stop for a flurry of pelting rain and another for blackberries! And on my return a traveler on horseback stopped to talk. How strange to find another traveling in the same manner as I. Only when the hour was late did I leave the panorama of *Llanquihué, Osorno, Puerto Octay*, and the green and yellow farm lands and return to the hotel. And here I found my fellow traveler--a welcome English-speaking companion. We dined together and walked together--out in the night which was brilliant with stars and a half moon. And when he slipped his hand into mine and later kissed me, I found myself wondering if the Nordics were in any way different from the Latins! A strange man whose motives I cannot fathom. A German who professes to hate the Nazis; a man on a strange mission; a man who would not tell his name. Was he trying to get information from me, or was he sincere? He seemed hungry for tenderness--something which I cannot give to a stranger. And when he wanted to come to my room, I found myself locking my door and going to bed. Another milestone in the road of experience.

Feb. 24, 1942--Osorno--Hotel Henrich

Yesterday morning I lingered in *Puerto Octay* to visit with my strange friend. I had breakfast with him, went with him to catch his horse, watched him make ready, and finally bade him good-bye at 11:00 AM! Then I, too, packed and made ready, but I waited until after *almuerzo* to take to the road. And then I pedaled away in a brilliant mid-day sun. Up the hill and away from the lake, looking back reluctantly at the red roofs of *Octay* and the pretty green surroundings--and wondering if ever again I would see *Osorno's* white beauty. Then into a level agricultural area with scattered trees and bountiful blackberries over a road where I could travel easily and quickly. How startling--this road without hills! Innumerable plodding ox-carts were my companions on the road, and I often hear the whir of threshing devices. In *Osorno* I finally located here at this poor hotel, glad of a place to rest and wash. And I had time before supper to walk a bit in the streets and sit a bit in the *plaza.*

February 24, 1942--Salto del Pilmaiquén--Refugio

This morning I set out bravely to attend to all my little businesses, but I didn't accomplish much more than to change a few dollars at a very low rate! I did, however, have a chance to see the town while waiting for the stores to come to life.

And I was amazed at the combination of old and new in the streets. The church, the German Institute, and many other buildings are modern to the nth degree, and beside them are old frame buildings which look as if they had weathered the centuries! When my sallies in *Castellano* proved fruitless, I sought out the British consul and showered him with questions. And then, tired of the trials of the city, I ate a bountiful *almuerzo* and prepared to leave. Gathered about my bike in the street was a crowd of men who asked a thousand questions and who wanted to snap pictures. I posed obligingly, but I felt apologetic for not being famous! I'm sure those men expect to see me in the movies and to tell their friends they knew me when--Then away to the east--out in the country again with its scattered trees, its ripened grain, its ox-carts, and its *huasos*? And there again loomed up my old friend *Osorno*! Slowly, slowly over the rough road--with frequent stops to gather blackberries. And in the late afternoon I arrived here at *Pilmaiquén*. Tea was being served within, and so I waited without where I talked with the chauffeurs! And a little later I walked down into the canyon with one of the bright-eyed boys here--a lad who had me to the very brink of the falls. A beautiful sight, the *salto*, with its torrent of white water, its rising mists and its luxuriant vegetation. Afterwards I indulged in the luxury of "*onces*," sitting by the window from wherever I could see the falls. And while daylight lasted I walked outside, looking, looking, looking. In the foreground the falls and on the horizon the volcano *Osorno, Puntiagudo*, and *Tronador*. A lovely sunset too. And a feeling of friendly warmth in my conversation with the farmer who stopped in the road to ask me about the price of cows in America. Then darkness and a warm, filling *comida* eaten by candle light, and afterwards a barrage of questions from the *señora* and her 4 boys. Bright moonlight and a chill atmosphere outside, and inside the warmth of candlelight and the coziness of a rustic room with a dormer window. Complete contentment.

February 26, 1942—Rio Bueno—Hotel Plaza

Yesterday morning I pedaled off to *Lago Puyehué* with the oldest son of the *dueña* of the *refugio*. What fun to have company! But the lad traveled faster than the slow, plodding tourist and when I stepped up my speed, I rode in fear of all the loose rock on the road! Oh me—The lake was all silver and gray in the gray of the morning and the road by the shore wound through alternating *bosque* and farm lands. In fact I liked the way so much that when my *compañero* turned back, I felt I must go on. And on I went—on and on— passing droves of cattle and oxcarts and *huasos*. And always in sight of the lake with the irregular shoreline and occasional islands at the far end of *Puyehué* I pushed up to see the much-talked-of hotel, and I went inside on the pretext of seeking photographs. A great barn of a place where all the aged and decrepit gentry had come for baths and stared curiously at my dusty and bedraggled person in the elegant midst. I beat a hasty retreat and spent the rest of the afternoon riding leisurely back to *Pilmaiquén* with many stops to look at the lake and the broad volcanoes at its head, for as the day cleared the lake's environs came into view. And there to the south were *Osorno* and *Puntiagudo* again! My *refugio* was doubly attractive after the austerity of previous places, and I devoured another *onces* there by the window in view of the falls and the volcanoes. Out in the yard later I rode one of the boy's horses for a couple of turns, using one of these strange Chilean saddles. And there too I made the acquaintance of one Walter Platts, accountant for the *Planta Electrica* which is being built at the *salto*. He wanted to practice English so he took me on an excursion across the river where the construction work was being carried on. We went into deep, dark *bosque* also to see other falls invisible from the *refugio*, and we saw a thousand fluffy bits of cloud turned to crimson by the setting sun. A nice chap, Platts—blond and blue-eyed but speaking Spanish like so many others in the south of Chile. Back at the *refugio*, I ventured to ask one of the boys where he got his north-European complexion, and with quick wit he answered, "*Soy*

Norte Americano; falta solamente la lengua!" After dinner more visiting with the boys, one of whom sang the national song of Chile for me. Then bed—by candlelight.

This morning I made an effort to get *desayuno* early but as usual it wasn't forthcoming until 8:00, so I had to be content with a late start. But with peak morning legs the road back to *Osorno* seemed easy and although loath to leave *Pilmaiquén*, I hurried towards town in order to arrive before the stores closed at noon. My mission—an attempt to find a new cable, and retrieve my 3 speeds. And I met with success! In one shop I procured the cable and a boy on a bicycle piloted me down a back street to a junky little shop where a mechanic agreed to do the work of installing the cable. I bought a *peso's* worth of grapes for lunch and stood by to see that nothing was injured while the holes in the attachments were enlarged and the cable was set in place with solder and a knot. Then I hastened to Hotel Heinrich to collect the things left in *Osorno*, and as quickly as possible I untangled myself from the curious and sought out the road to *Rio Bueno*. Frequent stops to adjust my new cable and also to eat berries, but always the luxurious feeling that I had plenty of time. What luxury to have 3 speeds once again! I scarcely dared change 'em! A good road and a lovely mild afternoon with banks of dark clouds filling the sky and reducing all the trees to sharp dark silhouettes, broad ones, tall ones, and capricious ones. And on either side the hills rising in multicolored ranks—red cultivated hills, yellow harvest hills, and blue and purple distant hills. A stirring afternoon which set my feet spinning on the pedals. Through *San Pablo* with its frame houses clustered on a hill, and thence to this *pueblo* where I found shelter in the hotel just as it commenced to rain. Before dinner a walk through the unpaved streets to look at the careless window displays behind drab wooden store fronts! And impatient waiting through the long, long hours till dinner time at 8:30!

February 28, 1942—Lago Ranco—Puerto Nuevo

Yesterday morning after breakfast I discovered that my temperamental tire was flat again. An old patch gone bad. But I stuck it down with a little more cement, crossed my fingers, and took off, hoping it would hold! I ran leisurely over to *La Union*, enjoying the wide open spaces and the dark clouds that still billowed about the landscape. And in *La Union* I rode up and down the streets and about the *plaza*, looking at the shops and the people trying to get the feel of these wooden towns of the south. Then back to *Rio Bueno* for almuerzo before trekking off to *Lago Ranco*. What small things shape my moods. At dinner the waitress stubbornly refused to bring me butter and I felt strange and unwelcome in the hotel. Not until I was back on the road again and some friendly tourists waved as they passed did my spirits bounce back to normal. And a fine trip I had here to the lake, rolling through large country with good farms and with *vistas* of deep blue ridges beyond. But although the land is cultivated, it is never bare of trees for the great ones are always left standing. Rail fences are typical in this part, and they are often built with great posts in which holes are hewn to carry the horizontal bars. I came upon *Lago Ranco* in the evening and after a refreshing dip, I spent the rest of the moments of daylight on the stony beach, just looking. What colors! The *cerros* which seem so carelessly piled about the lake took on a rich magenta, and the water of the lake, oily smooth, was like iridescent satin—purple, gold, orange, aqua—reflecting all the subtle color of sky and mountains. When darkness dimmed the landscape and only the moon seemed bright, I came in for supper—into this pleasant hotel with its rustic board walls and its fine outlook over the lake. Although I'm the only patron, I feel quite at home here.

March 1, 1942—Lago Ranco—Llifen—Hotel Ziegler

Yesterday morning, from my comfortable room, I looked out on a different *Lago Ranco—Ranco* in morning dress. Gone the vivid colors of the evening, and in their place, a silvery gray. A gray mist hung about the *cerros*, destroying all perspective and giving all the landscape the quality of a Japanese print. So different yet so lovely. I did not wander far, but instead sat on the beach to write, to eat blackberries, and to look. For I find that I absorb more of "the feel" of a place when I live quietly than when I indulge in a great lot of activity, so I am trying to train my restless spirit to rest peacefully without bounding hither and yon. After *almuerzo*, a little steamer came out on the lake and ran onto the beach, and Chester and I went aboard. First we steamed to *Lago Ranco*, the railway terminus and a lumber center. Here the main street is the railway track, and on every side are piles and piles of lumber. While the "*Saturno*" waited for the train, I walked to the station and on to the hotel. How sordid the town. Possessing nothing of the beauty of its surroundings. And I was glad when we moved out into the lake again and on to *Llifen*. Here my first thought was to find a room and with fingers crossed I inquired at the hotel. Vacancies, Allah be praised! And now I live in a gray board house at the foot of the jumble of *cerros* I had seen from *Puerto Nuevo*! A fine comfortable place with a lovely garden and a friendly German *dueño* who circulates amongst the guests and tends to all their wants. Last night after supper the moon shown brilliantly, creating a fairyland here by the side of the lake—a cold, surreal world with a lake of molten silver; *cerros* cast in ragged purple mold; and a garden of great white hydrangeas and fragrant roses—Beauty so intense that it hurt, and I felt vaguely discontent—a bit envious of those about me who were not alone but were secure in the warmth of companionship.

March 2, 1942—Lago Ranco—Llifen—Hotel Ziegler

Yesterday—*floja* again. After a late and leisurely breakfast, I watched others depart on horseback and then I wandered about to get acquainted with *Llifen*. Up the road to the few houses which make up the community, then back to the hotel and up a hill to a spot with a fine view of lake, hotel and *cerros*. Here I sat for a very long time to write and to enjoy the countryside. But at 12:00 I turned back to the hotel for an early lunch, and afterwards I went off on Chester in search of *Lago Maihué*. How people did stare! –I must have created a strange spectacle there on that road which knew only the tread of oxen. And I never found the lake! After pedaling 10 miles up the canyon and crossing a river, as per directions, I was told that the road was below. So I pedaled back and inquired again, only to learn that the road was above! Once more I turned back, but no likely looking road presented itself, so I gave up the ghost, too *floja* to make the effort. Back in *Llifen* I took tea, and then went back to the hills again to write and to watch the sun set across the lake. How peaceful there on a hill beside the lake at the mouth of the *Rio Calcurupe*. And the shadows in the ragged *cerros* grew long; and the sun went down in a ball of fire behind the *Isla de los Indios* in the lake. Beside me in a thicket, I discovered long tubular flowers, red and waxy, the national flowers of Chile. Perfection! Then with the coming of evening, I turned homeward like the boats on the river and the riders on the trail. –A rather lonely day because I was conscious that others about me were not alone. After supper I made plans to travel from *Llifen* to *Futrono* over the "*camino principal*" which was naught but a track; but Ziegler said that if I wanted to push, I could make it through. Then out of the corner of the *comedor* came an Englishman who dissuaded me from taking the trip— said the trail was a succession of bogs and fallen trees—utterly impassable. And then he kindly offered to take me over in his boat.

March 3, 1942—La Union—Hotel Union—10:00 PM

Yesterday the tide turned, and I was no longer alone. In the morning my English friend reneged on the trip to *Futrono* because of the wind which was driving up waves on the lake, but he suggested a "spot of fishing" instead. And always ready for anything, I was happy to go along. Equipped with ponchos and a packet of sandwiches we set out in his small boat; and a short way up the *Calcurupe* we set up our poles, set up a back to our seat, arranged some cushions, and settled ourselves, side by side, in solid comfort to hold our lines while the boatman rowed us to the most likely fishing spots! Fishing *de luna!* Done in good English style. All we had to do was pull in the fish! My companion caught a large one almost at once and later, with great excitement, I reeled in a small one. Than it was time for lunch, and we rowed to an "uninhabited island" which Turner claimed for his own. Here I was told to amuse myself while lunch was fixed for me, and I'll have to confess it was a luxurious feeling. My fish was filled with butter, wrapped in newspaper of the proper political cast, wetted, and baked in the fire. And it was served to me only after I was made comfy with blankets and pillows. It seemed as if I had never tasted anything better than that flesh which flaked off with neither bone nor skin. Delicious! And Turner had gathered berries to add to our menu and flowers upon which to feed our souls. Such a picnic! And I sat idly by while my sandwich was toasted and my pear was peeled. Then it was *siesta* time, and only after we were snuggled up under a poncho did I begin to learn about my companion. There it was again—an unhappy marriage and a great hunger for affection. And what had I to give? But I felt a bond of sympathy for this man, and I submitted to more caresses than is my want. When rain came we ducked under my green poncho and lay very close, but as his passion mounted I drew back and finally insisted on going. On the river in the rain we caught one more fish, and then, since the waves had grown to wild proportions on the lake, we left the boat on a bar and walked back to the hotel. More experience this day, and more food for thought.

This morning the weather had cleared and I started the day with a sense of well being. A double supply of bread for breakfast gave me assurance of sufficiency until evening, and I rolled happily down to the pier, ignoring the strangeness of a bicycle in the procession of oxcarts and horses moving toward the boats. Turner acted a bit frustrated—made a pointed effort to avoid learning my name—and I was troubled, for I knew I was the cause of his distress. But soon Chester and I were aboard the *Santa Lucia*, and *Llifen* was fading behind us—a memory of beauty and emotional intensity. In the company of a French family from the hotel I made a pleasant journey across the lake, and it seemed only a very little time until I had disembarked in familiar *Puerto Nuevo* and was back on the road to *La Union*. Again dark clouds brooded over the landscape, and the afternoon was one of light and shadow. But I was lost in thought, almost oblivious to the passing panorama. Why had an Englishman, a cold-blooded northerner with a hard set to his mouth, been fired with desire for me? Why had I felt an uncommon tenderness for this man with gray in his hair? Is it because I travel alone that men approach me so freely? Do they think I am ready to accept all things? And why do I sometimes respond to attention which lacks the depth of true friendship? Is it because my life has been so devoid of love that I grasp at anything? Or is it possible for a strong bond to spring up suddenly between 2 persons? How I wish I knew all the answers! Not wishing to reach my hotel too early, I stopped in a blackberry thicket and wrote for a couple of hours, and then rode in to *La Union* when the last rays of the sun gave the hills and the fields and the roof tops that mellow late afternoon light which I love so well. Here I met again the French family from the boat, and I had a drink with them before supper, so I felt quite at home here in this new hotel.

March 5, 1942—Valdivia—Gran Hotel de France—7:00 AM

Yesterday morning breakfast with my French friends and as they went off to the train, I went off on Chester. The rolling hills, the prosperous estates, the rows of slim poplars— all seemed as lovely to the north of *La Union* as to the south, but very soon I left the cultivated lands behind and entered a more mountainous section with fewer inhabitants. Here repeated fires had destroyed much of the timber and left the country rather desolate. What a pity to sacrifice those great trees just for the sake of a little pastureland. Climbing up and riding down over a road with a good surface was a real joy, and I liked the feeling of aloneness which the country gave me. A few trucks and a few little shanties built of loose boards leaned against each other were the only signs of life. But in our place a road gang shouted at me in a chorus, and I pedaled very fast without looking to right or left. Presently I entered a broad cultivated valley, and soon I was in *Valdivia*. Cobblestones, *que lastima*! How I hate 'em! But I cruised down the principal street and around a couple of blocks and finally located here because I liked the central part of the hotel with its skylight and its many plants. After a cleanup and *onces* I set out to find *Señora Mekes*, my table companion from "Trinidad," the jolly German I had met again in *Puerto Varas*. She welcomed me with open arms, introduced me to all her family, and insisted on my having another tea with all the fixings—cheese, jam, cookies! And since I had had no lunch I could do justice to another tea! Then I went with her and her family for a drive about *Valdivia*. We passed by an ancient Spanish tower, skirted the river front with its market, passed the *plaza*, went down the principal street, went out to the large new hospital, and finally went off into the country where the *quintas* with their wealth of growing things were enhanced by the light of the setting sun. We stopped at a farm belonging to relatives and here we looked all about the extensive and flowery gardens and sat long enough to take a couple of glasses of *chicha de manzana*. Then darkness, and I was delivered to the very door of my hotel. What a pleasant afternoon. How lucky I always am! And my memories of *Valdivia* will be warm ones because of the human associations here.

March 6, 1942—Valdivia—Gran Hotel de France—8:00 AM

Yesterday a day *con falda y sin bicicleta*. After *desayuno* I hurried down to the river and went aboard the "Bremen" (!) en route for *Fuerte Corral* in an open-air seat beside the warm stack, who should join me but another American from summer school in Santiago! Conscientious in

our efforts to learn Spanish, she talked in nothing else, and I
played the game too, although it must have appeared a bit
strange for 2 *gringas* to be talking together in bad *Castellano*!
Down the river *Valdivia* with views of pretty wooded banks;
and after two hours of sailing with stops here and there for
cargo and passengers, we arrived at *Corral*, a little town with a
jumble of wooden houses tossed up over the hill. I and my
fellow American scrambled up a narrow street and then down
and along the river bank to *Altos Hornos*, a plant for extracting
iron, but we didn't go in, for *Señor* Johansen, a relative of
Señora Mekes wasn't to be found. So we returned to Corral
and thence walked along the river in the opposite direction to
Amargos, a pretty spot with nothing much more than a hotel.
Here we went aboard the "Breman" again and soon were
cruising back to *Valdivia*. I had expected to stop in *Niebla*,
but decided instead to return to *Valdivia*, and 2:30 found me
again in the hotel looking for *almuerzo*! The plump French
dueña with the broad 3-tooth grin arranged a meal for me at
this late hour, and she stood by to visit while I ate. With
snapping eyes she explained that she and her family were all
"Free Frenchmen," and when I inquired about Nazis in Chile,
she said in a knowing way, "The serpent sleeps"! All
afternoon I walked and walked and walked—along the main
streets and the back streets along the river with its busy
market; back to the ancient Spanish town still impregnable in
feeling though hoary with age. I stopped at the *Intradencia*
where the *"unico Indio en Valdivia"* answered my "touristic"
questions and showered me with literature to take back to the
States, and I purchased flashlight batteries from a man with a
toothache. Then, *paseos* and business completed, I sat in the
plaza to watch the people pass—promenaders whiling away
the evening hours. The end of a lazy, happy day, a day of
bright sunshine, a day so clear that we could see *Volcán
Villarica* from the river.

March 7, 1942—Panguipulli

Ayer—one of those days so different from the thing anticipated that it will always be remembered. What a day! Leaving the comfort of the plants and the motherly *dueña* in my hotel, I rode out through the early morning activity in the streets of *Valdivia* and turned off into the country on the road which followed the *Rio Calle-Calle*. Here the road climbed hills for no reason at all, except perhaps to give the traveler a last view of *Valdivia* clinging to its riverbanks, and I struggled up stony *cuestas* in a torrent of perspiration. But the way was a pretty one with many panoramas over the river, and I traveled aimlessly content with the countryside. An Indian summer sun and the odor of apples in the air foretold the coming of fall. In *Calle-Calle*, I inquired about the river launch from a man so drunk that I was a bit frightened by his response but I managed to maintain my nonchalance and to hurry away as slowly as I dared! And on that launch I embarked upon another adventure, for there I met *Manuel Valenzuela* and his truck. I accepted a proffered ride, for I am beginning to feel pressed for time, and in that moment I was a bit weary of the continuos struggles with the rocks on the road. And a wild ride it was, slithering over the rocks and through the dust of country roads at high speed! With Chester bouncing about behind! And me praying to Allah that he'd arrive intact! But my *compañero* proved *muy simpatico* and when we stopped for *almuerzo* in a little hotel *in San José de Mariquina*, our acquaintance blossomed over 8 scrambled eggs and a bottle of *vino blanco* chosen by the flip of a coin! A friend of *Manuel's* appeared at the hotel too, so our party was a merry one. And I liked the informality of that small town hotel—a plain board building on an unpaved street from whence folks dropped in to chat. From *Lanco* I planned to continue *to Lago Panguipulli* by bicycle, but when we arrived in *Lanco*, I found my *compañero* turning toward the lake in his truck. This was not in the scheme of things, for *Manuel* was bound for *Temuco*, but he insisted that he had time to drive me up. And who was I to refuse a ride with a *buen*

Chileno! But he went a step further and took me over to *Lago Calafquen* en route! A beautiful lake this with its tiny islets, its silvery waters, its great snow-capped *volcán*, and its fields of yellow grain. We walked on the beach for a while to better see the lake, and who should I find there but the *Señora Piel*, the other German lady from my table on "Trinidad"! She and her family were picnicking on the beach, and we joined them for a while, accepting their sandwiches, wines, and *mate*—my first taste of *mate* and I liked it! Then on to *Panguipulli* where we stopped to watch the unloading of lumber from a little lakesteamer and to see the water take on the soft orchid and silver of evening. As *Manuel* lingered I began to worry about his reaching *Temuco*, but not he! After settling me in the nice little *Panguipulli* hotel, he ordered *refrescos*, and more time was consumed in *saludos* and conversation over 2 frothy *pisco* sours. By now it was truly late, so I urged *Manuel* to stay and have dinner with me, and he readily agreed. While waiting for the dinner hour, we walked on the hill in the bright starlight, and *Manuel*, like all the rest, wanted a kiss, but he didn't press the issue when I said "no"! Then back to the hotel for a long, conversational meal with another bottle of wine. And when we had consumed the last of that, *Manuel* still loitered! He seemed to prefer sitting in the moonlight to driving to *Temuco*! –and in the end he decided to stay the night and return in the morning if I'd go with him! And this I was quite willing to do for the sake of salvaging another day.

March 8, 1942—Pucón—Residencial Suiza—8:00 AM

We got up before 6:00 yesterday morning and left *Panguipulli* in the cold, moonlit dawn. Another *pasajero* joined us in our trek to *Lanco*, and when we arrived there we took breakfast with him in his hotel. Breakfast before 8:00 AM! Incredible! There I continued on to *Loncoche* with *Manuel*, and here was the parting of the ways. With plans to meet again in *Temuco*, we said good-bye, and he went north, while I climbed aboard Chester and departed for *Villarrica*. My way was a trail of dust—rich red powdery dust which settled over my hair and clothes and penetrated my pack. I and countless oxcarts were the only passers-by; not one single auto came over that road, and I can understand why. Here I was annoyed to be without my cyclometer, and I cursed the boys of *Calafquen* who took it from my bicycle, but cursing didn't help much! The countryside here was all more or less the same, and similar to that farther south. Cultivated lands containing great trees that were never cleared away, sturdy rail fences, blackberry thickets lining the road, and views of rolling blue hills beyond. Tired after a short night, a long day, miles of hard pedaling, and no food to restore my energy, I stopped in a convenient pasture and took a siesta. Then on to *Villarrica* and to the lake where I found a good road to *Pucón*. But my body was weary and the way seemed long in spite of pleasant traveling by the side of the lake, and happy was I to reach *Pucón*, a pretty *pueblo* snuggled in the lee of a peninsula reaching out into *Lago Villarrica*. Here I easily found the *residencial* I sought, and the tall *dueño*, with a *"como no"* to every question, made me comfortable. For half an hour I busied myself with emptying my shoes and socks, shaking my clothes, and washing my dusty person; and then *onces*, welcome *onces*--with brown bread and honey! After consuming every crumb, I went forth refreshed to see *Pucón*. And, per usual, I made the rounds of the town, the principal streets, the flowery *plaza*, the great hotel made exclusive with walls and fences, the beach—all the sights and sounds and *vistas* which the *pueblo* afforded. And I sat for a long while on the beach, first on one side of the peninsula where lake and mountains were utterly peaceful in the late evening light, and then on the other side of the peninsula where the sun sank as a great red ball with only a few frills of orange clouds and where *Volcán Villarrica* stood up white and lovely with a cap of fluffy white clouds. Walking home in the evening, I felt in *Pucón* the same atmosphere which I have felt in other towns in the south—an atmosphere which emanates from the unpainted board buildings with their broken window panes, white lace curtains, and crude board floors; from the many ragamuffins playing in the streets; from the horses standing in front of each

sign "*deposito de cervesa*"; from the gardens and fruit trees
protected by high walls; from the carefully attired *señoritas*
and *señores* apparently absorbed in promenading but forever
casting glances at one another; and from oxcarts and the be-
ponchoed horsemen moving through the streets.

March 8, 1942—Villarrica—Hotel Central—10:00 PM

    Floja again today—so *floja* that after a late breakfast I
wandered out along the highway toward Argentina and buried
myself in the first convenient *bosque*—an isolated spot where
I could read or write or stretch out at full length—secure from
the gaze of passers-by. But a young couple settled themselves
very near me, thinking that they too were alone, and I crept
away like a mouse to another spot! How good to just sit
amongst the trees and look at the *cerros* without feeling any
urge to climb them! I become more *Chilena* every day! And I
liked looking at *Volcán Villarrica* too, for like *Osorno*, it
stands up in snowy perfection. Back at my hotel I had lunch
in the backyard, and here I made the acquaintance of a family
from *Concepción* at whose table I sat. *Cazuela de ave* and
rosada. *Que rico*! –And in the afternoon I went with my new
friends for a dip in the lake—down in front of the great hotel
on a beach of black sand. Not until 5:00 did I finally get back
to my bike! What an hour for a Richardson to start traveling!
But I was refreshed by my swim, and besides, I'm very partial
to the late afternoon hours, so my journey was a pleasant one.
And how short it seemed compared with yesterday's trek over
the same road! With fresh legs, roads and rocks and hills
seemed utterly different. I arrived here in *Villarrica* just in
time to change my clothes and take a short walk in the street
with the rest of the public. And now, after a big meal, I'm
ready to "turn in" in anticipation of a hard day tomorrow.

March 10, 1942—Temuco—Hotel Fourcade—7:00 AM

    Up at 6:00 AM yesterday and off in the cool gray
dawn. Stimulating freshness. A deserted world. A feeling of

"going places"! Leaving the lakes, I entered a land of dry hills and scattered trees which vaguely reminded me of home, and I had the feeling that southern Chile was merging into the north. Autumn was in the air too. I felt it in the sweeping clouds, in the poplars silhouetted against the sky in the red and yellow appearing in the trees. Again I struggled with *muchas piedras chicas*, and when a young German asked me to ride in his pick up, I gladly accepted traveling with him from *Rio Allipén* to the *pueblo* of *Freire*. In *Freire* I took lunch in the hotel. And thence to *Temuco* the way was easier, so I arrived very much earlier then I had anticipated. A room and a bath were apparent in my mind, and after settling here and cleaning up, I walked out to see the city. *Mucho movimiento*! Quantities of people in the streets and amongst them many Indians and *huasos*. How different *Temuco* by day from the *Temuco* by night which I remembered! --And after touring the south, I more fully appreciate the "*edificación moderna y las calles pavimentados*"! Again I met the family which I had met in *Pucón*. And at 9:30 I found *Manuel Valenzuela* in *Hotel Central*. We spent the evening poking about the city and talking, and it was good to feel that I was not alone in *Temuco*.

March 11, 1942—Nueva Imperial—Hotel Teatro—7:00 AM

Yesterday I awaited *Manuel*, for he was to make a trip to the coast in his pick-up, and he had invited me to go along. Might as well see a little more of Chile I thought, so I changed my plans! All morning I busied myself in *Temuco*—bought a few necessities; adjusted and oiled Chester; looked with great interest at the colorful, the ragged, and the well dressed who passed in my street, a busy section just in front of the railway station. And at 2:30 *Manuel* came to tell me that his pick-up was still in the garage undergoing repairs. We killed considerable time walking across the town and stopping in the market and in all the saddle shops, but when we arrived at the garage, the mechanics were still busy with the truck. Here I found an English couple who was touring with a station wagon and I talked with them while I waited for *Manuel*.

When we were finally ready we drove off to *el cerro Nielol* where, after passing through deep and lovely *bosque*, we reached a high vantagepoint with a superb view of the city, the *Rio Cautin*, and the land of browns and tans and creams, which surrounds *Temuco*. By this time the afternoon had worn itself away, and since *Manuel* had a bit of business to transact, he dropped me off at my hotel with a promise to return at 7:30. I wrote a couple of long letters which the hotel personnel speculated on why I still waited there, and at 7:30 *en punto* (!!) *Manuel* phoned to say that he'd be along very soon. And come he eventually did, but it was dark now and time for *comida*, so we stopped to have a meal at *Hotel Central* before starting! Not until after 9:00 did we finally get around to leaving *Temuco*! –A journey in good Chilean style! But I rather liked the novelty of starting at night and the brilliant stars and the dark silhouettes of trees lent a charm to the landscape which only darkness can create. An hour's drive brought us here where we found the best hotel full and had to take rooms in this inferior place. *Manuel* was much concerned over the *chinche* situation, but the *dueña* assured us there were none in the hotel! Before turning in, we took a little drive, stopping by the river where *Manuel*, true to form, wanted to pet. But he is much less insistent then his fellow *Chilenos*, and I like being with him.

March 12, 1942—Puerto Saavedra—Hotel Central

Yesterday a crazy day which gave me greater insight into the ways of the *Chilenos*! After *café sin leche Manuel* went off to transact business, and I, to see the *pueblo*. Through all the principal streets I wandered up one side and back the other; and as I looked curiously at the Indian women with their lavish jewelry, at the men guiding their oxen with nothing more than a long pole, at the *huasos* with their colorful costumes; they in turn stopped to stare at the curious foreigner in *pantalones*. The streets were full of activity which gave life to the rows of shabby, unpainted buildings. Dust rose from the wheels of a myriad of crude oxcarts, horses galloped by; salesmen with baskets of notions lined the streets; hooded, sweating men carried sacks into warehouses. Sun and dust, activity and poverty. And I looked on with great interest. Leaving *Nueva Imperial*, we drove through a rolling land of brown and yellow, a land of potatoes and wheat. And at noon we were in *Carahue,* another dilapidated, dusty little *pueblo* overflowing with life and color. *Manuel* wanted film for his camera, but none was to be found, so he decided to call up *Temuco* and ask to have some sent to *Puerto Saavedra*. And this necessitated waiting until 2:00 PM for the stores to open! *No importa.* Business could wait, and we could wait—dawdling over *almuerzo* in the hotel and afterwards sitting in the garden. Before leaving *Carahue* we went down to the port on *Rio Cantin* where shacks huddled together in poverty and where small boats were discharging sacks of potatoes and wheat. Thence *Manuel's* business took us to *Trovolhue* along a road which followed the valley of the Imperial for a way and then off into the hills in a track of red dust. We put on overalls to protect our clothes from the dust and went into gales of laughter over the problem of adjusting his overalls to my size. In a cool refreshing bit of *bosque* we stopped to eat a melon, gather *copihues*, and take a *siesta*! And we reached *Trovolhue* a bit late! This little out of the way pueblo was teeming with children who had lived their lives so isolated from civilization that the appearance of a pick-up in their midst was cause for great excitement. They clamored aboard, ignoring Manuel's mandate of *"dos, no mas,"* and by the time we had slowly navigated the length of that rough street, we had a car load of ragamuffins who were all laughing and shouting and waving to their friends. *"Ave Maria, tanta gente!"*—as one woman exclaimed when we passed! Returning from *Trovolhue* we met a drunk in the road who created an unforgettable spectacle; he was galloping along on a horse, swaying dangerously from side to side, his beast completely out of control! We returned to *Carahue*, crossed the *Cantin* by ferry and doubled back to *Puerto Saavedra* on the opposite side. It was dark now, but this didn't seem to inhibit *Manuel's* speed, and we bounced in and out of all the

ollos in the road! Then our lights grew dim and a light rain
fell to add to the difficulty of driving. But *Manuel* sped on!
And we arrived *in Puerto Saavedra* at 9:00 PM–just in time
for dinner. After our meal we went out to the pier to wait for
the arrival of the *barco* "*Cantin*" with *Manuel's* film, but we
made ourselves so comfortable in the "*salon*" of another little
boat waiting there that the "*Cantin*" came and went without
our knowing it! Then we had to hustle down to another pier to
collect the films! What an unconventional way for me to
travel and what an unconventional way for *Manuel* to transact
his business! But we like it! And besides, this is Chile!

March 13, 1942—Puerto Saavedra—Hotel Central—8:00 AM

Yesterday morning I explored the town while *Manuel*
went off on business. And a forlorn little place it is with
weather-beaten gray buildings strung along an unpaved street
which lies beside the river. Winds blowing from the river and
bare hills rolling off to the east add to the desolate atmosphere
and yesterday there was no activity in the streets to brighten
the scene. Only a handful of oxcarts and *huasos*. Nets drying
by the river told of a fishing industry here, but no boats or
fishermen were to be seen. It seemed almost as if the coming
of autumn had driven the populace into hibernation and left
only the shells of their past activity in the villages. *Manuel's*
trip of *"una hora, mas o menos"* lengthened out into 3, and we
had a late *almuerzo* when he returned. Then he went off again
while I indulged in a *siesta*. And when he returned in the
middle of the afternoon, he decided that it would be better to
top off the day with a *paseo* and stay another night in *Puerto
Saavedra*! Se we bought cheese and bread and hired a boat to
row us across the river, whence a short walk brought us to a
fine beach on the open ocean. It was completely deserted, and
a faint sun was sinking in a bank of gray clouds, but the
warmth of companionship dissipated the cheerlessness of the
scene, and we had a delightful *onces* with thick cheese
sandwiches, hard boiled eggs, and a melon.

March 14, 1942—Puerto Dominguez—10:00 AM

Yesterday morning *"temprano"* we were to leave *Puerto Saavedra*, but by the time *Manuel* had put chains on the pick-up, made a business call, and bought some gasoline, it was 10:00! *Listo* at last, we drove off in the rain, but a short distance from town our road became a steep, muddy track where our truck slithered and slid to such an extent that even *Manuel* was skeptical. And ultimately we turned back! We had no alternative but to return to *Carahue*, and this we did, driving again through the valley of the *Rio Imperial* and crossing the funny little ferry which operates in the river beside the town. Here in *Carahue, Manuel* consumed considerable more time, while I sat by and watched the drama in the streets, completely fascinated. Oxcarts, *huasos*, basket salesmen. Ragged, barefoot men; women in shabby dresses and shoes. Indian squaws in shawls and elaborate head bands and necklaces, looking solemnly at trinkets for sale in the streets. A drunk who collapsed in the gutter and lay there unheeded by the passers-by. *Mucha gente* coming and going in the streets and sidewalks—an endless colorful procession. I like *Carahue*! We had *almuerzo* in a tumble-down little shanty by the river where we sat at a table with a couple of *huasos* and dined on smoked fish, tomatoes, 4 scrambled eggs, grapes, and *café con leche*. –While cats played at our feet, flies buzzed above, and all the people looked curiously at the queer *gringa* in *pantalones*! Then off for *Puerto Dominguez* on another road; and what a trip it was! Slithering through the mud, grinding up steep hills, following ruts so deep that the truck dragged, bouncing in and out of tremendous *ollas*! I breathed a prayer to Allah and marveled at *Manuel's* nonchalance! And all the while he was transacting business, stopping at every farm that possessed threshing machinery. In the evening we sighted *Lago del Budi* from our hill top road— a lovely irregular sheet of steely gray following the depressions in the bare hills. And just at dark we reached this little *pueblo* on the shore of the lake. While waiting for *comida* we explored the village, and then we took our meal by candlelight, just the two of us.

March 15, 1942—Puerto Dominguez—9:00 AM

Yesterday morning I lived lazily in this village which is such a *chicotito* that one can walk the main street in 5 minutes. Following a muddy path for *carretas*, I sought out a hill top as is my want, and there I settled myself in the sun to look out over *Lago del Budi* and over the little cluster of houses in *Puerto Dominguez*. The recent rain had washed the landscape; and the clusters of trees, the lake, and the hills rolling away into blue infinity were clear and bright. Below, life moved lazily in the village. And I was quite content to sit for a long time. When I finally returned to the "hotel", I found *Manuel* had arrived before me!!, and before going in for *almuerzo* we took another walk through the town. The mill seemed to be the town's general gathering place, and here oxcarts waited and Indian dugouts were moored while their owners loitered, *Manuel* to talk and I to look. Back home again we ate a hearty dinner, and then with *onces* in a bag we set out for *La Islet de los Conejos* in a rowboat. But the wind and waves on the lake were discouraging, and we turned back, choosing to row up the river instead of to the island. The river was narrow and lined with tulies, and our boat, large; and with a magnificent lack of cooperation we ran into the tulies, first on one side and then on the other! I got the giggles and could scarcely row! So our progress was slow and painful, and before we had gone far we decided to stop for a *siesta*! Then it was too late to go farther, and we rowed back to a patch of sunlight in which to eat our heavy cheese sandwiches and drink our hot coffee. Coming back through the village, the activity at the mill caught our attention, and we stopped to watch the Indians push off in their clumsy dugouts and paddle down the narrow estuary into the lake and the fading sunset. Then feeling too satiated with food to take comida, we went off to the tent of some gypsies whom *Manuel* asked to play for us. They had no guitar and so couldn't play, but the two young girls danced, and we sat around their little fire and talked. The old woman with a rag tied about her head, a cigarette drooping from her mouth, and a glint in her eyes sat by the fire and tended her pots of soup and coffee while answering *Manuel's* questions. It was a warm, interesting foreign picture. We took *comida* here by candlelight and then wandered off again into the night. Singing and loud voices from the village saloon told of the heavy drinking, characteristic of starved lives in isolated places. After walking the length of the main street, we sought out a haystack and made ourselves comfortable there in the fresh air and the star light, curled up under *Manual's* coat. As I suspected, *Manuel* wants more of me than a mere holding of hands, but he remains a perfect gentleman, and I have no fear of him nor am I repulsed.

March 16, 1942—Temuco—Hotel Fourcade—8:00 am

Yesterday morning after a late *desayuno*, I went off to the hilltop to sit again in the sun, while *Manuel* went to mass. How utterly peaceful and lovely this spot by the shore of *Lago del Budi.* Leafy patterns on the smooth trunks of the eucalyptus lining the road; a vast panorama of lake and field; an unconcerned little village lying lazily in a hollow by the water. I almost wished that rains would come to make the road impassable and imprison me here for the winter! For an hour before dinner *Manuel* and I walked again in the streets and followed the shore out to the rocky point where small boys bathed in the lake. A last *vuelta* in *Puerto Dominguez.* Then dinner, packing, good-byes—and once again we were bouncing along in the trusty "*camionetta Copec.*" With the son of the *dueño*, a passenger *atras.* The road back to *Carahue* was dry now, but instead of detracting from the wildness of the journey, it only added to *Manuel's* speed! And the road was full of oxcarts plodding along with sheathes of wheat and sacks of grain. Each time we passed I felt sure we'd clip off an ox or one of the solid wooden wheels of a cart, but *Manuel* seemed to be traveling under a lucky star! And we didn't even so much as run over a pig or a dog! We stopped at various farms and also in *Carahue* and *Nueva Imperial*, but we reached *Temuco* early for a wonder, *a las siete y media en punto*! And the last lap of our journey was a lovely one with long shadows across the landscape and with 3 volcanoes sharply outlined against the eastern sky. Back here in familiar *Temuco*, I luxuriated in hot water! And after I had washed and dined, *Manuel* came and we spent the evening together. I have grown very fond of *Manuel* with his little mustache, his hair slicked back, his happy-go-lucky ways, and his hearty laugh.

March 17, 1942—Victoria—Gran Hotel Royal—8:00 AM

Manuel assured me that he would call at 9:30 AM to let me know whether or not he would continue his journey north, and yesterday morning I waited for the telephone call. But after writing and mending until 11:00 without any word, I decided that my *Manuel* had made other plans!   --And I hastened out to buy a few necessities before the stores closed at 12:00. I indulged in an Indian curio too, bought hastily in the thought that this was my last opportunity. Then I rushed home to pack and eat before taking off on Chester. −And at this point the miracle occurred: *Manuel* called to say that he was continuing north in the afternoon! He had been skeptical the evening before, and I had decided that if *Manuel* was skeptical, there wasn't the remotest possibility of his going. But miracles do happen! And I was more than happy to go with him, for after traveling so long with company, the prospect of going on alone is a rather cold one. By 3:30 we were bounding along in the dust and heat of this great valley in the good *camionetta* Copec with "*el mejor chofer en Chile*" at the wheel! In *Lautaro*, we stopped for business and also to consume grapes and *pasteletas* and *helados*. Then on to *Victoria* with oxcarts scattering before us and a cloud of red dust rising in our wake! As the heat lessened and the sun became a fiery ball in the west, the wheat fields, the poplars, the distant hills and the occasional streams move themselves into a truly lovely panorama devoid of the hard intensity of midday. And once again I was thankful to be traveling at this hour. In *Victoria* we stopped here at this pleasant hotel where I have a room with an excellent view of all the activity in the street, a fine place to amuse myself while waiting for *Manuel*! At dinner we were both in a merry mood and fairly choked ourselves laughing while the rest of the people in the dining room looked on in wonder. Although *Manuel* went off on business while I explored the *plaza*. And when I came back to my room and lay down to wait for him, I fell sound asleep and didn't awake until 1:00 AM.

March 18, 1942—Hotel Savoy—10:30 AM

Yesterday morning I walked the streets of *Victoria* and waited for *Manuel*. −And I sat in my room and waited for *Manuel*! Life below was interesting. Quick stepping horses passed in the streets. Loiterers stopped to look over the heaps of fruit in the little shop across the way. Women bought meat in the shabby *carneceria* where assorted carcasses and joints were hanging in the open air. Men riding horses and carrying 2 cans behind their saddles, drew off milk by the liter. −A slow, unconcerned way of life permeated with the spirit of *mañana*. When *Manuel* was finally ready, it was noon, so we stayed for *almuerzo* in *Victoria*! And not until 2:00 PM, *mas o menos*, did we start for *Traiguen*! Great trees lining the road provided welcome contrast to the heat of the dry wheat fields and of the dry hills but in the village where *Manuel* stopped for business, the heat was oppressive. To refresh ourselves we consumed another melon, a juicy honeydew. And when we started north for *Angol*, the heat was waning, and evening was on its way. Up and down, up and down, through barren hills we went—our world, a world of brown and yellow, of rich warm browns and creams and tans. A *huaso* on a buckskin horse and wearing a tawny *manta* seemed as much a part of the landscape as the grass which had withered on the hills. *Manuel* followed our wandering road with his usual abandon, and at one point the sand and the pitch of the road proved too much for even the *camioneta Copec*. We bounced sideways and jammed cross wise in the road! And the engine refused to turn over. But with maneuvering and pushing we reached an incline and managed to roll with enough speed to start the car again! *Manuel's* lucky star stands by him! In a tiny *pueblo Manuel* stopped to search for bread and water but none seemed to be available. Finally at the *correo*, a *señora* agreed to sell us 2 rolls and 2 slices of cheese! And thus fortified, we continued to *Angol*, arriving just as darkness came. After a cleanup, a walk in the *plaza*, and a 9:30 dinner, *Manuel* still wanted to "*dar una vuelta*," so we went off in the pick up for a turn about the town. But we made the mistake of going down a back road, and when we tried to turn around, we rolled into a ditch of water where we stuck hard and fast! There was nothing to do but leave the *camioneta* 'til morning and return to our hotel on foot. Another adventure!

March 19, 1942—Los Angeles—Hotel Central—8:30 AM

Yesterday was a time of terrific emotional strain, for it brought the parting of the ways for *Manuel* and me; and my effort throughout the day to be nonchalant and gay sapped all my energy. Why I let myself go to such an extent, I do not know. It seems so stupid. And yet I can't avoid it. I wakened *Manuel* at 7:30 and we went off to extract the pick up from the mud. The efforts of a man with a shovel were futile, and we had to resort to a team of oxen—great beasts, who, with the aid of a racing motor, were able to pull us out of the ditch. Then we spent the rest of the morning in *Angol*, I puttering around my room and *Manuel* tending to his business. After dinner we loitered, conscious that this was the last lap of our journey together; and when we finally drove off to *Collipulli*, *Manuel's* speed was considerably tempered. From *Collipulli* I expected to go on alone, but *Manuel* studied his map and decided to go on to *Esperanza*, the northernmost *pueblo* in his district. He knew as well as I that there was no possibility of selling oil in this tiny village, but he said he'd go and see. And we stopped there at a farm to buy figs instead of to sell oil! Each of us ate a whole dozen! Then we crossed the river in a *balsa*, and *Manuel* drove me to the top of the hill before stopping for me to pack up. When his car came to a stop my heart sank, for I had no desire to go on alone. And the road wound away through a vast region of bare lonely hills. After depending on *Manuel's* direction and companionship for two weeks, I felt incapable of going on alone. We fell into each other's arms, and after a good-bye kiss, I fled with a lump in my throat and tears in my eyes. Pedaling helped and I pedaled mechanically, rapidly, glad of activity in which to lose myself. At least I had a goal, even if my going had lost all its punch. Through bare hills to *Mulchen*, and thence through more populated country with rambling farmhouses and rows of poplars. But the sun sank as I crossed the *Rio Bio-Bio*, and in a few moments I was traveling in the dark through terrain that was only a shadowy suggestion of reality. Rows and rows of tall poplars against a dark sky. And a thin slip of a new moon that soon sank from sight. I could scarcely see the road with my dim light, and I rode in low gear wondering when some hole or some pile of gravel would upset me. But curiously enough, nothing happened and after an hour of darkness, I reached cobblestone streets and knew that *Los Angeles* was very near. Stopping at the first hotel sign, I felt a sense of elegance as I walked into the central court and was shown to a room with modernistic chairs. But I wasn't equal to the 5 plate meal, and after consuming what I could I felt positively ill. A bad sign indeed when I can't eat! Usually I devour everything in sight!

March 20, 1942—Yumbel—Pensión "malo"—7:30 AM

Yesterday morning I took time to walk about *Los Angeles*, a nice little town with clean avenues and modern buildings. A turn through the principal streets with a stop at a bike shop and I was ready to pack up and continue on my way. Out of the city and away to the north, passing many oxcarts plodding townward, and soon I was traveling through brushy uninhabited lands. A truck carried me for a few kilometers, but the road was good, and I arrived at the *Salto de Laja* by

midday. Here I stopped to watch the water pouring over a
precipice and flowing away through a deep channel in the
rock, but a sense of loneliness caught up with me when I
loitered so I continued on my way. Just beyond the falls my
road forked and I turned off into a trail of sand which was
utterly discouraging. And henceforth walking and struggling
to push Chester became the order of the day! But the
countryside here was green with cultivated lands and rows of
poplars, and since I knew I could reach *Yumbel* on foot I gave
myself up to enjoying my trek. At one *ranchita* I stopped to
eat a whole watermelon, having no qualms over spending my
time in this manner! And the last lap of the journey to *Yumbel*
station where the sand was particularly deep, Chester and I
rode in an oxcart! The driver chattered in Spanish I couldn't
understand, but I smiled and answered "*Si*" to every "*No
cierto?*"! At the station I stopped to take *onces* and to watch
the life there, and when I continued my ride it was only a
matter of a few minutes before I reached *Yumbel Viejo*, my
goal. Here I stopped at the first *pensión*, and it seemed rather
picturesque with the courtyard full of oleanders and
hydrangea, but my room was a poor dark hole in the wall with
a dirty bed! Before dinner I took a walk through the town—a
sleepy little place with dusty streets and tumble-down adobe
buildings. And at 2:00 I turned in for a night of fighting fleas
and mosquitoes!

March 21, 1942—Concepción—Hotel Central—7:30 AM

Yesterday morning I was glad to gulp down a cup of
coffee and a roll and take my leave of that miserable *pensión*.
How refreshing the country after a bad night! And I rode out
in to it with soaring spirits, even though I had been warned
that mine was a *camino malo*. A vast country with distant
panoramas and a feeling of openness, and over all a clear,
crisp autumn air. In the village were vineyards and cultivated
lands and low rambling, adobe houses. But the hills between
were less friendly. Barren they were, with great red gashes cut
by winter rains—wounds only partially dressed by the

greenery of trees seeking a bit of moisture in that dry land. And up and down across this landscape I sweated, hauling Chester through deep sands in the valleys and up abrupt inclines in the hills. At one shanty which was overflowing with dirty-faced *niños* I stopped to eat grapes, and later I bought more grapes from an oxcart bound for town with its produce. Grapes to quench an endless thirst! And just when the heat of the day and the fatigue of my journey seemed overpowering, my road entered a highway! Incredible! And in a few moments I had arrived at *Florida*! Here I stopped for *onces* to replenish the strength in my weak legs, and I spent a sociable half hour talking with the driver of a gondola and watching an enthusiastic group draw numbers for the raffle of a goose! When the coffee and the thick meat sandwich had brought my muscles to life again, I was ready for another 50 kilometers, and I rolled on to *Concepción* over a road which seemed a boulevard compared to what had gone before. Down, down, down—praise be to Allah, the way was down! – Down a river valley, riding into the setting sun. And just at dusk, I reached the city—and the cobblestones that are so amazing to tired nerves. As I passed at a corner wondering which way to go, a pleasant chap on a bicycle became my self-appointed guide, and I was more than happy to just relax and follow him to *Hotel Central*.

March 22, 1942—Concepción—Hotel Central—very late!

Yesterday morning I wakened in a new city, and I went forth eagerly to make its acquaintance. Down *Barros Arana* I wandered intent on changing money and gathering information concerning the trip to *Chillán*, but *Cerro Caracol* caught my eye and I couldn't resist the temptation to climb to its summit for a panorama of the city. Up and up through pine woods I climbed, sharing the path with ambitious students who walked while reading aloud, and from the tip I looked down on a busy compact city. Following a road that continued farther, I reached a still higher point where a tower afforded a view of the *Rio Bio-Bio*. Then down by another road which took me past the *Barrio Universitario*, with its modern buildings and into the heart of the city once more. On every side are signs of the great earthquake of '39. Heaps of brick and debris, walls standing desolate and deserted buildings cracked and chipped, buildings repaired in a makeshift manner. But amidst this destruction are fine new edifices and everywhere construction work goes on. After lunch I took Chester off to a bike shop to which I had an introduction from a man in *Temuco*, and here a smiling *señor* supplied me with a new cyclometer and removed the "S" which has been in my front wheel ever since Chester came down in a tangled heap in the back of the *camioneta Copec*. Then I looked up the address of the Steffens, my friends from *Pucón*. Happy day! This proved an entrée to the home of a Chilean family. *Maria* was sick in bed, but I spent some time visiting in her room, and then I was invited to take *onces* with the rest of the family. A regular banquet with grapes, rice pudding, coffee, and bread! Afterwards we had music—the radio, the victrola, and the piano with *Señora* Steffens and her sister playing and singing. I was delighted to hear Chilean music, to be in the midst of a barrage of *Castellano*, and to have this opportunity to see the inside of a Chilean home. And all the while *Enrique* entertained me with his rhythmic responses to the music—*Enrique* the younger, who is young enough to be without inhibitions. After *comida* in the hotel, I walked again in the streets, this time turning off the avenue for the respectable and following another street which overflowed with the masses. Here was a medley of small shops, of street vendors, of fruit counters, of cheap clubs, of shabby promenaders, of horse-drawn cabs whose elegance was passé. But the streets were throbbing with life—and I looked on fascinated.

March 24, 1942—Chillán—Casa particular—8:00 AM

Day before yesterday, Sunday, was a very long and a very entertaining day. At 7:30 I knocked at the Steffen's gate according to directions which *Enrique* had relayed to me via telephone the night before. But *Enrique* still slept! However, he dressed hastily and appeared with a bicycle to accompany me to *la Boca del Rio Bio-Bio*. And off we went together, *Enrique* riding with speed and abandon, and I following more cautiously. The *Boca* proved to be a very pretty spot with a bit of open beach and interesting crags, and we scrambled over the rocks for a while before turning back. *Enrique* had to return to *Concepción* for mass so I continued on alone to *Ramuntelo*, riding through wind-swept hills where the road afforded views of a rocky coast and the open ocean. A lovely lonely way. For a moment I stopped at the *playa*, a crescent of white sand hemmed in by great rocks and green waters, and then continued to the bluff at the end of the road. Returning to *Concepción*, I couldn't resist the temptation to turn off and follow the strip of highway to *Talcahuano*, although I had no time to explore the *pueblo* with its docks. Riding back I pedaled at great speed, thrilled with the smooth road and a tail wind. Exhilarating after the plodding gait of the tourist! Another cyclist hailed me at the cross-roads, and it turned out to be Ernest, the younger Steffen, coming to accompany me back to *Concepción*. And once more back home I just had time to wash and change my clothes before hustling off to the Steffens for Sunday dinner. And what a pleasant meal it was with all the family gathered around and with the hum of *Castellano* filling the room. I, too, was included in the conversation and they all addressed me as Miss *Elen*, but I'm still unable to comprehend all. Meat, corn, and potatoes; soup; spaghetti; roast with salad; beans; grapes; meringues; *agua caliente*! Truly a bountiful meal! And I ate every crumb for I had had no breakfast and had pedaled far. After the meal we had music again, and again *Enrique* overflowed with the rhythm in his soul! And 2 of the children performed a stiff little minuet. Then it was decided that *Enrique's* friend, *Mario*, and I should make an excursion by bicycle within the city, and I rushed off to my hotel to change my clothes, always eager for more sightseeing. But a few minutes after I returned it commenced to rain, so we settled ourselves in the parlor instead of venturing out! Then it was time for *onces*! More

friends of the family were there for tea, and afterwards they
added to the volume of the *canción nacional*, which I specially
requested. By this time, the rain had ceased, and *Mario* and I
rode off to *Avenida Pedro Valdiva*, a fine residential street by
the side of the *Rio Bio-Bio*. We stopped there at a little zoo
with lines of stilted cages, but I'm afraid Mario didn't have the
true spirit of the naturalist, 'cause he made the rounds in 10
minutes! Then back to town we went again, but not home.
Instead we drew up at a fire station where the volunteers of the
Primera *Compañia de Bomberos* were having a glass of
ponche! *Mario* explained me to them, and I too was invited to
have a glass of *ponche*! Then we all went *arriba* where 3 of
the firemen entertained us with music, playing with great
enthusiasm. And I danced with a 4th! Then, after a tour of
inspection of their fine new building, we went below again for
more *ponche*! And I, in my faded parka and broken down
shoes was seated at the head of the table *"reina de los
bomberos"*!! *Mario* and I reached the Steffens just in time for
comida, and once again I joined the family in their meal!
Afterwards my *compañero—Mario* with the exaggerated
Oxford accent to his few words of English—suggested the
radio station, and off we went again, this time to a little downstairs broadcasting studio. And still later *Mario* lead me to the
press offices, *El Sur* and *La Patria*, where the night workers
were setting type and preparing photos. I felt like exhibit "A"
as the crowds gathered around me and were told in detail all
about me—my age, my work, and my mission! Not until 1:00
AM did *Mario* pilot me back to my hotel, and then I wanted
nothing more than to flop into bed and sleep.

And yesterday I took to the road again. *Mario* came at
9:00 to lead me out of the city, and thence I went forth alone.
Up and up and up through the hills which guard *Concepción*
and thence over the top, as it were, and down past *Florida*,
across broad, open slopes into the great flat valley which
stretches north and south through Chile. The day was brilliant
with droves of fluffy clouds and there was a tang of autumn in
the air which sharpened the landscape and accented the yellow
glow in the poplars and the rich purple of the fruit in the many

vineyards. And my spirits, too, were heightened by the keenness of the day. At one point I stopped to have my fill of grapes which grew by the side of the road. Then on through *Quillan*, a nice little sprawling town dressed with many trees, to *Bulnes* where I stopped for *onces* in an out-door dinning room under an orange tree. I reached *Chillán* at dusk and found all the hotels filled, but a lad from one hotel lead me around until we finally located a room in a private house and here I was glad to stay. *Chillán* is practically in ruins. Completely flattened by the earthquake of '39, it has been only partially rebuilt, and destruction is evident in every street.

March 25, 1942—Linares—Hotel Paris—7:30 AM

Yesterday morning I started north in earnest, and henceforth I travel in a direct line to *Santiago*. I thought I would take the train from *Chillán*, for I have been looking forward to seeing *El Capitán* in *Santiago* between March 21 and 28, but I just can't give up cycling, and I'm afraid that Chilean-like, the captain will forget our plans to meet again. So I'm sticking to my bicycle and reveling in the good roads and the beautiful Chilean countryside. All day yesterday I traveled along tree-lined lanes. Poplars, eucalyptus, weeping willows. And the produce of the countryside was on display in every fruit shop. There is an air of opulence here which is not to be found farther south and there are many great *fundos* in the country, *fundos* with extensive, rambling buildings and many trees and flowers. Off to the right rise the peaks of the *Cordilleras*, and they are beautifully clear in this autumn weather. I am forever thrilled with their wild, snowy tops. I passed through *San Carlos*, a *pueblo simpático*, and continued to *Parral* where I stopped at the hotel for dinner—a scattered sort of a hotel which shows the result of the earthquake. As I was leaving, a gentleman stepped out of the *plaza* and asked to see my passport. Told me also to stop at the *carabineros* in *Linares* for an official stamp of some sort. In the middle of the afternoon I bought a watermelon and sat down beside the railway and consumed the whole thing! And before the sun had set, I rolled into *Linares*. After cleaning up, I went dutifully forth to see the *carabineros*, but after a long and sociable chat, they told me I'd have to go to the *Intendencia mañana*! And this I resolved not to do! My day was rounded out with a walk through the principal streets and about the *plaza*, but I longed for a hill from which to view the mountains as they took on a rosy glow from the setting sun. At dinner the gentleman sitting at the next table proved to be an Englishman, and we talked across our tables for a very long time. Quite a surprise to find an Englishman in *Linares*!

March 26, 1942—Talca—Hotel Central—6:00 AM

What a day yesterday turned out to be! Phew! Shattered my hopes of cycling onto *Santiago*! And all because of my *caballito*! I rode merrily north from *Linares* passing into a land of scattered hills and vineyards, vineyards, vineyards. But off to the right the snowcapped mountains still stood guard over the valley. The opulence of the country seemed to increase, and I saw wealthy homes standing in the vineyards. An autumnal note was present too in the smears of red pepper and yellow ears of corn in the more lowly courtyards. In one vineyard, I stopped to eat the tiny bunches left by the pickers. Muscats in March! But ill-fortune followed my wheels, and just before reaching *Talca*, a soft tire hinted that all was not well with Chester. I patched the tube and blew it up only to find that it had to come off for another patch. And after an hour of sweating in the sun, the___thing was still soft! I limped on into *Talca* and stopped at the first "fix-it" shop, where I loitered for another couple of hours while the attendant put on four more patches. And then, in spite of the lateness of the hour, I started north again, hoping to reach the next *pueblo* before dark. But just as I passed out of the city of *Talca*, I felt the sickening thud of another flat tire! At this point I gave up and pushed Chester back to town prepared to stay the night in *Talca*. A small, dirty-faced boy attached himself to me in the capacity of guide. And a smiling man on a bicycle bought me 3 apples and conducted me to a shop where I could buy another inner tube. I made the purchase, although it practically depleted my funds, and it was installed while a crowd stood around and questioned me. Then 3 cyclists piloted me to the station where I inquired after trains and thence brought me to the door of my hotel. The rest of the evening I was content to just sit and talk to hotel personnel: the little school girls, their big brother, and the very large *dueña*. But my mind kept turning over the idea of going to *Santiago* by train, and I rebelled at the idea of deserting Chester. If only I had more pesos. If only my Chilean visa didn't expire the 28th. But I couldn't evade the cold facts, and the best I could do was to compromise with the idea of pedaling to *Curicó* and taking the train from there.

March 27, 1942—Santiago—Hotel Oddo—9:30 PM

And yesterday morning at 6:30 I pushed off into a cold, dark world. The streets of *Talca* were deserted, and the town slept. But as I pedaled deep into the country, the sun came over the mountains to chase away the chill, and I was glad to be abroad at this early hour. Hills to the right and hills to the left with a valley producing little more than a scrubby crop of bushes. But after *Molina* the countryside became lush with growing things again, and wagonloads of grapes were moving along the road toward a great winery. As I pedaled into *Curicó* another cycling enthusiast rode up to ask me whence I had come and where I was going. After piloting me into the heart of the city and around the *plaza*, he suggested that I should a*lmuerzo* in *Curicó*, and I had to confess that I didn't have the price of a meal! We tried to locate a place where I could change my U.S. dollars, but it was futile, so *Juan Toledo* asked me to his house for dinner. But he wanted me to stop by a photographer for a picture first! And I posed in the street with my bike, while a crowd gathered on the sidewalk! At his house *Juan* provided me with the equipment for a bath, and afterwards he showed me his room with the walls lined with racing trophies and photographs of cyclists. We had lunch in the patio, and I ate my salad, *cazuela*, beans,

and grapes as if I had never eaten before! Then *Juan* took me
to the station, took the wheels off my bike and prepared it for
shipping, and put me aboard my train, bag and baggage! What
kindness from an utter stranger. Although I hated to give up
cycling, I found much to interest me in my 3rd class jaunt to
Santiago. The crowds of ragged passengers, the baskets of
fruit, the crates of chicken, and the sacks of heavens knows
what which were all packed together in the coaches; the
salesmen who passed through the cars with their fruit, their
cheap clothing, and their diverse knick knacks; the stations
where women in dirty white uniforms were vending food from
baskets which they carried under their arms—whole roast
chickens, greasy joints, pig's feet, limp slices of onion soaked
in red sauce, and always the hot peppers of which the *Chilenos*
are so fond. And I stood on a back platform where I could
better see the countryside as it flew by. Acres of rich green
agricultural lands. In *Santiago* I was unable to pay for my
bike, so I had to take the train up town with my saddlebags
over my arm. I felt a little better when I saw another woman
on the train carrying a duck wrapped in newspaper, its head
tucked under her coat! No rooms were to be had at the
Claridge, so I came here, and after cleaning up, I went out to
mingle with the crowds in the street and to purchase fruit,
pastries, and ice cream for my dinner! A note from the
"nameless horseman of *Puerto Octay*" waited for me at the
Claridge, and I was pleased to be remembered, but there was
nothing from "*El Capitán.*"

March 29, 1942—Santiago—Hotel Albion—7:00 AM

For 2 days now I have drifted and rested here in this
city with its endless activity and endless crowds of people. I
have tried to extend my visa for Chile, but each time I have
had an appointment to meet the woman from the foreign office
who can arrange it for me, I have waited in vain, and now I'm
wondering what the outcome will be. Day before yesterday I
changed some money, window shopped, washed, wrote letters,
wandered aimlessly, and waited 2 hours in my room for the

woman from the foreign office. When I asked for mail at *Expresso Villalonga*, I was nearly bowled over to find I had some! Two messages from *"El Capitán"*! The rest of the day I walked with a spring in my step and a smile on my face! He doesn't know when he will have his vacation, but there's a slight possibility he may come to *Santiago* before I leave! I spent part of the day searching for another room too, for there were no meals served at the *Oddo*, and I found room without board very unsatisfactory. I wandered about buying fruit and ice cream and eating pastries and sandwiches in the arcades by the *plaza*. Not a very healthy arrangement! And who should I bump into in the street but the obnoxious American who had come down in the *Copiapó*! Per usual he was full of complaints and big talk.

Yesterday I continued my search for a room and again I waited on the woman from the foreign office without success. But in the afternoon I let business rest and went off to look up *Augusto Villanueva*, the gentleman I had met on the little boat coming from *Peulla* to *Petrohúe*. I found him in a great house down in the old section of town, and he received me with great hospitality. We visited for some time, took tea in the garden of his guesthouse, and then went off for an evening at the movies. So my afternoon was a sociable one, and I welcomed the stimulation of friends after a day alone in the impersonal city. After the show I moved over here to this hotel, but I find it unpleasant, and now I contemplate moving again.

March 30, 1942—Santiago—Mrs. Petre's—9:00 AM

Yesterday morning I hunted again for a place to stay, and at noon I moved over here to a little boarding house where I think I'll be content. At 1:00 I went to *Señor Villanueva's* home for lunch and we had our meal out in the garden—a secluded place surrounded by the house. How deserted that house seems! A tremendous place where only 1 or 2 persons live and where dust gathers in the unused rooms. The servant who brought our food came down a long corridor and across the garden like a ghost! After lunch *Señor Villanueva*, his sister, a friend, and I went off to climb *Cerro San Cristobal*. Around and around and up we went until we could look down on the whole of the city. And then at the top we took tea and danced with a crowd of other merry makers—a gay evening. It was dark when we started down, and the other woman took the funicular, while the *Señor* and I hiked down a shortcut. Then I came "home" to unpack, settle myself, and have supper in my new quarters. Yesterday was Palm Sunday, and all the people in the streets carried sprigs of braided palm and olive. But the approach of Easter seems unreal with the feel of autumn in the air.

March 31, 1942—Santiago—Mrs. Petre's—midnight

Yesterday was a sort of a homey day, for I can live here in my new *pensión* in a very informal way. Breakfast came to me while I was still in bed, and it was 10:00 before I had taken my turn in the bathroom and was ready for the day! Then I stopped to eat *pastelitas* as I wandered past the *plaza* on my way to the tourist bureau to inquire again about my Chilean visa! Later Mrs. Petre went with me to look up a *maleteria* where I could have my little suitcase repaired and where I could also buy leather to repair worn-out equipment. And I went on with her to the central market where she selected vegetables and meats for the day from the heaps of things on display. On the way home we met the "obnoxious American" in the street, and once again I listened to his tales of bad food and grandiose exploits. In the afternoon I went to the woman in the tourist bureau with determination, and instead of putting me off this time, they actually started proceedings on the adjustment of my expired visa. And the balance of the day I devoted to sewing a leather patch on the seat of my worn-out cords! In the evening I slipped out to walk a bit and to buy a kilo of grapes, and with this I finished my day.

April 1, 1942—Santiago—Mrs. Petre's—10:00 AM

What lazy days I am having now!—Lounging in my room until 10 or 11 each morning! Just as I was ready to leave yesterday, *Señor Villanueva* called and asked me to go with him to look at bikes and afterwards to take dinner at his home. We made the rounds of all the cycle shops, he in search of a bicycle and I in search of a Dunlop tire, but neither of us was successful. And at 1:00 we went out to his house for our meal. His mother, his sister, an uncle, and the 2 of us assembled in his mother's section of the great house and went into a rich dark dining room where we sat down to an elaborately served dinner. Afterwards we talked of politics and such until 3:00 when I had to go to the consular office for my visa. And now the negotiations are at last completed and I'm officially back in Chile with the privilege of staying on for 3 months longer! Yesterday afternoon I again went shopping with Mrs. Petre, and again I spent considerable time working over my travel-worn equipment!

April 3, 1942—Peñaflor—Residencial Quinta—9:00 AM

Day before yesterday was another lazy day. And not until 11:00 was I ready to sally forth! Then I devoted the rest of the morning to buying a pair of shoes! –A heavy pair of gunboats to replace the broken-down shoes which had suffered so in the mud of *Darien* and in the sharp stones of Argentina. After lunch I canvassed the *Alameda* for bike shops, walking close to the station down one side and back the other, but I am still unable to find a tire. Allah be with me when I start touring again with my tires from which the tread has been stripped! I took tea with Mrs. Petre, and in the evening we shopped, she to buy ham and I to purchase a strap and a jersey! I find Mrs. Petre very helpful and I like her. She's a bleached blond and has lived fast in her day, but she likes people and has adapted herself admirably to Chile. After *comida* we ended the day with a walk in *Parque Forrestral* where neon light and shadows created a fairyland in the midst of the city.

Yesterday morning I had a last look for a tire for my bike. And then, feeling the pressure of the city too much for me, I resolved to go out to the country. I packed up listlessly and at 3:00 PM pushed off into the traffic and cobblestones of *Santiago's calles*. Cars were jammed in the streets, and I soon discovered the cause: --uniformed men on parade in honor of the inauguration of the new president, *Juan Antonio Rios*. As I passed the *Barrio Civico*, I saw crowds gathering there, and mounted units, resplendent with uniforms and banners, were passing toward the *Casa Moneda*. The excitement and pageantry proved too much for me, and after pedaling around several blocks in a state of indecision, I turned and raced back to Mrs. Petre's where I parked my bike and changed my clothes before rushing out into the city to join the crowds. In the *plaza* I found a street roped off and lined with marines, and here I stood with hoards of jostling *Chilenos* to watch whatever might pass. Presently a band struck up the *cancion nacional* and several elegant black carriages drawn by handsome bays with red, white and blue braided in their manes, passed. But still the crowds waited, and so I crossed the street to a better vantage point and waited too. Then the carriages returned, and this time I recognized *Rios* as one of the occupants. The same face which I have seen on countless walls and handbills throughout Chile! And behind the carriages came contingent after contingent of marines. Not until the last man had passed did I return for my bicycle, and by then it was too late to think of going to *Curacavi* as I had originally planned. But I had no desire to stay another night in *Santiago*, so I pedaled off to *Peñaflor*, happy to be back in the saddle again. And I felt complete contentment as I came into this garden spot with its shaded avenues. Beside the road a woman was lighting a candle at a little shrine; and there was the smell of wood smoke in the air. Back in the familiar *quinta*, I wandered into the garden where grapes hung in the arbor and apples lay under the trees. A feast of fruit! And then dinner with roses on the table and conversation with my neighbors. And before bedtime the moon rose and shone brilliantly through the trees and vines of the *quinta*. How lovely, *Peñaflor*.

April 4, 1942—Curacavi—Hotel Central—9:00 AM

Yesterday I loitered in *Peñaflor* until after *almuerzo* for *Peñaflor* is one of my favorite spots. And I loved walking in the *quinta* where I could eat the grapes and apples, walking through the *pueblo* where *quinta* crowded on *quinta* with rank vegetation, and just resting under that luxuriant greenery. After a good lunch out under the arbor, I finally turned my spirits to the idea of moving on, and I sped away on Chester, turning the pedals easily and quickly there on the paved road. How luxurious after the roads in the south! Back to *Marruecos* and thence off to the left on the camino *Valparaiso*, a road which I had last traveled by truck. And how easy the *Cuesta Barriga* seemed when my legs were fresh! I wondered that I had ever thought it long or difficult! And I stopped at the top to eat an apple and to look back on the agricultural patchwork in the valley. Then down and down and on to *Curacavi*. Here I had difficulty in finding a room 'cause all the hotels were *chicititos* and the town was full of people. Finally I found *una pieza* in this tiny hotel—a dark little cubicle under the eaves of a rambling adobe building. But it opens out onto the patio with its garden, and all the earthen walks are swept neat and clean. After settling myself I went out to walk the streets, peering into the low shops and houses which crowded along the main thoroughfare and staring back at all the people who looked so curiously at me. Numerous bicycles in the street inspired me to take out Chester and ride until darkness drove me indoors. And then I looked forward eagerly to the evening meal, for my appetite had grown large with activity. A good meal it was, too, and I turned in quite satisfied with my day.

April 5, 1942—Pudahuel—9:00 AM

Yesterday morning I went off to explore the surroundings of *Curacavi*, and a dirt road soon drew me off into the country away from the highway with its speeding traffic. For 20 miles I pedaled on and not until I reached the *pueblo* of *Corombo* and the road which I had traveled on my return from *Algarrobo*, was I content to turn back. For curiosity always drew me on to the next turn, and I was delighted with the country there amongst the dry hills. Corn fields and green pastures and many cattle. And always the little, low adobe houses. But now there was a keen autumnal note in the air—present in the overcast skies and the cool weather, present in the cosmos, in the gardens and in the heaps of corn in the courtyards and on the roofs, present in the horses which stood waiting at the doorways, and present in the ragamuffins who played marbles in the dust. A sharp brisk atmosphere which added zest to cycling. And when I returned, the hour was late and I was tremendously hungry. A good dinner out in the garden and I was ready to pack up and turn back toward *Santiago*. A small boy with a bike load of bread accompanied me as far as *Miraflores*, chattering Spanish all the while. And when I reached the road which turned off for *Cuesta La Prado*, I couldn't resist the temptation to try a new route. So I turned off, replenished my water supply at a hovel at the foot of the hill, and started up on foot. −A long push up through scrubby vegetation, but from the top I had a lovely view of dim mountains and hills rising out of a hazy valley, and I liked the loneliness of the way! Then, suddenly, it was late, and as I rolled down, I realized that it would be dark before I found a room for the night. I could no longer see the road when I reached this little *pueblo*, and when I stopped to inquire for a *pensión*, I found that there was no place to stay this side of *Santiago*! So I sought out the *carabineros*, but they first asked if I had a *patente*, and when they found I lacked one, they were inclined to fine me 20 pesos!! --But I lingered and talked, and they finally waived the fine and helped me find a place to stay! I came here to a store to have supper and afterwards went to the house of one of the *carabineros* for the night. Two *señoritas* here made me very much at home, and the *carabinero* and his *señora* treated me to glass after glass of *chicha*. Their house was poor enough with mud walls and an earthen floor, and we all slept together in the same room! But this hospitality was genuine and I felt very grateful to them. I'll have to confess that the fleas kept me awake and tossing all night, and I found I had a cat for a bedfellow! But I felt a little soft when I heard the heavy breathing of the *señora* and her 3 small boys, 2 of them who were sleeping with their heads at opposite ends of a narrow bed! And they had a dog for a bed fellow!

April 6, 1942—Santiago—Mrs. Petre's—9:00 PM

Yesterday morning the sun was a welcome sight, and I was only too glad to leave that bed and my many crawling, biting *compañeros*! The ordeal was over at last—even though I must bear the welts for some time to come! Wanting to see the *2 señoritas* at the store before I left, I loitered in the little village and waited for them to waken. And how pretty and peaceful it was there. I had felt its warmth and beauty the night before when I had ridden out of the lonely desert into its few lights and its many tall shadowy trees, and now I found it equally *simpatico* by day. I walked back to the *laguna* and sat on its bank to write; and I walked in the other direction to the great *hacienda* whose fine house and broad gardens stood in stark contrast to the adobe hovels near by. Finally at 11:00 I had my coffee, said good-bye, and pedaled off to *Santiago*. But I did not stop; instead I turned south to *Maipú*, where a fiesta celebrating the historic battle of *Maipú* was in progress. After eating an *empanada* at the hotel (where I was unable to get a room for the night) I went back to the rodeo grounds where a row of makeshift restaurants had attracted the crowds. Here people were eating and drinking and dancing the *cueca* to the tune of tambourines and drums and beating on tables! What enthusiasm! The common people—ragged men and fat women with handkerchiefs in hand were stepping to lively tunes! I wandered up and down watching the crowds, the dancing and the circulating salesmen with their baskets; and I, too, was an object of curiosity with my bicycle, my tied-up pant-legs, and my leather-seated pants! At 3:00 PM I parked Chester and went into the little arena to see the rodeo, the main attraction of the day. And I found it most interesting, for it was so different from the rodeos I have known at home. The *huasos* looked very fine as they lined up on good horses wearing their colorful *mantas*, their round wide-brimmed hats, their black leggings buckled high above their knees, and their tremendous spurs; and their mounts were equipped with good *monturas* and finely braided headstalls and reins. The competition consisted of running a steer around the arena, pinning it against a padded section of the wall, and turning it back to be pinned in similar fashion at the other end of the arena. Always the *huasos* worked in pairs, and some of their horses performed beautifully turning their heads across the necks of the steers and forcing them to the wall where they were held fast by the weight of the horses. I watched until the hour was late and then rode away with the rest of the dispensing crowd—autos, pedestrians, *huasos*, gondolas, and even bicycles! Back to *Santiago* as the sun sank behind the hills and the *Cordillera* became rose and purple, and into the city as darkness brought out all the lights. Home again where a bath, a supper, and a flealess bed satisfied my every want!

April 7, 1942—Santiago—Mrs. Petre's—2:30 PM

    Yesterday was a social, civilized day in contrast to my wild, touring days! I slept late and topped off the morning with a walk downtown to ask for mail and to have a shoeshine in the *plaza*! And after lunch I made myself ready to go to tea with Mrs. Petre—the American women's tea. All dressed up with a hat and gloves, I felt quite elegant and I enjoyed the gathering with its familiar babble of English. Mrs. Petre and I visited a bit, ate 3 slices of cake (!), and scampered away to walk the streets before going home. But after dinner we went out again, this time to a movie which took me far, far from Chile.

April 10, 1942—Rancaqua—Hotel Santiago—9:00 AM

The 7th was another lazy day. I lay in bed until very late and then dressed in order to go to market with Mrs. Petre. We looked at the baskets of fat fish in the Central Market and then passed on to the *Vega*—a tremendous market across the *Mapocho*, a place in which I had never been before. Here was all the color and confusion of a popular market. Hoards of people crowded around the fruit counters in the open air section and filled the aisles in the great rambling building full of stalls for the sale of foods, hardware, clothing, furniture, everything--. Potatoes, squash, pots and pans, coats, meats, corn—all displayed in great confusion! Red peppers, tomatoes, grapes, avocados, apples. I was completely fascinated. Back home I wrote letters, wandered out to inquire for mail (always hoping to hear again from *El Capitán*), and went with Mrs. Petre on some errands. And in the evening the two of us went by *transvia* out to a cleaning establishment where I left my green dress. I have become quite chummy with Mrs. Petre in spite of the fact that I merely board with her, and this day she treated me to fruit and to 2 dishes of ice cream! She's a woman of the world from whom I learn of the world, and I like her humanistic philosophy, although I should never care to lead her kind of a life.

The 8th started off as an ordinary day and wound up as a very unusual one—for me at least! Discouraged over the prospects of meeting *El Capitán* in *Santiago* and weary of the city, I made plans to leave the following day—went to the tourist office for information, changed some money, kicked myself out of the lethargy of life in the city. After tea I went to call on the Pinstus, folks I had met in the south, but they were out, so instead I walked the streets enjoying the sharp silhouette of evening. Church towers, tall modern buildings, building balconies outlined against a rosy sky. And I wandered by the *vega* where I bought a *kilo* of grapes to eat in the park! There I sat alone while all the rest sat in twos! After dinner Mrs. Petre invited me to go to see a company of players, and we went down town to see *Olvido Leguia* and *Lucho Cordoba* in "*Yo Conocí Mucho a Su Papa*," a rollicking comedy that I managed to understand with Mrs. Petre's help. Afterwards we stopped for chocolate and toast and then turned toward home. But practically at our front door, adventure caught up with us in the form of 2 tipsy Englishmen. They spoke to us and we looked back and laughed and they turned and followed us! I was interested to see Mrs. Petre go into action. She slipped off her wedding rings and walked rapidly past our house out of earshot of the other boarders! Around the corner our pursuers caught up with us and asked if they might join us, and Mrs. Petre answered with a charming "yes"! This was my first experience in being "picked up", and just for devilment I decided to see it through. So we walked on together, I with pudgy, bald Charlie and she with tall, tipsy Jim. We picked up Charlie's car and started the rounds –first to the Ritz Taproom where we had strong drinks and danced on an illuminated floor, and then to the *Refugio* where we had weaker drinks and danced on a plain floor. As the evening wore on voices became thicker, laughter more boisterous, talk more ridiculous, and our companions more bold. But I could not tolerate the touch of my escort, and I had not consumed enough liquor to lose my sense of discrimination, so Charlie accused me of being in love with Jim and probably regretted the several hundreds of *pesos* that he was spending on me! Mrs. Petre wanted to go on to another cabaret and finally succeeded in getting our escorts underway, but thank fortune the next place was closed! So we managed to get home at 6:30 AM! Drink had gone to Mrs. Petre's head by then, and she was swearing like a trooper and walking with an unsteady gait. Getting the key in the keyhole and walking upstairs were problems that needed my help! But ultimately we got to bed, and I chalked up another escapade to experience.

And yesterday morning I left for the south—after 2 hours of sleep! My legs didn't function with their usual vigor, but when I reached the country, I drew a deep breath and traveled with more spirit. Tree lined roads, vineyards, cacti-covered hills, opulent *haciendas*——these things I love. A detour to *Morros* and back to *Buin* delayed me as did the loss of the nut that holds my back break in place; and shadows were long when I came pedaling slowly into *Rancagua*. Nearly 60 miles on 2 hours of sleep and no lunch! But the countryside was green and the mountains near, and I liked the region at once. I stopped in a poor little hotel, unpacked, washed, and went out to see the town. But en route I discovered a much better hotel and made up my mind to change. So I thought up a ruse, and when I asked the *señora* the cost of room and meals, I told her the price was too high and I would have to move. Her price was high, but I felt like a culprit as I lied about my small amount of *plata Chilena* and the dire necessity of spending very little. She became oily smooth, but I stood firm and smiling, leaning heavily on my inability to speak Spanish! And finally I pushed off and came here, relieved to have a comfortable room and a clean bed and towel. But I was no sooner settled than 2 girls from the other place knocked at my door and said it would cost me nothing to return and spend the night there. The *señora* liked me, they said! But I was skeptical, and discouraged them by pretending not to understand. What was their game, I wondered. When I was finally left alone, I went out again to walk the streets and look in the small shop windows, and at 8:30 I returned to devour a big meal and go wearily to bed.

April 11, 1942—Baños de Cauquenes—Hotel Rio Claro

Qué bueno dormir toda la noche! And I felt better after a good night's rest. But I spent the morning in Rancagua, for I had only a few kilometers to pedal during the day. I like to know the small towns of Chile, and I never tire of walking the streets, so I was content to poke about *Rancagua*—up and down the main thoroughfare, around the *plaza*, down to the station, and through the market there where eager salesmen trying to interest me in buying *manzanas*, *uvas*, *paltos*, and *gallinas*. A *gringa* was fair prey, they figured! I looked at wares in a saddle shop and was sorely tempted to buy but fortunately I resisted; and as yet I travel without a heavy pair of spurs or a bulky headstall in my pack! I also stopped at Braden Copper and Co. hoping to get permission to go up to their mines, but they answered me with a flat "no." And then it was noon and time for dinner. And before long I was pushing off for the *Baños de Cauquenes*. Up towards the hills along the *Rio Cachapaal* away from the heavy traffic of the "longitudinal *sur*" and through country with pleasant farms. The day was gray and the poplars, yellow fingers against the sky. And leaves were falling from the trees which lined the road. Winter is on its way. A short trip brought me here where I have taken a room in an unpretentious hotel in preference to the great ones across the river. After *onces* I walked out and a vineyard attracted me towards the hills where I could walk and eat grapes at the same time! *Que rica!* And at dusk I came back to sit by the river for a while before going to dinner. My table companion proved to be a German Jew who told me of her scattered family with tears in her eyes. And thus the suffering of the war was brought forcibly home to me who has forgotten it in my pursuit of selfish pleasures. I rarely read or talk or think war these days.

April 12, 1942—Rengo—Hotel Comercial—8:30 AM

Much of yesterday I spent at the *baños*. A pretty spot in the hills with a river of green water in the canyon below and with tall trees clustering about the hotel. After *desayuno* I walked across the river to the hotel which is a small village in itself. But I continued on up into the brushy hills, and when I returned I passed across a suspension bridge into the park behind the hotel. Here the leaves were yellow and heaps of them had fallen in the pathways. And I sat there where autumn had saturated the air, and cracked black walnuts! After *almuerzo* I had determined to push on, but instead I walked back across the river again with my German table companion. And instead of pedaling with determination, there I was loitering in the patios of the hotel and wandering through the baths! At 3:00 PM I suddenly decided to go, and I hurried back to my room, paid my bill and left in a flurry of activity. I would go to *Rengo* I thought and my feet turned rapidly, whirling me down out of the hills. But I was brought up suddenly by a loud report and a whistle of escaping air, and for the next half hour I had to repair a very flat tire! This delay should have sent me to *Rancagua*, but I just couldn't resist the yen to try and reach *Rengo*, so I turned south on the longitudinal sur! And I pedaled as fast as I possibly could— bouncing and clattering over the bumps and bumps in the road, and praying to Allah that my defective rear tire would hold out! And the evening grew darker and darker! All things were homeward bound at this hour—all except Helen. The oxcarts and the dark shadows of men moved with the assurance that welcome shelters awaited them; while I hurried in the insecurity of night and an unknown destination. I was conscious of walls on either side of the road and of trees and of low houses, but I had to keep my eyes on the road to avoid an upset. A wild, exciting ride! Night had come and all was very dark when I reached *Rengo*, and the streets here were very dark too. The only light came from the flicker of candles deep within the buildings, and I thought I had come to a land where electric lights were unknown. But just as I reached the corner of the *plaza* the lights came on and the city took shape. And there I was at the front door of a hotel where I took refuge for the night in a tiny room, scarcely large enough to contain both Chester and me. After dinner I wandered out for a walk in the plaza, and I stood with other passers-by to listen to a band play a piece before it moved on to another part of the town. Then, as I was passing into the court of the hotel, a Chilean spoke to me asking if I were a *Norteamericana*. And he shook my hand and asked me to go for a walk! I went, of course, for it is my policy to never, never, miss anything, and I welcomed a little company after several days alone. We walked down the main street to the station and back to the *plaza*; and before we parted, my new friend had suggested that he go with me on an excursion by bicycle the following day!

One never knows in what spot he will encounter unexpected experience! That is one of the great joys of travel.

April 13, 1942—Rengo—Hotel Commercial—9:00 AM

Yesterday morning I wakened to the tune of the *cancion nacional* played with gusto by a band in the *plaza.* And after coffee *Manuel* procured a bike, and we rode off to *Pelequen.* The spirit of companionship sharpened the excursion and sent a joyousness surging through me, as my legs turned effortlessly and we rolled past farmlands and hills. In *Pelequen* we stepped into the church to see the *Santa Rosa de Lima*, a much-venerated saint; and then, by way of contrast, *Manuel* sought out a restaurant where we sat beneath a grape arbor to drink a pitcher of *chicha!* Thus *Plelequen*, which I would scarcely have noticed had I been alone became a place of *buen recuerdos.* But on our return I felt a bit light-headed— as if I were on board ship—and I wondered if *chicha* were really as impotent as I was assured it was! Back in *Rengo,* *Manuel* asked me to come and meet some friends, and after being introduced to several girls and fellows I found myself going with the crowd to the *Club Social*—faded parka, patched britches and all! We all sat around a large table and had a drink and a meat sandwich while conversation flowed and it must have been two o'clock before we came back to the hotel! Then I went into a hearty dinner, while *Manuel* disappeared. In the afternoon the spirit of Sunday crept inside of me and I changed into my best clothes and went out to walk the streets! All of the iron doors were rolled down and the shops locked and barred, but I walked the length of the town in spite of the fact that I couldn't window shop. And then I sat in the *plaza*, feeling very much like a lady! But not for long, 'cause I was presently seized with a desire to cycle and I took off my finery and went back to Chester! Out of the town I pedaled, selecting at random a road that lead toward the mountains. That great impressive mass of the Andes which always draws me toward it. And I found myself in a truly beautiful spot, a river valley with the rambling intimate farms that I love, protected by hills and lying under the spell of the *Cordillera*. How lovely it was there in the late afternoon with the yellow poplars catching the last rays of the sun and with the hills and mountains taking on the soft purple of evening. And I shared the road with all the inhabitants—young and old—who were passing a leisurely Sunday out of-doors. I rode until my way became a stony path and then, reluctantly turned back into the setting sun, pedaling into *Rengo* just at dusk. Again I changed my clothes and sat in the *plaza* to pass the time until *comida*. And who should pass by but my friend *Manuel*! He wanted to go to the movies, so we went in to see the better half of a typical American film before coming here for our meal. And then, as if we hadn't had enough for one day, we went back to the *Club Social* where all *Manual's* friends had gathered for a dinner party! We joined them in wine and conversation and then we danced the night away to the tunes of the radio! The Chilean way of dancing rather floors me, but I entered in as well as I could, considering the fact that I have no rhythm in my soul and that I cannot speak the language! To bed at 2:00 AM!

April 14, 1942—Rengo—Hotel Commercial—8:30 AM

Manuel's "*Hasta mañana*" kept me waiting here at the hotel yesterday morning. I watched for him during *desayuno*, and afterwards I sat in the patio to write—sat, in a conspicuous place where he couldn't miss me! Only once I ventured out to window shop a bit and to watch the Monday morning activity in the streets. But at 12:30 I decided that further waiting was futile, and I went in to *almuerzo* with plans to move on in the afternoon. And then *Manuel* appeared! Such is the way of the *Chilenos*! I couldn't guess what his motives might be, so I decided to just follow along and watch. During our meal his brother came in, and *Manuel* informed me that he was angry because he, *Manuel*, had not returned to his *fundo*. So I thought of course that *Manuel* would hasten away at once. But not *Manuel*! He suggested that we *vamos andar un ratito*, and we walked down to the station and along the tracks to the auction grounds where we looked about the sales-stand and all the stone-paved little corrals.   Then back to the hotel where Manuel suggested we *vamos arriba en bicicleta*. Might as well, I thought, for I can always put off leaving until *mañana* and I can't always *vamos arriba* with *Manuel*! So he rented a bike and off we went—back up the road which I had traveled the afternoon before. But bad luck shadowed me, and twice my back tire wilted to the tune of escaping air. We fixed it up with my last patch, and I traveled on in fear and trepidation, expecting every bump in the road to send it flat again and to send me hiking back to *Rengo*! We turned off the road I knew and followed a branch that took us up the other side of the canyon.   Here *Manuel* knew everyone, and he greeted them all with a "How do you do?"   And finally we came to a lumping halt in the front yard of one of those little adobe houses, Manuel jumped off his bike and greeted all the people there with *abrazos*! He ordered coffee and while it was being prepared, we went for a walk up along the edge of the hills where we could look out over the valley. Through thorn bushes and black berries with one step to rest in a straw pile and with another stop to inspect a little tile factory where tile lay, drying in the sun. Back at the *señora's* we sat down to a table under the fig tree and had coffee *sin leche* with *pan amasado* and fresh cheese. And the *señora*, who lacked front teeth, stood by and exclaimed "*por dios!*" over the fact that I had come alone all the way from North America! There were figs to eat too—dead ripe--And I had a glimpse inside the house where food was cooking over an open fire on the dirt floor. A dark, windowless house where people sat around the fire on low stools. It was dusk when we finally left that house, but our way was down hill and we traveled quickly. At one house the screams of a frightened woman brought *Manuel* up short, and he exchanged some sharp words with a drunken man who was attacking the woman with a club. For a moment I thought he would make for *Manuel* too! But we didn't linger.   Instead   passed   on   to   *Cerillo*   where   *Manuel* reported the incident to the *carabineros*. And there in *Cerillo* we stopped to hear a friend of *Manuel's* play the piano! We sat in a room lit by candlelight and perfumed with the scent from a boquet of roses, and listened to the *señora's* enthusiastic playing. And when she played dance tunes, we danced on the board floor! Before we left she served us preserved figs. And then we rode off into the night. My flashlight served to light our way for a while, and then it went out and left us to guess at the way. How uncanny to ride without knowing when your wheels are going to catapult over rocks or flounder in sand! But we didn't have far to go, and part of the way some kind people in an auto lighted our road. Back home once more I changed my clothes and rested a bit and then went to *dar una vuelta* with *Manuel* again. We walked down to the station where we looked at all the posters in the waiting room and thence turned back towards our hotel, but we met friends of *Manuel's* en route and stopped to have a social visit on the street corner! We even danced there on the sidewalk to the tune of music from a near by circus! Back here we found more friends, and we all went into the bar to drink *chicha* and to roll dice! And so the evening passed. But before turning in *Manuel* suggested another walk and we went out once more into the deserted streets. This brought the climax, for in a very dark street I found myself in *Manuel's* arms! My hulking, likable farmer friend, *Manuel*, who had made not one advance, was a true *Chileno*!

April 15, 1942—Rengo—Hotel Comercial—9:30 AM

And yesterday I lingered again in *Rengo*, the town I expected to pass in the night! *Por que?* Because I was to go back to *Cerillo* with *Manuel* to take tea with the *señora* who had played the piano for us there. Before venturing out on Chester again I bought patches for my tires and a new globe for my flashlight, and then I went off to explore the environs of *Rengo*—off to *Malloa*. How beautiful the countryside is here! Adobe walls, rows of poplars, tree-smothered *casitas*, vineyards, orange orchards. Lovely intimate country. And yesterday was a clear autumn day with gold in the trees and with the *Cordillera* standing sharp and near. I rolled along narrow roads where houses and orchards crowded together, and I had the feeling that all the world was muffled with trees. Behind one hedge row I could see horses trampling out the grain from a pile of straw. Fall! Instead of coming in for dinner, I ate the 16 apples I carried in my pack, and I delayed returning to Rengo until mid-afternoon. Then I stopped at the hotel for a moment to freshen up before going to *Cerillo*, and, lo and behold, my tire went flat as my bike stood in my room! At least I was lucky in choosing the place for trouble! Later, as I pedaled toward *Cerillo* I wondered if *Manuel* would really be there, and I delayed beside the road to give him plenty of time to arrive. But the moment I stopped, my ____ tire collapsed again! A hasty repair proved insufficient and after another mile or so I had yet another flat! Such are the joys of cycling! Being close to *Cerillo*, I decided to continue on foot, and once in the village, a kind *señorita* provided me with a little gasoline with which to clean my tube, and I put on yet another patch. It was late now and *Manuel* was no where to be seen, so I turned back pondering over the unpredictable ways of the *Chilenos*. And a man passing with a horse and buggy stopped to tell me that *Manuel* was in *Rengo*! I had no sooner cleaned up after my return than he knocked at my door and asked me to go with him to see Romeo and Juliet at the local theater! A peace offering! After the show we walked toward the station—apparently the most favored walk in *Rengo*—and en route we picked up another of *Manuel's* friends, a funny little fat man who kept me laughing with his imitation of the Yankee way of speaking and with the way he spit "shooore" out of the corner of his mouth. We stopped for a round of *chicha* at a hotel near the station and after reconnoitering we returned to the same hotel for dinner. *Manuel* rushed out to buy *paltos*, and we had salad, soup, and beefsteak at 10:00 PM! And red wine! The rest of the evening I walked with Manuel who was pleading for a kiss all the while but was ever a gentleman. We sat in the *plaza* and discussed love. And by way of variety we went over to the police station to see the *carabinero* who had been murdered a few days before! He lay in a casket heaped with flowers in a brightly lighted room and people were coming in all the while to pay him tribute.   This was the first time I had ever looked on death, but even that swollen face with blood at its mouth did not seem so terrible to me as I had thought it would. Always I find that knowledge of things feared dispels the fear that surrounds them.

April 16, 1942—Curicó—Gran Hotel Comercio—10:00 AM

And yesterday morning I finally pulled myself together and left *Rengo!* *Manuel* had promised to wait for me, but he slept through the morning, and I left without even saying good-bye—left with that unsettled feeling that I always have when I leave friends I'd like to know better.   Pedaling south was a pleasure for the way was varied—hills, cultivated lands, and an occasional river—but best of all I liked the lanes lined with golden poplars where I rode across bars of sunshine and shadow.   Once I stopped to greet the curly-headed, grinning truck driver I had met before on the road to *Malloa*. But I made few stops, pedaling through *sin almuerzo*.   And I reached *Curicó* comparatively early; had time to wash and go out to see the town before dinner.   I walked all the principal streets, as is my want, and ambled through the poor section where one always finds the greatest activity.   And en route I bought the biggest apple I could find and also a little packet of ground corn from a small boy with a bucket of coals to heat his wares.   –Just enough to hold me together until 8:00 PM! Then I sat in the *plaza* until dinnertime and watched the world go by.

April 17, 1942—Curicó—Gran Hotel Comercio—8:00 AM

Yesterday morning I played very, very lazy—got up late, dallied at breakfast, wrote, washed clothes.   And then I walked the streets again where I discovered the market in a patio at the center of a block of small shops.   Here I bought a kilo of *uvas negras* and a *kilo* of *uvas blancas*!   The Richardson yen for fruit getting the better of me again!   And I enjoyed just looking at the riot of color in the vegetables there. After *almuerzo* I collected my wits and set out to find *Juan Toledo*, the chap who had been so kind to me when I was in *Curicó* before. His family welcomed me with genuine hospitality bringing out *chicha* and *torta*, and I sat down to visit with them while I waited for Juan to return. And how good it was to see *Juan* himself again! Just like meeting an old, old friend! I asked him about repairs for my bike, and he obligingly gathered up Chester and me in his car and drove us from shop to shop, doing what he could to adjust my wobbly brake and my leaky valve. The kindness of the *Chilenos* seems to be limitless! The balance of the afternoon I spent here in my cubbyhole of a room, but in the evening I ventured out to walk in the *plaza* once more. Quantities of others were there too, and from the vantage point of a bench I watched them go by while I listened to a band's intermittent tunes. There were school girls in black walking very fast and young men walking deliberately and nonchalantly, there were *señoritas* dressed to be seen and young blades eager to look. There were old and young, rich and poor. All the populace seemed to be there. But most interesting were the tattered ones who came to hear the music—hungry for a little beauty in their lives. Sitting alone I attracted attention, and I smiled to myself as I watched the tactics of a young man near me. He looked my way, changed his seat to the one next to mine, looked again, and finally spoke to me. He had recognized me as the lone cyclist. We talked and joked, and all the man's comrades gathered around! A chummy gathering! And when we parted, I had an invitation to breakfast and to see the town! Back at the hotel I waited for *Juan* who came at 9:30 to have dinner with me. But our dinner conversation was rather hit and miss, because I find it difficult to understand *Juan's Castellano*.

April 18, 1942—Curicó—Hotel Comercio—9:00 AM

Yesterday morning I went over to *Enrique's pasteleria* for breakfast, but I went early, and when I didn't find him there, I shipped off for a trip with *Juan*! Premeditated intrigue! And what a glorious day I had! We pedaled out of *Curicó* for 18 kilometers. Eighteen kilometers of country road lined with the tall *alamos* I have come to love so well. Eighteen kilometers between rows of fingers of gold! And out there in the country we stopped at the *fondo* of a friend—stopped for a visit and spent the day! We ate figs and *uvas coloradas* from the arbor. Then *almuerzo* was spread for me, and we sat down to dine with the *señora* and her dark-eyed daughter who moved deliberately in and out with the various *platos*. *Cazuela*, a vegetable hodge-podge, macaroni, and a great plate of fruit set out on the table of a windowless room whose only light came from the wide doors opening out on to the front yard with its arbors and trees and flowers. And our table shared the room with a bed, a sewing machine, and a dozen sacks of wheat! After dinner we joined the rest in the work of husking a great pile of corn in the front yard but no one worked consistently. We stopped to eat chestnuts, and walnuts; to play the victrola and dance; and I went off on a neighbor's horse to bring in the cows! At 4:00 we were still there at the farm, and so, of course, we took *onces* with the family—*onces* of steak and onions, tea and bread. And not until 5:30 did we finally say good-bye and turn back to *Curicó*. But we chose an auspicious hour, for the sun went down with magnificent color and the poplars fairly glowed in the evening light. Gold, gold, gold! A world of vibrating gold. And others, like ourselves were moving homeward along those glowing lanes. Back in *Curicó* I said good-bye to *Juan* and his family and retreated early to my room in anticipation of moving on the next day.

April 19, 1942—San Fernando—Hotel Español—8:30 AM

Yesterday morning I wakened to another flat tire, and weary of my futile attempts to repair an old puncture, I took Chester to a *taller* and turned the job over to him. But I hovered around just to make sure that nothing went amiss. Can't bring myself to trust anyone else with my trusty bike! Twice I stopped in at the *pasteleria* to ask for *Enrique*, but he proved too elusive for me, and I gave up the idea of seeing him again. And the last shreds of the morning I devoted to packing and setting everything in order so that I could eat at 12:00 *en punto* and pedal away early. But just as I was consuming *plato no. 3, Enrique* arrived! He talked while I finished my meal, and then he suggested that we go climb a hill before I left! Being a true Yankee, time seemed sort of important to me and I didn't relish the idea of traveling after dark, but I decided to assume the Chilean point of view and let time "go hang"! And with this I changed to street clothes and went off to *Cerro Condel*! At the summit were a virgin and an ornate iron cross bearing an iron hand. And away from the foot of the hill stretched the vast farmlands that surround *Curicó*, while to the east the Andes stood up sharp and clear. A fine view. All the while we walked *Enrique* talked with great eloquence. He told of his work as an inventor, of his past in a revolution, of his religion of science, of his love of women! He related the legend of the iron cross, spoke of the history of *Curicó*, told of a volcanic eruption which blacked out the city! But my skepticism rose in direct proportion to his mounting eloquence! Back at my hotel once more, I bade *Enrique* farewell and hastened away with all possible speed. And the kilometers slipped away much faster than I had expected. I was conscious only of the power in my legs, of the great mountains beside me, of the golden trees which barred my road with shadow. And just at sunset I reached *San Fernando* and found a room here in this friendly hotel. I walked the streets before dinner, listening to the band, that played on the corner and watching the crowds; and I made the acquaintance of one *don José Dios* who lives at the hotel. Later he brought me a little packet of *pastelitas* and invited me to the show! And so I spent the evening watching an Argentine production and killer-diller western! Just another of those unexpected happenings in the life of a lone tourist.

April 20, 1942—Rengo—Hotel Comercial—9:00 AM

Yesterday began as a lazy Sunday and ended with a breathless trek, for by now I start my day so late that I have a hard time getting places before dark! I dallied over breakfast and talked to my Spanish friend *Don José*. And then as I ambled out toward the street, the smiling elderly *señora* of the hotel stopped me to talk and to introduce me to a *Chileno* who had a son in the U.S.—a son at International House in Berkeley, of all places! After more talking, I went out with this man for a *paseo* in the streets down the principal thoroughfare and around the *plaza*. With the sun shining brilliantly and the *Cordillera* rising sharply at the end of the street. We stopped at a *pasteleria* for *refrescos* and *pastelitas*, and I was surprised to find my quiet, softspoken friend repeating the same old compliments—*"simpatica," "bonita"*! Back at the hotel I dined leisurely, packed leisurely, and talked at length to my friends. Then I suddenly realized that I must be on my way, for it was 2:30 PM! So off I went into the sunshine—off to the fork in the road where my adventurous spirit turned me toward *San Vicente*. Through pretty country at the foot of a hill along a river to this new *pueblo* which was sleeping in Sunday tranquillity. I pedaled around the *plaza* where people loitered, and past a company of *bomberos* who were rehearsing in full regalia—splendid black and white uniforms. Then I turned toward *Rengo*, following a new road. Stopping to inquire about the way, a fat *huaso* informed me that my road didn't go to *Rengo*, and when, on the strength of my map and a guide post, I insisted he fairly spat out, *"No hay!"* –And with this I retreated to another branch in the road which proved to be *el camino Rengo*. But there was a *cuesta* which had to be navigated on foot. And I found the nuts holding my wheels had to be tightened. And once I fell as I passed an oxcart. And all these delays combined with the lateness of the hour sent me racing breathlessly with the coming night. Around the skirts of the hills and back into the valley on the familiar *Malloa* road. And I reached *Rengo* when the mountains before me ever rose of purple and darkness were quietly closing in. Back to a poor little room in the same hotel where I freshened up and hurried out into the streets, hoping that perhaps I might find *Manuel*. In the *plaza* were some of his friends and I shook hands all around, feeling quite at home. And later as I sat in the *plaza, Manuel's* brother came by! I walked with him to the station and we visited at great length, but his resemblance to *Manuel* fairly hurt, for I wanted to see the other who was in *Santiago*. Just before going to sleep, a strange note was tossed through the transom of my room, and later there was a knock which I did not answer. I spent a restless night—wondering.

April 21, 1942—San Bernardo—Hotel Plaza—9:30 AM

Yesterday I started the morning for once! Leaving *Rengo* with regrets! I rode the dusty, bumpy road to *Rancagua* with sort of a heavy heart, for the leaves which fluttered down from the trees reminded me that this was the autumn of my stay in Chile. In *Rancagua* I bought a kilo of grapes which I ate by the wayside before jolting along to *Hospital*. But even with a kilo of muscats to cheer me on my way, the road seemed long. I felt as if I were forever pedaling up hill, and each sickening thud of my back wheel left me wondering just how much longer my worn-out tire would last! In *Hospital* I inquired for a room at the hotel, but one look inside the place convinced me that I'd sleep in any pasture in preference to it. So I marshaled my dwindling energy, and decided to push on to *San Bernardo*. And on I came, my good legs turning obediently in answer to my mind! The detour around *Buin* seemed discouraging but, as if the gods were with me, the last kilometers were smooth and easy, and I rather enjoyed the race with darkness, for the trees were lovely in the dusk, and candles burned at the little shrines by the road. I came into town with a feeling of satisfaction: a sense of peace in the darkness, in the smell of wood smoke, in the security of a town. And I was grateful for a room where I could wash the dust from my body. Before dinner, I went out to walk in the shadows of the trees which line the streets of *San Bernardo*.

But the hour was early when I sought the warmth and rest of a bed.

April 23, 1942—Santiago—Mrs. Petre's—10:00 PM

Santiago *otra vez*, and the lazy, luxurious life of the city. Day before yesterday I loitered away the morning in *San Bernardo* where I walked the streets, treated myself to a kilo of grapes, wrote a letter home and cleaned and oiled my good bike, Chester. Then I stayed for dinner which lead to altercation over my bill, but I stood firm in what I thought was right, and pedaled away leaving a very annoyed maid. Back to Santiago at top speed—whirring along just for the sheer joy of racing on a paved road! And the populace stared at the spectacle of a girl riding thus on a bicycle! Through the heart of the city, too! But I have long since become hardened to the stares and smiles of the *Chilenos*, and I don't care a whit what people think of me. Returning to Mrs. Petre's was like coming home, home to a place where I could take a hot bath and flop! But I was soon in the streets again, bound for my mail and enjoying those keen moments of anticipation before I learned there was nothing for me. Disappointed I returned to loaf away the evening.

And yesterday was another lazy, disorganized day— filled with nothing. After lying abed most of the morning, I finally stirred myself and went to talk with the American consul about my Argentine visa. And on the way home I dropped in at the Claridge where to my great surprise, I found my old friend *Señora Meches*! How good to meet this smiling warm-hearted German again! Her good humor is contagious. The afternoon and evening I dawdled away over 2 kilos of grapes and a dozen apples brought to comfort my restless spirit!

April 24, 1942—Santiago—Mrs. Petre's—10:00 PM

Yesterday morning I went to the *Vega* with Mrs. Petre, to that colorful market which has more life than any other spot in *Santiago*. And while she selected fish and corn and squash, I watched the people swarm by and listened to the venders hawk their wares. One salesman answered her with an "O.K" and a "'ank 'ou", and one employed sleight of hand to fill her bag with little, dried-up *paltos* in place of the large, luscious ones she selected! On the way to the market I met one of the chaps whom I had met in *Rengo*—a friend of *Manuel's*! And both Mrs. Petre and I had a good laugh over the spectacle of a man on a second-story balcony nonchalantly sawing a couple inches off the bottom of one of his doors! After lunch I donned my one and only dress and went out to tea with *Don Augusto Villanueva*. We met at the bank, visited in the *plaza*, and went to the *Lucerna* for our tea. A popular tearoom with a jazz orchestra. Afterwards we went to the Anglo-Chilean institute to hear a lecture, but it was all in Spanish and much of the thought was lost to me. When I returned, I was very disappointed to learn that I had missed the visit of the *Chileno* I had met in *San Fernando*.

April 25, 1942—Santiago—Mrs. Petre's—9:00 AM

Yesterday morning to the *Vega* again, to that hodge-podge of color and activity that forever fascinates me. Bright red peppers; narrow passageways; ragged children with platters of carrots or a handful of garlic for *"un peso, un peso, un peso!"*; stalls stacked full of pots and pans and baskets; wagon loads of corn and potatoes and apples, heaps of grapes and tomatoes and avocados; old men standing with sacks— waiting for someone to hire them to carry their purchases; portable stoves with a few coals and dishes of hot *empanadas* and fried fish; people buying, people selling, people going, doing, going. Coming home we stopped to buy watercress from a ruddy man with a low-crowned hat set squarely on his head and a sprig of cress hung over one ear. He told us with a grin that he had just come from the police station where he had been taken for selling in the streets without a license! After lunch I went back to the Argentine consul and discovered that I could get to B.A. on my present visa, but when I returned to the American consul I found that my passport was already on its way to Washington. Such are the trials of the tourist! Now I must wait here until the thing returns, fretting all the while for fear that snow in the mountains will block my trip across the *Cordillera*. Blank space in my day I filled in with mending and getting my things in readiness for the trip ahead.

April 26, 1942—Santiago—Mrs. Petre's—10:00 AM

Yesterday morning I went off with Mrs. Petres to try and discover the truth about whether or not I must have a Chilean *carnet* in order to leave the country. We went first to the Chilean-American Institute in *Calle Paris* where we didn't learn much but where I found a girl from Porterville! *Qué chico el mundo!* And then we went to the *Investigaciones* where we were sent from one person to another until we learned that they could tell us nothing without seeing my passport, which is now in Washington! The press of business over, we went to the *Vega* to buy. And then I hurried home, gulped down a hasty lunch and went off to *Señor Tarrago's* for coffee. After a good visit with the little professor; I came home to tea and in the evening I went out again to walk the streets with Mrs. Petre. We made ready with great care and from the fire in her eye, I thought that Mrs Petre would surely find some romance amongst the crowds in *Estado* and *Alemada*. But there was nothing interesting to be found aside from a few approving stares, and after a dish of ice cream we came meekly home.

April 27, 19942—Santiago—Mrs. Petre's—10:00 PM

Yesterday was Sunday and a day of unforced marking time. At 11:00 I went with Mrs. Petre to the English church where we alternately knelt and stood and where all the loyal subjects of the king were praying for success in war. Then to the Central market for a few odds and ends. —And to see if the fish man was there—he with the neatly pressed suit and the smiles and the *"muy buenos dias."* In the afternoon I wrote and consumed quantities of grapes and apples. And also dropped in at the Claridge in search of a little gasoline which is not to be found. The balance of the day I devoted to the practical work of washing clothes.

April 28, 1942—Mrs.Petre's—10:00 AM

Yesterday I began the day under the pressure of things that had to be done. And the brilliance of the sun spurred me on, for I longed to spend these glorious days in the *Cordillera* instead of in *Santiago*. So I bounced hopefully off to the American consul, only to be told to come back at noon. And at noon I was told to come back at 4:00 PM. I walked aimlessly, sat thoughtfully, consumed one snack of food after another; and all the while I rebelled against the turn of events that had sent my passport back to the states. At 4:00 I returned and was sent to be interviewed by one of the officials from the embassy. He questioned and cross-questioned me, asked my family history and my purpose in traveling, why I had come to Chile and if I intended to ride my bike farther, where I had been and whom I had met. Then with the suggestion that all Americans should be aiding in the war effort and with a warning against people who might approach me for information, he let me go. And the consul gave me a letter to the effect that I did really possess a passport! The hours before dinner I spent in walking restlessly--. Out through *Parque Forrestal* where the benches along the dark paths were crowded with couples making love; down to *Plaza Italia*; and back to *Cerro Santa Lucia*. And all the while the moon shown with such splendor that it only added to my restlessness. After dinner I made an effort to patch my front tire. Lavished all the care on it of which I was capable.

April 29, 1942—Santiago—Mrs. Petre's—10:00 AM

And yesterday morning my tire was still flat! But I had weightier business to attend to, and with my letter from the counsul in my hand, I went to "*Investigaciones*" to find out the truth about the *carnet*. The answer was "Yes, you must have one," and anxious to save time, I opened negotiations at once. But when I was asked to pay $262.00 for my stamps, the shock took all the wind out of my sails, and it was a pretty dejected foreigner who stood by for finger-printing, cross-questioning, and photographing. Back here at the *pensión* I had a pow-wow with Mrs Petre and others in the house, and decided to go to the office of foreign affairs to ask more questions about the *carnet*. But their answer to me was the same. And so I turned my attention to Chester and his weak tires. The only available new tire in his size was in a German shop, and I found the price had gone from $100 to $150 within the past couple of weeks, but it was absolutely essential that I purchase it. Then the *dueño* wanted $10 more for putting the darn thing on, and irritated, I hauled my bike home to do the work myself. Before dinner I walked with Mrs. Petre out into the bright streets amongst the usual crowds of *Chilenos*. And the early coming of darkness coupled with the chill of fall made me think that a cozy place in which to spend the winter would be preferable to the open road on a bicycle!

April 30, 1942—Baños de Colina—11:00 AM

Yesterday morning my tires were hard and round— just cause for a celebration! And I resolved to linger no longer in *Santiago*. So I packed my goods and chattels, went to market one last time with Mrs. Petre, and confronted the American consul for a true statement of when my passport would return from Washington. I had to replenish my dwindling *plata* too, for I had little left after the heavy expenses of the last few days. But by mid afternoon, everything was ready, and, with 2 pieces of Mrs. Petre's cakes inside of me and 2 more in my pack, I set off for *Colina* and points north! With a sense of relief, I rolled out of the city and into the roominess of the country, but it seemed a little sad in the late afternoon with the gray of autumn veiling the hills and with the slow oxen soberly plowing the brown earth. In

Colina there was no sign of a hotel, so I pushed on to the *Baños*, following a river valley into the hills, and I kept watch for a likely thicket in which to spend the night for I knew the hotel would be expensive! But as the sun set behind the hills and I approached the welcome light of the hotel, I decided to treat myself to a room here, and here I have stayed. –Here in this tremendous and ancient establishment with its 40 employees and its 6 paying guests! But I find it a pleasant place with its rambling buildings, its large patio, and its intimate circle of hills. And last night when the moon flooded all with its cold and lonely light, I was quite content to be here. Before dinner I went to look at the baths—large pools of green water, all named for saints. And after dinner I sat in the saloon and visited and joked with 3 Italians and 1 Spaniard. More practice in *Castellano*. And much laughing with the elderly *Italiano* who told us of crossing the *Cordillera* in the early days. –*"Siete dias en mula y dos meses en cama!"*

May 1, 1942—Los Andes—Gran Hotel, Francia—9:00 AM

Back on the road again! And happy in my vagabond's life. Back to the uncertainty of unknown ways, to the "*Que lindas*" and "*Adios, señoritas*" of men in the road, to the hard climbs and the beautiful vistas of Chilean countryside, and to the insecurity of never knowing where I'll rest at the end of the day. How I love it! Yesterday morning I loitered in the hills at the *Baños*, content with the tranquillity of the place. Following a trail out along the hillsides, I came to a vantage point where I could look out across the valley and to the hills beyond. And there I met the Spaniard of the evening before, all wrapped up in a blanket. We walked back together, pausing to watch the arrival of the gondola from *Santiago* with its small dribble of passengers, and chattering in *Castellano* all the while. Before dinner I made ready to leave, and when I went in for my meal, Chester stood waiting at the dining room door! The elderly Italian came bringing me candied fruits, a half a goat's cheese, 3 crackers, 2 lemons, a big delicious apple, and a bottle of wine – *"el mejor que hay!"* And I left with a bountiful *onces* tucked in my pack! Starting the day so late but wings to my feet, and Chester fairly purred through the valley to the foot of *Cuesta Chacabuco*. But here all purring ceased! And my wheels turned slowly as I struggled to keep the pedals turning. Up and up and up—11 kilometers in low gear—with perspiration streaming down my glasses. But the climb was worth the view from the summit, and as I sat down under a thorn bush to eat my cheese and crackers and apples I could look across the hills with their scrubby vegetation to the rugged *Cordillera* beyond. Thereafter my way was down, and my aching back could rest. Down out of the dry hills and into civilization once again. Adobe walls, lovely country. The Chile that I love. And beyond the walls I caught glimpses of the rosy mountains of evening. Lights were burning when I came into *Los Andes*, and the activity of the town drew me out into the streets before supper. Out to the *plaza* with its many trees and gay fountain, where I sat to listen to the music of the band. And as if for my special benefit, it played *Hay Carramba, Que Felicidad!* A full moon looked down on the *plaza* full of promenading, and made me happy with its clarity. Good weather ahead, perhaps.

May 2, 12942—San Felipe—Hotel Europa—9:00 AM

But yesterday morning dawned gray, *que lástima!* – and once again I watch the mountains anxiously. I passed the morning pleasantly in *Los Andes*, loitering over coffee and doing a little writing before I ventured forth. And then I walked out to make the acquaintance of the town—up and down, around the *plaza*, down to the station—getting the lay of the streets, noting the roads leading out of town, and always peering into the shop windows to see what *Chilenos* buy. And after dinner I was ready to travel on "*inmediatemente*". Down the river valley towards *San Felipe*, past the prosperous *fundos* which make this section an oasis amongst dry hills. I rolled easily, silently, happily. But I took time to turn off and pedal up to the *Baños de Jahuel*, a luxurious resort in the hills. Here I parked Chester beside the elegant autos, and clad in my travel-worn cycling garb, I went to see the swimming pool, the gardens and the hotel itself with its tiled walls and neat arbors! I had resolved to stay the night if I liked the place, but the loungers and knitters didn't interest me and after a brief visit I was content to roll back down the hill. Here in this *pueblo*, I found a pleasant room opening on to a tiled patio decorated with potted plants. And after the usual "bath in a wash basin" I went out to take a walk before dinner. I always go out with sort of a swagger too—as if to show those who laughed at the bedraggled cyclist that after all she can be a lady! I found the *plaza* full of life, and there I stayed to watch the *Chilenos* taking their leisure. Boys were playing hockey on skates in one section, and around the central fountain the crowds were promenading in twos and threes and fours. I alone came *sola*. *San Felipe's plaza* differs from others in its Grecian note; urns and female figures in marble decorate its walks!

May 3, 1942—Quillota—Gran Hotel—9:00 AM

Another gray, forlorn day—a cold day. And once again I spent the morning in town. I walked the streets which seemed deserted compared with the evening before, and I sewed the patch back in the seat of my slacks! All the while I bundled myself up in my coat because of the chill in the air, but my hotel was cheery enough with its black and white tile, its plants, and its smiling service. After a good warm *almuerzo* with soup and *agua caliente*, I packed up and left with the hotel personnel standing curiously by. But my heart wasn't in this journey down the *Rio Aconcagua*; my thoughts turned up the canyon toward the *Cordillera* and Argentina. Nevertheless, I must pedal with purpose, for I had more than 60 km to travel before I could stop for the night. So I hurried down my pebbly road, and as I warmed to the activity of cycling, all ennui left me and I reveled in the brushy hills, olive green and brown beneath the low-hanging clouds; in the river spread thinly over its sandy course; in the occasional intimate *poblaciones*. Life was good—as ever. At one point in the road I met a troop of uniformed men who seemed a bit incongruous in that isolated spot. From a distance I thought they must be *bomberos* or *carabineros*, but they were like nothing I had ever seen before! Costumes of bright red and blue with caps covered with spangled things. And one of their number sporting a mask with horns! *Que curioso!* And in that same road I met an old friend—the gentleman with the green car—he of the staff of *La Union* whom I had met months ago near *Curacavi*. But this time he was honeymooning with his bride! One never knows what the road ahead will bring forth! I rolled into dusty, busy *Calera* just at dusk—time to stop—but *Quillota* was near and a better town, they said, so on I went. Never know when to call a halt! And once again I found myself traveling on the edge of night—down shadowy roads where rocks and pits remained a mystery until my wheels reached them! But *Quillota* proved to be a good little town, and a friendly *carabinero* directed me to *Gran Hotel*, a dim, deserted place where Chester and I found lodging. Out in *los calles*, by contrast, there was plenty of activity, and there I stayed until dinner time, walking up and down with the crowds and ambling about the *plaza* where the usual band music had attracted the usual listeners. Famished I bought a kilo of grapes and at 8:30 devoured a welcome dinner. Then I went to bed for warmth, thinking to read and write until late, but my eyes were too heavy for anything but sleep.

May 4, 1942—Limache—Hotel Central—8:00 AM

And yesterday morning I wakened to a room flooded with sunshine! Happy day! Of course I can travel in the rain, but the longer the winter holds off, the better I'll like it! --So I lay abed and luxuriated in that light and warmth; and I delayed so long that the big tousle-headed waiter in the *comedor* scowled from under his gray bush when I came for a late *desayuno*. But I soon left him in his dim quarters and went out to see *Quillota* by day. And once again I found the streets crowded even though this was Sunday. After walking the streets for some time, I retired to the *Plaza* to sit and watch and watch and watch. There were the usual ragamuffins looking for shoes to shine. There were the usual coaches drawn up to the curb—horse drawn coaches with the driver sitting high and cab slung low behind. And there were the usual promenaders: old men, *señoras* with children, adolescent boys and girls looking at each other, and a few young bucks who assumed a disinterested air. I noticed one young man looking at me, and I decided to play the game—a game which became so absorbing that I loitered in the *plaza* until late afternoon! He looked several times, and I looked back. Then I smiled. And he smiled back each time he passed my bench. Eventually he took a seat opposite me, but before long he joined some friends who were sitting beside me! And then just when we were side by side I had to dash off for *almuerzo! Que lastima!* But the afternoon found me in the *plaza* once again, and there I found the same young man once again! He and a couple of companions followed me wherever I went, always choosing to sit on a bench near me, and all afternoon we flirted at a distance. Life in the Chilean manner! But at 5:00 I decided it was time I started my cycling day! So I left that lazy, peaceful, Sunday *plaza*, and in 10 min., more or less, was on my way, rolling along an asphalt road to *Limache*. And all the while I looked out across acres of artichokes and cabbages and lettuce to the bushy hills standing guard over the valley. Neat, gray-green hills rising vivid and sharp in the autumn air. Hills washed with yellow light as the sun went down. In *Limache* I found this dim and dusty hotel and soon I was out in the streets to explore the town. But the town too was dim, and almost deserted with scarcely half a dozen persons in the plaza. Quite a contrast to *Quillota!* And for want of anything better to do, I had an early comida and went to bed. *Que lastima que no puedo encontrar un otro pueblocito como Rengo!*

May 5, 1942—Olmué—Hotel Ingles—8:00 AM

Yesterday I dawdled again. Only 8 kilometers of cycling! That ought to qualify me for a *bien buena Chilena!*

But I did start early—or at least by 10:00 AM! En route I stopped to buy a dozen big apples and I continued my way with my saddlebags bulging and an apple in my hand. Eight kilometers in cheery sunshine along a road which took me to the foot of a semi-circle of hills and into this little *pueblo* which has more hotels than any thing else. But the season is past, and the *pasajeros* have vanished, and I have this hotel practically to myself. But I like it 'cause I have a pleasant room opening onto a patio, and I can wander around the *quinta* and eat chestnuts, and grapes and apples. After lunch I dallied in the garden and walked through the little *pueblo* which seemed to be sleeping in the heat of the afternoon. And after a hearty tea I walked to the neighboring village of *Granijo,* farther up the canyon. As I passed beyond the *pueblo* the sun was sinking, and the hills were lovely shades of blue and green. And I climbed up a hillside to sit amidst the cactus and thorn bushes and watch the light fade away from the landscape while ox carts lumbered home along the road below. Then I walked home into the blazing glory of the setting sun. Home to a good *comida* and a sociable evening of conversation with a young Italian and his wife who work at the hotel. A lazy, sunny day of rest in anticipation of harder days to come.

May 6, 1942—Lampa--Pensión "La Quinta"—9:00 AM

And yesterday morning I started my day with real purpose! Got up, dressed, and set my bike in order as if I really intended to go places! Then I had to wait for *desayuno* 'cause no rational *Chileno* gets up at 8:00 AM when the mornings are cold!. So I waited, for I couldn't think of cycling without *café con leche y pan con mantequilla.* But by 9:00 I was on my way, pedaling up the canyon toward the *Cuesta Dormida*, up through those beautiful gray-green hills with their dressing of low bushes. Up and up and up, *casi 10 kms. a pie.* And when I was within a few meters of the *cumbre*, a truck stopped to ask me to ride! Irony! There was scarcely any traffic on that remote road, but I didn't feel lonely in those hills for high above were mines with buildings clinging to the slopes, and occasionally I heard the shouts of men on horseback driving pack burros through the brush. At the summit I stopped to look back on *Olmué* valley and to look ahead to the *Cordillera*. And sitting on a rock in the sun, I lunched on 3 apples. Thereafter my way was down—down past road workers who lay sleeping by the side of the road or comfortably sprawled across wheel barrows, past houses so intimate with the road that I practically rode through their dining rooms, into a narrow canyon with a good stream of water and many trees and cacti. *Un camino de segunda clase!* In *Tiltil* the *vistas* broadened and the road improved, but strangely enough, the country here seemed more lovely, more desolate than the hills above. And my system began to grumble over the apples inside, so I sprawled in the shade of a thorn bush for some time. Later the whistle of a train and the hearty wave of a friendly engineer and the invitation to ride of another truck driver lent a bit of kindliness to that desert land. And *Lampa* with its many trees and low houses seemed like a veritable oasis! Here I decided to stop for the night, and a handsome *carabinero* helped me to find a *pensión*—a little group of adobe huts in a thicket of fruit trees and vines. Before dark I walked through the village with the daughter of the *señora*. A rambling garden *pueblo* whose inhabitants, I thought had never before seen a *gringa*! But at one point a woman rushed up, and who should she be but one of the passengers from the little steamer on *Lago Ranco*! We embraced and talked excitedly like old friends, and I was practically overcome with surprise! Last night I dined by candle light on a bare table in a room with an earthen floor. But there were flowers on the table and the *señorita* played a victrola to entertain me. And I slept in the *señora's* bed (possibly the sheets were clean ones?) in a tiny room whose walls were profusely decorated with pictures and calendars.

May 7, 1942—Santiago—Mrs. Petre's—9:00 AM

Yesterday turned out to be a day of accomplishment for me. After breakfast I took leave of my *pensión* and turned again toward *Santiago*. But before I ever left nice little *Lampa*, a thorn punctured my tire, and I had to stop in the streets to fix it! A delay of slight importance, however, for I reached "home" before noon. A bath, a meal, a few pleasantries, and I was off to complete arrangements for leaving Chile. The American consul returned my passport (at long last!), the Argentine consul assured me my visa for Argentina was still good, and *Investigaciones* delivered my new *carnet* and gave me a stamp of *salida* without the payment of $150. But I had to talk fast for this! I stopped to ask a few questions of *Señor Nagel* and spent a sociable hour visiting with him and others in the office. I collected a letter from *Expresso Villalonga*, and was thrilled beyond measure to receive word from "*El Señor Copec*"—my *Manuel*. I stopped at the Claridge to say good bye. And I looked up *Señora Bunster* with whom I had a very pleasant visit. Thus flushed with the joy of human associations and with the success of business I came home to dinner and to preparations for leaving Santiago. But all day I moved in the city with a heightened consciousness of its personality, for I knew my time here was short. I looked at faces, and at buildings, and at all the activity in the streets with the thought that perhaps I might never see these things again. And in this mood, I stood brazenly by to watch a funeral procession take shape. Watched the elegant black coach topped with a black cross and drawn by 4 black horses, watched the attendants deck it with many wreathes, watched the pall bearers carry the casket to the coach, and watched the procession move away.

May 8, 1942—Esmeralda—"La única casa rspeta por acá"

And yesterday, after a last flurry of activity, I pulled myself together and left *Santiago*. But I left later for I had many errands to attend to. I had my old tire vulcanized—a spare to carry for good luck, and I had new rubber heels put on my shoes. I refilled my bottle of oil, bought a Chilean flag, and made a trip out to *Tarragó's* to collect my lost gloves. I tied up and sent off all my surplus *"papeles"* in the hope that they would eventually reach Porterville. And I bought a goodly number of Argentine *pesos*. Then I went home to eat a farewell kilo of grapes and to pack up my good Chester. But the tea hour arrived before I was ready to go, and it was 5:00 PM! Thus, with the sun sinking, I left *Santiago*—never to return. Down toward the cemetery, passing the white coaches for the dead who are too young to have sinned and out *Avenida Independencia.* —With Chester loaded to the hilt and a spare tire dangling behind! And with all the populace turning to whistle as I passed! I welcomed the country where I was less conspicuous and where I could travel freely. And after a pleasant evening trek, I reached *Colima*, just at dark. But the hotel was full! And there was nothing to do but travel on. Here in *Esmeralda* I went to the *carabineros,* my old stand by, to ask where I might find a room, but they said there was nothing short of the *Baños.* And it was now pitch dark. But on second thought, they said there was one respectable house in town, and they brought me here, where the *señora* agreed to take me in. And I have spent another unique night! I had supper with the *señorita* who sort of took me under her wing, and afterwards we visited in the street, the center of a curious laughing crowd. Across the way was a *quinta* where we went to hear a man and woman play a piano and drums, and then we returned here to listen to the radio and to watch the men playing billiards. Never will I forget the picture in that room. Ragged men, all in black slouchy hats, intent on their cues and balls. A lame chap with shining eyes. A boy who could scarcely reach across the table to play his game. Dim light. Mud walls. Low ceilings. And when the radio gained enough *fuerza* to be heard across the room, the *señorita* and I danced with a couple of the village lads! By 11:00 PM I was too weary to stay awake longer, and I retired to my little box of a room and to a bed that was not clean. Little streaks of blood on the sheets told of others who had slept there before me and who had battled with the insects! Pleasant prospects for the night! –But what could I say or do when it was only by a streak of good fortune that I had a room at all? I went to bed with all the nonchalance I could muster and with the hope that my constitution was still fool proof!

May 9, 1942—Los Andes—Hotel Español—7:00 AM

And yesterday morning I wakened quite rested and with no more welts than I have acquired in other places! After *café sin leche* and *pan sin mantequilla* in the backyard, I pushed off into the brilliance of a perfect day and rode the old familiar *camino* back to *Los Andes*. The *Cuesta Chacabuco* seemed shorter this time, for I did not expect it to be short, and the view from the top was quite changed. With a clear day, the folds of the hills and the skyline of the *Cordillera* were sharpened, and I could see the details of the agricultural patchwork below. Once again I thrilled to the road sweeping down out of the hills into the poplars and walls of the country surrounding *Los Andes*—only this time it was hot and lazy in a mid-day sun. And I was more than content to find a room where I could actually wash, brush my teeth, and sleep in a clean bed! After a very good *almuerzo*, I went out to look up information concerning the roads and trains to *Mendoza*. But I found myself so weary physically that I did not do anything more energetic than sit in the *plaza* and watch the world go by! In the tourist office I found a boy interested in collecting stamps, and when I gave him a few, he fairly overflowed with touristic information and pamphlets. Back in the *plaza* for the balance of the evening, I amused myself watching one man in particular—a man who was all bundled up in a brown coat and who walked back and forth in front of my bench, stopping to look at me each time he passed. Finally he sat down on my bench staring at me all the while! And as I left the *plaza* on my way home, he whispered, *"Adios, señorita,"* as I passed!-- another romance in the making! But I went home to dinner and to my comfortable room where I could read and write and sew, and prepare myself for the long, long road over the mountains into Argentina.

May 9, 1942—Juncal—Pensión Juncal—10:00 PM

Phew, what a day! *Más que 50 Km. de subida! Y todas las horas desde 8:00 en la mañana hasta 4:00 en la tarde sin comiendo!* I left *Los Andes* immediately after *desayuno* and pedaled off with a beautiful day and a merry mood, off towards the glorious ragged peaks that had been so tantalizing when last I was in *Los Andes.* At long last I was on my way to the *Cordillera!* Up the *Aconcagua* I pedaled, past various *casitas* and tufts of poplars, but always in the shadow of the *cerros* rising on either hand and always thrilling to the height and to their rugged beauty. A lovely winding trip over a road which climbed so gradually that I could pedal the whole of it with the exception of the bit rising above the gorge known as the *Salto del Soldado.* In *Rio Blanco* I had expected to stop for the night, but I arrived there at noon and found the hotel a bit austere, so I decided to travel on to *Portillo.* But I didn't anticipate a road *tan malo!* Almost immediately it commenced to climb at such a pitch that I couldn't possibly ride my *caballito,* and there was so much loose rock on the road that pushing became a task of sheer endurance! Up and up and up—far above the houses and poplars—beyond all habitation, and into a land of rock and silent peaks. With the river dashing through the canyon below and with snow-splotched *cerros* looming above. Beauty to compensate for my toil. But as the hours passed my progress became slower and slower. Thin air and hunger combined with hard work. And when I finally came in sight of a house, I walked right in and asked for bread! And I chose the right place for a young telegraph operator there immediately set about preparing *onces* for me. Grapes, a banana, tea and bread. Mana from heaven! And for two hours, I loitered there. My host assured me that I could find a bed in the *pensión* above, and I gave up the idea of going on to *Portillo.* The old line of least resistance! We went *arriba* together, and here I've been ever since. Spent the evening dining and talking with my new friend, and watching all the employees of the railway who have come here to dine. And now the radio blares and the waitresses dance with a couple of the young blokes who linger on. Little did I expect to find such gaiety here in these rocky heights!

May 11, 1942—Hotel Portillo—8:00 PM

Yesterday morning I dressed quietly in one of the rooms which I shared with one of the waitresses and passed through a room where 2 others slept—out into a crisp clear morning with the sun just flecking the tops of the *cerros* and the creek noisy in the canyon below. The black and dirt of the railway junction seemed tawdry in contrast with the grandeur of the mountain above, and I walked a way down the track to be alone with beauty. Already, at this early hour, men were coming for *desayuno* at the *pensión*, but I waited for David, and the 2 of us had breakfast together—a lengthy, sociable breakfast of eggs and coffee and *"pan del campo."* We loitered at the table a very long time, but I needed to travel on, and eventually we walked back to his house and my bicycle, and I took leave of that lonely chap with his drab little telegraph station and his cat and chickens. Once again my way was up, but I had only 8 hours to travel and could afford to go without haste, stopping often to catch my breath and to look in awe at the *cerros* with their streaks and patches of snow and their rich warm colors. How glorious to be alone in such a spot! And not another soul passed in the road. Rather suddenly I came upon this hotel, my destination, and immediately I became the center of a curious questioning crowd. Almost before I knew it, I was installed in a comfortable room and was feeling very much at home and very exhilarated over the wildness of the peaks all about. Then there was *almuerzo* with half a dozen others here in this great living room—a meal for a king—soup and tender steak and grapes and an apple! And afterwards I went off with a couple of *pasajeros* (with a car) to *Laguna del Inca*, a lovely green lake in the lap of the mountains just a short way above *Portillo*. Later in the afternoon there was time for a hot shower (!!) and clean clothes and a bountiful tea. And all the evening I visited at great lengths with the young chaps in charge of the hotel and 3 *Norte Americanos* on a photographic mission and an official of the *aduana*. We spread out maps and talked of travel in South America and of the war and of many things. And 3 of us sat up until past midnight enjoying the fire and talking Spanish. The surprise of the day was the arrival of another cyclist! A man from B.A. on his way to *Santiago*! And I was more than pleased to see another bike in touring trim.

Today has been a happy lazy day idled away in this beautiful spot where there are so few of us that we make an intimate group. In the morning I took coffee with my 3 compatriots who dashed off to get their station wagon aboard the train at the mouth of the tunnel. As I watched them go I wondered how many times I would regret the fact that I did not accept their invitation to ride to B.A. Then I bid the cyclist *"vaya bien,"* feeling quite plutocratic over the fact that I was luxuriating here for the day. Later I went with some of the hotel personnel to *Laguna del Inca* to obtain some bread for our meal here; and our excursion included a tour through the construction camp there, a look at the round houses at the foot of the up-ski, a visit to the station master, and a ride back on a railway dinky. Our day was punctuated with trips down to the track to watch the trains go by, a major diversion here, and one train brought a personable young man with whom I danced and drank toasts before and after dinner and ultimately bid fond farewell as he passed on a down train. Once again the dark eyes, the little mustache, the flowery compliments that I have come to know so well! And all day I have taken my leisure here in this great room with its lighting fixtures of skis and its cheery fire. And all day I have peered anxiously at the weather, for this morning, clouds came floating in and they have gathered in forbidding gray banks above the mountains. It just can't snow, for I must pass the *Cordillera* and enter Argentina before my visa expires on the 13th.

May 13, 1942—Puente del Inca, Argentina—the Barracks

Yesterday morning I wakened very early—full of excitement over my anticipated trip. But when the 1st gray streaks of day lit up the world, I could see that it was snowing in the mountains above. My heart sank. It would be impossible to pass *El Cristo* and *Uspallata Pass*. But if I started early perhaps I might pass through the tunnel and reach Argentina in spite of the weather. At 7:30 I was packed and ready to go, but *desayuno* wasn't forthcoming until 8:00, and I couldn't climb mountains in the cold without food. So I waited, but with tremendous impatience, walking from window to window to look at the weather, incapable of sitting nonchalantly by the fire. When breakfast finally did arrive I ate enough for 2, and then rushed away to start the long push up. As a parting gesture, the hotel personnel presented me with 3 cans of apricot jam! I had absolutely no room for such a gift and it was very heavy, but who was I to refuse 3 cans of jam! If it became the straw that broke the camel's back at least I would have tried to carry it with me!

Out into a cold gray world I pushed, and as I struggled up the first incline, snow commenced to fall. Surely the gods had willed that I should not reach Argentina. But as I topped that incline and entered a sort of a lap in hills, the clouds thinned, and a weak sun came through to illuminate the rugged, snow-dusted crests and to gladden my spirits. At *Caracoles* I scarcely paused, and ignoring the clouds which were sweeping in, ignoring the snow in the road above, ignoring the tales of 10 kms of impossible road, I turned up toward *El Cristo*! And strangely enough the road didn't seem so hard. To be sure there were curves where I needed every ounce of strength to push my heavily loaded bike and there were snow banks and places where the road was washed out, but the incline was possible, praise be to Allah! And I loved the wild desolation of those mountains. And I looked back, with great satisfaction at the loops of road below where a single bicycle track in the snow was the only sign of life. As I topped the pass and came upon the great black Christ the wind was so chilly that I sought refuge in Panagra's radio station where a genial man insisted that I sit down and have a cup of coffee with bread and cheese and *dulce*. And I was more than glad to rest in that clean, warm room. There I made the acquaintance of the Argentine soldiers stationed there and went out to watch them ski for awhile. Their leader, a man who spoke English, asked me in to the *refugio* where he wrote a letter for me, a letter to an officer in the army camp in *Puente del Inca* where I wanted to spend the night. And then he walked a way down the road with me and wished me a warm *"vaya bien."* So my memories of the summit are pleasant ones.

And never shall I forget the beauty of the trip down! As I passed below the summit I looked out across the valley of the *Rio Mendoza* to a whole range of mountains—high and grand and looking a little like stick candy with their streaks of snow. And as I wound further down into the valley, colors became apparent in the sides of the mountains—brick red, chartreuses, steely blues. The road was excellent, but I had to stop often to warm my icy fingers and to walk the chill out of my feet. No matter. With such sheer magnificence on every side, cold fingers and toes were immaterial. In *Las Cuevas* I passed the *aduana* without difficulty. The official took my passport to make arrangements to extend my visa, and inspection of my baggage consisted of nothing more than a slap on the outside! Then on to *Puente del Inca* in the cold of late afternoon. But here the full force of the colors in the hills was brought home to me. Never before in my life have I seen such color! Rich dull reds, tawny oranges, tans, the blue green of old copper, creams, deep blues, magentas, chocolate browns, grays—all sweeping down the soft shoulders of the mountains, down into a valley of chartreuses—the yellow-green of a carpet of low plants. And the gray of the afternoon seemed to accentuate the color by contrast. In *Puente del Inca* I traveled to the barracks with my letter in hand. And I was escorted into the officers' quarters and welcome warmth. Here I could spend the night, they said. And I sat there amidst those stern bearded men whose requests brought the clicking of heels and the undivided attention of the underlings, thinking how varied had become my experience in South America! I dined with 3 while another played the guitar and still another a harmonica. But the exertion of a long, hard day sent me early to bed.

May 14, 1942—Mendoza, Argentina—Hotel Europa

And yesterday morning I wakened to look out on a world of white! Snow! Was the weather going to stop me here after crossing the summit? Not knowing what else to do I waited to have breakfast with the others and to ask their advice. And then I took still more time to go with one of the officers to see the *Puente del Inca*, a natural bridge formed by the deposits of mineral waters and undercut by the river below. A little shrine there attested to the fact that folks believed themselves cured by the waters issuing from the rocks. By the time I had returned to my room the day was brighter and less forbidding and since the snow was not deep, I took leave of my hosts and rolled on down the canyon, a white canyon with white *cerros* rising on either side. Down into the black cavern of a canyon below—a land below the snow where once again there was color in the hills. In *Punta de Vacas* I stopped only long enough to ask about the way, and then on a broad, fine road I sped on towards *Uspallata*. Turning to look back at *Vacas*, my bike skidded out from under me, and Chester and I went down together with a crash! I thought surely something must be broken, but fortunately nothing was, and I pedaled on more cautiously. Then a truck stopped to ask me to ride and although I was happy pedaling in this beautiful country, fear of *mucha subida* and inability to reach my destination before nightfall caused me to accept. And then I regretted my move because the trip down the canyon was beautiful beyond description with jagged colorful peaks above and the river far below. The road too was good, and there I was riding down hill after all the trials of the climb on the other side! The irony of fate! We stopped for lunch amidst *Uspallata's* golden trees. Steak and fried potatoes in a hovel. And I decided to go on to *Mendoza*. We were out of the canyon now and in the low deserty hills of the pampas, and when mist closed in about us, I felt completely isolated from the world of men. But there was my friend the truck driver, a ragged little man who took off his wedding ring and tried to hold my hand! After an eon in the mists, we arrived in *Mendoza,* and I came to this cheerless room, too weary to search further. I asked the truck driver to come for dinner, for I wished to repay him in some measure. And come he did— an hour before dinner! In a brown suit without a shirt! And I had a devilish time getting rid of him. He wanted to spend the night with me!

May 15, 1942—Mendoza—Hotel Italia—9:00 AM

Yesterday morning I wakened with a restless feeling and sense of dissatisfaction over the fact that I was in *Mendoza* and not still in the *Cordillera*! But there were things to be done and the 1st was to find another hotel, a more cheerful place. In the tourist bureau was an amiable man who told me all concerning the roads, the country, and the hotels, and with a little shopping I found a much better room at smaller cost. When I paid my bill, I was charged 50 cents for breakfast. I cornered the waiter and extracted the overcharge from him and left without giving a tip, in spite of the fact that a couple of little girls ran after me, asking for *propina*. Here in my new location I drowned this unpleasant experience in a tremendous *almuerzo*. And then I went off in search of *Cerro de la Gloria* and a view of my surroundings. Up on the hill I made the rounds of the zoo, a nice park where the animals were kept in a more or less natural environment. Long brown cats, long-legged wolves, alpacas, curious beasts. And then I climbed to the top of the hill to see the monument to liberty of *San Martín*, and to look up to the *Cordilleras* and out to the endless *pampas*. A beautiful warm clear day. En route I found a companion, a little man from B.A. whose nose was a bit large and whose eyes were too close together. But we made the trip *ajunto* and afterwards visited the park with its natural woods and winding roads and lakes.   Back home I went off to the neighborhood of my 1st hotel, thinking that perhaps my friend with the truck might be returning to *Vacas* and I might be able to intercept him and go back once more to the *Cordillera*. And sure enough, there he was in the street, but without his truck!   After a *vuelta* down to *Calle San Martín*, we parted company and I came back to wait for my friend from the *cerro* who had asked me to a movie. In the mean time, a chap from the hotel made himself known to me, and he came to bring me a map and to tell me that I was beautiful and he was in love with me! The Argentines seem to be more or less like the Chileans. Later I spent the evening at a poor movie, trying to evade holding hands and craning my neck to see the Spanish captions because the sound effects were too distorted to be intelligible!

May 16, 1942—Mendoza—Hotel Italia—past midnight

        Yesterday was an aimless sort of a day of nothingness. In the morning I settled myself in the bar to write, but at 10:00, the narrow-eyed man of the *cerro* appeared, and when we commenced to talk, others from the hotel gathered around—an Italian, a traveling salesman, a blond boy. Soon there was a heated conversation underway, with all talking at once and pronouncing judgment on Chinese and Negro culture! And I became an interested listener, trying to keep the thread of the ideas! Then the morning was gone and it was time for lunch! In the afternoon I settled myself to write again, but at 2:00 the narrow-eyed man of the *cerro* returned, and when he suggested a *paseo*, I acquiesced. We went off by bus to a military airfield where a soldier guided us about and thence we walked back to the field where *San Martín* marshaled his men for the trip across the Andes. All of the country about *Mendoza* seems to be dedicated to the memory of the *Liberator*. Back home once more I told my "shadow" that I was going *arriba en camion* and wouldn't return for 2 days. And I did want to go back to *Puente de Vaca,* but the weather was ominous, and I preferred to stay in my comfortable hotel. Before dinner I went for a *paseo en coche* with the young blond chap and his mother—down the principal street, up to elegant *Hotel Plaza* for a look at the lobby and casino, and thence to the park. After dinner I met a *señorita* here who speaks very good English, and we talked until very late—with one of the waiters sitting eagerly by to study our English!

May 17, 1942—Mendoza—Hotel Italia—11:30 AM

Yesterday morning no one was abroad, and since the weather was still unsettled, I settled myself in the now deserted bar and actually did write letters! All morning I wrote letters! Then the day cleared and I was sorry I hadn't gone off for a *paseo* in the *cerros*. Such is life! But I managed to salvage the afternoon, for Chester and I spent considerable time milling about the environs of Mendoza. Out to *Sauce* and *Borballon* where the countryside is a succession of beautiful vineyards, with some of the vines trained as high as trees. Paved roads with canopies of branches overhead. And *vistas* across cultivated lands to the foothills of the *Cordillera*. A rich land! Back in town I sought out the park, and there 2 small boys piloted me about the roads and the lakes, and showed me the way to the *casas colectivas*. Here on the outskirts of the city, I was surprised to find rows of 2-story modern buildings divided into apartments for working people. Back home once more I took a little time to work on my bike, and then scrubbed the grease from my hands and went out with *Mario,* the traveling salesman for a *vuelta.* We stopped for a drink, and spent several hours visiting over wine and olives and crackers and peanuts—and dancing, returning to our hotel for a very late dinner. Dinner now became a sociable affair for the young Italian with a friend came to talk with me and afterwards Mario moved to my table. The latter suggested a *cine* after dinner, so off I went again to see an Argentine film. And by the time we had returned, *Mario* had become so intimate that he was quite insistent about spending the night with me. These Latinos are all alike, every last one of 'em! I find the city of Mendoza a tight modern place overflowing with activity. And then many *plazas* and tree-lined streets give it the atmosphere of a garden. What a contrast there is to the Chilean towns! Buildings are more modern, window displays are less careless, stocks are more complete. People are taller, sharper featured, better dressed. There are fewer hovels and fewer rags, more autos and gasoline. Gone are the ox carts and the familiar brown uniforms of the *carabineros.* And over here they speak a different language! *"Che"* for *"mire,"* *"nafta"* for *"benzena,"* *"te"* for *"onces,"* *"neumaticos"* for *"foros,"* *"manteca"* for *"mantequilla"!* *Que dificil!* And I have to travel on the lefthand side of the road.

May 18, 1942—Mendoza—Hotel Italia—8:30 PM

Yesterday—another day whiled away in *Mendoza*—here in this informal hotel where I feel very much at home. A lazy, cold Sunday. I wakened to the sound of rain and reluctantly gave up the idea of a trip into the hills, sitting indoors instead and watching the weather hopefully. Writing, talking, watching the weather—thus I passed the morning. But in the afternoon I ventured out to try and exercise a little warmth into my chilly self. Up and down *Calle San Martín* and around *Plaza San Martín*—looking, looking, looking. Modern buildings, beautiful woolens, the familiar gaudy earrings in the windows. And all the world seemed to be looking at me! I felt like exhibit A! And I also felt cold, so I bought a kilo of cookies for the warmth in their sweetness! As I sat writing in the bar before dinner, Hugo, the blond Italian, came to invite me for another *paseo en coche,* and with him his mother, and a couple of other girls and I went to the club by the side of the lake in the park. Here we looked at all the shiny trim racing boats, and the others played pingpong, and I danced the *tango* with *Hugo!* And very presently it was 9:00 PM and we had to return to dinner. Afterwards I looked at photographs with the young Italian with the flashing white smile—photographs of North Africa where he had seen military service and photographs of Italy which he loved so well.

May 19, 1942—La Paz—"Hotel"—7:00 PM

And yesterday I thought I'd leave Mendoza, but circumstances altered my plans. As I walked briskly down *Las Herras* to tend to last minute details, *Hugo* and his family picked me up for another *paseo!* And off I went with them *en coche* to see the ruins of a couple of churches shaken down in an earthquake in the 1880's. Afterwards *Hugo* went with me to the tourist bureau and also to change some money and en route he became so enthused over the idea of a *paseo en bicicleta* that he decided to rent a bike and join me! So we hustled home to have dinner at 12:00 and by 1:00 we were on our way, pedaling off toward *Maipú*. Presently *Hugo's mama* and *papa* joined us, following along in their auto to see that the bold *gringa* didn't spirit their son away! We all stopped together to see *Bodega Giol*, largest *bodega* in the world, and there we saw wine, wine, wine! It was flowing through pipes to barrels where men tapped with hammers to determine when the barrels were full. It was passing through filters. It was stored in great casks holding hundreds of liters. *Viño Toro.* And we sampled the claret so clear and red. Then on to *Lujan* with *mama* and *papa Hugo* still following! Here was country typical of *Mendoza*. Acres and acres of vineyards, all in autumn reds. Paved roads, overshadowed with weeping willows and plane trees. *Alamedas* framing the hills beyond. Beautiful, rich farm lands. And the cerros shrouded in dark clouds seemed awe-inspiring—mighty! Beyond *Lujan* we visited the *"Dique"* where water flowed for irrigation. And thereafter we started bravely off on the longest road home. But *Hugo's* legs cramped, and we turned back to *Lujan* and a shorter route. And we stopped for *café con leche* in the *pueblo* amidst the curious stares of the people in the streets—a welcome interlude. Then back to *Mendoza, Hotel Italia*, and *comida*—with little Helen consuming soup, rice, fish, beefsteak, stewed fruit and tea as if she'd never eat again! Early to bed in anticipation of a long day ahead.

And this morning in the dark and the cold I looked out at a starless sky, and knew that I could loiter no longer in *Mendoza* waiting for clear weather. Methodically I packed my things, each in the same old place, and after coffee sickishly sweet with sugar and a double on bread, I pushed off in the dark before anyone else was awake. Left the hotel where I had been so happy—where the waiter with flashing eyes spoke to me in English, where the bathroom was clean and my bed was clean, where the light was bright enough to actually see by, where the table was set with care and the food was bountiful enough to satisfy even my appetite. And where I knew everyone. Left a life of comfort and pleasant associations for the open road which forever draws me on. But as I clattered over the cobblestone of the city and sped away on the smooth road leading to *San Martín*, my thoughts turned back to the *Cordilleras*, and I felt a little nostalgic for the wild heights which I would not see again for a very long time. Behind me they were wrapped in clouds. And the sun, too, disappeared in clouds after lingering for a moment as a glorious band of red above the horizon. Thus, on a cold morning I pedaled off on the long, long road to *Buenos Aires*. Vineyards and tree-lined roads graced my way at first. And as the day grew older, a weak sun shown through the thin yellow strands of the willows. Then trees and vineyards were gone, and there was nothing but *pampas* as far as I could see— grasses, sand, and thorn bushes! With the clouds billowing over head and with Chester and me rolling smoothly, steadily on across a lonely land. Once we stopped to finish the cookies and later to take refuge in a wash and to dine on bread and strawberry jam. Here I rested too, for the sun was warm, and my legs were weary after pedaling against a head wind. But we managed to reach *La Paz* before dark—after nearly a hundred miles of *caminando*. And I had time to change my clothes and walk about the town before the sun went down. A small town of the plains with a few stores and a couple of hotels, unpaved streets and a forlorn *plaza.* And now I wait in a cold *comedor* for dinner—food to satisfy a gnawing hunger.

May 21, 1942—San Luis—Hotel Roca—8:00 AM

Pampa, pampa, pampa. All day yesterday I trekked across limitless pampas—a land of sand and thorn bushes. A vast, lonely land brushed with wind and canopied with scudding cloud. I shared my ribbon of road with trucks carrying wine to B.A., and occasionally I passed a forlorn little collection of mud houses, so I was not really alone. And I found a beauty in the *pampa.* The gray-green of the thorn bushes tapered off to a deep blue in the distance. And all the world out there possessed a horizontal feeling. The horizon itself—an infinite ring. Distant hills lying in long, low waves. Fingers of clouds following the line of the horizon. A silvery sliver of lake measuring itself along the horizon. A rosy glow over *La Paz* drew me out of the hotel and on to the road before the sunrise lost its glory, although I was loath to leave the warmth of my bed. And in a few moments the *pueblo* was lost in the thorn bushes, and I left as if I alone moved and breathed in this wasteland. At the great white arch which marks the boundary between the provinces of *Mendoza* and *San Luis* I was obliged to stop and show my documents, and I delayed a few moments to answer the questions of the curious crowd which surrounded me and to drink the small glass of whisky which the *dueño* of the bar proffered. On again and up, for now the road began to creep up over a broad *mesa* and toward hills in the distance, a slight elevation which gave me a better view of the sea of *pampa* across which I had come. Occasionally I passed great carts drawn by 6 mules and loaded with wood wrung from the skimpy trees of the *pampa,* the only industry in this region. An obnoxious truck driver followed me for some time trying to persuade me to ride and later another of the same vintage stopped when I stopped beside the road. The latter talked of politics and sneered whenever I said I did not understand, so I pulled Chester out of his grip and pedaled on. Long before I reached *San Luis,* I could see it before me, looking almost like the *pampa* and yet somehow different. And as I drew near, its church steeple, its huddle of buildings, and its tree-lined streets seemed like an oasis of civilization in a land of nothingness. And the *cerros* behind it, sharply wrinkled in the late-afternoon sun, were a bold contrast to the level *pampa*. Here I found refuge, and went out before dinner to see the town. A nice little place with bright shops, a *plaza* reverberating with radio music from loud speakers, and its many people in the streets. At 9:00 I devoured a tremendous meal and went wearily to bed.

May 22, 1942—Villa Mercedes—H. Progresso—8:00 AM

With only 100 kms. ahead of me yesterday, I dallied. And then as I left the hotel, the *dueño* told me of a fine *paseo* in the hills only 30 kms! But I just couldn't miss any thing, so off I went to the hills! And it was a lovely *paseo* with the road, winding through the hills, passing a deep gorge and climbing up for a view across an artificial lake. There were houses tucked into the folds and valleys of the hills, and the countryside was intimate and very pretty—a contrast to the *pampa* below. There was *pampa* below. There was *pampa* grass too, white plumes along the gullies. And I loved the gray-green, sharp-featured *cerros* with the road winding in and out, up and down. But I couldn't stay. I needed to return to my long, long road across the *pampas*. And by mid-day I was on my way to *Villa Mercedes*. A few turns and ups in the low hills at the foot of the *cerros*, and I reached the "highest point between B.A. and *Mendoza*." And thence my way was more or less down, and I glided along with little effort. The countryside was different now. The thorn bush dwindled to mere scattered patches, and there were vast areas of dry lands, scratched a little here and there as if someone might once have had an idea of producing something. Cattle were feeding on these lands and I saw an occasional drove moving along near the road—poor, scrawny beasts prodded on by *gauchos* as poor as the cattle they herded. All day the hills of *San Luis* were in view behind me, and off to the left another hill kept me company—bits of variety in the landscape. At one of the desolate, treeless, little railway stations I stopped to buy heavy, flat rolls taken from a gunny sack full of bread, and later I picnicked on the plains, opening my last tin of *"mermelada"*, with fond memories of *Portillo*! As I approached *Villa Mercedes*, the thorn bushes were larger and the agricultural lands more prosperous, and I felt the nearness of civilization. In a moment I was in the heart of it, an object of curiosity in search of a haven of solitude. And glad to disappear into a hotel. In conventional clothes I went out to walk the streets and to look at the stores and the people before coming in for a late dinner and a welcome bed.

May 23, 1942—Rio Cuatro—Hotel Victoria—9:30 AM

Yesterday I felt unhurried, for my legs had proven themselves equal to the demands of my trek, and kilometers seemed nothing on the good roads of the plains. Leaving *Villa Mercedes*, I lost myself in the sandy tracks of the country and I had to push myself through to the pavement asking the way of everyone I met. Thence I followed without difficulty for I could see the road ahead stretching on to infinity! Stretching on through country which became more and more prosperous. More and better cattle, horses with some degree of quality, acres and acres of land utilized for the production of grains. And dotting the endless fields were groups of trees which told of houses there—and life. Gone now were my friends, the hills, and slight undulations in the plains provided the only variety in the terrain. At lunchtime I took refuge behind a pile of gravel, the only place on the *pampa* where I could find seclusion from the road! Then on and on and on. And the breeze which had been brushing back my hair became a strong head wind. On and on and on. The wind seemed a mighty force holding me back. On and on. I felt as if I were climbing the highest peak in the *Andes*. On and on and on. And my bones ached, and I was weary beyond measure. But at long, long last I arrived. *Rio Cuatro* at last! And I came grateful to this hotel which had been recommended to me in *Mendoza*. A sponge bath and a change of clothes revived me and I was ready for a *paseo* through the streets to look and look and look. Here as in other Argentine towns, I find evidence of the wealth of the country. Modern buildings, well-dressed people, many automobiles. Ever so much more opulence than in Chile. But life is cast in a very similar mold. People promenade in the streets and in the *plazas* and take their appetizers in the bars. The men size up the women from head to toe, and the women look coyly back. Radio music plays in the *plazas*. Men gather in knots to talk, talk, talk with emphatic gesticulations. Thus all passed the hours before dinner. And I pass the hours walking *"para conocer, no mas."* But always I am eager for dinner and am early in the *comedor*. And good the Argentine meals tasted to a hungry cyclist! Bowls of soup with cheese, platters of rice, platters of tongue or liver or kidneys, platters of tender beef, dishes of fruit, and a hot drink to take the chill out of one's system. All is served family style—an abundance of everything. And butter is served *"sin vale"*! Other things about the hotels are better too. Waiters' uniforms are cleaner, baths are cleaner, lights are brighter, patios are neater. But there are no heating systems, *que lastima*!

May 24, 1942—Santa Rosa—Hotel Torino—7:00 PM

All day yesterday I rested in my comfortable hotel in *Rio Cuarto*. A day of ease and feasting. An interlude in which I gathered strength for more pedaling. Sleeping late, dawdling over coffee, writing—thus I whiled away half the morning. But there were errands to attend to before the shops closed at noon, and I went out to look up the Automobile Club of Argentina to ask a round of questions about the road to *Cordoba*. I bought food too, figs, and peanuts for my lunch on the road, but they proved so tempting that I ate half of them in my room! After a tremendous *almuerzo*, I disciplined myself to the task of mending and didn't venture out again until late afternoon. Then I went forth to see the opening of festivities for the celebration of *Veintecinco de Mayo*, Argentine's

independence day. I had seen evidence of the coming *fiesta*
earlier in the day: blue and white emblems on the white
uniforms of students, store windows decorated in blue and
white, flags flying from buildings, autos, bicycles. And now
the townspeople were gathering at the *municipalidad*. The
flag was solemnly lowered to the tune of a bugle corps, there
was a sonorous speech, and then the dignitaries moved down
the street, a band followed, and all the populace fell in behind,
filling the streets from curb to curb. I followed too, excited by
the music and by the torches which were carried by the throng.
A motley, noisy crowd, exuberant over its *fiesta*. In *Plaza San
Martín* we came to a halt at the foot of a mounted figure of the
hero, and while the wind whipped the flags into rippling blue
and white, the crowd sang the national anthem and listened to
another speech. Then the procession moved back to the center
of town before disbanding. Since the hour was too early for
cena, folks amused themselves, walking around and around
the streets which surround the *plaza*, the *señoritas* passing in
one direction and the *señores* in the opposite one. Back home
I made preparations for an early departure, but I went to bed
disquieted by the sound of a strong wind outside.

May 25, 1942—Cordoba—Hotel Cordoba—10:00 PM

    And the wind was still blowing when I wakened
yesterday morning and got up in the cold starlight before
anyone else stirred. A hasty breakfast of bread and cheese and
I pushed off into the darkness at 6:30! An incredible early
start! But there were *caminos de tierra* ahead and hills and
heaven knows what. In a moment I was out on the *pampa*
again following the beam of my flashlight, alone in the dark
and the silence! With Chester I was able to follow a newly
made highway and thus avoid the detours, but the *Argentinos'*
quaint custom of tossing rocks and thornbush into roads closed
to autos kept me on constant vigil. As I left *Rio Cuatro*, there
was no smiling *señor* to hold up a bottle of *refresco* and bid
me stop, as there had been when I entered the *pueblo*, but out
on the *pampa* a *señor* in a hovel by the side of the road invited

me to stop for *mate*! And I sped on my lonely way in the darkness. Presently a dull orange streak in the east foretold the coming of day. Brighter it grew and brighter, changing from orange to a vibrant mass of fiery red. And its light revealed the unbroken rim of the world out there beyond the fields of chocolate earth. How immense, the *pampa*. Then the sun came up as a great red ball, only to disappear again in the gray of a forlorn day. A cold day. And a cold wind blew in my face. My hands grew icy on the handlebars and my feet numb on the pedals as I rolled along that road which forever disappeared into infinity. On and on and on, stopping occasionally for a few figs to replenish the fires within—fires exhausted by the cold and the effort of pedaling against the wind. A range of hills on the left gave promise of *sierras* ahead, but ahead I could see nothing but the endless prairie. Was it possible that within the day or within a lifetime, I could reach hills again? Then from *Berrotaran* I saw their form in the distance. Hills! And it mattered not a whit that the pavement came to an end, for my *camino de tierra* lead into the hills. And I was eager to feel the weight of the hills on my pedals. Then, with the first ups and downs, the sun came out, and my world was gay once more. Contentedly I pedaled in and out, up and down, through those bushy, lovely hills, and with a sense of satisfaction. I stopped to eat my bread and cheese on a hillock where I could look across their surging greenery. In the afternoon I reached *Rio Tercero* with its dike and its great artificial lake, and here were resort hotels, boats, and Sunday holiday seekers. On a hill top I stopped, to eat peanuts and enjoy the surroundings before pedaling on to *Santa Rosa*, but even so I reached the *pueblo* early and had plenty of time to explore its unpaved streets and wander down to the river below and to buy a loaf of heavy white bread that I like with my cheese. A peaceful, scattered little village, *Santa Rosa*, with its gay white houses set hit or miss on the slopes. Popular in summer, it is almost deserted now, and I found myself practically alone in my hotel. But that didn't lessen the beauty of a chicken dinner!

May 27, 1942—Cordoba—Pensión "Velez Sarsfield 311"

And the 25th, the day of *fiesta*, dawned clear and cold and bright with a feeling of gaiety in the air. I took to my road, through the hills with great gusto, but the cold in the shadows was so intense that I had to resort to wearing a pair of socks on my hands! And my windbreaker was clammy cold on my bare arms. But the wind was with me, praise be to Allah! And the curves and ups and downs were a never ending joy to a cyclist fresh from the *pampas!* Wooded hills! Oaks and well-fed thorn bushes. And frequent villas with their bright white residences. I pedaled slowly for I loved those hills, but before noon I had rolled out of them and was on the plains of *Cordoba*. *Alta Gracia* drew me aside for one kilometer and I climbed up its sloping street to the *plaza* and the old church, gray with age and possessing the solid architecture of the colonial period—substantial round arches and heavy square lines. I stopped for a moment to visit with a couple of young cyclists, and then I was on my way again, searching for a likely luncheon spot. I found it in a cornfield behind a screen of trees, and here I rested long enough for my one and only slip (washed the previous evening) to dry in the wind. Then on to *Cordoba!* Sliding easily along a level, paved road with a tail wind to cheer me on. And with umbrella trees to remind me of home! In town, I found crowds of people dispersing. I had just missed the *fiesta, que lástima.* And I was a poor, befuddled stranger wondering where to look for a place to stay. There would surely be hotels near the station, I reasoned, so I inquired about the way, and crossed the center of the city with mouths dropping open as I passed. At *Hotel España* I answered the questions of a curious crowd and was directed to *Hotel Cordoba* where I escaped the stares of the curious in a not-too-good room. Presently, I was in the streets again in more conventional attire—walking, walking, walking, to orient myself to the new city, the largest I had yet visited in Argentina. Bright lights, streetcars, tall buildings, modern window displays—dazzling to a girl from the hills! And in *Calle San Martín*, I joined the promenaders who had crowded the autos out of the thoroughfare. Until the dinner hour, I walked and looked, excited by the city's concentrated activity.

And yesterday too was a day of orientation. First of all I went to the tourist bureau where a very pleasant *Señor Rocca* showered me with literature, told me of *paseos* in the *cerros*, and sent me to a *pensión* that he said was good. Banking on his judgment, I moved without first going to see, and I was disappointed to find myself in a dark and dirty place where floors were cluttered and servants untidy. But the sun was bright outside, and outside I would stay until I found another place. In *Plaza San Martín*, I sat to look at the great cathedral, one of the best examples of colonial architecture in Argentina. A grayed and massive edifice with the solidity of round arches and unadorned square lines. Above on the hill I wandered through *Parque Sarmiento*—under the trees, besides the lake and along the bluff where I could look out across the city with its countless church steeples and domes. And in the evening I crossed the river to look up *Tomas Pastorino*, a student from summer school in *Santiago*. But since he was not to be found, I returned to the center—to the bright lights and the promenaders of *San Martín*, a never-ending source of entertainment. And before retiring to this dark hole in the wall, I found a better *pensión* and made ready to move again in the morning.

May 28, 1942—Cordoba—Pensión Martinez—8:30 AM

Hoping that the *dueña* wouldn't see me leave for *"una vuelta en los cerros"* in skirt and silk stockings (!!), I pedaled hastily around a corner and headed for my new quarters. But a couple of policemen stopped me almost immediately and asked a hundred questions, more curious than suspicious. And as we stood there, a crowd gathered around, passing from one to another the surprised exclamation of *"sola"! * Finally a man stepped forward and spoke to me in English, and before he left he gave me his card and asked me to come to his home in the evening! Then I pushed my way through the curious and escaped into my new room, a room with light where at last I could make myself at home. Always in the streets to get the feel of the city, I wandered aimlessly about, picking out the old colonial buildings with their grayed, massive architecture, and wondering at the proximity of the old and the very new, for one finds both side by side in *Cordoba*. After lunch, I called *Tomás Pastorino* by phone, and he cordially offered to come and take me for a *vuelta en la ciudad*, an invitation I was glad to accept. How pleasant to meet again an acquaintance from summer school! First we went to the cathedral and passed through its holy ancient doors (I bare headed!) to see the splendor within. The richly decorated dome and the vault of the nave, the altar of silver, the floors of tile. The square columns so massive that they give the appearance of a wall and one feels that he is in a church without columns. Within as without, there is a feeling of great weight and solidity with none of the soaring grace of the Gothic churches, but with a beauty peculiar to massive architecture. From the cathedral we went up to *Sarmiento* Park and to an exposition of products from the province of *Cordoba*. Broom fibers, marble, mica. Corn, cheese, mushrooms! Machinery. And who should I meet up there but my old friend from the tourist bureau, *Señor Rocca*. He introduced me to the head of the exposition who told me that that house was my house, and he also introduced me to a maker of cakes who brought out a box and treated us to *dulces de leche* and to turkey sandwiches! Finally *Tomas* and I broke away in time for a walk through the park. Along the bluff where we could look out across the city and down at the zoo, past the great cage with its assorted birds, including condors, past the Greek theater, past the swimming pool. Then back to the city once more. And in a few moments I was on my way to visit the *señor* of the morning. I found him in a luxurious book-lined study, taking an English lesson from an American woman. But the lesson ended when I arrived, and we talked of cycling across the *Cordillera* and the curiosity of a woman's traveling alone! Then with a *copita* and a bourbon we dispersed, and I hustled home to the warmth of soup and a bed.

May 28, 1942—Carlos Paz—Hotel Plaza—9:30 AM

And today the persistence of clear skies and sunshine lured me back to the open road—back to pedals and sweat and the uncertainty of the unknown—back to the thrill of unexpected adventure. For my home is the open road; my life the turning of pedals—wondering where the night will find me, what the future will bring. Glorious freedom! But first there were errands in *Cordoba*—bread and cheese to purchase—and gloves for the morning chill. Then out of the city on the road to *Carlos Paz*. En route another cyclist joined me—company as far as *Yocsina*, and the kilometers slipped quickly away. Then hills again and happy pedaling. But a strong wind bore down upon me, and I found myself walking up hills which were scarcely hills at all. And the bunch grass bent low and silvery under the force of the wind. But the sun continued to shine and the mica, which is everywhere, sparkled under its rays. And soon I was rolling down to *Lago San Roque* in spite of inhibited progress. Here I trekked aside to follow the road to the *dique*, a road which winds along the lake providing pretty views of all its inlets with their harbored boats. And high on a brushy knoll where the panorama of lake and hills was unimpeded, I stopped under a thorn bush for bread and cheese. At the *dique* a group of tourists shook my hand and wished me *buena suerte*, and a *trabajador* wanted to treat me *to una cosita*, but I declined and rolled back along my way—back toward *Carlos Paz*. Here I found a comfortable room, and went out almost at once to walk about the *pueblo*. Signs "*a la cruz*" drew me off on to the hillsides, and I climbed up towards a cross following sighs of "tighten your cinch," "rest your horse," "climb slowly." *Arriba* was a fine view of *Lago San Roque* and of the hills rolling away on all sides, hills which looked as if they had been formed by some giant's hand crumpling the *pampas*, hills softened by the gray-green of thorn bush, hills purpling in the distance. And as I walked down again, the sun set in a mass of golden clouds and a fall moon rose behind the hill with the cross. Thorn bushes were angular against the gold; hills were purple against the gold. And the scattered white houses of *Carlos Paz* seemed warm and friendly. The hours before and after dinner I whiled away in conversation with the *señoras* of the hotel and with a couple of *pasajeros.*

May 30, 1942—Hotel El Condor—9:00 AM

Yesterday morning was gray with clouds and surprisingly warm and tranquil. No breath of wind stirred. And I pedaled out into the silence with a sense of relief. Before leaving *Carlos Paz* I went up to *Villa del Lago* for a view of the lake. Gone the white caps of the day before, and mountains and sky were mirrored in its placid depths. A very different *Lago San Roque.* Turning up the long road to *Miña Clavero*, I wound at first through brushy hills. Then up and up and up. I climbed until the brush had disappeared, and the hills were clothed only in bunch grass. Yellowy green, dark spotted with Aberdeen Angus cattle. Broad, rolling *pampa.* At *Copiña* my road plunged abruptly into the rocky heights, coiling back and forth amongst great cliffs and gorges of gray stone. Below, the land from which I had come was opalescent in the almost-light of the veiled sun, but the rocky peaks beside me were darkly purple under storm clouds. And the rocky slopes up which I struggled were gray, gray, gray. Lunch of bread and cheese failed to renew the force in my legs, and I was walking now pushing up and up. Up and up in a lonely desolate world of gray rock forms and purple beyond. An Indian road worker told me there were yet 6 kms of *subida* ahead, and with crossed fingers I watched my cyclometer turn, wondering if there were 6 or 60 kms of climbing. But the Indian was right and at 6 kms I reached the high *pampa* of *Achala*, a land of rock and bunch grass. Here the dark clouds swirled low, and within another kilometer my world was enveloped in mist. A lone hotel ahead offered refuge, and there I would treat myself to tea (with plenty of sugar) and wait for the clouds to dissipate. But the mists blew endlessly by, and the fires of snug *Hotel El Condor* proved so inviting that I decided to spend the night! And a pleasant evening it was, too, spent in the cheer of the fire in conversation with a blue-eyed, amiable French chap, a fat Swiss lad whose words were full of humor, and an Englishman who was bound for the States on horseback. Fires! I didn't have to go to bed for warmth!

May 31, 1942—Miña Clavero—Hotel Petit—9:00 AM

Yesterday morning I looked out again at a gray world. Disappointment. But the clouds were higher, and one could see across the *pampa*. I must go. First, *café*, however, and methodically I cleaned up a basket of bread and a dish of jam. Then good-bye to fires and friends, and off across that cold, windy land. Clouds raced across the *pampa* and the grass lay flat beneath the wind. But there was a lightness about the day, and occasionally the sun came through. There was light and shadow on the *pampa*. And as I passed *La Posta* and began to descend, the sun came out! My road spiraled downward as it had come up—wind amongst great piles and shoulders of rock. And below lay a level valley. I traveled slowly, stopping often to look down through canyons of stone to the valley where there were the white buildings of *Miña Clavero*. And presently I arrived. Riding through the village in search of a hotel a crowd of schoolboys ran after me laughing at the strange spectacle of a girl alone on a bicycle. And there was such a multiplicity of hotels that I was completely confused. In *Petit Hotel* I escaped from the curious and discovered I had arrived in time for dinner, happy day! 3 slices of ham, a bowl of soup smothered in cheese, 2 tremendous breaded cutlets ringed around with lettuce, 2 eggs, 2 rolls, an orange, a banana, and a cup of tea loaded with sugar! My appetite knows no bounds these cold days! After such a meal I was ready for more activity, and I went off on Chester to reconnoiter the environs of *Miñas Clavero*. Across the river I rode through the other half of the town and followed the road to *Villa Dolores* for a way—down the valley with hills on either hand. But I didn't choose to go down far, for the climb back would take the strength I needed for the business of getting back to *Cordoba*, so I turned aside and followed the road to *Nina Paula*. A pleasant road which led up into the rocky hills, and from which I could look away to other hills darkly blue and purple under a cloudy sky. Once I stopped to make a place for myself in the soft grass of the *pampa* and to write. But I moved on when the passers-by became too numerous. And always there are passers-by in this country, no matter how remote it may seem. They go on foot and on horseback and on mules with their legs swinging like pendulums to keep the animals moving. Back in *Miña Clavero*, I changed my clothes and went out for a walk in the village. Through the center, across the river on stepping stones, and into the tourist bureau, where I talked at length with a couple of young chaps who were curious about my journey by bicycle. Unpaved streets, a few shop windows, a few food stores, many hotels—and many loiterers. This is *Miña Clavero*. But it had its charm, for a river runs through its center, and hills rise all about it. Topping off the day with half a chicken and a steak, I went to bed in search of a little warmth.

May 31, 1942—Salsacate—Hosteria Pocho—9:00 PM

Early this morning, when the world was still very dark, I wakened to the drip, drip, drip of rain. And the idea of spending the winter on the open road lost all its appeal! But with the coming of day the rain ceased, and by 10:00 with an ample *desayuno* inside, I was ready for the road once more. Off to the north, up the "level valley" which almost at once presented a rocky incline. And I climbed in a world wrapped in gray clouds. *Cerros* were there on either side of me, but I could not see them. And below, *Miña Clavero* was only faintly discernible. This time my climb was a short one, and very soon I was rolling along a valley which was truly level. A ribbon of hard dirt road over which Chester ran silently and easily with no wind to hold him back. Few trees, much bunch grass, no vistas. But gray days have their lighter aspects and presently I could make out the forms of hills about me. Better to mark time and wait for the day to clear, so I loitered 2 hrs. over bread and cheese out there on the open *pampa*. And when I traveled on, the sun had come through, and I could see at last. Once more the hills were my companions. In the vicinity of *Ambul* I entered a veritable forest of bushy little palm trees, and I was as delighted with their silvery foliage and their lovely silhouettes against the cloud-strewn sky and the dim, orchid mountains that I turned aside and rode down the road to *Ambul*, just to be amongst the palms. They provided a fitting setting for the white-washed adobe houses with the smooth bunch-grass thatches. I reached the little village of *Salsicate* early in spite of myself, and the rest of the afternoon. I sat on the front porch of my *hosteria* writing, visiting with the *dueño* and keeping an eye on the street where passed the populace. I, too, went for a *vuelta* through the unpaved streets, but my cycling garb made me conspicuous, and I didn't stay long. After supper the little girls of the *dueño* entertained us with songs and readings. An informal family affair, only 4 boarders, and the rest, family.

June 2, 1942—Tanti—Hotel El Bosque—9:00 AM

Yesterday morning at 6:00 the moon was so bright I thought the day had come! I got up to find Chester with a wilted tire! *Carramba!* And I had to make an early start too. With the aid of a flashlight I went to work and patched 2 holes, the result of a thorn and a bit of glass. And the rattle of tools and the swish of escaping air roused the household, so I was actually able to have *desayuno* at 7:30! Excited by a clear morning, I rolled happily on my way at 8:00. And mine was a beautiful trip. Winding up through wooded hills, with an occasional palm to add zest to the landscape, and looking back at the hills of *Salsacate,* one a perfect volcanic cone with its base lost in a dense white mist. But there was no mist in my hills, and in brilliant sunshine, I climbed up into an intense blue sky. Back and forth and up until, with a last look back at the tiny, far-away houses of *Salsacate*, I passed over the top and onto the *pampa* of *San Luis*. Here the road swept up and down through a land of grass and rock with great stony gorges falling away to the right and with *Los Gigantes* rising in rocky prominence. A lonely land, its life confined to an occasional stone hut and an occasional rider passing over the horizon. On a point high above one of those yawning gorges. I ate my bread and cheese in the warmth of the sun, all the while looking down into the gray-green depths where a little band of sheep fed amongst the rocks. As I passed *Los Gigantes* and began the downward trek, I left the brilliance of the summits for the mists of the valley, and it was suddenly cold. Down, down, down. Wheels whirred as my feet rested idly on the pedals and my body grew chill. And in the valley ahead, I could see *Lago San Roque* and the white buildings of *Carlos Paz* and *Tanti*. Down, down, down. *Tanti* at last. And after riding the length and breadth of the *pueblo*, I returned to what appeared to be the last place to stop. Here I found welcome shelter, a fire, a chicken dinner, and the friendly curiosity of the *dueño* and his *señora*. And a brilliant starlit night gave promise of a fine day ahead.

June 3, 1942—La Cumbre—Hotel La Serrana—7:30 PM

But yesterday morning the clouds floated in, and the mists lay stagnant in the valley below. I must be on my way, for with winter so close, every rain-free day is a precious thing not to be wasted in the cold bowels of a hotel. Far better, the life of the road where the turning of pedals sends warmth and spirit surging through me. So I followed the open road— down to the edge of *Lago San Roque* and thence off to the north, rising gradually upwards in a broad valley, but always following a range of *sierras*. Some times the mists lay cold and thick about me, foreshortening my world, and other times they parted and shared with me the beauty of the hills and the cloud-darkened landscape. I rode quickly through *Cosquin's* busy center, running away from the laughing, staring crowds and noting only the large hospital, the narrow church on the hill, and the *plazas* which are rare in these hill *pueblos*. But I liked *La Falda's* cheerful cluster of buildings at the foot of the sierras, and I pondered stopping here, for the day was growing gray and grayer, and I was thinking more and more of some pleasant place in which to weather the coming storm. Better to go on. Perhaps I could reach *La Cumbre* in time for dinner. But no it wasn't possible, and I resigned myself to bread and cheese in the shelter of a gully! And practically in the lap of *La Cumbre*, as I discovered when I traveled on! Then came the rains, and it was a wilted, rain drenched traveler who interviewed the sour *señora* and took refuge here in spite of her. A hot shower, happy day! Or at least fairly warm one! And then out into the streets in search of *la fabrica Rosario* to which I had a letter of introduction from the "cake man" of the exposition. But the *fabrica,* I learned, was out in the country, so I passed the time walking the streets until the rain sent me scampering back to the hotel—back to hot coffee and the sweetness of jam and too much sugar, fuel to combat the cold. Then with a lull in the rain, I ventured out again to better know the village and its guardian hills. *Exposiciones Indigenas* drew me out of the streets to look at the handiwork of Indians, and in the 1st shop I lingered long to talk with the Russian-Jew who was the proprietor—talk of war and not of Indian cultures. Back in my hotel I dined and retired to the sound of pelting rain outside, and thus nourished the idea of spending another day in *La Cumbre* was born and reared.

And today has been the day of leisure. Rain, rain, rain—an endless downpour which drowned every vestige of desire to go back to the road. All day I have stayed in doors to study my *guia* and to painfully compose in bad Spanish letters to my friends in Chile. This morning I shopped a little for a more cheerful hotel, but gave up the idea of changing. And after tea when the clouds lifted and light came in around the edges of the world, I walked out into the fresh air and the rain washed hills to find the little old *Capilla del Roque* of the Jesuit fathers with its several venerable old trees, yellowed and dripping. En route I found a sign "Picadilly Circus, 10,872 miles"! Even *La Cumbre* has its English touch! Walking the streets of the *pueblo* in a wider arc gave me a greater familiarity with the place, but the time between rain and darkness was too short for much exploration. A fleeting interval in a gray and mournful day.

June 5, 1942—Capilla del Monte—H. Petit Central—9:30 AM

As if some force in the world were balancing the scales of cheer and gloom, yesterday dawned with an amazing brilliance, pouring light and vividness into the sky, into the hills, across the white buildings of *La Cumbre.* And I was excited by the day's invitation to come forth. With Chester, I went off for a *paseo* to the *Estancia Rosario,* to the cake factory in the hills on the road to *Ascochinga.* And here *Señor Viglianco* showed me the rooms stacked high with jars of *dulces,* the great copper caldrons where sticky solutions bubbled, and the tables where a man was creating *alfajores.* And I came away with a kilo of *dulce de la leche* to add more *peso* to Chester's load! Back in *La Cumbre* I consumed an *almuerzo* of prodigious proportions, drew a smile from the sour *dueña* as I paid my bill, and pedaled away in the sunlight. Through the hills to *Cruz Chica, Cruz Grande,* and *Los Cocos,* a woodsy road overshadowed by *cerros* on either side. And back to the broader valley at *San Esteban.* For a while I stopped to lie in the sun amongst the thorn bushes, but restlessness soon urged me on to *Capilla del Monte.* And here my lucky stars brought me to the door of the *"Petit Central"* where I found two *chicas simpaticas,* one the daughter of the *señora,* the other a *pensionista.* With them I visited at length and with the señora who dropped in to ask if the *Norte Americanos* had *mal corazon* towards Mussolini! After a sociable tea, the *chicas* and I went out for a walk through the town and up to the church. Deep red light on the hills and a lovely sunset. And with a *señorita* on either side of me I felt as if I were a part of the life of the *pueblo,* not just a stranger looking on. We all had supper together, the Italian *señor* and *señora* and their vivacious daughter, the *pensionista,* and I— an informal family meal with the *señor* spitting on the floor and saying "C'mon, Butch" in Yankee English! Afterwards the three of us went to the movies, American productions whose sound effects I was able to decipher with the aid of the Spanish captions! Jayne Pitt and Slim Sommerville way down here in Argentina!

June 6, 1942—Capilla del Monte—H. Petit Central—8:00 AM

I found *Capilla del Monte* so pleasant that I changed my plans and stayed in town yesterday—a pleasant day passed in the company of two *señoritas* of the hotel, one a serious and pretty student, the other a devilish young one who dances as she serves the table and who laughs and laughs and laughs. After a 10:00 AM breakfast, *Zulema* and I went off to visit "*El Zapato*", the rock which resembles a shoe. Out in the wide open spaces, it is situated amongst other rocks, and its stony prominence affords a fine view of the *pueblo* and its hills. After dinner *Zulema, Yolanda* and I, all three, went up into the hills for another *paseo*—up to the plant which purifies the town's water supply and beyond to *La Toma* where stream and canyon and hills form a woodsy retreat. *Cordoba's Sierras* are very pretty but not to be compared with the breathless grandeur of the *cordillera*, and I couldn't help smiling to myself at *Yolanda's* naïve query as to whether the *cerros* to the east were as high as *Capilla's* mountains! All day long the sun shone brightly, and I had a vague feeling that I should be on the road, but unfortunately I can't stretch the sunny days to cover all the things I want to do. And I find the life of a vagabond is the richer for its moments of leisure—moments devoted to companionship and to the sheer joy of just being. At bedtime, I said good-bye to all the hospitable folks of the hotel and made ready to roll on my way at the first sign of dawn. Back to the road again after another interval of relaxation.

June 7, 1942—La Granja—Hotel La Granja—4:00 PM

And yesterday morning I carried out my plans in spite of the cold, forbidding day. As I pushed my loaded Chester through the doors of the hotel, *Yolanda* came out in her nightie and bare feet to urge me not to go, but I felt I must be on my way and on I went. The forlorn grayness of the early morning resolved itself into rain before I had gone far, and all day it rained, the wind whipping the dampness into my face and blowing back my hair in wet stringlets. Hour after hour I rode in a gray and timeless world. No arc of sun to mark the passing of the hours. Few other persons to share the vastness of the country. Lonely hills dimmed by rain. And dimmer still in my eyes, for I couldn't use my glasses. Riding alone through the dripping thorn bush, clad in a clammy poncho without any idea of where to find warmth at the end of the day, I might have been unhappy if mine weren't a wild, lone spirit. But I found beauty in the wet landscape, the misty hills, and aloneness has no horrors for me. Rather I find it a time when I can lose myself in the world about me, can become a part of the earth and the heavens. And with a strong body and strong legs, the discomforts of the road and the length of the journey have no significance for me. And never a day passes which does not have its diversions, its facets of joy or color or adventure. After leaving the broad valley of *Capilla del Monte*, I climbed up and over a ridge and dropped down into the red landscape of *Ongamira, Ongamira* with its strange smooth red rock forms. And here was a *pensión*. I would stop and have coffee! How good—3 cups of *café con leche* with great slices of bread and *dulce de leche*. And I was loath to go back to my wet poncho and my wet road through the hills, so I loitered to talk with the men of the *pensión*. Then on along a narrow, cultivated valley with little groups of wan yellow trees to mark the location of the houses. And up into the hills once more. At this time a breathless man from *Ongamira* overtook me, and in rapid Spanish, only half of which I understood, told me of a truck in which I could ride to *Ascochinga*. My heart sank. Here I was being herded into another truck while the memories of *Uspallata* were still fresh in my mind! I didn't want to ride in a truck! I liked my rain-streaked world! But I couldn't tell a breathless man, that I wouldn't ride in his old truck! He walked along and elaborated the difficulties of the road: the sand, the mud, the hills. And with true Latin gallantry he tossed rocks at the black Angus bulls and herded them out of our way. But fortunately the truck wasn't leaving for a while, and I explained to my friend that I would pedal along in the road until it came and then ride the rest of the way. Then I shook his hand with a *"muchisima gracias"* and fled! I would hide in the bushes when that red truck came my way! But it never came, and I rode on in peace—up and down through the dim, brushy hills. A lake, yellow trees, and the silhouette of domes and towers were my introduction to picturesque *Santa Catalina* which is dominated by its ancient church. Here I stopped to walk around the gray and venerable edifice. Heavy round arches and the simple geometric lines of the other colonial churches and the mellowness which only age can give. And out at the side several curious men stopped their work of skinning a great bloody beast to stare at the beponchoed *gringa* who wandered around the church! Thence on to *Ascochinga*—up and down once more through the lovely green hills. A soft front tire grew softer and softer and I had to accept what I didn't want to believe: a thorn had punctured my paper-thin *goma*. Nothing to do but to stop under a dismal thorn bush and repair the damage. By now it was growing cold and I was eager to find shelter, but *Asochinga* had little to offer. I would try *La Granja*, and my lucky star brought me to this hotel. From the first moment when the plump Hungarian *dueña* greeted me with a smile I have felt at home. And where I found an open fire and a room with private bath and hot water, and was served a hot and bountiful tea, I was completely happy! What more could any wet and weary traveler want. All evening I sat by the fire visiting with the German *dueño*, the 2 ladies who live here, and the 2 other *pasajeros*, one a Hungarian architect, the other a Spaniard. And when I went to bed there was a hot-water bottle *en mi cama! Hay carramba, cuanta felicidad!*

June 9, 1942—La Granja—Hotel La Granja—9:00 AM

The hot water bottle must have won me 'cause 2 days later, I'm still here! Day before yesterday I wakened to the sound of rain, but I wasn't perturbed 'cause it was an excuse to linger on. And all day I sat by the fire in the pleasant company of the others here in the hotel. Outside it rained and rained and rained, but I didn't venture out. Just sat inside by the fire, going no further than to my room and to the table where I consumed great pots of hot milk and tea with long and innumerable platters of hot food. A life of ease and comfort, *sin* tired muscles, *sin* hunger, *sin* cold. Music and companionship and warmth. And another hot water bottle! In the afternoon it snowed, and we learned form the radio that a foot of snow covered *La Cumbre* and *Capilla del Monte.* Once again I had escaped in the nick of time!

And yesterday, I talked myself into staying another day. It wasn't hard! In the morning I went for a *paseo* with the Hungarian and the Spaniard. Armed with walking sticks, we went off briskly but the somewhat fat Hungarian slackened at the first hill. And then there was a ditch to cross. The slight Spaniard scurried around for rocks to make a bridge, while the big [Hungarian] placed them in the water. Then the Spaniard tossed one into the mud, and Arse [the Hungarian] was spattered with mud from head to foot! We couldn't help laughing as he wiped the black dirt from his boyish face and sputtered, *" Hombre, hombre, mire a lo que hace!"* On the hill above, we could look across to higher hills in the distance, hills white with snow. And these hills so intrigued me that after dinner I started towards them on Chester! Back to *Ascochinga* and up the road to *La Cumbre.* But it seemed like a new region to me for the sun shone on the hills, and they were green now instead of gray. My way climbed up and up and up—up out of the woodsy hills and into the bare grassy ones. Up where there was snow lying in the shadows. And where I could look down on *Ascochinga* and out across the vast level expanses beyond. I wanted to reach the top and look down on the *La Cumbre*, but the hour was late and after reaching a point where I could see across to many hills powdered with snow and after pausing for a sociable chat with a road worker, I turned back. Rolling downward was easy but cold, and my feet and hands were icy when I reached this haven of fire and hot tea. But I had memories of a church steeple, and tree forms against a cloud-strewn sky and memories of pale, chartreuse hills and of a wintry stream overshadowed by a great yellow willow—all these memories for my pains. And my tea tasted doubly good for all the cold and the exercise! And I felt doubly content in the warmth and companionship of the evening.

June 10, 1942—Cordoba—Pensión Martinez—6:00 PM

Yesterday morning was hard and clear and cold and frost-encased. As white as if snow had fallen and as cold as the north pole! With features so distinct that nothing was left to the imagination. Again I sat by the fire. But when the sun had risen high enough to shower its warmth on *La Granja*, we all sat on the porch in the sun. Then, presently it was noon, and after another hearty dinner, I reluctantly turned to thoughts of moving on. I didn't want to leave this happy spot, but vagabonding leads me away from life's joys as well as to them. And I felt a strange something when I said good-bye to Arse, as if there were some bond between us—Strange. But the open road and the hills and the sun soon captured my mind, and I idled carelessly along, loath to leave the *sierras*, happy in the winding road. And the sun. I would stop for the night where ever my spirit willed. But none of the little villages along the way caught my fancy, and in *Rio Ceballos* I decided to go on to *Cordoba*. Down out of the hills, past the luxurious chalets of *Villa Allende*, and into the city, hustling to my *pensión* as quickly as possible to escape the curiosity of the multitudes. And here I found hot coffee and a hot bath. And feeling spirited I went for a walk in *Calle San Martín*—just for the fun of the lights and the crowds. And when a mustache and dark eyes breathed *"Que hermosa!"* into my hair, I soared to the top of the world! Before dinner I called

Tomás, and the sound of a friendly voice added to my contentment, even if the entangling of *Castellano* over the telephone was an ordeal. All seemed right with the world. And then the tide turned, and my spirits deflated like a tire with a slow leak. I think the *dueño* must have been suspicious of me, for when he took my name he talked a lot about the police, as if preparing me for something which he anticipated and I did not. Then they came, 2 of them, and for an hour I showed my possessions and explained my being here. They looked at my things, inspected my documents, cross questioned me, and laboriously wrote down the names of all who have given me their names and addresses. Meanwhile the *dueño* stood by saying, *"Pero Ud no es mala. Buena niña, linda.."* And the police assured me that this was routine activity. I answered with a polite, *"claro,"* but I thought— "phooey!" For I have lived long enough and traveled far enough to know when I'm under particular suspicion. And when they left with my Chilean *carnet*; the green card which is all that the official at *Cuevas* gave me in place of my passport; a number of my names and addresses; and my diary, there wasn't any doubt in my mind as to what they thought I was. Ironically they wished me pleasant dreams, little realizing that I would pass a tranquil night, for they did not know what I knew—that my belongings, my words, and my actions were all free of any subversive element.

And this morning my 1st duty was to go with the *dueño* to the police station. I passed through the arches and along the halls of that austere building with a set to my shoulders which bespoke the Richardson stubbornness. I would convince them all that I was innocent. And I was told to come back later, the inspector wasn't in! Thus with part of the morning left to me, I dropped in at the tourist office and here I learned with a shudder that the only *casa de cambio* in *Cordoba* was paying no more than $2.60 for good American dollars. As I walked out I tested the strength of my legs, wondering if I could pedal to B. A. before my *pesos* expired, and I came to the conclusion I would expire, as well as my money, en route! I must have more *pesos* at any price. But first I would try the banks. And the first one I approached was eager to take a travelers cheque at the old rate of $4.00. That's one good thing the war has done for me: it has cut down tourist traffic to the point where cheques sell at a premium. I was delighted. The hours between lunch and the time of my return to the police station I spent in walking the streets—up and down, up and down—noting the design of church towers against the sky, the square solid fronts of the houses with their large doors and grilled windows, and the glimpse of patios to be seen through open doors. And in a sentimental moment I sat in a park to reread my letter from *"El Capitán"!* Then I went back to the police. Two new ones questioned me, and they pried into my motives, until I almost felt as if I did have a secret mission! Why was I in Argentina? Why was I alone? Why was I not traveling in the interests of my profession? Did I want to talk over their radio transmitter? Did I write daily to the States? Did I send telegrams? Why was I carrying Chilean documents? Why was my passport in B.A.? Why? Why? Why? And my simple answer that I traveled only because I loved to travel seemed entirely too simple for the grave implications of all these questions. Then they told me frankly that they suspected me of having interest in the politics of their country. What could I say? Just the same old thing, over and over again. But eventually they agreed to return my documents. And I was conducted to the lower regions where another gentleman with a great book bearing my name took down all the details of my appearance, extracted a photograph from me, and conducted me to yet another dept. where yet another man made 4 sets of my fingerprints. Then with a final volley of questions, my things were put in my hands and I was wished *"feliz viaje"!* But I didn't feel like a happy tourist, rather I felt like one with those numbered faces hanging on the walls!

June 12, 1942—Cordoba—Pensión Martinez—8:00 AM

Yesterday morning I felt alone and a little forlorn. The folks of the *pensión* eyed me suspiciously. The folks on the streets passed indifferently. I would go to the tourist office and talk with the pleasant *Rocca*, but he was out. I would stop at the A.C.A. for information about the roads ahead. But I was not a member of the club and my reception was a cool one. So I just walked aimlessly through the streets looking for postcards and *fajas* (sashes). I wanted to see *Tomas* again before leaving, but he hadn't called, and I hesitated to take the initiative. Then as I stepped out of my *pensión* for another walk in the streets, I almost bumped into him! *Que bueno!* We talked at great length, and he promised to return in the afternoon. I felt immeasurably better. At 3:30 he came, and we went out to look at things of interest in the city. There were innumerable old churches to be seen and we went into first one and then another, I with a white handkerchief dangling about my ears, and he with reverent crosses and kneelings. In *la Compañia de Jesus*, we looked at the richly decorated vaults and domes and at the ornate altar carved from cedar by the hands of Indians in the long, long ago. And a *padre* unlocked a great door with a 300-year-old key and showed us a still older chapel, less ornate, more primitive, but not lacking in painted vault and carved woodwork. Beside the *Compañia,* and a part of it, is the university, 2nd oldest in South America. We walked into its patio and out again, and thence past the *Colegio de Monserrat* within whose venerable walls *Tomas* had studied. We stepped into the *Monasterio de los Teresas*, also, another old church, and paused to look at the impressive gray walls of the cathedral and at the *Capillita* as we walked across *Plaza San Martín*. In *La Casa del Virrey,* which is now a historical museum, we spent only 10 minutes in which to see the great spurs, queer stirrups, and other regalia of the colonial period as well as the furniture of another day: chairs with tooled leather seats and backs, ornate pianos and tables, much carved wood. In the *Capilla San Roque* we saw all the little silver offerings to the saint who heals the sick. In the *Merced* we looked at the altar of green onyx from *San Luis*; and in *Santo Domingo* we smiled at the English flags taken from the British in the battles of *Buenos Aires*. As we walked through the streets, we stopped to talk with *Tomás'* friends met en route, and we spent some little time looking for a particular book which *Tomás* wanted to have. Then there was the refreshing pause for coffee in *Calle San Martín* and the visit to one of *Tomás'* friends in a newspaper office where I met *Señor Rocca* again! In the evening we went up to the observatory but found it closed, so we walked back through the bad section of town and along *Plaza Paseo Sobremonte* to look at the *Palacio de Justica.* Back home once more, I felt warmed by the companionship of the afternoon and completely content with my day. I find *Tomás* a very pleasant companion, a gentleman without being forward, a guide with endless patience.

June 13, 1942—Rio Primero—"Bar and Hotel"—7:00 AM

Yesterday morning I decided against an early morning start and a long, long trek. Better to lie in bed until the sun warmed the world. Better to go for another *paseo* with *Tomás.* And in the afternoon I could clip 50 or 60 kms off of the trip to *San Francisco* and then reach that pueblo easily the following day. *Tomás* came early and we climbed up the hill to the art museum where we spent some little time looking at the paintings of artists from *Cordoba.* Many were done in the modern manner. Many showed that they had been inspired by the *Sierras of Cordoba.* None were outstanding. Better than any of the canvasses was the view from the porch of he museum: *Cordoba* in brilliant sunshine. Cream and white walls. And shadows. With the *Sierras* rising beyond. Back at *"Pensión Familiar"* I gathered my things together and packed each in its same old place, a task that has become almost as routine as the turning of pedals. Then I cleaned the grime of the *Sierras* from Chester's black frame, and at 2:00 I said good-bye to the *señor* and *señora* who had been overly affable all day. Pedaling through the heart of *Cordoba* took courage, but I made it! With complete indifference to all who turned on their heels to watch me go! And in a few moments I crossed the river, turned down a back street and stopped at

Pastorino's as *Tomás* had asked me to. Here I met his genial little mother, who made me feel truly welcome in spite of my costume and my unconventional way of travel. And his sister served me coffee. After much visiting and a trip to the parlor to see the family portrait, *Tomás* gave me 2 letters to friends and a handful of photographs, and we all drank a glass of wine to the success of my journey. Then they sent me on my way with a hearty handshake—and a sense of joyousness which lasted all the day. My last view of *Cordoba* was one of a city of sunlight. White walls, red roofs, and, of course, church towers. And I felt reluctant to leave this place I knew for the unknown places ahead. But the open road soon won me, and I felt exhilarated as I whirred along through the brown and the green fields of the country. The withered grasses by the wayside had no counterpart in my spirits. And I looked back with a feeling of familiarity to the range of *Sierras* behind me, watched the sun set behind their sharp silhouette. *Rio Primero* proved more attractive than I had anticipated and a good room added to my contentment. The mustachioed *dueño* of the hotel and all the personnel covered their curiosity with nonchalance and silence, but the townsfolks eyed me through the door as I sat writing in the barroom. And I smiled to myself as I went on writing.

June 14, 1942—San Francisco—Hotel Plaza—7:30 AM

By the shadowy flickering of a pale candle, I prepared for yesterday's trip. But it was light when I pedaled out of *Rio Primero*, and a cloudless sky gave promise of a fine day and a warm sun to drive the chill out of my toes. Eagerly I waited for its appearance, but I was destined never to see it throughout the day. For within a few kilometers a south wind blew in a bank of clouds too deep and gray for the sun to penetrate. And I rode in their shadow, stopping occasionally to walk the life back into my feet. –90 miles of Argentina's level lands. 90 miles of brown fields and green fields. Brown fields where 6-horse teams pulled long discs. Green fields where countless horses and cattle fed. Brown fields dusted with the pale green of new grain shoots. Rich lands these. Only an occasional bit of thorn bush now and most of this preserved as little roadside parks. Houses scattered sparsely across the country. Small towns at long intervals. At noon I secluded myself in a thorn-thicket to eat my bread from *Arroyito* and my *dulce* from *La Cumbre*. But another on the road saw me stop, and he turned and drove back with his horse and high cart. As he climbed through the fence to my hiding place, I received him coldly, and in my iciest Spanish asked, *"Que quiere?"* Smiling he stretched himself out in the dry grass, but to all his questions I answered with a short "yes" or "no", and all the while I conspicuously flashed my knife in and out of the can of *dulce*! Eventually he realized that he was <u>not</u> welcome, and he went his way, leaving me in peace. All day I rode quickly and easily along a smooth and windless way, down a road whose only deviation was an occasional turn to cross the railroad track. And I reached *San Francisco* by mid afternoon. The friendliness of the people, rather than the elegance of the place, attracted me to *Hotel Plaza*, and here I stopped. But shortly I was in the streets again looking for the *señorita* for whom *Tomás* had given me a letter. Unfortunately she was away, so I spent the rest of the day looking about the town—walking through the principal streets and past the large *molino*. And by 8:30 I was more than ready for *cena*!

June 16, 1942—Santa Fé—Hotel Colón—10:00 AM

Day before yesterday, Sunday, was a long and arduous day. No 7th day of rest for me! In the early morning I heard the sound of rain, but I only snuggled deeper in the warmth of my bed. And when it grew light I found the rain had stopped and the weather was warmer than usual. On to *Santa Fé*! Out across the level lands once more! But the clouds lay in long streams and a diffused light from behind them gave life to the greens and browns of those level lands and sharpened the silhouettes of leafless umbrella trees and windmills. Not for long, however. Before noon grayness eclipsed the light and the wind blew stronger and stronger—always *"en contra."* Pedaling became an effort. Cold penetrated to the core. And I knew there was rain in the darker clouds blowing in. I ate a hurried lunch in the protection of a ditch by the side of the road, smearing *dulce* thick on my bread to fortify my body against the cold and the rigors of hard pedaling. Then on into the wet with my slicker flapping uselessly about me and my clothing soaking the rain. *Que linda viajar en bicicleta!* And thus I arrived in the city—all wet and wilted, a dejected figure in a dripping green poncho. My kingdom for a warm hotel! But I took the first one that would have me, and 10 minutes later I was luxuriating in a tub of hot water! Nothing else mattered. I would give up the life of a *viajante* and spend the rest of my life in hot water*!* *Que bueno!* But I did emerge in time for dinner. And straight-away went to bed.

And yesterday the clouds had vanished and the day was clear and cold—so cold that the wind whipping through the streets cut like a knife and there was irony in the brilliance of the sun. First I must know *Santa Fe.* And all morning I walked about the center of town—*Calles San Martín, 25 de Mayo,* and *San Geronimo.* Narrow streets but full of life. In the afternoon I went farther afield. Down *Boulevard Galvez* to the waterfront and along the industrial section. Thence to the far end of town, to the government buildings, and beyond to the park by the water. In the office of the A.C.A., I met a friendly welcome and secured the information which I sought, and this, with the aid of a cup of hot coffee, served to enliven my cold spirits, energized me to the point where I decided to call on *Julio Cesar Bonazzola,* the *señor* I had met in *Trinidad.* I found him in his office in *Calle San Martín,* and he was most hospitable. Showed me all the diplomas and certificates in his office, and he asked me to dine with his family. And at 8:30 I went to his house on Chester, dressed in my best blouse, and with my long coat flapping in the breeze! And there was *Julio* in a fine home with a good wife and 5 children! He was now a family man. No longer the "bad boy" of *Laguna San Rafael*"! He sat beside me at the table, heaping

my plate with good things and after our meal he called up
friends until at least 5 had dropped in to join our group.
Coffee and wine and photographs and much, much talk. An
English Mr. Foster and an Argentine Mr. *Cuneo* who spoke
English. An evening of warmth and contentment. I stayed
until midnight, and then *Señor Cuneo* piloted me home in his
car. Welcome my room after that fast cold ride!

June 17, 1942—Hotel Colón—past midnight

And *Cuneo* told me that he would call to show me
something of the town in the morning but I passed his
promises off as Latin froth, and was very surprised when he
did call—with a car and two friends! Off we went—down
Blvd. Galvez to the river with its bridges and its industry,
passing the ferry slip and the docks, and stopping to eat *asado*
at one of the little open air restaurants for laborers. Then
Cuneo introduced us to the plump and smiling *señora* and to
the old man, telling them with enthusiasm that I had come by
bicycle from California! And between mouthfuls of bread and
meat I had to explain that I had come from Chile. A mariner
who asked a question was also brought forward to be
introduced and he stayed to talk for *un rato*. A handsome man
with the sharp, far-seeing eyes of the sea—eyes which lit up
like sun on the water when he smiled. With hearty hand
shakes we left this place and went on past piles of *quebrado*
logs and metaliferous earth, back to the center of town around
the *plaza* where the governor's palace and the courts of justice
are located, finally arriving at a "butter factory." Here a
kindly old man showed us through the plant which is
completely equipped with modern American machinery. We
saw the bottling machine, the pasteurization tanks, the
revolving butter tanks, the machinery for slicing and wrapping
butter, the freezing machinery, and the cauldron for preparing
dulce de leche. And I came away with the gift of a cube of
butter and a glass of *dulce*. *Despues* I returned to my hotel
and ate a hurried lunch, for I planned to take the 1:30 ferry to
Paraná. But I waited for my bus on the wrong corner, and

when I finally got aboard the right one, I knew I was too late for the ferry. But then on the self same bus was *Cuneo* smiling broadly from behind his little black mustache! He had come to ask questions because he had told the press about me, and they wanted more details! But I wasn't interested in publicity, and tried to evade the questions. As we walked away from the vacant ferry slip, who should we meet but *Julio Cesar*, out for a drive with his wife and oldest boy! And for want of anything else to do, we got in the car and went along. *Julio* stopped to talk with a fisherman—a man with a fine strong face and keen eyes. And we all went to look at the boat club, climbing to the top of the building for a fine view of the *Rio Paraná* and all its flooded lowlands. Thence we drove to *Rincon*, across those same watery lands and past many little houses of rushes, the *ranchos* of the *Criollos*. *Rincon* seemed to be a citrus center with groves of tall trees and with heaps of oranges, mandarins, grapefruit and sweet lemons on every side. *Julio* bought and we all ate! Back in *Santa Fe, Cuneo* took me in hand, and I followed meekly—right into a nest of newspapermen with cameras and pencils! Unhappy day! And they told me that an "American boy from B.A.," wanted to talk to me over the phone. A United Press correspondent! I decided I might as well talk and at least straighten out the misinformation that *Cuneo*, in his enthusiasm, had passed along. So I answered the questions as best I could, smiling at the thought of my friend's words, "I tell lies sometimes, but never mine!" After the newsmen were satisfied, we went to an insurance office where *Cuneo* asked a friend to look out for me while he went to work. But I felt quite able to look out for myself, and after visiting awhile, I took my leave. I visited several churches but found them uninteresting after *Cordoba*, and so I gave up sightseeing and went home to write. Before dinner I walked the length of *San Martín*, for *Cuneo* had said he would meet me "somewhere," but I didn't find him in the streets, so I went home to dine and sleep.

June 18, 1942—San Lorenzo—Hotel Victoria—9:30 PM

And yesterday morning I wakened very early. I would go to *Paraná* on the early ferry, I decided on the spur of the moment. So I hustled out of my warm bed into the cold streets, and at 8:00 I was aboard and moving out onto the river. Away from *Santa Fe* and down the long artificial channel towards the river and the distant huddle of buildings that was *Paraná*. The sun came up a ball of fire, spreading a rosy glow over the muddy water and melting the frost on the decks. Fishing boats on the water and poor little houses on the banks of the canal. And on the ferry, a truck driver who straight-away began to plan an evening with me! I walked away. A river full of brush-clad islands with muddy water lapping about them. A broad river. And it was nearly 2 hrs. before our boat passed the bluffs at the foot of *Paraná*. Hills! Low ones, but hills. With the city following their ups and downs. Until 2:00 I stayed there in the capital of *Entre Rios*, getting to know yet another Argentine city. *Café* in the *Plaza Hotel. Calle San Martín* and *Plaza San Martín*. The cathedral. And finally *Urquiza Park*, draped along the bluffs by the water front. A bright day which sharpened the white buildings of the city, the church towers rising skyward and the boats lying in the harbor. Homeward bound on the ferry I had to ward off the advances of the boat hands, but I found it pleasant to talk with a Frenchman who, like myself, preferred the freshness of the top deck. Back again in my room I turned hungrily to bread and butter, but right in the midst of it the phone rang, and *Cuneo* invited me to tea. I met him at the Ritz where he introduced me to Mr. Brek, "the American boy" from B.A. And over café and pancakes we talked and laughed at great length. *Cuneo's* jokes keep me highly amused, for he tells them in broken Yankee English and laughs with great *gusto* himself. Eventually he had to go back to work, leaving Mr. Brek and me to entertain ourselves, and we made a night of it. First we walked to *Julio's* office where I wanted to return a book and say good-bye. Then we stopped at a *cafeteria* for a drink, and afterwards hunted up a restaurant where we had dinner together. Thence to a movie, a Russian picture with a German theme and Spanish captions! In a theater which advertised *calefacción* but turned off the heat after the crowd was safely inside! As we left the theater who should we meet but *Cuneo* who had been looking for me all evening! So we stopped to have tea together again, laughing over the picture salesman who spoke to us in American slang as we passed. And it was past 1:00 AM when I finally returned to my room.

June 20, 1942—Rosario—Hotel Universal--9:00 AM

Next morning, day before yesterday, I left *Santa Fe, Cuneo* came to see me off and the *dueños* of the *Colón* looked on in stark disapproval. But with wheels under my feet I could run away from all the curiosity and disapproval of the crowds and retreat to the refreshing impersonality of the country. The day was bitterly cold, and the wind from the south blew stronger and stronger cutting through the meager protection of my cotton clothing and decreasing my speed until the hope of reaching *Rosario* had "gone with the wind." The country was more thickly populated now and the towns less forlorn. The richness of the province of *Santa Fe* was everywhere apparent. Good lands producing oranges, grains, truck crops, and rich pastures. There are fewer horseman in this region, fewer of those men with the boots and baggy breeches and with the queer saddles made of two rolls of leather covered with leather and sheepskin pads and possessing round stirrups with a half-moon opening for the toe. But horses and carts are still common, and horses furnish most of the power for farm machinery. I even saw a blindfolded horse trotting around and around to operate a water pump. The publicity I received in *Santa Fe* is bearing fruit already, and people ask me if I am the *Norteamericana* who has come from California by bicycle! Why can't the newspapers and the radio tell the truth? It was just dusk and very cold when I arrived in *San Lorenzo*, and here, with the aid of a couple of highway police, I found a room in the cheerless *Victoria.* It was too cold to shiver in an unheated room until dinnertime, so I lunched on bread and *dulce* and went right to bed to get warm.

And yesterday I came on to *Rosario.* Although I started late, the day was cold, and there was frost on the cabbages and ice on the puddles. It was only a short while until I was in the city, but here I found cobblestone, and bumped painfully along to the center. A confusion of autos and streetcars and bicycles! But I found my hotel easily and was glad to retreat to a bath and conventional clothing. And a good dinner! Then I was ready to see the town. First I went to the English cultural school, the one in which *Zulema Campos (Capilla del Monte)* had been a student, and here I sat by the fire and talked with one of her professors, a dark man from India, who told me that the school had been established to counteract German and Italian propaganda. At 6:00 I returned to visit a class in conversation where old and young were learning to speak English by playing games. And afterwards I walked through the city, drifting automatically into the principal streets where the crowds surged up and down. *Calle Cordoba* and *Calle San Martín.* Narrow streets with bright lights and bright window displays. Streets where people came to look at each other, to talk to their friends, to listen to the newscast. I mingled with the crowd, but a girl can never lose herself in a crowd in Argentina. She is always looked at. And I find it difficult to accustom myself to the stares of the men who look her over from head to heels and who bend down to get a better look at my legs!

June 21, 1942—Rosario—Hotel Universal—8:00 AM

Yesterday morning it was cold and I didn't venture out until 11:00! I'm degenerating into a hot house pansy!— Spend most of my time in bed with a blanket around my shoulders! But when I did venture out, I found a *fiesta* in progress. It was Flag Day, and *Calle Cordoba* was decorated with blue and white bunting, and crowds had gathered in the park in *Avenida Belgrano* to watch the marching of men. I, too, watched the helmets and bayonets and the tramp, tramp, tramp, of many feet moving in unison. But it was the faces that held my interest, in faces of men who kill, not of men who think. After lunch of bread and butter I went further afield in *Rosario*. *Calle San Martín* to *Av. Pellegrini*, from which a collection of vegetable wagons drew me to a further street. Here I found a tremendously big market, encircled with wagons and full of the noise of buying and selling. But it was evidently a wholesale market, for no women were there, and when I walked through, I was so uncomfortably the center of attention that I retreated quickly to the *avenida* where it was proper for a lady to walk! In *Parque Independencia* I enjoyed the trees and gardens and ponds before returning to the center by way of *Blvd. Orono*, with its palatial homes, and *Calle Cordoba*. And then I was ready for a hot bath to soak out some of the chill! Afterwards I sat in the lobby to write. *Cuneo* had said he would come to *Rosario* Saturday, and perhaps he would. I would wait. And sure enough, in he came! With the same happy smile and with *recuerdos* and a newspaper article for me! We talked, stopped for an elaborate tea at the Palace, walked in *Calle Cordoba*, and returned to my hotel where we talked some more. A pleasant evening.

June 22, 1942—Pergamino—Hotel Sarmiento—8:00 PM

Yesterday morning I wrote again, waiting for *Cuneo* who had said he would come, but in good Latin style hadn't said when! At 11:00 he appeared with a nephew and again we visited, and he invited me to the football game in the afternoon. What a game! We stood up for all of the 90 minutes; everybody stood. And the crowd shouted with great enthusiasm. Injured players lay as if dead on the field, while one man ran out to them with a suitcase and another followed with a hot water bottle. A little water sprinkled on the head brought them back to life as good as new! Men who scored were lovingly mobbed by their fellows. And the referee was mobbed without love when he called fouls. Players shook their fingers vociferously in his face! I found the game very entertaining and the crowd equally so. Score: Rosario—4, B.A.—0. And no necks or legs were broken! After the game, *Cuneo* introduced me to his *señora,* and the 3 of us went together to the center for tea. A warm *confiteria* with delicious cakes and steaming drinks. The afternoon's refreshment—which I have come to like so well. But after tea, *Cuneo* and his wife returned to *Santa Fe,* and again I was alone in the city. And I felt doubly alone. For awhile I mingled with the life in *Calles Cordoba* and *San Martín.* But shortly I went back to my hotel to write letters, for I feel less lonely when I visit on paper. Another guest at the hotel approached me, and we talked for some time in English. He had been to the States but was now connected with the *Departmento de Hacienda* of the government. We went out for coffee and *panqueques* American style (!) and stopped by to see the night club with the tropical atmosphere—the *"Caribe."* And it was past midnight when I finally got to bed.

But I wakened at 7:00 this morning, as is my wont. And the weather was warmer, Allah be praised! --Back to the road once more, the old restlessness of spirit moving me forever on. *Rosario* was wrapped in fog when I left my hotel, and when I went down along *Avenida Belgrano* to see the waterfront, I found the river completely hidden in gray. Only the cranes were discernible, dark silhouettes in the mist. In a short while I made my way out of the cobblestones of the city and rolled freely down the open road. Once again my way followed the River *Paraná,* but as before I saw it seldom. A few rises in that level land brought it into view, and then it was gone again. Rich loads beside the river. Fruit trees and truck crops. And the mists rose and the sun brightened the dead corn stalks and the leafless trees. Only thin clouds veiled the sky this day—so different from the wild, billowing masses of the trip from *Santa Fé* to *San Lorenzo.* As I approach B.A. the towns are larger and more frequent, and I do not want for hotels. In *Villa Constitucion* I stopped for *café con leche* and later I bought oranges to slack the bitter sweetness of *desayuno.* But most of the day I traveled steadily on, and I reached *Pergamino* comparatively early, for the head winds

were less strong than before. But I was weary, none the less.
After a bath, I wandered through the streets and down to the
plaza where the tall church steeple rose dark against a darker
sky. But long before dinner I was here in my hotel, hungrily
waiting for the savory meat and soup. And now I lingered by
the stove, too comfortably warm to move.

June 23—San Antonio de Areco—Hotel Plaza—8:00 PM

        Last night after a hearth meal, I slept the sleep of the
dead, waking this morning at 8:00, which is late for me. And I
hurried into my clothes so as to get back to the road before too
late. Outside was a dense mist, but I didn't mind because it
insulated the world against bitter cold, and I could ride without
iciness in my hands and feet. But the wind still blew, a strong
head wind which held me back like a gigantic force and
necessitated a tremendous pressure on the pedals. And when
the mist turned to rain, which the wind whipped through my
clothing, I looked for a place where I could take *desayuno*. In
Viña I found it, the far corner of a dark bar room which I
shared with truck drivers! But the jugs of coffee and milk and
the loaf of bread tasted like nectar of the gods! Thereafter I
rode without stopping. Across vast pasture lands dotted with
cattle and horses and an occasional clump of trees to mark the
presence of a house. Into the wind. Terrain which gently rose
and fell. Frequent *arroyos* with sluggish streams. And here,
as in all parts of Argentina, a multiplicity of bird and animal
life. Little rodents without tails scamper across the road.
There are strange round mud nests perched on posts. And
flocks of birds hover over the newly turned earth where pass
the eight-horse teams. I see yellow and rusty-colored birds,
birds with long necks, birds with long legs, hawks, owls,
countless birds--. Here at *S.A. de Areco* the police stopped
me, and when they discovered I had no *patente*, they took me
"inside" for questioning. But after a little conversation they
shook my hand and bid me "*vaya bien*"! Although it was not
late, I was quite ready to stop here, and after a short *paseo* in

the *pueblo*, I went to bed to rest before dinner! Pedaling against the wind is beginning to tell on me!

June 28, 1942—Buenos Aires—Jan's--Anasco 4

Buenos Aires at last! And such a round of activity that I have given up writing for all of 5 days! My diary lapses while I flit from one thing to another without an interval of solitude. On the 24th I left *San Antonio de Areco* in the heavy mists of early morning—left that nice little town with the narrow streets, compact buildings, neat *plazas*, and *vistas* of rolling plains beyond. Wet streets, and a gray day. And wind again! Before reaching *Pilar*, I stopped for *desayuno* in a bar where the floors were sawdust strewn and a crowd of youngsters were noisily gambling. Then on to B.A., non-stop through the country which gradually lost its vastness and became more intimate. In *San Miquel* the *camineros* stopped me, asked for my *patente*, ushered me in to explain to the chief. But our conversation grew sociable, the *patente* was forgotten, and I was asked to dine with the *camineros*. A couple of us sat down at a table covered with newspapers and littered with the food and dirty dishes left by others and we dined on *puchero*—a great dish of it—and soup, with bread and wine. And I tried to be nonchalant as I used my second-hand silverware! All the while the others stood by asking questions and making jokes at which they laughed but which I only half understood. From their office I called Jan by phone and was amazed when I actually heard her voice. But I was relieved by the warmth of her reception and my doubt as to whether or not I should go to her home were melted away. With voluminous directions and handshakes all around, I left the *camineros* and turned into the outskirts of the city. A crossroads brought me to a halt, and I sought directions from more *camineros*. More questions—and a glass of water and a cup of hot milk to cheer me on my way. More directions too! Turning and dodging in the city destroyed my assurance, and I stopped to ask the way of a policeman. More questions and directions! I thought I'd never get to Jan's! Cobblestones also. But the excitement of traffic stepped up my speed. In *Rividivia* an aristocratic-looking couple stopped their car to ask me if I'd come from North America and they spread out a map and told me exactly how to reach Jan's! A few more blocks and I arrrived. A modern apartment with the same old Jan! and a genuine welcome. A bath, clean clothes, and 2 letters from home! And an evening of visiting with Jan and making the acquaintance of her husband and child.

On the 25th Jan hustled around and set her house in order so as to take me downtown. My first day in the heart of B.A. Subways, tall buildings, smart shops, and crowds of well-dressed people. A great city with the atmosphere of a great city. At the U.S. consul's I learned I'd have to go elsewhere to get my passport. In the Bank of Boston I found I could still change traveler's cheques at a good rate. And at *Expreso Villalonga* I found mail. Mail! More than 30 letters from family and friends! Happy day! In the afternoon Ines Rosenbusch came, and we went back downtown to pick up her car at the garage and to go once more for my passport. At the office of immigration we found it, and I took it back into my possession with a sense of relief. We drove along the waterfront and past the dock. Ships and cranes and cargo— that exciting part of a city which has in it the romance of far away places. And the great expanse of yellow water which is the *Rio de la Plata*. Back up town to the U.S. consul once again, for I must begin at once to get the necessary visas for further travel. And then to the Omega Club for tea—high up in a tall building where one can look over the jumble of Renaissance domes and square modern towers which make up the city and out across the port to the *La Plata*. Over all yellow haze from the burning of corn in place of coal— symptom of the maladjustment of a war-torn world. Back home, Mrs. Rosenbusch, Jan's mother-in-law, and Martha Mendez dropped in to visit. And with all the activity of the day, I had to sit up very late in order to read to the end of my many, many letters—welcome letters from Chile and Panama and the States.

On the 26th I was fired with a desire to answer letters, and all morning I wrote, visiting with friends whose letters brought them close to me. At noon we all went over to the Rosenbusch house for dinner and there I met the doctor and other members of the family and I found myself in the midst of a delightful family group. Five people whose hospitality reached out and took me in—and whose merriment was contagious. A dark room warmed by an open fire; a tiny walled garden where each plant was a special friend; a long table which symbolized the unity of all who belonged to that home. In the afternoon I returned here to a tea which Jan gave for a couple of American women –Mrs. Shilenburger and Mrs. Hopkins. And we spent an American afternoon with English and open-faced sandwiches. Later Mrs. Rosenbusch and her sister dropped in, and there was visiting until 8:00 PM. But after all had gone and we had had our dinner, I went back to letter writing in the quiet of the night.

Saturday, the 27th, I called up some of the folks whom I had met along the way and who had asked me to look them up in B.A. The voices of Erwin Minder and the mother of *Hugo Bassi* sounded familiar, and I was sorry to say "no" to invitations to meet them in the afternoon, but the day was fine and we had planned to go to the zoological garden. But Jan was slow to get things done and the child caused a commotion and by the time we finally got underway, it was too late to go anywhere! So we had tea at the Rosenbusch's and spent a pleasant evening in that very pleasant home. Then at 9:00 we all went off to have dinner, with the Hopkins and the Shilenburgers—dinner at *La Cabana* where the steak was 2 in. thick and where we had a mixed grill of *chinchulines* and other assorted organs and where we topped off the meal with a baked Alaska which looked like one of Greenland's icy mountains!

July 2, 1942—Buenos Aires—Jan's Anasco 4

Sunday, June 28, was a family day with the Rosenbusch's. Early in the morning *Inés* came with "Tanti

Trudy" and the 3 of us joined them in a trip to *Tigre*. A beautiful day. We drove out a long way in the car—out of the city limits, along *Av. General Paz*, and out to the section where are all the boat clubs, dozens of them, one for every nationality. Jan, *Carlos*, and I went by launch to *La Marina*, a large and imposing club where we took out a row boat for our trip to *Tanti Anitas*. The boat was a light little thing which skimmed along without any effort, and Carlos and I rowed the 7 kms. to *Tanti Anitas* island very easily. It was a pretty trip too, along a narrow waterway with other boats and past numerous islands, all separated by little canals. Disembarked at the island, we met *Inés* and the 2 aunts, and we went for a walk out to the plum and apple orchards. Here the delta land has been cleared and canals dug for drainage, and the rich soil produces good fruit. We had dinner then in the house on stilts with everyone chattering happily. And afterwards we went for another *paseo* in the orchards. Huge snails lay by the canals, their insides eaten by birds. And in the trees were the silk cocoons of insect pests. Though its winter, *no mas*, pussy willows were out, and Jan gathered many for the house. Before leaving we had a bountiful tea with the "*tantis*," and then Jan, *Inés, Carlos*, and I rowed back to the club with a cargo of oranges and apples. This time the current was with us, and we traveled amazingly easily. A hot shower at the club and back into the city as the sun set and the moon rose. Through old *San Isidro* where all the buildings are built one against the other. At the Rosenbusch's we had our supper, a large and happy family group, and afterwards played tiddlywinks until time to come home to *Anasco*. A fine *dia de fiesta*.

June 29th we again went to the Rosenbusch's, this time for *almuerzo*, but I did not go until late, for I wanted to write letters and I left after dinner in order to be in *Anasco* when Erwin Minder of the *Copiapó* arrived. What fun it was to meet an old shipmate again and although I had not known him well before, I felt as if he was now an old friend! We went down to the waterfront for a walk, looking out across the *La Plata* and watching the boats in the harbor. Two great gray ships bore the flags of Norway, and several were painted with the blue and yellow of Sweden. Back up town we stopped for tea at the New China. Cakes and music and walls painted with scenes from Peking. And thereafter we went to a movie on Custer's last stand and a picture [set] in Shanghai. *Norte Americanos* would have gone home by the time the show was over, but it was time for dinner in B.A! So we stopped for soup and a cutlet! I find Erwin very congenial for he likes sport and travel which are so dear to my heart. And my heart skipped a beat when he slipped his hand into mine! Neither did I sleep so well as is my wont!

June 30th was a day of inactivity. Not once did I venture out, but I watched it rain from Jan's comfortable apartment. And spoiled baby Dorley made enough commotion inside to vary the monotony. I wrote letters, mended, and hoped for a phone call which didn't materialize. And at 6:00 my friend *Hugo Bassi* whom I met in *Mendoza*, came to call. It was fun to see him again and he talked long to *Carlos* and Jan who understand so much better than I. But after dinner I went right to bed, exhausted from an emotional strain.

Yesterday, July 1, was also a day of inactivity. I'm degenerating into a lounge hound! In the morning, I wrote and wandered aimlessly about because my eyes bothered me; and after dinner I actually took a *siesta*. Then there was tea with *Martita* as a guest, and after supper *Inés* came with the car and we all went to a movie—a very bad one.

July 7, 1942—Buenos Aires—Jan's

Thursday, July 2, was warm, praise be to Allah!—And memorable because Erwin asked me out for the evening. I met him at his office in *Corrientes*, and after wandering about the streets, including narrow *Calle Florida* with its fine shops and crowds of promenaders, we went up to his *pensión* in *Santa Fé*. Here I looked at photographs which took me back to days in Japan, and then we had dinner there in the room with Erwin's roommate, a young Japanese. All very pleasant.

Afterwards we went to town, spending the evening in *"Sevilla"* where there was Spanish music and dancing and where the waiter who served our tea wore an atmospheric costume. I felt very gay there amidst the crowd, and I enjoyed the evening no end.

I can't remember what happened July 3rd, so it must not have been a very outstanding day! In the afternoon *Inés* came with the car and Jan and I took Dorley to the doctor. Afterwards, we two went to the Methodist Church bazaar and where Jan stocked up with miscellaneous supplies.

The fourth of July was cold enough to be Christmas! Sharp and bitter. But when Carlos came home from work, we all went off to the Zoological gardens. Myriad of birds, many native to Argentina. And interesting animals from these parts. Long-legged red foxes, strange rabbits with long, thin legs; huge guinea pigs; small ostriches; *peccaries vicuñas*; *llamas*. And an anteater wandered at large, a "feather duster" as Carlos called it! After tea we came home, but we stopped at the neighborhood market where I stayed with *Carlos* to look at the fruits and vegetables and all the various meats. Such quantities of meat! All freshly killed. Counters selling tripe and intestines and brains and livers! And stalls where chickens were killed and dressed "while you wait." We also stopped to look at the assorted meats and the endless variety of cakes in a *confeteria*. And we ate a slice of hot bread topped with cheese and tomato in a specialty shop.

Sunday was another family day. At noon we all gathered at the Rosenbusch's where we had a delicious turkey dinner. Such a mad house of conversations!—With every one talking at the same time and with me understanding only about half of the machine-gun Spanish! Afterwards *Inés, Carlos, Marta, Enrique*, and I went for a *paseo* in the car. We stopped to look at the Congress building en route and to see the fountain with its bronze horses. And then we continued to the port. In *Puerto Nuevo* were crowds of people, for here some of Argentina's war ships were open to inspection. *Enrique* was not satisfied until he found a former colleague who would take us to see the engines. But we never got any farther than the officer's lounge where we had a cup of coffee and passed the time of day! Then back to the Rosenbusch's for tea and finally home to the apartment for supper.

Yesterday was a quieter day, one of the days that passes and leaves no memories in its wake. Just writing and reading and the daily round of living in the family of the younger Rosenbusch.

July 16, 1942—La Plata—Hotel Savoy—10:00 AM

Unrecorded weeks are slipping by me now, for the soft life of the city dissipates my will to write. On Tuesday, July 7, I made a weak effort to entertain by asking Jan, Carlos and Erwin to have dinner with me downtown. We all met at the *"La Estancia,"* and after letting Erwin know that we'd probably be late, we actually were on time and had to wait for him! Sitting on hide covered chairs, we consumed the thickest, tenderest steaks I've ever encountered. But the show we went to afterwards wasn't quite so successful. Greta Garbo in a comedy slightly risqué! To top off the evening, Carlos invited me to have coffee at the *Confiteria Ideal.*

On Wednesday, July 8, I finally got around to working on my good Chester who has stood deserted for so long. In the seclusion of the basement, I set to work taking off the wheels and washing away the dirt and grease of Chile and Argentina. After lunch, with hands still grimy, I went downtown on business. Went to the bank to inquire about getting more money from home (!), went to the American consul, and then dashed off to see if I might recover my passport at *Dorsena Norte*, but I arrived after hours! At 4:30 I met Jan in *Corrientes*, and after tea we went shopping, surging along with the crowds until after nightfall when the city was gay with lights. After supper at home, we went out for a walk with *Carlos*, down busy *Rivadavia* to a shop where we all had hot *pisa*.

Thursday, *Nueve de Julio*, was Argentina's great day—a holiday with festivities and parading and homage to *San Martín*, for on July 9, 1816, independence came to

Argentina. *Inés* came for dinner and afterwards, she and *Carlos* and I drove to the line of parade to watch the marching men. Such a mob! Humanity, so deep, that it was impossible to see the street! But we found a bit of high ground which gave us a vantage point, and even I could see the parade when it came. Hundreds of men in gala. Infantry, cavalry, artillery. Bright uniforms, fine horses, faded flags which had seen the march of history. An impressive display of the military power of this proud country. While across the street civilians pushed and crowded, and mounted police mercilessly rode them back. Then came a shower of rain which melted away the crowds and we secured a place in the front row! And here we stayed until the last division rode past, their blue and white banners vivid against the gray sky. As we drove back into the city we passed the port where every boat was gay with flags. And, appropriately we stopped in *Avenida 9 de Julio* to have tea at *El Gitano*! Afterwards we returned to the elder Rosenbusch's for dinner, another of those noisy, amiable family gatherings with their good-humored banter and their spirit of unity. And still later *Inés* drove a crowd of us back to the city to see the lights which blaze only on the 25th of May and the 9th of July, *Plaza de Mayo*, was lovely with all its buildings illuminated— *La Casa Rosada, El Cabildo, la catedral*, and best of all, *el Banco Nacional*. And other parts of the city were gayer than usual.—A great day, *el Nueve de Julio*.

Friday, July 10, was another quiet day. In the morning, I went to market with Jan and stood by while she bought meat and vegetables from the various stalls and counters, and then I walked with the baby by way of helping with the household. In the afternoon, I went to town to try and recover my passport from *Inmigración*, but after spending an hour in walking from office to office, I learned that I must come back another day. Then I looked for a friend who wasn't in, shopped for a good belt which I couldn't find, and returned home disgusted with my day's accomplishments! In the evening, John, a cousin, came to dinner, and he kept us amused with his tales of his 3 children.

Saturday, July 11, I went back to Chester again—finished cleaning him up, put him back together and surveyed his gleaming frame with satisfaction. He was ready for the road once more. And in the afternoon, Jan and I went for another *paseo* with *Carlos*. –By subway to *Calle Callao*, and thence on foot along that street to *Recoleta*. Here we spent considerable time walking amongst the monuments and reading the names of noted persons. I was amazed to find the crypts so large and to see the caskets standing in elegantly decorated rooms. Best of all I liked the fine doors. There were old brick monuments, narrow and tall, and great new monuments of marble—all crowded together as if it were a privilege to lie in *Recoleta* and many insisted on occupying a bit of its small space. Names great in history were on the tombs, and names of wealth. Hundreds of thousands of *pesos* devoted to the memory of the illustrious dead.

Sunday, July 12—to the Rosenbusch's again. And after dinner we all drove to the museum of natural history. Here for an hour we looked at birds and animals of Argentina and also at some ethnological collections. But the museum is new and only a few things are on display. On the way home we stopped at a *panaderia* for *media* and *lunas*, and who should we meet there but *Tanti Anita* and Mrs. Merlynoff who asked us to their house for tea. What a house, the house of Merlynoff! Rooms so elegantly furnished that one walked on tip toe and spoke in a whisper! Mirrors, crystal candelabras, orchids. And we had tea in the basement! For dinner, we returned to the Rosenbusch's, and we topped off the day with a show, "*Que Verde Era Mi Valle*" with a short on *Nahuel Huapi*. The latter even drew out Dr. Rosenbusch, who seldom goes to the movies.

Monday, July 13, I just lived, *no mas*. In the morning, I gave Chester the final touches and worked over my equipment—symptoms of a growing desire to return to the road once more. And in the evening, I screwed up my courage and phoned Brok, the American boy of *Santa Fé*. His voice was hospitable at the other end of the wire and he laughed with the same old gusto. We talked for at least an hour—the longest phone conversation I've ever had! But I guess that's to be expected of a telephone man!

Tuesday, July 14, was a day of great goings on. In the morning, Mrs. Rosenbusch came to help Jan prepare for a tea party, and I took Dorley out to the park for an airing. Then I went home with "Aunt Dora" for lunch, and afterwards we went off to *Inmigracion* to see about my elusive passport once more. Thence began a round of office hunting, the same thing I had gone through before. From *Mesa de Entradas* to *Disembarco* to *Estadistica* to the *Secretario* to *Señor Carnevale* and back again to the beginning for a second round! I got the giggles. But finally we found a *señor* who knew where my passport was, and we learned that it had been held up because my name was not on the list of those who had entered Argentina Feb. 13. "Come back again later!" From *Darsena Norte* I hurried home to Jan's tea and here I met a crowd of Rosenbusch's relatives. We drank tea and sampled cakes, and they talked and I listened. But at 7:00 I could linger no longer, so I said good-bye and "*tanto gusto*" and rushed off to meet Erwin. He met me at Peru station, and we went to his *pensión* for dinner. A friend of his came too, one Ernest P., and we had such a jolly time talking that we spent the evening there instead of going to a show. Much more fun. And I still smile at the memory of Ernest's tales of his experiences on the farm! Erwin and I stopped for tea in *Caballito*, just next door to home, and when he finally left me in *Anasco*, I found myself locked out. –Had to wake the household in order to get to bed!

Wednesday, July 15, saw me back on the road again! For a short trip only, but with the same old exhilaration. As I packed my things, I loitered, for I always find it hard to leave a place where I have stayed long enough to feel at home. But once I was in my *pantalones* and felt the turning of pedals under my feet, my spirits reacted with their usual verve. Through the heart of B.A. I rolled, ignoring all the stares and remarks. Down *Rivadavia*, on foot across *Plaza Once*, and off along *Paseo Colón*. I had no difficulty making my way through the heavy traffic with its hell-bent *colectivos*, but I crossed the interminable cobblestone which jolted one until he feels like egg nog. As I left the dingy, outlying districts of B.A. and entered the country, I breathed deeply again and felt the thrill of the wide open spaces. Green grasses and trees, and rich soil bearing carefully tended truck crops. I felt like a colt just turned out to pasture. How good to be again amongst the growing things. And to add to my contentment, the road was made of shaped cobblestone laid in fan-like patterns, not the rough stones of the city. At dusk I reached *La Plata*, and a friendly policeman directed me into the city. A pleasant gas station man also answered my questions. And with all this help I arrived at the Savoy Hotel with little trouble. Here I changed and walked the streets a bit before dining on a dozen apples and flopping into bed. I was weary after a night of visiting and afternoon of travel.

July 17, 1942—La Plata—Carmen's--48-756—2:00 PM

Yesterday morning it rained and I slept late and devoted much time to writing. Then as the rain cleared and my eyes tired, I went out to make the acquaintance of *La Plata*. In front of the hotel was *Plaza San Martín*, formally arranged and beautifully cared for, and bearing in its center the inevitable monument to the famous general. In the town are many large and imposing buildings. *La casa del gubierno, la legislatura, el teatro Argentino, los tribunales, la municipalidad, la universidad.* But the general feeling is of lowness, for there are few tall buildings. And this feeling is emphasized by wide streets. Tree lined many of the streets, and just now there are trees hanging full of oranges in some of the *calles*. Very pretty. I wandered leisurely on my way thinking to look for another cheaper hotel, but I looked up *Hugo Bassi's* address, and here I have been ever since. *Hugo* was away, *que lastima*, but his aunt, *Carmen*, was here, and she took me right in. We had *almuerzo* together, and then we went to her club where she played for 2 hours and I looked on. Then we had tea together and looked for a room for me without success, so she asked me to come here. And after supper of *pisa* we went to the Savoy, collected my things, and pushed Chester back to *Calle 48*. Here *Carmen* fixed a bed for me on the floor, and after a couple of oranges we went to bed, she to knit and I to write. I am very content here, for I have company to talk Spanish once again.

July 18, 1942—La Plata—Carmen's at 48-756—9 PM

Yesterday, the 17th, I had a fine time doing nothing. *Carmen* and I slept late and after coffee she tended to the house and I went off to the post office. Then it was time for *almuerzo!* And we dined out to save housework. In the afternoon we ran a few errands coming home for *mate* and later for chocolate and *churros*. The *mate* we took in good Argentine fashion—from a gord full of *yerba*, sugar and hot water—both using the same *bombilla!* In the evening, *Carmen* invited a friend to join us, and after promenading for a while, we stopped at a *confiteria* for a *copetina*. Here we passed much time sipping vermouth and spearing olives, potato salad, cheese, and shellfish with toothpicks. And afterwards we stopped for *pisa* and muscatel wine! Then a bit more promenading before we returned to our beds, our nightly fruit, and our respective knitting and writing.

Today we have also done a lot of nothing. Got up at 10:00! And went out to find a glorious spring day giving brilliance to all the light colored buildings of the town. A few more errands and a visit to some of *Carmen's* relatives. Then back again to the *Teritoria* for another hearty meal. *Despues* we went to "the club," but while Carmen sported there to maintain her figure, I chose to walk in the sun. And I wandered off to *"el bosque"* where there were trees and grass and folks out to enjoy the day, afoot, on bicycle and in autos. Returning early to the club, I watched the playing of volleyball, basketball, and *pelota con paletas*, and there I took a welcome hot shower along with Carmen. The balance of the evening was spent in a *confiteria* over *copetinas* of vermouth and the usual peanuts, potato chips, and party sandwiches.

And now we're back to our beds again, knitting and writing. What a life!

July 20, 1942—La Plata—Carmen's—48-756—9:30 PM

Our lives a round of *paseando, comiendo, y durmiendo*—so we pass the time, Carmen and I. Yesterday we got up early—at 9:00! And often chocolate for me and *mate* for her, we went to mass, mass in the great cathedral in *Plaza Morena*, with me carrying *un libro de misas* and wearing a black lace veil! A gothic cathedral with pointed arches rising skyward, but lacking the mellowness of old glass and worn stone. Here the populous knelt while *padres* chanted and Helen looked on, wondering at the intricate form enveloping Catholicism. And afterwards we went below to see the casket containing the remains of *Rocho*, the founder of *La Plata*. After church it was time to eat again and we indulged in *raviolis* and *asado* at the "American Bar"! Then off to the museum which is considered one of the best in South America. Here were fine collections of shells and minerals and prehistoric animals which I found very interesting. And when we left it was so late that we hadn't time to go to the football game! But we did walk past the playing fields, which were packed with enthusiastic spectators, before returning to the center for *el cine*. Here we met *Carmen's* friend, Fannie, and spent the rest of the day watching 2 films, one a ridiculous Hollywood product, and one a very good Argentine movie. All the rest of the townspeople went to the show too, and the house was packed! And when we left, the streets were lined with young men looking at the *chicas!* Such is the life of the Latins. From the movie we went to the Teutonia for beer and *fiambres*, and after that we were ready to come home to our knitting and writing.

Today was another day of great doings. Got up early again—*a las ocho y media!* And went off to meet Fannie Resnicovsky. She took us to see the *Colegio Maria Auxiliadora,* a Catholic school for girls, and here *la Hermana*

Directora showed us all through the institution with its large paved patio and its light, airy dormitory. In the classrooms the girls all stood up and said *"Buenos dias,"* and laughed as the director joked with them. I was introduced as a professor from California and felt like exhibit "A" as the youngsters eyed me curiously but in the chapel I was most awkward. Here *Carmen* practically had to pull me to my knees by the back of my coat! From the school we went to the cemetery with its many *bovedas*—elegant marble mausoleums housing the caskets for the dead and the monument of the living. Carmen took flowers to the tomb of *Vuotto* and showed me where her *padres* rested, the mother and father on the first floor and the others in a vault below. An elegant hand-made curtain hung at the door and hand worked cloths covered the caskets. Nothing seemed too fine or too costly for the dead. Leaving the cemetery, we went back to dine in town, to the *"Era"* where we spent 2 hrs. over *polenta*, an Italian dish of corn meal. Then the afternoon being fine, we went off to walk in the *bosque* where we had our pictures taken by one of those professionals that haunt all places frequented by the people. Here we looked about the sporting clubs too, places where folks go to participate in their favorite sport. And later, after tea at Carmen's, we went to Fannie's for a cup of cherry brandy, followed by an excursion up town for *pisa*!

July 27, 1942—Jan's—8:00 PM

Tuesday, July 21, I came back again to the city where there is so little tranquillity that I cannot write. A fond farewell to Carmen and I rolled away, stopping only once to answer the questions of a curious policeman. I took time to go down to the port, but the shabby environs, and the few boats seemed depressing and I didn't like the scum who loitered there so I hastened away. --Back to the road to B.A. and to the refreshing country. Presently, I was in the city again, battling with the unpredictable traffic. Cobblestones, *colectivos*, detours, and people who turned on their heels to watch me pass! Even the sophisticated *porteños* find me a curiosity!

Welcome the refuge at Anasco 4! And the bath and the settled feeling of being home.

Wednesday, July 22nd, I went downtown. In the afternoon because official offices seem to open only in the afternoon and with Jan because I needed reinforcement for my incomplete Spanish. First we tackled *Darsena Norte* and *Inmigracion*, where once again we made the rounds to *Mesa de Entradas* to *Disembarco* to the offices *arriba*. And at last, praise be to Allah, someone there seemed to know about my passport, and when I said I needed it, he made an effort to hurry it through for me. I was so used to being asked to come back again that I was amazed to actually find myself walking out with that indispensable green document! A trip to the Brazilian and Uruguayan consulates yielded nothing, and after *panqueques* and milk and a bit of window-shopping, we came home in time to fix up and rush over to the Rosenbusch's for dinner. A pleasant evening with the family and with Mrs. Hopkins and Shellenberger.

Thursday, I went off to town again, this time for the whole day. To the Boston Bank for *plata* and to see the Uruguayan consul, who, after asking my nationality assured me that there were no difficulties involved in entering his country. The war and the alignment of the South American republics on the side of the Allies seems to have facilitated travel for me. At 12:30 I met Brok and a friend and we all had lunch together, followed by café at the American Bar. Brok is his same old jovial self, but I didn't like his friend, so I wasn't sorry when we parted at 2:00. Later I came away from the Uruguayan tourist office with a load of literature, and at 4:00 I met *Inés* who took me to the A.C.A. where I received even more literature! I feel so indebted to *Inés* for the time she has devoted to me that I took this opportunity to ask her to tea, and then I embarrassed her by almost not tipping the waiter!

Friday, July 24, I had to go to a doctor in order to get a certificate of good health to present to the Brazilian consul, and for lack of another better, I went to Dr. *De La Torre* recommended by the consul. After assuring me that a girl never went alone to an Argentine doctor, Jan accompanied me.

We were ushered in ahead of everyone else and after one look at my robust self, the doctor wrote out the document without further ado. Then he held Jan's hand and put his arm around me. Price: $5.00! With a little time left, we went to a couple of bike shops to inquire about *gomas*, but they were so scarce that I put off buying, and we hurried home to prepare for a company dinner. *Poncho* and Kiki came for the evening much to *Carlos'* disgust when he found Dorley coming down with a cold.

Yesterday, July 25th, after pondering the tire situation, I decided to buy at once, and I went back to a shop I knew to purchase a Dunlop. Went by bike too, getting plenty of excitement out of racing with the traffic, but per usual, I ignored the whistling, shouting multitude. For dinner I went to the Rosenbusch's who were having a special feast of *asado*, and the lamb that was flattened by cutting down the middle and then roasted over coals in the patio, was perhaps the most delicious meat I have ever tasted. I like the freshly killed meat of Argentina ever so much better than the aged meat at home; it's tastier and more tender. After dinner *Inés* invited me to the *Colón* Theater to hear Brailowsky in a piano concert. And in mended stockings and a borrowed hat I joined the crowd that streamed through the theater doors. Women whose appearance had been ordered and reordered and who gave the impression that every movement was disastrous to the set of the curl and the hang of the fur. We climbed up to a plush-like box where we looked out on the great red and gold horse-shoe of the theater with its seven tiers of humanity, and I felt very elegant, as I looked down on the packed house where all were listening in absolute silence to the notes from the flying fingers of the artist. The appreciation of the audience was genuine, and thundering applause brought Brailowsky back for many encores. I was impressed.

August 1, 1942—Buenos Aires—Anasco 4—10:00 AM

Sunday, July 26, I went to the *Bassi* home for dinner, and I had a delightful visit there in that middle-class family. I hadn't seen the *señor* nor the *señora* since *Mendoza*, and they seemed like old friends! *Hugo* was there too as well as his brothers and 2 cousins, and I was surprised to find *Carmen* in B.A. What fun to chatter in Spanish again and to be a part of an Argentine family. Not truly *Criollo*, for the father is Italian, but typically Argentine because of its admixture of blood. According to Latin custom, we visited at the table long after the meal was cleared away. And then we went for a *paseo* in nearby *Palermo* park. A beautiful sunny afternoon which brought crowds to the out-of-doors and which had something of spring in its softness in spite of the fact that trees and rose bushes had not yet come to life. Only the flowering quince gave promise of what was to come. We walked through the rose gardens and to the Spanish patio, all of tile, and around the lake. And then it was time to go home for tea and cakes! After another hour of visiting around the table, it was time for us to leave, and I came back in a packed colectivo—one of those little buses which travel with such speed and abandon, typical of B.A.

Monday, July 27, dawned ominously warm, and rain and wind came to mar the day. In the afternoon I ventured out to the Brazilian consul and walked through the grayness to *Retido* Station to try and find a *guia*. But I had no success, and I came home a bit depressed. The weather and my spirits had conspired to dull the brilliance of B.A. with her fine white buildings and her many wide avenues. And an indefinable restlessness was urging me back to the open road.

Tuesday, July 28, was a beautiful day. Once again B.A. weather had given proof of its changeability! And after dinner I pedaled off on Chester to meet *Hugo*. En route some young blade snapped to attention and with raised hand, shouted "Heil Hitler" as I passed! Again I was reminded that I look very much like a German. *Hugo* was waiting with a borrowed bike and the 2 of us rolled away to *Tigre*—Through *Palermo* and *San Isidro* on excellent roads and stopping at *Las Barrancas* to go down to the beach and the yacht harbor. Clear sunlight that danced on the water, on the white boats, on the white buildings of B.A. further down the river. And a fresh feeling in the air that sent us racing on our way. How exhilarating to pedal along together, handle bars low, pedals turning easily, wheels whirring rapidly! The never-ending thrill of cycling. In *Tigre* we rode beside the canals past anchored boats and deserted clubhouses, and we followed one road leading out into uncleared delta land, over-grown with willow. There with a glass of "toddy" and a piece of "budin," we raced back to B.A., stopping only in pretty *San Isidro* to go inside the church. I came in hot and late, and bathed and dressed breathlessly before rushing away to meet Nick Shriber who waited for me downtown. We went to the Boston Bar to pick up the rest of "the boys" before going out for the evening and here Harry Bateson and Charlie Merten joined us over gin tonics and peanuts, potato chips, and pastries. Then after a look at the bowling alley and the games upstairs, we went to the City Hotel to pick up Arthur Martin and to have another round of drinks. We picked up another girl here, much to my relief, and thus, with the party complete, we went to dine at Coraggio's in *Entre Rios*. *Helados* in an atmosphere of merriment with singing waiters who flirted with all the girls and accepted drinks from everyone. They even sang "A Bicycle Built for Two" in broken English! For variety we decided to go elsewhere for café and after driving to the *Boca* and smelling the pungent smells and looking at the dim, drab buildings and the hulks of ships lying in the port, we stopped at the Liberty Inn. Then in a room full of blue smoke and merry sailors we had our café and assorted drinks while talent from the floor sang to us and a fat lady officiated behind the bar. Tiperary and Loch Lomand with everyone joining in. And a tipsy lad, in derby hat and long black tie who ate beer nuts and operated soda bottles for our entertainment. Nick invited 2 of those British lads to join our table, and one, the be's'n John, was so far gone that he called me "his California poppy"!! We stayed until far, far into the night, and finally, when the Liberty closed up, we saw our salty friends to their homes.

Wednesday, July 29, is a day that has left no memories. Just a day of living with time to write and wash and think and to visit with *Carlos* and Jan. One of those days of doing little which are indispensable to the keenest enjoyment of the days of doing much.

Thursday, July 30, was a fine day that made me want to cycle, and in the morning I went off on Chester to explore the city—off to the west along *Rivadavia* and then to the north where cobblestones interfered with Chester's smooth speed. Coming down wide *Juan Justo*, I was stopped by policemen who inquired for my *"patente."* And with all the nonchalance at my disposal, I lied. *"Si señor, yo tengo uno de los Estados Unidos,"* I said pointing to my PNCA plate! They looked at the plate and at me and at one another, and having never seen such a license before and not knowing what else to do, they told me to *"Siga, no mas!"* What a relief! In the afternoon I cycled again, out toward *San Martín*, but I returned in time for tea, and Jan and I visited at such length that I had to hurry in order to keep a date with Erwin for 7:30! He met me at the Peru station of the *subteraneo*, and we went to his friend *Ernesto* Pfister's *pensión* for the evening. There we ate carrots and talked and dined, and Ernest asked *Tola*, a negro boxer from the States, to come in! A great black fellow with a soft drawl. I shall never forget his tales of trying to fight his way through a crowd to his own fight in *Santiago* and of his fear of a Latin *señorita* who wanted to marry him! To top off the evening, the 3 of us went to a German beer garden where we had rum punch while an orchestra played and others danced.

Friday, July 31, I spent a lazy afternoon visiting with *Tanti Dora* who was in bed with an earache. For tea I walked to the home of Norma Ferran, whom I met in the south, and joined her mother and grandmother and a friend for a couple of hours of visiting. Their home for dinner and off to a show with a Mr. Drysdale, also met in the south, one of the "English Five." We saw an amateur production, "The Country Girl," given to raise funds for English prisoners of war, and it was an unusually good musical comedy. Then *café* at "The Ideal" and home very late.

Aug. 3, 1942—Buenos Aires—Jan's—7:00 PM

Saturday, August 1, was a very American day. At noon I went out to *Colegio* Ward to have lunch with the directors of the school. They showed me about the campus, and with them I watched a *fútbol* game and attended a faculty tea. It was interesting to see the plant of a school in *Buenos Aires*, but schools have little romance for me! The day was warm and the humidity so great that water was streaming down the walls and lying all over the floors. Something new to me. I came back to town in a bus with some of the American High School students and made my way home just as an electrical storm was breaking. And as if sparks from the heavens had entered our household, *Carlos* and I had a terrific political argument at dinnertime!

Yesterday, Aug. 2, was truly a memorable day. Early in the morning, Drysdale picked me up, and with a couple of others we drove to the *San Isidro Club* where *Martin* and Merten were waiting with a yacht. Rain had fallen through the night and the day was dark and forbidding—so much so that I had expected the party to be called off. But Nordic blood is more sporting than Latin's, and those English lads were laughing at the weather and rearin' to go. *Qué suerte*! No day is ever lost when it is met in the spirit of fun. We put our wraps and baskets of food aboard, and the men put up the sails and started the motor, and under combination power we left the harbor and turned up the *La Plata*. Gray skies and gray water. Misty bits of woodland on the banks for all the world like hills. Rushes in the water to remind us that the *La Plata* is not deep. A fleeting bit of sunlight which caught the yellow ripples and dressed them in silver. A lovely, lonely day with no one else abroad. In the cabin Arthur started a primus and made *mate*, and we passed the gourd from one to another until all had had their fill. *Mate amargo*. Then Drysdale and Mrs. Allbright cooked sausages! From the *La Plata*, we turned up the *San Antonio*, finally stopping at a small clubhouse where another English couple was waiting for us. And these folks already had a fire going so we started our *asado* immediately.

Half a lamb and several yards of *chinchulinis* (plaited guts!).
Then we hovered around in a hungry circle, waiting for the
meat to cook, but the only visible results were the fountains
that broke from the *chinchulinis* and sprayed the lookers-on!
After 2 hrs. we sat down to a table loaded with meat and
bread, and with greasy hands and faces we ate until we could
eat no more. Then back to the river again, this time with 8
passengers. Out in the river as a strong wind was blowing,
and after reeling in the main sail, we shut off the motor and
really sailed. What fun! The boat dipped until her decks were
flooded as she scudded before the wind. And we dodged the
boom as we tacked back and forth. Then we women were sent
below, out of the spray and the activity of the men, but we still
watched. I watched them as they struggled with the ropes,
dripping wet. A true landlubber, I felt sure the boat would
turn completely over, but the men nonchalantly sailed toward
the misty form of the *San Isidro* church. And the only
[problem] occurred when we were nearly home. We ran
aground almost in the front yard of the club and freed
ourselves only with the aid of a tug! It was dark when we
finally went ashore, and we were so wet that Arthur's *pensión*
in *San Isidro* looked awfully good. A place to change. And
we stayed on to see movies of the south of Chile and to have
dinner together. I returned home a happy girl, content with the
comradeship and joviality of the day.

August 4—Lujan—Hotel Commercio—9:00 AM

Monday, the 3rd, was another rainy day which inspired
me to do nothing. In the morning I went down town and
hunted banks in an effort to decide what to do with the $1000
draft recently received from home. But I came to no decision!
And in the evening who should call up but my old friend
Cuneo. He and his wife came out for an hour's visit before
dinner, and it seemed like old times to see him again. The
man who calls himself "publicity"! And after they left Paul
came to dinner, so the evening at *Anasco 4* was spent in
visiting.

But today the program has been different because I decided to come to *Lujan* on the spur of the moment. And after finally getting through coffee, packing Jan's last minute arrangements, I pedaled away on Chester. Out of the city on *Rividavia*, and clear to *Lujan* in the self same street. Well built up countryside. But enough gaps to show the green of winter rains and the early yellow flowers of *mimosa*. Muddy tracks leading away in the country made me glad I was rolling on concrete! And made me wonder what Brazil would bring! A fresh breeze cleared the skies and *Lujan* seemed brilliant when I arrived—as if washed and dried. And I liked the town at once with its narrow, friendly streets and its great church and its open, paved *plaza* giving an uninterrupted view out to the country beyond. To solve the hotel problem I stopped at one recommended by the *camineros,* for I had no time to lose, and almost immediately I was in the streets again, ready to see the town. First the church whose tall spires dominate the town and the surrounding country, a church famous for its healing virgin, a place of pilgrimage for devout Catholics. A gothic style edifice built in the usual form of a cross, it possesses a solemn religious atmosphere which inspires reverence in all— even a heathen like myself. For half an hour I wandered through its interior noting the rich altar, the countless little figurines brought by the pilgrims and hung in plaques on the walls, the votes of thanks to the virgin, and the little virgin herself in a special chapel behind the altar. Material manifestations of a human desire to lean on something omnipotent outside of the world of reality. And at the front door of the church were stalls and hawkers to sell spirited offerings *"barrato"* to all who wished to make a display of their reverence! From the church I went to the museum and here I found a wealth of military things. First the annex where was Argentina's first locomotive. Elegant old carriages used by officials of the past, the saddles used by the men who rode horseback from B.A. to New York, and a great oxcart said to have been used by *San Martín*. The altar was made of *quebrado* with hide-bound wheels and a cover of rushes –all so heavy that a oxen was needed to pull it—but as if the maker had a touch of delicacy in his soul, he had hung a lacy bit of knotted raw hide at the front. The museum proper was a rambling colonial building, perhaps the *cabildo* of times gone by and the worn pavement of the courtyards, the rusted iron grills, the thick walls and the bright tiles of the window sills gave it the mellowness and beauty characteristic of ancient things. Inside were all manner of things reminiscent of Argentina's history. The usual flags and guns and *recuerdos* of military exploits. But much more interesting to me were the great spurs, the *boleadoras*, the wide soft saddles, and the queer bone furniture of the *gauchos*. Also interesting was the thick-walled jail with its wooden clamps for heads and legs. At 5:00 I was unwillingly ushered out of the museum, and after tea at the "Munich," I walked the streets until bedtime.

August 10, 1942—Buenos Aires—Jan's—8:00 AM

Wednesday, the 5th, I visited an *estancia* near *Lujan*. Leaving down the wide avenue in front of the church, I walked and asked questions as I went. Then through the mud of a country lane to the fine buildings of the ranch. Mr. Garlir, the *administrador,* met me with cordiality and showed me all about the place which was devoted exclusively to horses. We looked at the stallions, and the mares and the tiny colts, and then walked out across the pastures to see the yearlings. A sunny spring-like day; and the green grass and the fine horses made my blood run high. After looking at everything, we returned to his pleasant rooms and had a whisky and soda followed by a delicious lunch in front of the fire. Then back to town in a carriage drawn through the mud by a good team of brown mares. And in a little while, I was packed and pedaling away from *Lujan*, returning to B.A. through country fragrant with *mimosas*. Head winds and hard pedaling heightened by the company of another cyclist who joined me in *Liniers*. The cobblestones and traffic and finally *Anasco 4*. And I left my refuge only to take some mimosa to *Tanti Dora* in *Acoyte*.

Thursday, the 6th, I spent in preparing a dinner for Erwin and *Ernesto* and *Inés*. Jan went with me to buy fruit and vegetables and assorted groceries, and the afternoon passed in a flurry of activity. I found cooking quite an adventure here where I had no recipes, no measuring cups or spoons, no standard products! And my limited Spanish was futile in directing the maid! But things went along, and I enjoyed my guests after the work was done. *Carlos* couldn't be here, but at least we had a couple of men, and *Ernesto* was his usual entertaining self. The boys stayed until late, coming back after a false start for the door!

Friday, the 7th, I had an early lunch in order to spend much time downtown, but per usual; I accomplished little. Again I tried unsuccessfully to solve the problem of my bank draft that is something of a lemon. But I gave this up and went to visit *Cuneo* and his wife instead. They went back to town with me, leaving me at the door of the Methodist church where I met Jan. And we had tea at the bazaar that was in session there, bowing and smiling to all the good ladies of the church. Then we made a hurried exit and dashed for *Constitución* to say good-bye to Paul. But we arrived late! So after looking about the station a bit, we made for home.

Saturday, the 8th, I spent the afternoon with Carlos who felt that I should be shown around. We went off in the car for *Parque Lesama* and the museum, but found the museum closed, so we concentrated on the park which is located on a hill and therefore very lovely. We explored the *Boca* too, driving past the old dilapidated buildings, the bridge which operates as a movable carriage, the wool market, the *figorificos*, and a myriad of small boats lying at anchor. There was even a church boat there! Then we drove back past *Darsena Sud* and around *Plaza San Martín* and across to *Calle Bolivar* which is one of the oldest parts of the city. Here is a church which is said to have withstood the early invasions, and here are many old houses. In another part of the city we stopped at *Mercado Abasco* and went below to see the meat auction. Rows and rows and rows of carcasses sold in quick succession by chanting auctioneers to buyers who indicated merely by an imperceptible movement of head or hand. Nearly a thousand halves of beef were sold that day. From below came a strong odor of *mate* while above was the refuse of vegetable sales completed in the early hours of the morning. All the romance of commerce and growing things combined into one. But we had to hurry through in order to appear at the Rosenbusch's household for a 7:00 buffet. And what a buffet! More than 20 persons and a table loaded with bits of this and that. Much visiting and eating and a late return home.

And yesterday, the 9th, found us again with the Rosenbusch's although I was loath to refuse an invitation to spend the day with Drysdale. *Inés* and Dr. Rosenbusch came early, and we all drove together to the *Exposición of the Sociedad Rural* where an exhibition of horses was in progress. A *gaucho* in full regalia held me fascinated. His saddle was the usual 2 rolls of leather padded with soft skins, but his stirrups were of silver as were the bands on his rawhide headstall. And *adelante* he carried a *boleadora* while *atras* was a lariat. He himself was in gala with baggy britches, silver spurs, and a wide belt hung with silver coins. In the horse barn they were judging the *Criolla* horses, blocky little animals, who now have a registry of their own because of their usefulness on the *estancias*, and we watched them take their turns, the roans and pintos and buckskins and blues. Then we sat in the grandstand to see the judging of more aristocratic polo ponies and saddle horses. After lunch at the Rosenbusch's we returned to the stock show, and after looking at sheep and dairy cattle, we went again to the ring, this time to see the judging of driving horses. There were *lechederias* and *panaderias* and all manner of commercial conveyances painted with elaborate designs and drawn by good horses that stepped with pride and that wore brass-laden harnesses. Some of the animals were almost obliterated under brass! And little bells tinkled on the harnesses. I was interested to see such good quality horses hitched to wagons, for I had already noticed them in the streets of the city. And the enthusiasm of the on-lookers would have been a pleasure to any lover of useful horses.

August 16, 1942—Buenos Aires—Jan's—8:00 PM

Monday, the 11th, found me in the streets again, this time canvassing the bike shops for a gear cable of good imported steel; and I finally bought one which will prove its worth later. As I worked my way downtown from *Congresso*, I stopped at the *Mercado La Plata* to look at the fancy food stuffs available in B.A.—gleaming fish, attractive fresh vegetables, polished fruits, marbled meats. All manner of good things to eat. Stalls and hawkers...with an aristocratic air, catering to wealthy homes. A market occupying a full block in *Avenida 9 de Julio*—"widest street in the world." In the afternoon, Jan and I went again to the Rural Society, but per usual we were late, and the Arabian horses which we went to see turned out to be Hereford cattle! But fine cattle they were, all shined up for the show and so fat they could scarcely walk. After watching the judging for a while we went to the barns to see the horses and Shorthorns and pigs. And out of the corner of my eye, I was also watching *peones* who were dressed in their Sunday best for this greatest event of the year. Rags decorated with silvery belts or a new hat. For tea we had hot cheese *pisa* and then hurried home to change and go to the Hopkin's for dinner. Sophisticated Mrs. Hopkins sitting in discomfort while the untrained laundress officiated as maid! And on the way home *Carlos* paid tribute to the American meal by stopping for a round of *pisa*!

Thursday, the 11th, Jan and I spent the morning preparing *almuerzo* for Dr. Rosenbusch, *Tanti, Dora, Inés*; and afterwards *Inés* and I rushed down to *Congreso* to meet *Enrique* who showed us through the building. Upstairs the rooms of the finance commission and the military department, and downstairs the presidents' rooms, the chamber of deputies, the senate, the *comedor*, the *sala de pasos perdidos*, and the elegant reception room with its deep carpets, ornate chairs and tremendous candelabra hung from the high dome of the building. Most interesting was the automatic voting system of the *camara de deputados*—each seat with 280 electrical contacts so that any deputy could vote from any seat with his own particular key, all votes being registered on the walls above. Throughout the building there was a cold official elegance, as if to impress all who entered there; but there were other earmarks of officialdom also: job seekers in the halls, too many employees, café served throughout the day. After completing our tour with a trip to the extensive printing dept. in the basement, *Enrique* gave me a card to an official in *Darsena Norte*, and I went off with *Inés* to try and get permission to return to Argentina after traveling to Brazil. "Easy," they said,--just get a letter from the American consul stating what I wanted to do. So I went to the consul only to be assured that I could get nothing to facilitate my return to this country. I had arrived at the end of a blind alley.

But Wednesday, the 12th, I went packing back to the American consul, for *Carlos* and *Inés* had exploded over an American's presuming to know an Argentine's business. And again I meekly asked for the necessary letter. But they issued no such letter, I was told, and the only document I could get was a certificate of good conduct! Tired of offices, I spent the remainder of the morning buying an umbrella for Jan, but the afternoon found me making the same old rounds. *Darsena Norte* again, this time with Jan and *Inés* only to learn there the same thing I had already heard from the American consul—no possibility of getting advance permission to return to Argentina. Futile Enrique's pull and my several trips to town! Leaving *Inés*, Jan and I went to inquire about passage across the river to *Colonia*, and at Milanovich we discovered a new angle: I could not purchase a one-way ticket to *Colonia*! Had to buy one to *Montevideo* or *Fray Bentos* instead! Unforseen complications.

Thursday, the 13th, I forgot official business and spent the day playing. In the morning, I had to deliver a package to *Carlos*, and he took time out to show me through the Institute—all the crowded rooms where vaccines were being prepared amongst a confusion of test tubes, cultures, medicines, incubators, and rat cages. Then home to a company dinner for *Marta* and *Enrique*. And later *Inés* and

Tanti Dora came to take *Marta,* Jan, and I for a drive in the country—out to *San Martín* and around to *San Isidro,* with a turn about the campus of the veterinary school en route. Pink blossoms of flowering peach and yellow blossoms of *mimosa,* with a feeling of spring in the air. A beautiful day punctuated with tea at one of those great old houses along the river. And I arrived home just in time to change and dash downtown to meet Drysdale at the Boston Bar. He and Merton were waiting, and they ordered me drinks with a "side car" for me. And before long we were joined by another couple and a girl. An English gathering with the exception of my Yankee self. Drinking and peanuts and sociability. And then to the *Parrilla* for dinner, a meal notable for its first course of snails and muscles and squid all steamed together and served in a kind of a soup. Drysdale's suggestion that the best way to handle snails was to separate the meat and eat the shell was rather well taken! But we had *bifes* and *panqueques* to balance the score! And then we whiled away the night at the *Tabaries,* "best night club south of the equator." Singing and dancing with "exotic" ladies standing by and with an opportunity to dance ourselves to the tunes of a "college boy" orchestra! A night of joviality and thick blue tobacco smoke.

Friday, the 14th, I made preparations to leave, for my English friends had said they would take me by private launch to *Colonia.* Another trip in the *Rosamar* and evasion of the official difficulties of the crossing—Too good to miss. So I went to *Expresso Villalonga* with my tale of difficulties in drawing traveler's cheques and they told me that they would honor nothing short of a ticket to Paraguay! Great guns! But as we talked, they softened, and finally agreed to sell cheques on the basis of a ticket to *Colonia.* So I bought the cheapest ticket I could get (an air ticket), endorsed my draft over to *Villalonga,* and purchased my cheques with a sigh of relief. Their stamp on the back of my ticket made it impossible to return, but I was willing to sacrifice *12 pesos* for the privilege of buying cheques, and the ticket would make a good souvenir! In the afternoon Dr. Rosenbusch came to say good-bye, *Tanti Dora* bought me a lovely "going away" purse.

Tanti Trudy came for a farewell embrace and *Inés* left a nice leather folder for my documents. Goodbye, goodbye—and I felt a tugging inside as I prepared to leave the hospitable family. But there was little time for sentiment for Jan and I had to rush downtown to collect quinine ordered by *Carlos*, to change the date on my air ticket (in the thought that I might get a refund on the other side), and to buy Uruguayan currency. The packing interrupted by dinner and a visit from Erwin who came by to say goodbye. And a toast in liqueur to the success of my journey! Then more packing—And headaches over the effort to get everything inside my small bags! At one o'clock I gave up and closed my pack without my new purse and with baggage bulging from under the flaps. *Listo!*

Saturday, the 15th, I wakened late, and rushed madly to get underway, for I had to be at *San Isidro* at 8:00 AM. At 7:30 with Chester sagging under baggage and with a hurried breakfast inside of me, I said goodbye to Jan and *Carlos*, and rode away in the rain. A dismal day with B.A. clad in gray, but with fiery excitement inside of me. And I pedaled madly! How far *San Isidro* seemed—Keep 'em turning! And at 8:30 I arrived, full of apologies to Merton and Martin who met me at the station. But they countered with long faces and the confession that they could not get a boat. Pin pricks in my balloon of anticipation! I could change my plans however, so I chattered gaily over the tea that Martin ordered for me in his room, and I thought and thought about how to get to Uruguay. Then I called Jan and retreated to *Caballito* with the rain blowing in my face and with the "crew" of the *Rosamar* piloting me by car. Anticlimax. In the afternoon I went with Jan and *Carlos* to the Rosenbusch's where everyone greeted me like a long lost friend and where I had to tell the whole story of my futile ride in the rain. *Que verguenza!* But it seemed no more than natural to be again in their midst and I took my tea with the usual gusto. Afterwards I went home and spent some quiet hours reorganizing my wet pack, and I anticipated going early to bed, but *Carlos* and I became involved in an argument and until midnight I countered his devastating attacks on America and Americans.

August 19, 1942—Colonia, Uruguay—Hotel Beltran—9 PM

The whole of Sunday, the 16th, *Carlos* devoted to me—a sort of going away spree. In the morning we went off to town and spent our time just poking about. Stopped to look at armadillos, all cooked and ready to eat. Went to the laboratory for a while and left with the image of Suzy, the spider, eating a tiny pink mouse. Walked along the arcades of *Leandro Alem*, the "bad, bad" section of town. Went into the parochial post office and climbed to the top floor. Passed into the cathedral and around the kneeling throng to the tomb of *San Martín*. And had time only to walk in and out of the *cabildo* and in and out of the office of *La Prensa* before meeting Jan and *Marta* who came by car. With them, we drove to *9 de Julio* and walked through the fish department of *Mercado La Plata* before going to *Los Patitos* for lunch. *Pescaray, dorado*, squid, muscles, eels, snails, and masses of shrimp as an appetizer for our duck! –A visual appetizer, *no mas*. After lunch we hurried out to the races and took paddock tickets so we could see the horses before and after the races. Very nice to watch the excited animals and the satin clad little jockeys, but we all bet on the wrong horses! De Camps from the institute was there, and with him we watched the testing of hearts and the taking of temperatures before sending the animals to the track. After 3 races we left the excitement of horses and betting and went to the Rural Society, where the official opening was in progress. Such crowds! We parked the cars so far from the entrance that we were able to see the Botanical Garden *en route*! And inside we couldn't get near the central ring where dignitaries were speaking and champion animals being shown. But outside we were able to watch the parade of animals to the ring. The fat brushed-up bulls and the neat high-stepping horses. A social event this, with well-dressed men and sophisticated women pressing in from all sides. After the showing we rushed over to the entrance gate in order to see the grenadiers in their colorful costumes and President *Costillo* in his special coach all leaving the exposition grounds. Then we looked about the fowl barn, the sheep barn, the short horn barn, and the pig barn, after which we had tea and went home. But not for long. Before dinner *Marta* and *Enrique* called, and we all went down town for the evening. First *pisa* in *Corrientes*, with great slabs of it! Delicious! Then "*café puro do Brazil.*" And lastly "*bebidas con espectaculo*" in a downstairs hall. Spanish singing and dancing with the crowd joining in and with everyone in a merry mood. When we finally dragged home to bed, I counted mine a complete day.

Monday morning, the 17th, I went back to the business of getting out of Argentina, and Jan went with me. Before asking for a refund from S.A.N.A., I explained my problems to *Expreso Villalonga* so that there would be no question about my traveler's cheques. And then I found that when asked to return the money on my ticket, S.A.N.A. was willing to carry my bicycle! But a new angle presented itself: before leaving Argentina with a bicycle I must have permission to export steel! I must get a letter from the American consul and permission from the *aduana* officials! *Cuanta felicidad!* Leaving countries seems to be much more complicated than getting in! But Monday afternoon was a holiday, and I could do nothing more, so I forgot difficulties and luxuriated in visiting the Rosenbusch's who were celebrating *Carlos* and Jan's wedding anniversary. After a delicious dinner there, a crowd of us went to the *Sociedad Rural* to see the auctioning of animals. With patience, we were able to crowd into the room where Herefords were being sold by Arturo Bullrich. $63,000 for the 3rd prize animal, more than for the 1st and 2nd premiums. Rebellion against an American judge whose decisions were not liked. We also watched Frederico Bullrich selling shorthorns and talking to the *estancieros* whom he seemed to know. But most aggravating to me was the sale of Arabian horses at 1000 and 1100 pesos. A gift, *no más*—with very little interest in the sales. –And "me with a bicycle and no room for an Arabian!" *Qué lástima!* Before leaving we walked through the draft horse barn and went to see the display of grains—wheat, oats, barley, flax, corn, and many others. Then we retired to Acoyte for tea and supper. Another pleasant day spent in the warmth of Rosenbusch's hospitality.

Tuesday, the 18th, I went forth to collect permissions, reinforced with *Tanti Dora's* speed and efficiency. First we went to the American embassy and to a Mr. Nyhus who very kindly agreed to write a letter describing my journey and asking consideration for my bicycle. Then *Tanti Dora* insisted on buying another purse for me, and we found a flexible blue one, guaranteed to adapt itself to any shape in my pack! After lunch at *Garth y Chaves*, we went to the *aduana* and there we spent the rest of the afternoon. Starting with the doorman we went from office to office until we finally reached the 3rd floor and an official high enough to give us the necessary permission. Then we bought *papel sellado* and sat and talked and sat some more and eventually learned that my papers would be ready *mañana*. Success! Back home I went to work on Chester who was rusted and stiff from exposure, and after cleaning and oiling him, I installed my precious new tire and tube. Then I packed, said good-bye to Erwin over the phone, and drank again to the success of my trip—this time with *Marta* and *Enrique* who dropped in for a short visit. I was ready to leave at 3:00 PM the following day, but I still had my fingers crossed.

August 20, 1942—Carmelo—Hotel Carmelo—8:00 PM

And yesterday I actually did it, actually managed to get out of Argentina! All morning I worked over my things, trying to shake them down into smaller space, trying to find a place for the things sent from home and for the new *recuerdos* from friends in B.A. *Cuantos difficultades*! And when Chester was finally packed, his saddlebags were bulging, the top of his suitcase showed a gap, and 2 spare tires dangled aft! Dinner, good-byes, and off into the streets again, with a farewell ride down busy *Rivadavia*. And shortly I was back as the *aduana* waiting for my documents. But they weren't ready, and I was lead from office to office for the necessary signatures.　At 2:30 I had to be at the airport, and at 2:20 I was still in the *aduana*, but my urgency seemed to impress the officials, and they took time out from their coffee to send my papers through.　It seemed an eternity before everything was ready and when the documents were finally in my hands, I rushed downstairs without waiting for the elevator!　By this time it was impossible to ride by bike to *Puerto Nuevo*, so I hailed a taxi, stuffed Chester inside and urged the driver to fly to my plane.　What indignity to arrive in a taxi!　But at least I did arrive!　And there were *Tanti Dora, Tanti Trudy*, and *Tanti Anita* waiting for me.　I was in such a dither of excitement that I could scarcely organize myself enough to weigh in, pay over weight on my baggage and convince the man in charge that my bike must go.　Saying good-bye was only a matter of minutes, and I had no time for sentiment or to miss Jan and Carlos who hadn't arrived.　Nor did I have time to take a last look at B.A., all bathed in brilliant sunshine, and to wonder if I'd ever return.　I had only time to realize that I was leaving the port and the *3 Tantis* by launch, that I was climbing up and down into a comfortable seat, that Chester was rolled into the aisle beside me and that with a whir of motors and a spray of water I was taking off into the air over the *Rio La Plata*. Below was murky water with a path of silver leading to the sun.　Nothing more.　But in a moment I could see the undulating land of the Uruguay side and in 15 minutes we settled down again amidst spraying water.　*Colonia*, my first step on Uruguayan soil!　On the pier I loaded Chester and rolled to the *aduana* with everything aboard.　A short inspection and I was pedaling through the streets, so happy to be on my bicycle again and traveling in the sun that I rode a way into the country just for the sheer joy of cycling.　Then back to find a hotel and to walk out into the streets.　An old town, *Colonia*, with a feeling of age in the rough cobbled streets, in the low thick-walled buildings, in the tempo of the people.　And picturesque too with its narrow streets leading to the river, and with its rocky shores where clothes were drying in the sun.　At dusk it was lovely with its buildings sprawled over prominences rising out of a river of blue and gold.   I liked *Colonia*. And she yielded a doz. bananas for my supper!

This morning I went back to cycling in earnest, leaving *Colonia* at 2:00 and turning up the river toward *Carmelo*. Another brilliant day with spring heavy in the air. Grainfields green in the sunlight, willows lacy with new leaves, quinces and *mimosas*, bright with bloom. And my road lead up and down, up and down across farmlands which rolled away to the river. Cattle, sheep, and horses all fed in the same pastures, and at one point I saw ostriches too in the fields. At mid-day I stopped on an isolated hill to loll in the greenness, to eat bananas, and caramels, and to write, write, write. A horseman came up to question me, and passers-by stared curiously, but I went on writing. And it was past 4:00 when I rode off again into the sun. Shortly I turned down a tree-lined avenue and crossed a bridge into *Carmelo*, and after cruising about the streets for a while with a crowd of boys panting after me, I found a room here. Then the routine of unpacking and changing clothes and I was ready for my usual walk. Down along the river and back to the *plaza* and through the main streets with a stop to buy oranges for supper and another stop to ask questions about the road ahead. There is a familiarity in the way of life here in Uruguay—in the loiterers outside the bars, in the women standing in the doorways, in the laughing school youngsters in white, but the streets of the town bear new names and dates and on every side are products with strange names. I <u>feel</u> that I am in a new country.

Aug. 22, 1942—Mercedes, Uruguay—Petit Hotel—10:00 AM

And yesterday morning, the 21ˢᵗ, I was initiated into Uruguay with police for breakfast! Just as I was preparing for an early start, a stern gentleman appeared at my door to question me about my life, and he asked me to go to the *comiseria*. So I packed up and pedaled to headquarters, bag and baggage, in the hope that I might yet get away early. But there I was held for nearly an hour answering the questions of first one official and then another. Why was I traveling alone?

What nationality was I? Why had I stopped at a German hotel? Didn't I know that Germans were enemies of North Americans. Then they looked at all my documents, took down a volume of notes, and allowed me to go my way. As I pedaled out of town another cyclist joined me—spoke to me in English and said he was a German refugee. But his Spanish had no German accent and his questions made me suspicious. Were the police still checking on me? I was vague in all my answers, and I turned the tables by questioning him. But he stayed with me for 20 kms. and I was too uncomfortable to enjoy the bright sunlight and the blazing green of the rolling countryside. Then he left and from *Agraciada* on I rode in peace. The road was of earth now and bumpy from the mud of recent rains, but I traveled easily, reveling in the joy of being alone with spring. Vast expanses of new grain, occasional houses, many sheep and cattle. Peach trees in pink bloom. New lambs. Long-legged birds standing in the ponds. Cardinals with brilliant red backs. With the softness of spring on every side, I could not understand the many dead animals, which lay by the side of the road. They seemed incongruous. Much more in keeping was the wagon drawn up by the side of the road with the horses unhitched with the man making *asado* over a small fire. Through *Dolores* I rode – a country town lazy in the mid-day heat – and just beyond, amongst the trees by the river, I stopped to eat oranges & caramel. A man with a sack over his shoulder stopped to keep me company and we talked about Uruguay and watched the traffic on the road. Truck loads of flour; horsemen driving cattle; wagons with 7 horses hitched. When the heat had dissipated a bit I went on my way to *Mercedes* – a pretty town built over the hills beside the *Rio Negro*. And just at dusk I was out exploring. Down to the river where the ferries were plying back and forth and around the plaza with its church towers and dome. Then a visit to the *comiseria* to avoid suspicion on the part of the police. And afterwards dinner and to bed. I begin to notice other differences here in Uruguay. The people of the country speak in a sing-song manner, and there are evidences of Uruguay's stand in the war. Posters of allegiance to Roosevelt

and Churchill. And people like the boatman by the river who
shook my hand because of my nationality.

Aug. 23, 1942—Mercedes—Petit Hotel—7:00 AM

Yesterday morning, the 22nd, light streamed into my
room to announce another cloudless day. How lucky I am in
my wandering! And I luxuriated in the tranquillity of a day in
town. After café, a short *paseo* in the country. Out past an
airport and up to the very doors of an *estancia*, with the road
following the crests of hills along the river and then turning
away between rows of China berries and eucalyptus. Lovely
views across the river and the rolling countryside. Olives,
grapes, and peaches—unusual in this vast granary. A feeling
of intimacy which I never once felt on the plains of Argentina.
And always the softness of spring in the air, which unlike the
gold of autumn, becalms my racing blood and tempts me to
stop and lie in the green and the sun. And stop I did, out there
in the pastures where the sun was melting away the dew on the
grass, and where I could write undisturbed. Back to town
again at mid day, back amongst the low buildings with their
solid fronts lining unpaved streets and with their curious
population peering out to watch me pass. Dinner in
pantalones. And off again for another *paseo*, a longer one to
Fray Bentos. Across the *Rio Negro* in a one-auto *balsa* and
off into the country, hurrying in order to return before dark.
But before I had climbed the hills away from the river, a
policeman on a bike came alongside and motioned me to stop.
The same one who had hailed me below with a "psssst" and a
wave of the hand and whom I had ignored as fresh! He was
panting like a hot dog and irritated as he ushered me back to
the *factura* for questioning. And I was irritated to be taken
from the road and sun. Where was I going? Why? Didn't I
have documents other than a passport? For half an hour I was
detained. Then back to pedaling through the ups and downs of
Uruguay's springtime greenness. Approaching *Fray Bentos*,
the road was lined with China berries and there were willows
and flowering fruit trees in the hollows. Pasturelands were

dotted with the blue-green of new thistle leaves and with the bouncing white of new lambs. The feeling of springtime permeated to the core. Then I was in the dusty streets of *Fray Bentos*, riding over the hill to the docks beside the river and around to the gates of the *Anglo Frigorifico* which was closed to visitors. A sleepy little town with many loiterers, but pretty in its vantagepoint above the *Rio Uruguay*. In the late hours of the afternoon, I turned back to *Mercedes*, happy in the lengthening shadows. Flocks of little green parrots flashed vivid green from the skies as if competing with the green of the pastures. Lambs scampered to their mothers. And just at dusk I came again to the *Rio Negro* which reflected its boats and willows and caught the sunset colors in its waters. Home, dinner, and to bed in anticipation of a long day on the road.

August 24, 1942—Colonia Suiza—Hotel Klein Flottveck

And yesterday, the 23rd, was a long day on the road. More than 100 miles of pedaling! A constant turning of pedals from 8:00 in the morning until after dark. Away from Mercedes with a last look at its cluster of white buildings strewn over the hills and its pretty surrounding farmlands. And all into limitless pasture lands. Sheep and cattle and a few ostriches. And a road rolling on and on. Few houses and few people. Wide open spaces. In a dark tumbledown *almacen* I bought hard bread (out of a gunnysack) and a little can of meat for my lunch, and I disrupted the gambling game of the rustic men within by my curious appearance out of the nowhere. Lunchtime found me settled on the green of a pasture near *G.E. Rodo*, alone except for an occasional passing horseman. One even stopped to chat. Asked me if I was selling something! But I didn't rest long for a fresh wind was blowing and dark clouds rolling in. By mid-afternoon I had reached *Cardona*, a handful of houses on the plains, and I resolved not to stop, for it seemed windblown and forlorn. Just a question about the road from one of the loiterers at the bar, and I was on my way towards *Rosario*. And the road turned and went with the wind! *Que lindo*! I fairly flew with the wind. A noise from behind like the bellowing of a bell, and I stopped to find a uniform on a bicycle pursuing me. Drat the police! They always seem to show up just when I'm in a hurry. Nothing to do but return to *Cardona* to answer questions and show my documents. But at least the policeman too had to ride into the wind as we returned to town! It was 4:00 o'clock before I was on my way again, riding past the natives who stared at the girl taken in by the law. 60 kms. to go. But it seemed like a dream with *viento en favor*. Pedals turned easily. Hills seemed as nothing. Up and down, up and down. I sped. And the wind swept away the clouds; and spring was there in the lambs in the fields and in the red verbena by the side of the road. Before *Rosario* I took a side road to *Colonia Suiza*, a bad road but a lovely way. Intimate farm lands in the mellowness of the setting sun. There I was in the village, cruising up and down in search of a Swiss or German hotel, for I anticipated a clean room and good food. But the hotels were located out of town, and darkness came before I found one. A question of a man on the road brought ready help. He, a Turk, went with me and asked questions until we found the hotel I sought. How welcome the German hospitality! And although I was almost alone in the hotel, I was quite content with my homey room and a good chicken dinner.

August 25, 1942—Montevideo—Dante Hotel—8:30 AM

Yesterday morning, the 24th, I didn't leave as early as I should have, for I was loath to go from the pleasant *Colonia Suiza*. Not until past 9:00 did I get underway. Out on the long straight road to the capital, up and down but forever straight. And a wind blew stronger and stronger, filling the skies with the gray, cold clouds of winter, dulling the green of the fields, dissipating the softness of spring. Blowing from the side at first, it soon changed to a head wind that sent discouragement through my struggling legs. More and more force was necessary to turn the stubborn pedals. Hills became mountains, and pedaling downhill became as necessary as pedaling up. Kilometers lagged. Wind whistled eternally through my wheels and hair. Would I ever reach *Montevideo*? With head down, I scarcely saw the forlorn gray world across which I rolled, noted only the occasional thickets of trees which cut the wind and the road posts which marked the kilometers. By 9:30 I had used up the energy from my good breakfast and I stopped in *Santiago Vazquez* for café. Welcome rest. And the knowledge that *Montevideo* was near made the rest of the trip easier. There was the *Rio La Plata* again. And more houses and orchards to cut the wind! And in a moment I plunged into the city, trying to think of all the reasons why I could hold my head high and ignore the laughing crowds. But I too, saw the picture of a funny, sunburned girl, hair streaming out behind, a curiosity amongst the streetcars and autos. *Montevideo* was impressive, with tall white buildings and broad avenues, but I had eyes only for a hotel into which I could escape from the crowds. Into *Av. 18 de Julio*, the heart of the city. A question of a friendly policeman. And hurried negotiations for a room here which I received in spite of my wild appearance! What crowds gathered about my bike during the few moments I left it in the street! One would have thought that an important person had come, or that there had been an accident! But it was only overloaded Chester who jammed the sidewalk with a milling mob! I could scarcely get back to him! And it was with relief that I saw him disappear up the stairs. Welcome rest. And a change of clothes, so that I too could be just another in the crowd. Then out into the streets for my first introduction to *Montevideo*. Up and down *Av. 18 de Julio* from *Plaza Independencia* to *Plaza Cagancha*. Fine buildings and good window displays—just like any big city. But the people are not as well dressed as in B.A., and there's a marked increase in the number of Negroes.

August 26, 1942—Montevideo—Dante Hotel—7:30 PM

Yesterday, the 25th, was Independence Day in Uruguay—a day of fiesta. And so I lay in bed with the spirit of fiesta in my soul. And sunlight streamed in my window making my blue and white room very gay. Unusual in this land of somber interiors. And the reason I stay in this hotel which is not very good. Down in the street later I found the sidewalks lined with chairs and the crowds gathering to wait for the parade, and I too waited although I hadn't the slightest idea how long it would be. An hour, or perhaps 2, I stood while the people packed in 4 or 5 deep on either side of the street. Then a ripple through the mass of humanity, *"Alli viene,"* and I knew the parade was on its way. Marines from Brazil, marines from Argentina and marines from the USA. Even I broke out with nationalism and clapped enthusiastically as the Stars and Stripes went by followed by a contingent of men who seemed to tower above those who had gone before. Then followed Uruguayan military units, a small number of men who made up in elegance of uniform what they lacked in numbers. Plumed hats and red-striped pants. And noisy bands and a very few good horses. In a few moments all had marched by and a vanguard of workers organizations filled the streets chaotically. U.S. flags and Union Jacks, Soviet flags and Uruguayan banners all together. There was no doubt where Uruguay stood in the war! After lunch I went out to walk farther afield, to know Montevideo better. Down *Av. 18 de Julio* to *Parque J. Battle y Ordoñez* in search of the oxcart monument. A lovely park with grass and trees following the ups and downs and with views across the multitudes of white houses sweeping off to the *Rio de la Plata*. Crowds of people were there to enjoy the holiday in the sun, and I mingled with them. At last I found the monument I sought, *"La Carreta,"* and it even exceeded my expectations. 6 oxen hitched to a *carreta* followed by a man on horseback and 2 more oxen—all in bronze, and placed on a grassy knoll above a pond so as to form a keen silhouette against the sky. Powerful. And full of the pride which the Uruguayan feels in his rustic pioneers. Just below the monument I saw the reason for the crowds in the park: the Stadium *Centenario*, packed to the brim and a *fútbol* game in progress. Such enthusiasm! Even those outside had caught the spirit! All the people about me were having *mate* and buying food from the many vendors, so not to be outdone, I bought 5 cents worth of peanuts and sat on the grass to consume them! From the park I walked and walked and walked. Down *Av. Brazil to Plaza Pacitos,* a semicircle of clean sand outlined with modern buildings. Thence along the shore to broad *Av. Artigas* and on this street to *Constituyente* which took me back to the center of the city. With aching feet I returned home happy in my day of fiesta. All day I had been alone but I had felt as one with the holiday-seekers, with the sparkling modern buildings, with the wind-swept atmosphere.

And today I have continued my exploratory gyrations. In the morning I visited the Touring Club and *the Oficina de Turismo* to inquire about the city, this Republic, and the roads to Brazil, and my way took me towards the harbor into the old part of the city. In *Plaza Independencia* I paused to admire the great statue of General *Artigas,* and at the *Plaza Constitución* I stopped into the cathedral. Then I wandered out to the waterfront where I could look across the *La Plata* which is like a sea and back at the jumble of tall buildings which mark the center of the city. Old dilapidated buildings and down-at-the-heels life exist there by the water, unmindful of their incongruity in the very shadow of the smug, commercial section of town. After lunch I resorted to a streetcar and took a long ride around the bay to the *Cerro* to which *Montevideo* owes its name. Climbing upward across country I passed hovels which were depressing even in bright sunlight and with relief I reached the green carpeted, wind-swept summit where the old colonial fort is located. The simple, massive form of the edifice tells of early days, but over the colonial skeleton is a modern veneer which destroys the essence of age. Inside are cannons and guns, flags and gold braid—*recuerdos* of Uruguay's fighting days. But outside is a panorama which is much more impressive. Extensive views of *Montevideo* wrapped around its neat bay, of the country to the west, and of the murky *La Plata.* With the city very white in the bright sunlight and the country very green. For tea, I bought another 5 cents worth of peanuts, and then didn't know where to put them or where to eat them! Coming back to town I stopped at *Parque Prado* to walk through the formal *Rosalinda* where no buds yet show. And thence I walked back here along Av. *Agraciadas and Calle Paraguay.* Another pair of tired feet! But I am now well oriented in *Montevideo.*

Aug. 28, 1942—Montevideo—Dante Hotel—7:00 AM

More business yesterday morning. To the bank which doesn't open till 12:30! In search of a map of the road ahead and bike shop. But my wanderings took me down towards the waterfront again and I was irresistibly drawn to the boats. Past the tremendous *aduana* building at the water's edge. One of the Mihanovich steamers which runs to B.A. lay at the wharf. And farther down was a 4-masted schooner flying the Brazilian flag. A multiplicity of ropes and folded sails that made me want to see her in action. Few boats. And most of the docks barred to the public. After lunch I went back to the City Bank of NY to reassure myself in the matter of cashing cheques. And almost with a sense of relief I found I could. I also found the rate so much higher than in B.A. that I had lost $1.50 on the exchange over there. Oh me! If one could only know in advance! Finances settled, I hurried home, changed to cycling togs and went off on Chester to make the most of the beautiful day. First to a bike shop to have the pedal cones tightened and to buy spokes, and thence off to explore *Montevideo's* famous beaches. Down to the water at the foot of *Calle Sarandi* and from there along the *ramblas* which skirt the water front all the way to *Carrasco.* Scallops of fine boulevard. Sparkling sunlight reflected from the water. A series of curving beaches. The whitest of sands. And an endless chain of residences and hotels facing the water. A beautiful ride. First *Ramirez* Beach with a turn about lovely *Rodo* Park. Next *Pocitos* with its crescent of fine buildings and its popular promenade. Then, *Bucio* where the water harbors a whole flock of little sail boats. *Malvin* next, a more modest resort. Following are several small beaches and finally comes *Carrasco*, a long strip of sand dominated by the large casino. Here ends the seaside road, and I turned into the residential area to make a loop around the tree-lined streets before returning to the beach avenue again. One almost feels as if he were in a forest there in the streets of *Carrasco!* Back to *Montevideo* by the same road, always enjoying the sand and water and the sparkling whiteness of the buildings. And at sunset I rounded *Ramirez*. An orange sky reflected in the river. The city, an irregular silhouette with the *Palacio Salvo* rising high and looking as if it stood with folded wings. Lights in the blackness of the silhouettes. A city with the warmth and the heartbreak, the busy and the jobless, which all cities know.

August 30, 1942-- Piriapolis – Hotel Uruguayo – 10:30 PM

Friday, the 28th, I started the day with ambitious plans but accomplished little. There are so few things which can be done in the morning in *Montevideo!* First I went to the automobile club for information about roads to *Rio*. Walked the whole length of Av. *18 de Julio* and back by way of *Constituyente*. And the early afternoon found me in the *Palacio Legislaturo* after walking down and up *Agraciada*, which sweeps to the very doors of the building. A magnificent building it is too, not as much for the style as for the materials—granites and marbles of Uruguay. Outside white unpolished marble; inside, a great variety of polished stone. All colors are there—gray and purple and blue and green—lovely soft colors following into one another. Columns of red granite. And in the "*sala de pasos perdidos*" a floor of intricate design, all done with inlaid marble. The assembly rooms are elegant, but simpler, more modern than those of the Argentine legislature and throughout I found this building more to my liking. Two guides showed me around from the1st floor to the highest tower with its fine view over the city. But they make me uncomfortable with their familiarity. One used the old "*Qué simpática!*" gag, and the other asked if I wouldn't like to go to the *Solis* theater! From the legislature I went to the American consul, just to be sure my passport was all in order and from there to *Pocitos* and *Calle Cololo* where lives the *señorita* to whom I had a letter from *Tomás*. But she was not home, so I went out to *Instituto Crandon*, only to find that the director also was away. As I walked home, I improved my time by shopping for Brazilian currency and I discovered to my horror that the sailor from the Brazilian boat had recently been paid in *pesos* and had bought all available *milreis*! Frightened, I walked down toward the harbor into the commercial part of town, but *"no hay"* were the words which came from all of the *casas de cambio*. *Qué cosa!* Tired, I sat in *Plaza Independiencia* to watch the people and to think. And there I stayed until supper time.

Saturday, the 29th, I was up early, for I wanted to complete my business and go for a last bike ride about the city before leaving *Montevideo*. But I was so early I had to wait for offices to open! Had my shoes polished to kill time—first time in ages—and I was skeptical as to whether or not it was customary for a *señorita* to sit so boldly in a shoe-shine shop! Then more time searching for Brazilian money which I finally located in the *Banco Commercial*. *Que suerte!* Not until after 11:00 was I off on Chester for my last spin about the city. Out to *Colón* where avenues are lined with great eucalyptus trees and there are many pretty *quintas*. And then across country to *Bucio* beach where I found a solitary spot in which to stop and eat the 2 "poisonous pastries" I carried in my pack. Here I would rest and read for awhile, but Chester came down with a flat tire and left me with time for nothing but repairs! A hasty return, a change of clothes, and I was off to take tea with the *Señorita Ofilia*. I was a lady again instead of a bedraggled cyclist! And I had a delightful afternoon visiting with the *Gamundi* sisters who later took me to see Disney's Fantasia. We dined on sandwiches and cookies carried to the theater and returned home very late. A long day for me.

And today I started the long, long trek towards *Rio*. Another brilliant day with the city crystal clear as it came to life in the morning light. An ideal day for the open road. And I left very early, sneaking along *18 de Julio* and *8 de Octubre* scarcely noticed in the almost-deserted streets. But already a market was in progress in one section and the streets full of flowers and fruit stalls. Out into the life-giving country, into the land of green grass of flowering trees. I didn't care if there was a head wind! Or if the hill were endless. Trees and truck gardens and newly green willows. At mid-day I turned down to the beach, *La Florista*, and ate bread and cheese by the edge of the water. The pines and eucalyptus woods tempted me to enter and rest, but I need, must pedal on my way. Once as I stopped by the side of the road, a policeman came to check on me, but he was quite affable, no bother at all. As I neared *Piriapolis* in the late afternoon, the country changes. It was more open here with views along to the beaches, and there were high hills. A few kilometers of deep eucalyptus trees and I arrived at this village by the sea which is almost all hotels. Rest and a short walk, and I was ready for dinner and bed. Tired because I had eaten little and traveled far.

September 1, 1942—San Carlos—Hotel Concordia—6:30 AM

Yesterday morning, Aug. 31, the skies were gray with clouds brought in by the wind which blew all night. My luck was changing. Would it rain just as I reached *Treinta y Tres* from whence I needed 5 days of rainless weather to reach *Porto Alegre*? *Quién sabe*? I left *Piriápolis* early—rode away from its crescent of beach and deserted hotels into the thick woods and hills which form its background. And thence through *Pan de Azucar* into the open rolling country once more. Extensive pasturelands and the characteristic horsemen with their long, all-enveloping white ponchos. Saddles with solid trees, much sheepskin padding, and flimsy little metal stirrups. My road climbed over hills from which there were sweeping views of Uruguayan countryside and rolled past occasional bits of eucalyptus woods. Hungry for want of breakfast, I pursued a red *panaderia* car until I finally overtook it and was able to buy a loaf of bread and cheese. And then I stopped by the side of the road for the usual bread and cheese. At noon I arrived here in *San Carlos* and since I liked the place I decided to stop. But I was so full of bread and cheese that the soup, peaches, fish, and *dulce de leche* had lost their usual appeal. In the afternoon I pedaled to *Punta del Este* for *paseo, no más*. Pedaled easily without my usual cargo. Through *Maldonado* with its blue-domed church and down to the long beach which curves away to the cluster of white buildings at *Punta del Este*. An elegant resort with many beautiful residences and large hotels. The first of the ocean beaches, it has the quiet waters of the river on one side of the peninsula, and the breakers of the Atlantic on the other. For diversion, I bought a dozen oranges and stopped in a solitary spot behind the bushes along the beach to rest and read. Then suddenly it was cold and I rode away to *San Carlos*. A very gray afternoon. Gone the keenness of detail of the preceding days. Everything clothed in a gray overtone. In town again, I changed and walked out. Around the *plaza* with its old-looking church and through the streets. In a grocery store I stopped to ask a question and spent a sociable hour talking with the genial store keeper who had foods from all over the world. Then a good dinner and early to bed in preparation for a difficult day ahead. Cross-country on earth roads to *Minas*. But the sound of rain unsettled my plans! And more plans would have to wait on the weather.

September 2, 1942—Pan de Azucar—Hotel Nuñes—10:00 PM

All day yesterday, the 1st, I sat indoors listening to the rain pouring outside and wondering if there would ever be a lull which would permit me to be on my way. But there was no break in the continuous downpour. The "*tiempo de Santa Rosa*" had arrived. So I sat in my bare room and wrote letters going no farther than 3 times to the *comedor* to take my meals. And the folks who came to eat in that small town hotel eyed me curiously, the *señora* and *señorita* in black, the *estancieros* in boots and baggy trousers. But I quickly disappeared in my room, leaving them to speculate. At noon I found myself with a table companion, someone who took it upon himself to find out about me. And in the afternoon, this man came to my room with a *cafecito* and stayed long to talk. But the night brought problems. One of the *estancieros*, looking doubly fat in his baggy pants, came to my room on the pretext of borrowing "*un libro muy interesante*," and he lingered. So when my table companion came to the door I urged him to come in. Safety in numbers! But therewith began a contest of time, each man waiting for the other to leave! One read a newspaper through 40 times, and the other stared stupidly at my English guide, and I mended and packed and hoped they'd leave before dawn. But neither stirred and at 11:00 pm I took the initiative, telling them both they'd have to go and let me sleep. The one I had urged to come in went away in a rage, and the other practically had to be pushed out. *Qué cosa!* Why I permit such situations to develop when I can foresee them in advance is more than I can understand. It must be my endless curiosity about human nature. But I was truly irritated when one of the "gentlemen" returned to my room after I had gone to bed. Which one it was I never knew, for I didn't turn on the light. To his "*Dígame una cosa*," I replied with a sharp, "*Vaya inmediatamente*," and he went. I turned over and slept to the sound of pounding rain.

And this morning I resolved to go, come what may. Restlessness sent me on my way in spite of gray skies. Refreshing, the open road. But before I had even gotten the rhythm of the pedals, I was turned back by flood waters which had risen over the bridge across the river. Men on guard there suggested I try the railway bridge and I took their suggestion. But as I paused at the station to ask permission, the skies grew almost as black as night and heavy rains commenced again. Enveloped in visor, hood, and poncho, I limped down the tracks and across the bridge and back to the highway, laughing at myself all the while, in high spirits despite the nasty weather. But 10 kms down the road my spirits collapsed when I discovered I had lost my 2 spare tires. After carrying one tire all the way from Santiago and another from B.A., I had to lose them in Uruguay! And I was depending on them to see me through to *Rio*. With hope, I turned back, searching the road and asking all passers-by if they had seen my *gomas*, but fate was against me, and I found no trace of them. Again I turned toward *Minas*. But when I reached this town, I was so thoroughly soaked that I thought it best to stop. So again I spent the afternoon in a small hotel hoping for better weather. More letters and a walk out to buy stamps was my only diversion. But for sociability, I lingered to talk to the man in the post office and the chap in the bicycle shop.

September 5, 1942—Montevideo—Hotel España—10:00 PM

The past 3 days have been so filled with confusion and doubt and shattered plans that all my energy has been consumed in trying to reach some decision, in trying to bring order out of the chaos in my mind. September the 3rd, I left my cheerless hotel in *Pan de Azucar* and went back to the road with joy, for the skies were clearing and the sun coming through. A gay inviting day with welcome warmth to dry the wet clothing which I wore. At the *Solis* river I found an expanse of water across the road, but it was not deep, and I pushed Chester through the muddy current, stopping for a sociable chat with men at the other side. Then on to the point where the roads forked and I turned toward *Minas*. Now I'm really on the way to Brazil, I thought. And I enjoyed the ups and downs and the many *montes*. But there were crude shelters of branches amongst those eucalyptus groves where the woodcutters lived in poverty. Before long I sighted the houses of *Solis* and I decided to go on to the country beyond before stopping for lunch—the lunch I was destined never to eat. For on the outskirts of the town I was stopped by a policeman with whom I walked for a while before we were picked up and driven to the *comiseria* where I was held until mid-afternoon. Questions, questions, questions. With the solemn procedure of being ushered from the office of one official to that of another until the highest had satisfied his curiosity. Then just when I hoped to be on my way again, I was told I must go on to *Minas* by omnibus. Why the intense concern over me here? I was irritated not to be able to ride my bike when the day was so ideal. And I disliked the trip by omnibus with me in cycling clothes and all the passengers looking at me and my police escort. In *Minas,* we descended at the *comiseria,* and I was highly irritated to find Chester's cyclometer broken, but no one cared for that, and I was ordered from office to office with more than the usual dispatch. More questions but always the same ones and I knew them now by heart. *Nombre? Edad? Nacionalidad? Soltera o casada? Motivo en el viaje? Itinerario en Uruguay?* I answered mechanically. Then followed orders I couldn't understand, and as a man took my money I began to realize the meaning of what was taking place. They were putting me in jail! And a man with keys was waiting. Tired from lack of food and an afternoon of grilling, I lost control and gave up to tears which came in spite of me. Why was I being held? What had I done? How long would I be there? Would I be permitted to get in touch with the American consul? Only vague replies which gave me no hint of what might be in store. And I was too choked with tears to ask further. I could only wait and hope. Down a long hall of barred rooms I was lead, then a door was opened and Chester and I were ushered inside. A clanking of steel, a turning of a key in a lock, and for the first time in my life I knew the meaning of the loss of liberty. And I felt utterly hopeless and alone. More tears before I could get hold of myself and take note of my quarters. A large room with adjoining bath and with four beds. But there was only one other occupant, a dark woman who seemed quite affable when I was finally equal to conversation. A few minutes later a couple of bowls of nondescript stew were brought to us, and I ate because I was hungry, but the atmosphere of a stained table, crumbs from previous meals, a chipped enamel bowl, and a spoon which had a taste all its own were not conducive to appetite. Food gave me staying power, however, and I was able to retrieve the sense of adventure with which I face new experience. Life looked better and I could joke with the guards and officials who came at regular intervals to request my papers and documents. Tired at last, I crawled in under the ponchos on my bed, but I slept with my clothes on for there were no sheets and I never knew when I'd have to get up to produce more papers.

And yesterday morning before daybreak I was roused once more. *"Tiene que marchar,"* they said. With a clank the door closed behind me and I took leave of my brown companion and was transported bag and baggage to the station. At 6:00, while the moon and stars were still shining, the train started for *Montevideo* carrying me reluctantly with it. With me went a large genial woman who immediately set me at ease and also a stern policeman who kept vigil by my side. Reserved at first, we were all the best of friends after the 4 hrs. of journeying to the capital. Descending from the train we were met with a battery of newspaper men and as we left the station we were surrounded by clicking cameras and a curious crowd. I was confused and unhappy in my tramp-like costume, but the grim march of events were beyond my control. I was taken immediately to *Investigaciones* and there kept in custody the rest of the day. I was detained first in one office and then another and then another, always with someone on vigil, and at regular intervals officials came to question me. The same old set of questions. Name? Nationality? Age? And why was I in Uruguay? I waited and waited and waited. And wondered what I had done and what they would do with me. At noon, I had coffee to carry me through the afternoon, and I waited and waited and waited. Part of the time I was kept in a small room with a gentleman who was busy marking newspapers. Red lines under the names of all Nazis and suspected Nazis. A notebook of subversive elements. But my interest caused him to put away his work and turn the key on his books. I was dangerous. In the late afternoon I was taken to another office whose elegance bespoke chiefdom. From here would come the final verdict. A Mr. Wright from the U.S. Embassy was brought in to interview me, and I was relieved to think I could explain myself to a countryman. But he too was suspicious and I immediately retreated from his attitude of smooth superiority. More conversation. And at length, I was permitted to change my clothes and go freely forth. But Mr. Wright held all my papers. I thought with a smile of the calendar in the *comisería* in Minas, *"Tradición de Libertád."* And the police official on the train who had spoken in glowing terms of freedom in Uruguay. How to get into the hotel was my problem. There I was in the *comisería* with a bicycle which marked me, and my picture was spread across the front page of every newspaper in Montevideo. I suddenly felt deflated and unequal to the task of handling my own affairs, but there was no one else to do it for me. So I left my bike and took a taxi. At Hotel Dante I paused but I couldn't face people I knew, so I came on here where I was given a room. My name and my baggage revealed my identity and I felt like a hunted rat, but the people of the hotel were very kind. I bought a paper to read the lies about me and retired with thankfulness to the security and comfort of my room.

September 7, 1942—Montevideo—The Hall's—10:00 AM

Saturday morning the 5th, I was refreshed and hopeful, and I shopped for a tire and a cyclometer in the fond hope I might continue cycling. At 9:00 I went to the American embassy to get the final verdict from Mr. Wright and he returned all my papers and documents with the suggestion that I go home at once. There were no direct orders in what he said to me, but I felt the pressure behind his words amounted almost to an order and I felt apologetic to the U.S. government for what I had done! I would give up the idea of future travel. Struggling to reorganize my disrupted plans, I was glad to come here in the afternoon to talk with the Halls, kindly folks who had been called upon by the Rosenbuschs to get in touch with me while I was in trouble. I called up Tanti Dora to reassure worried folks in B.A., and she pleaded with me to come back. The Halls also urged me not to go to Brazil, and my mind was made up. It was pleasant to have tea and to talk and forget my own troubles. But in the evening when I was again alone, I brought newspapers to read about myself, listened for conversations in the streets, and felt the eyes of the world fixed on me—some with wonder, some with suspicion.

Then I turned to the isolation of my room and read my diaries until late, wondering if then I might find some clue to the suspicion of my fellow Americans.

Yesterday, the 6th, I spent in friendship free of suspicion. In the morning I left the hotel and moved here to the Halls who had kindly offered me a room. And then I went to the Methodist Church service, stopping en route to walk through the flower and fruit market in the streets and to answer acidly the questions of a reporter from *"La Razon"* who recognized me. After church, Mr. Legg asked me to his home for dinner and there with his family and a Mrs. Schroder, a Miss Wait, and a Miss Cruser, I had a very jolly time. Americans who understood me! Later Miss Wait showed me through Crandon Institute. And in the evening I went with Miss Cruser to the young people's meeting at the house of Mrs. Bals. A good supper and a pleasant time.

September 10, 1942—Montevideo—The Hall's—8:00 PM

Monday morning, the 7th, I had promised to return to the embassy to tell them what I planned to do, and return I did. Bars and police aren't necessary to make me keep my word. But over the weekend, I had had time to see myself in a new light and to talk with others, and the idea of returning was becoming less and less attractive. I stopped at a tourist agency to check and see if my Brazilian documents were in order and then I went back to Mr. Wright with determination. I had done nothing. I wanted desperately to go on. My papers were in order to go to Brazil and to no other place. I would continue my trip with the concession that I'd give up Chester for a while. And Mr. Wright again relieved me of my passport! "For checking," he said. I can be reasonable if approached in the right manner, but this continued suspicion on the part of my own government is making me more and more stubborn. If they'd only tell me what they thought I'd done. In the meantime I remain a virtual prisoner without even a substitute for my passport that would permit me to travel in Uruguay while I wait for the "powers that be" to satisfy themselves on my innocence. In the afternoon I returned to town to find out what returning to Argentina would involve, and I also went back to the U.S. embassy for more information on my passport. Nothing new.

Tuesday, the 8th, I spent the morning writing letters which will probably never reach their destination, but none-the-less I wrote hoping to get in touch with friends. And in the afternoon, Nellie and I went for a *paseo*. Down through the heart of the city and back to the *Rambla*, stopping at the *Tienda Inglesa* for tea, and passing through lovely *Parque Rodo* where the lawns are sprinkled with flowers and where new greens and a sweet fragrance add to the feeling of spring. Montevideo's white buildings and *Palacio Salvo* are very familiar now. I feel at home. Gone the flags of the 7th, flags for the celebration of Brazil's independence day, flags of the U.S., England, Uruguay, Brazil, Russia, and even China.

Yesterday, the 9th, I was called to return to *Investigaciones* and there *Señor Alonzo* had a letter from Jan sent to me in *Treinta y Tres*. And he asked me to read it and translate it! Probably thought it contained some subversive element to which I would react in some particular manner. But it was nothing more than news of the family! For lunch I went to the Legg's again and afterwards with Mrs. Legg to work at the Red Cross. We walked through the springtime beauty of the park and *Avenida Artigas* and spent a sunny afternoon sewing, tea included. Then I hurried home and off to the *Gamundis* for the evening. Through ordinary streets where boys played at *fútbol*, folks stood at front doors or behind the grills of open windows, and knots of conversationalists loitered in front of vegetable shops. A slow easy-going, before-supper-kind-of-life in an ordinary work-a-day world. Ordinary people leading ordinary lives. At Gamundi's the family greeted me with hospitality and we laughed together over my recent predicament. Two chaps from summer school in Santiago also dropped in to add to the merriment, and I was warmed by the jolly crowd. Then, before coming home, Ofelia, Irene, and I went down to the *rambla* for *cena* of *pisa, faina,* and *zu-zu*.

September 11, 1942—Montevideo—The Hall's—9:00 AM

Yesterday more letters to the folks in B.A. who are expecting me back. An attempt to explain the feelings and desires which will carry me on to Brazil, passport permitting. The longer I think about it, the more determined I become. From a distance my recent experiences seem ridiculous rather than serious, and I think I can avoid similar trouble in the future. The girl who was ready to return to B.A. on the first boat and later timidly thinking of taking the train to *Rio* is now ready to pedal on as originally planned. *Vamos a ver.* In the late morning I went out to buy some old newspapers carrying articles about me, and I slipped unobtrusively into the offices of *"La Razon"* and *"El Diario"*, but I was recognized both places. And as the crowd gathered about at *"La Razon"*, I beat a hasty retreat to avoid more photographs! In the afternoon I went to the Brazilian consul and laid my case before him—said I was the *"espia"* who wanted desperately to go to Brazil. And he was encouraging. Then I went off to buy a tire and to search for another *cuenta kilometer*. The latter is not to be had in *Montevideo*, but tires are numerous, and the chap who sold me mine gave me a special price when he learned who I was! Threw in a reptile's leg as a *recuerdo* too! Back to the American embassy I found Mr. Wright and his colleagues in a merry mood. I feel almost undressed when I confront them 'cause they've read my diaries, but I can't help laughing when they mention, "staring stupidly at papers." And when they make me laugh I can't even be irritated with them, although they refuse to help me in any way. It's going to be a contest between their hard-headed "diplomacy" and my stubbornness—stubbornness which gains momentum every day. Business done I wandered off to the *Rambla* and then to *Parque Rodo* where I sat and read, marking time until the hour when Mrs. Hall's tea guests should have gone home. But they were still here when I arrived, so I had a visit and a piece of cake in spite of myself!

September 13, 1942—Montevideo—The Hall's—9:00 AM

Friday, the 11th, I went to visit *Violeta Cavallero's* school for the poor in *Malvin*. Such poverty! In a poor little church, she was working with the ragged group. Baggy clothing hung on their frames. Rags and dirt. But laughter and contentment with all, for they knew nothing else. Songs and games and play "work." And something to eat. So little with which to meet such need. On the way home I bought cala lilies which are so abundant now and struggled home on a crowded bus with my arms full of the white blossoms. In the afternoon Nelly and I walked down past Crandon to the home of a friend, one *Tota Gomez*, where we stayed for tea. An attractive, exuberant girl who served a beautiful table and then showed us her home and garden. Here I was surprised to find a house full of American and English things and a family permeated with propaganda of the moment. They were members of the Bellows Club, paying one cent for each enemy vessel sunk in the war. They were reading ally literature, wearing "V's", working at the Red Cross, and fully expecting the powerful U.S. to win the war. —Wish I, too, could be so optimistic! And in contrast with the sentiment in Argentina, they felt grateful to the English who had built the railroads. Proudly, they told me that in days gone by, their father had bought all their clothes from Montgomery Ward and Co.! And their feeling for the states was almost one of worship. I walked home through springtime flowers and warmth with food for thought.

Yesterday, the 12th, was a day of nothingness. In the morning I went hopefully to the embassy, only to learn they could tell me nothing of my passport. It was being "worked on" in B.A., so they said. Why are they holding it so long? If they want to certify it, that can be quickly done through the *Santiago* office. If they do not want me to go to Brazil, they should have a simple policy of "no." Only a few days ago my passport was considered in order, but now they must "work" on it. Being just a simple soul, I can't understand these things. Neither can I understand their refusal to help me in any way or to give me a letter with which I could at least travel in Uruguay.   And I am irritated by their attitude that, as an American, I should conduct myself in a better manner.   True I ride a bicycle and am therefore unconventional.   But I have made friends for myself and my country by being decent, by going abroad with the idea of liking the people and looking for the good.   Never have I been guilty of the critical attitude and the blustering braggadocio of the typical American tourist who is hated all over the world.   All I ask is recognition of these things and permission to go my way in peace!   But I am held as a thorn in the flesh while diplomats decide how best to get rid of me.   Oh well—*paciencia*.   In the afternoon I repaired my equipment and set my things in order.   And this only heightened my irritation for it revealed how many things are missing from my baggage.   A photograph of Chester and me, 2 pictures of Chilean *huasos*, a newspaper clipping, and more. Little things to be sure, but things carefully sorted and saved from the great quantity of things I cannot carry.   And then my heart sank at the discovery that my green silk dress was missing.   I knew exactly where it had gone—into the hands of my cellmate in *Minas*—for I had found my suitcase rummaged there but had missed nothing until the present.   I am trying desperately to keep my memories of Uruguay untainted by this experience, but I find it hard to be charitable in the face of a broken cyclometer, an injured gear cable, missing possessions, and endless days of lost time.   *Paciencia!*

September 15, 1942—Montevideo—The Hall's—9:00 AM

Sunday, the 13th, was another "churchy" day, but I am more than grateful to the Christians here who treat me like a person.   Heathen though I am, I cannot escape the recognition that the church molds fine character, and seen in this light, it becomes a good thing in spite of the orthodoxy which I myself cannot accept.   After a Spanish service here at Mr. Hall's church, I went off to dine again with the Leggs, walking down *18 de Julio* and *8 de Octubre* which have become so familiar. The flower market which sprawls for 2 blocks along *18 de*

Julio is now a riot of color! Fresias, poppies, snaps, pansies, calendulas. And the leaf buds are breaking open on the trees which line the avenue. I spent a pleasant afternoon with the Leggs. They're real people. And before leaving I walked out to the park with Mrs. Legg and the children. Deer and ponies and *salchichas*. And a stadium reverberating with *fútbol* enthusiasm! In the evening I went again to the young people's meeting, this time to the home of the Coates. A long and welcome walk with the group from the church. An outlet for energy no longer expended on pedals. *Violetta* talked, her eyes full of enthusiasm for the God in which I cannot even believe. And there was warmth and companionship. But my mind was captured by the young Norwegian there, symbol of the country and the people I always love. In his Nordic reserve I felt the depth and the painful beauty of the fjords and I remembered again the far-seeing eyes of Hans. Old memories stirring. Ashes fanned to live coals.

Yesterday, the 14th, I spent the morning writing, venturing out only once to look for mail at the embassy. In the early afternoon I returned to inquire about my passport, and I came away with the same old discouraging replies which left me in a stupor of futility the rest of the afternoon. I feel so bitter in the face of official power—just another atom, powerless to protest. And yet I feel that I am being dealt with in a most unjust manner. I have been as honest and as frank with the U.S. officials as I know how to be, and yet I have received not one single honest explanation from them. I don't even know what in reality roused the suspicions which brought about my trouble. And now they refuse to tell me why my passport is being held indefinitely. I would expect such treatment from the *Criollos,* but I thought Yankees were different. I also thought consulates existed to aid their nationals, but I was naive. Never have I asked anything of my government abroad, for I feel that my problems are mine to work out as best I can, but now when for the first time I truly need help, my government steps in unasked, not to help but to hinder. The State Dept. is so busy currying the favor of the South American republics, so busy dazzling the populace with propaganda of the northern colossus, that it is annoyed by a tourist suspected of espionage. A crackpot riding a bicycle ought to be removed as soon as possible. The fact that I have been the victim of a mistake is immaterial. The fact that I am a human being with feelings and desires and even rights is not considered. My losses and disappointments are overlooked. I am approached as a public nuisance who ought to gracefully pack up and go home. But childlike, I consider myself entitled to the same privileges which other tourists enjoy and I shall continue to ask for them. In the late afternoon a *Señora* came for tea, and afterwards *Violeta* and another dropped in, so I forgot my troubles in an interlude of sociability.

September 17, 1942—Montevideo—The Hall's—9:00 AM

Wednesday, the 15th, I went again to the embassy, hoping to learn something definite of my situation. Nothing. Only the smooth grins which said as plain as day: "Aren't you sorry you didn't do what we suggested you do?" My feeling of discouragement knows no bounds. They can keep my passport for a year, and I have no recourse but to accept it. In the afternoon I ventured out timidly on Chester, wondering what might be in store for the "*espia,*" but all went well, and I pedaled joyfully to *Pocitos* and out *Ave. Artigas.* New leaves on the trees. And sun. And in me a passionate longing to leave the city and pedal off into the country which always brings new life to my mind and my body. In the evening I went with the Halls to visit friends across the street, wealthy traveled people with whom we visited until late, staying for coffee and cake.

Yesterday, the 16th, I did little. Wrote, mended, thought. Tried to counteract the bitterness which grows within me. At 3:30 I met Margaret Forsinan at Crandon, and we had tea together at her home and later walked in the park. More of the exciting new greens of spring. And conversation about the foreign policy of the States. I find that others here have encountered the same "helpfulness" at the embassy which I have come to know so well. Later I came home hoping to arrive in time to see the funeral procession of ex-president *Terra*, but it had already passed and only the crowds of people remained in the streets. Official homage had been paid to the dead, but that the people resented the dictatorship was apparent in the fact that they carried on their business as usual.

September 18, 1942—Colonia Suiza—Klein Flottbeck

And yesterday came the ultimatum. Beating my usual path to the *embajada* in *Agraciada*, I found Mr. Wright unusually affable. He shook my hand. And then, in words full of smiles, he told me that the State Department had asked for my immediate return to the USA. These words cut deep, but I said nothing. The atmosphere was too saturated with a you're-getting-what-you-asked-for attitude. Later Mr. Meninger officiated at the death of my passport, striking out permissions and sprawling new regulations in their place. I was given 2 months in which to get home. When I summoned up enough courage to ask what I had done to deserve such treatment, he snapped back in anger that they didn't want me running around South America getting myself into trouble and expecting others to get me out! I said nothing more, for there was nothing more to be said. Words of mine were obviously not wanted. As I walked away from the office my first reaction was one of relief. At last I had an answer, knew what I must do. And after battling official difficulties for so long, there was a sense of ease in the fact that major decisions had been made for me and I had only to follow their lead. I could even be gay at dinnertime. But afterwards as I walked out with Nelly to get my Argentine visa, to ask about boats and to browse through the old section of the city and the port, I became very sad. I turned in upon myself and thought, for this thing which had come to me was one of the most momentous of my life. Dreams and hopes and desires for the year to come were ashes. And I felt the sting of punishment in what had been done. But punishment for what? I had gotten into trouble with the police, but I had done nothing wrong. In the face of strong suggestions that I go home, I had said that I would continue in what I believed was my right to travel as other tourists were traveling. But that right proved to be an ethereal thing which wasn't really there. I was a special case because I rode a bicycle and got myself into trouble and I could take my choice of going home or being sent home. With the Richardson stubbornness, I persisted in the path which lead to being sent home. And they had their point. I was a tourist without motive, a crackpot adventuress who would take advice from no one. And to a degree they were right. But underneath that stubbornness were very human desires. A love of travel and of the out-of-doors which is almost a passion. An emphasis on the living present born and bred during these years of war. A feeling that this is my last chance to see South America. A hesitancy to confront war-torn America with my philosophy of pacifism. Desire so strong that I must go on, must risk the possibility that I might not be dealt with as a human being. I played a losing game, and in defeat I felt futility—as if the walls of officialdom were so high and so broad that a mere person like myself could beat himself against them endlessly without being noticed. All these thoughts and sensations surged through me as I walked, and only once did I stir out of myself to note the hull of a Swedish ship and to thrill to her clean whiteness and her blue and yellow flags. Göteburg written on her hull stirred exciting memories. After tea I packed, hardly able to collect my wits, let alone my possessions. And I called to say good bye to friends. I also called Mr. Wright to ask if I might ride my bicycle to *Colonia*. But when he said no to that and also to my going by omnibus I decided that he was not motivated by a spirit of justice, and I made up my mind to go in spite of him where *Alonzo* of *Investigaciones* assured me I would have no troubles with the police. After *cena* I called for the last time on the Gansundis, enjoying once again the friendliness of the 4 sisters. And one of the chaps from summer school in Santiago dropped in again to eat *pisa* with us and to add to the fun of my last night in *Montevideo*.

September 19, 1942—S.S. City of Colonia—1:00 PM

And yesterday morning, the 18th, I left *Montevideo* in the gray mist of early morning. An alarm at 6:00 ended a wakeful night, and after a few moments of packing I was ready again for the open road. Good byes to Nelly and Mr. Hall who came to the door in their robes. And I couldn't help saying, "*La espia se va,*" and waving gaily to a couple of policemen who had watched me with great interest as I packed up. Then the familiar streets of the city, gray and deserted and soon the country with the long straight road rising and falling ahead. How good the pedals under my feet! How good the sun and the green grass and the red verbenas by the side of the road. And I needed the fun of cycling and the peace of the country to clean the bitterness and futility from my mind. The only blot on the day was the fact that I was doing what I had been told not to do, and this I did not like even though I felt perfectly justified in it. Easy miles rolled away. Five oranges sustained my energy and I looked forward to dinner in *Colonia Suiza*. Then a uniform stepped out into the road and stopped me. Allah be praised! Was I to go through that again! I thought everyone in Uruguay knew me and that all the questions I'd answered, I would now be free. But no! Where are you from? Where do you go? Who are you? And my name gave me away! I must wait until they communicate with the *jefetura* in *Sorianas*. Damn the *jefetura* in *Sorianas*! They had been the source of all my original troubles, and now I was beholden to them again. For 3 hours, I waited, but the police were very affable. They treated me well and invited me to dine on their soup and salad. And I was in no hurry. But I had misgivings about what might happen. Suppose I had to confront Mr. Wright again! Heaven forbid! Eventually I was permitted to continue my way, and by mid-afternoon I was back at the familiar hotel in *Colonia Suiza*. Tea. And the peace of a country place, with land and orchards. Orchid wisteria against a sky now gray. And the simple German servant who walked with me about the place and showed me her system for selecting fertile eggs by dangling above them a gold ring on a silk thread. Dinner of *sopa, carne, polo, panqueque,* and *naranjas* followed by the comfort of a hot shower and a room flooded with moonlight. Peace, peace, peace.

September 20, 1942—Buenos Aires—Jan's—9:00 PM

Yesterday morning, the 19th, I wakened early and shortly after 7:00 I rode away, reluctant to leave pretty *Colonia Suiza.* A short cut took me around a *comisería* and thus avoided interference which might mean serious delay and I pedaled with purpose for I had to reach my boat by mid-day. A faulty cable annoyed me no end, but cycling was fun, and I loved the ups and downs of Uruguay in spite of the disaster that the country had brought to me. Another *comisería* had to be passed on the outskirts of Colonia and I approached it with fear, wondering if I could pass without being seen. But no, an officer stepped out and once again I was answering the questions that were now so passé. Time! This once it was important to me. And I told the officer I had to make that boat. He asked my name and with dignity and self-confidence I looked him square in the eye and said, "Helen Richardson." *"Siga, no mas,"* he directed me. And with relief and thanks, I went my way. In *Colonia* the *aduana* officials recognized me, with the result that I had to tell my story to all of them. And the boat company sent me to the Argentine consul just to make sure that I was "in order." On the deck, the usual crowd gathered around, more interested now than ever, and the official who checked my passport said, *"Muy conocida!"* I was infamous! Three hours on the river passed pleasantly. *Colonia* and the rolling hills of Uruguay disappeared and the city of B.A. took form as the sun beat endlessly down on the muddy, *La Plata.* *Darsena Sud* with the many masts and stacks was interesting, exciting, full of the flavor of far-away places which every port possesses. But after the "City of Colonia" had docked, all romance was lost in the routine of *aduana.* My scanty and worn equipment looked too ridiculous to merit official interest, but the authorities said I would have to leave my bicycle. Again I felt flat. In cycling clothes and with saddlebags over my arm I must make my way through the heart of the city. But when an official from the *aduana* helped me to the street car and a young man from the boat bought my ticket and a man from the subway carried my bags to *Añasco 4*, I felt like I hadn't been so badly received after all. And here at Jan's I was welcomed back as if I hadn't been a bad child. How glad I was to just relax and visit and forget my troubles for a while. And after tea, *Inés* and Mrs. Rosenbusch came to welcome me back to the fold. Home again!

September 22, 1942—Buenos Aires—Añasco 4—8:00 AM

Sunday, the 20th, was like other Sundays which have gone before. A lazy morning was followed by dinner at the Rosenbusch's where we gathered with the same old jovial spirit. And afterwards we drove to *Palermo* and walked in the park which is now full of spring time loveliness. Wisteria and many blooming things. And crowds of people. For tea we went to the house of *Mendez* where many of the family had congregated. Five of the Kurths! And others. A happy babble of conversation which would drown anyone's troubles. And at the close of the day I felt ready to face Monday's business of going home.

But yesterday I accomplished little. Most of all I wanted to talk with Mr. Nyhus at the U.S. embassy, for I am still looking for a frank explanation of why I am being sent directly home. But I was unable to see him, so my trip to town degenerated into a visit to *Expreso Villalonga* where I was greeted as *Mata Hari* and where I spent a sociable interlude as I gathered data on boats and planes and trains. In the afternoon I sorted over my junk with an eye to going home by plane, discarded things no longer useful and wondered if I could get Chester and a toothbrush within the 25 kilogram limit. And for *cena* I went again to the Rosenbusch's in order to have a visit with Mrs. Hall who had just arrived for a church congress.

September 25, 1942—Buenos Aires--Añasco 4—8:00 AM

Tuesday, the 22nd, I spent the morning puttering around and in the early afternoon I went to see Mr. Nyhus, full of questions and hoping for a suggestion as to how I might yet salvage some travel experience from my broken plans. He was very, very nice and he not only assured me that there was nothing disastrous in my canceled passport, but he said he could see no reason why I shouldn't go up the Pacific coast making stopovers wherever I liked. I was grateful for his moral support and I went away with a bounce in my stride. I could go by plane, cutting down the traveling time to a few days and leaving more than a month for sight seeing along the way. At least I could see a little of Bolivia, Peru, and Ecuador. I was satisfied. The Bolivian and Peruvian consuls yielded nothing but locked doors. But the Colombian consul gave me a visa *en seguida* and I was encouraged to find that no notice was taken of the limitations in my passport.

Wednesday, the 2nd, was a whole day of business. In the morning I went again to the Peruvian and Bolivian consuls where I found that *nacionalidad Norte Americana* was an open-sesame to easy permissions. And when *Villalonga* secured a place for me on the Sunday plane to La Paz, I was pleased with the successes of the morning. In the afternoon I went off to *aduana*, wondering what negotiations would be necessary to retrieve Chester and how hard-boiled the officials might be. But I found that the doorman and the secretaries and the chiefs all knew me now and they were all very affable and helpful. They gathered around in knots in each office. I entered and they asked a thousand questions of what had happened in Uruguay. In fact they asked so many questions and devoted so much time to coffee drinking that I was obliged to wait 9 hours for the necessary documents. But I was permitted to bring my bike in without charge, so I counted the afternoon a success.

Thursday, the 24th, was a long and eventful day. In the early morning, I trekked out to the Panamanian consul, fortified with a receipt for the $150 which now must be deposited by all who pass the canal. And I secured my visa without trouble. Then back to the center to talk to the Mexican consul and thence to Villalonga to actually buy my Panagra ticket. I felt extravagant as I counted out more than $600 worth of traveler's cheques—money carefully hoarded in anticipation of another year of travel—but, like a condemned man, I wanted to make the very most of my last days abroad and only by air could I see anything of the countries to the north, so I felt justified. Better to invest in experience than to save for a war-exhausted world, I was saying to myself. *Villalonga's* pert Italian conducted me to Panagra for final arrangements and I had uneasy moments as my passport was checked and doublechecked. Perhaps they would send me to Chile in order to live up to the letter of Montevideo's sentence. But they gave me the ticket on the promise that I would get a U.S. visa before leaving. And then I forgot all problems in an unexpected surprise. A chap stepped up and asked if I were Helen Richardson, and in utter amazement I recognized Page Smith, an old classmate now flying for Pan-Air. How small the world! And as if surprises never go singly, I bumped into *Leoncio Andrade* out in the street! The doctor from Santiago whom I hadn't seen since I refused to make a weekend trip with him to the *Cordilleras*! At lunchtime I was disturbed over the new problem of a U.S. visa, now that I had recovered from the surprises of the morning and had time to think. After *Montevideo's* experience I expected no quarter from American officials and I had no desire to seek them out. To go to the U.S. embassy here would mean returning home via Chile and since in my mind that was an arbitrary stipulation, I was anxious to avoid it. I prayed for some loophole by which I could evade U.S. officialdom until back on my own doorstep. I had no desire to see plans wrecked and dreams shattered by naively walking into another consulate. So I went to *Villalonga*, told them frankly what was on my mind, and asked if I might get my ticket without the visa. I could go to *La Paz* they said. Relief. And I started again my quest for visas. With a letter from the

Boston Bank in my hand I found the Guatemalan consul much
more hospitable than before and in addition to my visa he gave
me a card to relatives in Mexico!   But Ecuador was
disappointing.   No visas without special permission from
Quito and a wait of several days—conditions which
eliminated me.   So I finished the day with a stop to have
pictures taken, and then rushed home to help with the meal
because I had asked Page to come out for the evening.   Page
with the same look and laugh of the schoolboy but with the
worldliness of much living.

September 26, 1942—Buenos Aires-- Añasco 4—9:00 PM

Yesterday, the 25th, was another long, long day.   What
time one can consume in the red tape of traveling!   I had to
pick up my new photographs and carry them to the Mexican
consul.   And then there was Chester to rescue from the
aduana.   But, wonder of wonders, I didn't have to wait and I
felt quite at home there in *Darsena Sud* where I knew all the
officials.   To pedal again was good, and in spite of street
clothes I rode all the way to Panagra's office.   But, per usual, I
was an object of curiosity, and one man stopped to ask about
my *"raid"*.   In the afternoon I shopped for a suitcase and
decided against buying one.   A box would do as well.   I
shopped also for dollars and after passing up bills so ancient
that they looked foreign, I finally bought a hundred for $70
worth of pesos.   Allah protect me in the job of transporting
them all the way to the States!   I'll earn my $30 profit!   Before
leaving the center I stopped at the Mexican consulate again to
collect my last visa, and thence I went wearily home, ready at
last for the long trip north.   For *cena*, we all went over to the
Rosenbusch's.   Another good-bye party!   With *Tanti Trudy* and
Tanti Anita there and also *Marta* and *Enrique*.   One of those
jolly family gatherings which I like so well and which I shall
miss when I leave B.A.

September 27, 1942—Tucuman—Hotel Playa—10:00 PM

And yesterday, the 26th, I completed all last minute details. All morning I packed and unpacked and packed again. My baggage seemed pitifully small, but with my bike weighing 18 kilos, I had to reduce my personal things to 7 kilos. What a job! Over and over again I sorted my things— worn "treasures" which I hated to discard because they had served me so well for so many months. But many had to stay, and I was annoyed at the tenacity with which I clung to things—mere things. I must learn to place experience before things. So little by little the discard heap grew. Faded blue cords which, with the aid of a leather patch, had seen me through nearly 10,000 cycling kilometers. Chilean shoes which had trudged across the *Cordillera*. A flashlight. A spare tire. My impermeable. A spool of thread. A spare strap. Everything not absolutely essential. But try as I would, I couldn't bring myself to part with my tools and saddlebags. Perhaps I would be able to cycle some along the way and I must always be ready to take advantage of the opportunity. By noon the packing job was done, and in the afternoon I rested and walked with Jan and *Carlos* to see their new house in *Parral*. And I thought. For the 3rd time I was ready to leave B.A. and I looked forward to the trip ahead with mixed feelings. I was quite ready to leave—had been ready for weeks—but I felt a smoldering resentment against the injustice which forced me to go at once, forced me to give up my bike, and forced me to spend all at once enough dollars for a year of life abroad. Waters, mountains, heat, cold—these things I could meet philosophically, but somehow I couldn't reconcile myself to the arbitrary dictates of another human being, a man empowered to sit in judgment on others merely by his official position, a little man whose own cramped life held no understanding of other lives cast in a different mold. To him I couldn't explain my fierce joy in a fresh day and a flower by the side of the road, nor could I talk of my love of knowing the world. I could only meekly say yes when ordered to give up the things which meant most to me. There was an abyss between us spanned by his power but not by his understanding. And as a boy who steps on a caterpillar, he carelessly crushed my dreams. "For the war!" What had my going home [anything] to do with the war!—Except to have embassies abroad free to gather more dust!

September 28, 1942—Tucuman—Hotel Plaza—11:00 PM

Yesterday morning I wakened early, full of the excitement of going away. A last breakfast with *Carlos* and Jan, and I went off with *Carlos* who carried my 7 *kilos* of things bundled up in my disreputable saddlebags. By subway to the office of Panagra where I waited for the bus to take me to the airport. And as I rode out of the city, I couldn't help noticing the *Buenos Aires* I was leaving. Broad *Av. 9 de Julio.* The *Congreso* with its park in front— strip of green now bright with flowers. *Rivadavia* and *Anasco 4.* Large, modern, cosmopolitan—an impressive city. And yet there were cows in the street driven by a man who sold fresh milk! Far out in the country we stopped at the airport of *Maron*, and after the formality of inspection we went aboard our DC 3. I sank into a comfortable seat in the back where the wing didn't impede the view and waited anxiously for the take off. Humming motors, bumpy taxiing, down the field, a pause, racing motors, and then the plane surged forward into the wind, and we rose almost imperceptibly into the air. A thrill went through me as we left the ground, but I looked down on the earth of Buenos Aires with the feeling that I'd never see it again. From the air I watched the earth flow by. A rich agricultural patchwork of green and brown with scattered houses. Squares, rectangles, parallelograms of cultivation. And there was *Lujan* with its tall church—and *Haras,* Argentina. I could even see the fillies grazing in the field! Once again I was riding the airways, only this time there were Stars and Stripes on the wings instead of the Rising Sun. At noon a tray was set in my lap, and I dined on pork and potatoes, a tangerine, and a piece of cake. But much more interesting was the panorama below. As time passed, the cultivated lands below lost their richness and bits of brush land were interspersed with the field crops! We were nearing *Cordoba*. Then suddenly we were there, winging over the mass of white buildings which make up the city. And beyond I could see the shadowy forms of the *Sierras*. During our 10- minute stop I called *Tomás* by phone, and it was good to hear his voice again, but I had my usual difficulties understanding what was said over the phone! Then back to the air again, flying northward over the Sierras. *Lago San Roque* and *La Falda* tucked in their places on the other side of the hills. Crumpled, deserty hills which were so familiar. The red earth forms of *Angamira* and even the *pensión* where I had stopped in the rain months ago. Then on into unknown lands. Desert lands with low brush, all laced with animal paths and criss-crossed with roads. A great expanse of white salt passed beneath us. And again we came to cultivated lands. *Tucuman* with its mountains to the west. Here we descended again and my bike and bag were taken from the plane, for I planned to stay over a couple of days. With my usual independence I started to pack up my bike, but I found the Panagra personnel ready to take care of me, so I relaxed and let them do it. They brought Chester and me here to my hotel and secured my room for me while I just came along. How easy! And I was glad to relax a bit after the excitement of the day. But not for long. With an unknown city outside, I couldn't rest. A desire to know drew me out into the streets, and I went in search of *Armando Cecilio*, another acquaintance from summer school in *Santiago*. But he was not home nor was he at the university. A *portero*, however, showed me a little of that institution, and the rest of the afternoon I spent in poking about wherever I pleased. Around the principal streets—*Las Heras, 24 de Septiembre, Mendoza*—noting where shops where Chester's newly broken gear cable might be repaired and where I might buy cycling sandals to replace the abandoned Chilean "gum boats." In the evening the *plaza* claimed me and there I sat to listen to band music and to watch the crowds of people pass. Soft air and the odor of orange blossoms reminded me I had come a long way. Spring was coming to B.A., but summer was approaching *Tucuman*.

September 29, 1942—Tucuman—Hotel Plaza—9:00 PM

Yesterday morning at 9:00 *Armando* came to the hotel in search of me. The same old *Armando*. And he devoted the morning to showing me about. First we went to the old building where the declaration of independence was signed in 1816. And thence to *Parque 9 de Julio* where flowers bloomed on every side—phlox, gerbera, roses, Paraguay jasmine. Masses of color in formal arrangement. Here we collected cotton from the bursting pods of the *palobarracho* and we stopped to see *Tucuman's* 1st sugar mill. Primitive wooden rollers turned by mule power and copper cauldrons for evaporating the syrup. By contrast we visited next the *Ingenio Guzman*, largest sugar plant in *Tucuman*, and I was amazed to see the massive machinery for crushing the cane and the giant tanks for reducing the juice. All was quiet now for the season runs from June to August, but the plant is capable of producing 500,000 kilos of sugar per day. Clustered about the central plant is a veritable town, complete with stores and church. And as I walked down its broad, dusty street lined with low, flower-smothered houses I couldn't help thinking how very different was the atmosphere here compared with that of other parts of Argentina. Back at my hotel I prevailed upon Armando to stay and have dinner with me, and we laughed together over experiences in Chile, recalling words peculiar to the *Chilenos*—*onces, benzuna, wawa, manteca, gondola,* and the like. Afterwards *Armando* went to his work and I to do errands. First, there was Chester to be repaired, and I took him to a man whose shingle said "Raleigh." And next there were shoes to be bought—light ones which wouldn't increase the *peso* of my pack. By 4:00 I was ready to meet Armando again, and this time we went to see the university's zoological museum. Here I was introduced to a number of professors and I was shown about the collection of birds and animals and the library with its precious old books. Then we returned to the house of *Cecilio* where I met the family and took tea with *Armando*. A jovial family gathering whose spirit warmed me more than the *copetina* I had with them. At dark I returned home to revel in my room with its facilities for writing and its view over the street and *Plaza Independencia*—a vantagepoint clear to the hearts of the Latins.

And this morning *Armando* came again to help me see *Tucuman*—this time with a car and friends. All together we drove out of town and up The *Cerro*, a way that lead us along avenues lined with *paloborrachos* and through *quintas* green with fruit trees and bright with flowers. Beautiful countryside, luxuriant and intimate. As we climbed into the hills we could look down on the green and yellow of the valley, but I was more interested to see the vegetation of the hillsides. It was so thick as to be almost tropical, and the great trees were draped with vines and ferns and plants of the air. There were *paloborrachos* with their large pods bursting into snowballs of cotton and crowned with exquisite pink blooms. I loved it all, for it had something of Panama in it, and yet it was not Panama, but *Tucuman*. At the summit we stopped to look at the magnificent new *hosteria* not yet open to the public, but we were cheated in our view, for we had climbed into the clouds. Shadowy mountains and valleys gave only a hint of the surrounding country. When at noon I was left again on my doorstep, I ate a hasty bit of bread and cheese, changed, and sallied out on Chester just to amble around and enjoy the country. Toward the hills as is my want. But I turned off and followed country roads to *San Pablo*. As in the morning I found the country pretty and green and lazy, but now in the afternoon sun it was perfumed by the odor of petunias, umbrella trees, orange blossoms. There was no cane in the cane fields, only crushed bits in the road to remind one that this was Argentina's sugar center, but men were working the earth in preparation for next year's crop. A diversion in my cycling was the young blade who galloped out of a field, asked if I were *señora* or *señorita*, and invited me to cycle with him *Domingo!* I hurried away before he decided to give up his horse and take to his bike, *hoy dia!* From the valley I turned up the road towards *Villa Nouques*, back again into the hills with their luxuriant vegetation. But I traveled slowly now, and I could better see the broadleafed plants, the slim creepers, and the lovely purple and yellow flowering things. Reluctantly I turned back to the city for a long drink and a bath before sallying out to walk in the streets lazy with fiesta and to pass the evening in the *plaza* where a military band played martial music. How these Latins do love music! It always draws them out in crowds. Even a poor hollow-faced, bare-foot boy sat quietly there on my bench. Dirty, ragged, sad-eyed he listened to the music.

October 2, 1942—Salta—Hotel Plaza—12:00 Noon

September 30th I spent part of the day in *Tucuman*. *Armando* came again in the morning and took me to see the university.   The physics dept. with its many English publications, the museum with an interesting Indian collection, the 2 telescopes which *Armando* himself had made, the library, and the dept. of architecture where students were drawing. We visited at length with a Hindu Naranjan Sin G H Kang and a professor Felix Cernuschi, and the latter invited us to have a drink with him before lunch. Afterwards I had to pack and collect a letter from *Villalonga*, and then it was time to go to my plane. A chap came to my door, announced himself as Panagra and took charge of my baggage and bicycle, while a car picked us up outside! *Qué facil*! I'm not accustomed to being looked out for in such style! At the airport I found Armando with a gift for me and we sat and visited until the plane arrived from B.A. and was ready to leave for *Salta*. How good *Armando* was to me during my short stay in *Tucuman*. I shall treasure the *faja* and the little *boleadora* that he gave me. Per usual I sat on the edge of my seat, the better to see the panorama passing below. Time seems more precious than ever before and I feel that every moment must be packed with seeing. A few moments of cultivated lands, and then we flew on over an uninhabited desert-like section. Low bushes. And earth crumpled into sharp-edged hills. A sandy river bed with a curving wisp of water. A bank eroded into pillars of sandstone. A mass of blue mountains to the west. And we flew low close to the hills and the mountains. Just an hour and we were approaching *Salta*. The valley widened here, the mountains stood up high in the west and there below were the clustered buildings of the city. *Salta!* Another name on the map was coming to life! Efficient Panagra service soon deposited us, bag and baggage at our various hotels, but I wasn't satisfied with mine and I changed over here to a better place at the same price. Then there were still a few hours of sunlight in which to make the acquaintance of the town. And I walked about, getting the feel of the low familiar buildings, the slow life in the streets, and the pleasant, shady *plazas*. Always I felt joy in the mountains rising out beyond the city. Having made the acquaintance of one *Eduardo Gitlin* who was on my plane, I had company at dinnertime, and afterwards we went to a movie and topped off the evening with café and peppermint in the bar of the new *Hotel Salta*. Life in *Salta* was sociable and fun.

And yesterday, October 1st, I spent a long day in knowing *Salta* better. At 7:30 I rolled off on Chester, a bit groggy from the late hour of the night before, but quickly enlivened by the feel of the pedals. A turn up to the *Guemes* monument at the foot of the *cerro*, a few *vueltas* in the northern part of town, and then out on the road to *Jujuy*. But I was far from alone on the road, for I shared it with many Indians bound for town.

"*Un saludo grandote para Ud, Helen, la simpatica americanita, cuya amistad me cuesta dejar.* I desire for you good luck in your life and remember me." Eduardo Gitlin, Salta, Oct 2/1942—Rep. Argentina

They passed on horseback and on mule back, the women riding sidesaddle, clad in bulging shirts and men's hats, and carrying 2 baskets of *verduras* slung from the saddles with pointed leather skirts protruding fore and aft. Some of the women carried babies in their arms. Some of the men drove little burros loaded with *leña*. Stolid faces. Rags.

And also in the road were school children in white. Brown faces which turned 1st in amazement and then in laughter as the funny *gringa* passed. But I was too absorbed in the panorama to care who laughed. My road followed a valley guarded by erect desert hills and holding a river that seemed too small for its broad sandy course. But wherever man had put water on the land, it had lost its parched brushiness and had bloomed as a garden. Lush bits of vegetables and fruits were scattered along the way. And little adobe houses were shaded by great trees. Weeping willows raised luxuriant green tops. And I followed on always looking forward to the mountain *vista* beyond each turn. A chap in a pickup stopped to chat and I talked with him a long while, for time meant nothing now that I had no goal. But before noon I turned back, riding lazily in the heat but anticipating *almuerzo* after a morning *sin café*. And I met again the traffic of the morning going home with empty baskets and packsaddles. And *almuerzo* was good! I ate again with Eduardo, and we took *café afuera* in one of the bars that are so typical of this land. Places where one can always find men drinking and talking at all hours of the day and night. Not until 4:00 was I ready to go out again. And this time Chester and I turned west toward *San Lorenzo*, a pretty little settlement at the foot of the hills. Here the paved road stopped but a dirt road lead on into the hills, and I couldn't resist. On amongst those crumpled tops, dark against a dark sky, following a river valley holding vegetable gardens and even a large country house in its lap. Pretty. Intimate. The afternoon waned as I turned home, and looking back toward *San Lorenzo*, the mountains were olive green from diffused light that passed through some gap in the clouds. And the sun setting behind distant blue mountains punctured the bank of clouds with shafts of light. Great drops of rain fell as I entered *Salta* and I sped to my hotel, ready to stop now that day was done. A 9:30 PM dinner was welcome, and again I took *café afuera* with *Eduardo*. Afterwards we walked in the streets and in the *plaza*. And as we sat to rest amongst the shadowy trees of the *plaza*, conversation turned to serious things. We talked about why I thought myself a "*bechu [?] raro*," and next thing I knew *Eduardo* was suggesting we marry! But he hadn't any tendencies toward kissing or holding hands, so I didn't object! Strange are the ways of the Latins!

October 3, 1942—La Paz, Bolivia—Sucre Hotel—8:00 PM

Long, long ago, yesterday morning, I didn't get up so early as is my want. Too little sleep. Too many things to do. Days too packed. And then I spent a prosaic morning at the bank, in a saddle shop trying to make up my mind about a bridle, and at the hotel desk, writing. After lunch, topped with *café* at *Hotel Salta*, I again went off on Chester, This time on the paved road to *Cerillos*. Luck pedaling in the shade of roadside trees with vistas of gray hills and gray skies. From *Cerillos* on to *La Merced* with its interesting, deserted old brick church. And farther still. –The call of the open road! Dilapidated adobe houses. Strings of jerky hanging in the sun. *Gauchos* in baggy breeches. And on the road more *gauchos* with red ponchos and riding little mules. Saddles with pointed skirts. A lazy tempo there in the country and in the country towns. Back in *Salta* I was not ready to stop, so I turned and pedaled up the zigzags to *San Bernardo*, a hill overlooking the town. Late afternoon light gave an ethereal aspect to the dust rising from *Salta's* streets and accented her church towers. In the road was a little band carrying some sort of a sacred cargo—an image bedecked in gaudy fashion. But at the *cumbre* there was no one, and alone I stood at the foot of the cross to watch the light fade from the hills and the lights come on in *Salta*. Then home in the soft protectiveness of night. Dinner and café again with *Eduardo*. But I insisted on going home early because I wanted to be fresh for the day ahead. However, *Eduardo* came to my room and we talked at such length about the war that the porter had to tell us to be quiet! Once again I went late to bed.

And this day has brought a change so great that I can scarcely comprehend it. Accustomed to the slowness of a bicycle, I look back on my travels by plane in wonder and disbelief. I am incapable of absorbing the "feel" of what I see, and I wonder if I was really there at all. At 7:30 this morning Panagra called for me, and I went off with a roll in my hand! The usual formalities of getting aboard and then we were whirring away, winging over the hills of northern Argentina, the same sharp brushy hills which I had seen in my cycling about *Salta*. A sea of clouds hung in the valleys, and the hills stood as ranges and isolated islands. *Jujuy* and *La Quiaca* were not to be seen. But as we climbed upward over the rising terrain, the clouds disappeared, and we looked down on a bright panorama of Bolivia. To the east, dark, shadowy hills, and to the west the light pastel colors of dry lands bathed in sunlight. Table lands cut with red gashes. Mauve hills with purple canyons. Strata tilted and folded by some omnipotent yet capricious power. Wild, sharp, barren lands. A confusion of earth forms too—wild and too remote to be harnessed by the hand of man. And yet there was life there. Canyons held thin laced streams, and occasional habitations raised their heads in defiance of the vastness and the solitude. Higher and higher we climbed. Up into this air where whiffs from the oxygen tubes were necessary to clear away a drowsy feeling. 19,000 ft. And below the wild hills united to form the *altiplano* of Bolivia. To the east and to the west the rugged peaks continued, only here they were higher, more rugged, snow streaked. But below the land was almost level. Gullies feather-stitched the rounded contours. Bushes stippled the lines of the gullies. There was a predominance of warm rose colors as if here the climate was mild, but the air held a biting chill. Yet still life persisted down in the desolate land. Tiny squares—adobe walls—enclosed the houses and the animals of some hardy souls whose natures were accustomed to the nothingness of the *altiplano*. Then we flew low, and suddenly there was a town. *Uyuni* with its earth walls enclosing wretched huts and with its small lake of water surrounded by llamas. We landed some distance from town, and I had my first close up of Bolivia. A red, yellow, and green flag and little, stolid, dark-skinned soldiers. Cold air. Level lands. Distant mountains. Flying again to the north we passed a great expanse of white—the *Solara of Uyuni*. And farther still there seemed to be water. Perhaps it was only a mirage, a trick of the desert. No, it was water. Water lying in thin puddles as if the earth could not absorb it. And then we passed a real lake, a large body of water—*Lake Poopó*. Below us over the surface of the water flew flocks of flamingos, flashing bits of pink and white. Life on the *altiplano*. And as we left the lake behind, we approached *Oruro*, a mass of buildings huddled at the foot of a hill. Here again we stopped for a few moments, but the town was a distant thing, and I enjoyed more the view of the mountains to the east, rugged tops dusted with new snow. Mountains which stood off to the east during the rest of our flight to *La Paz* and which filled me with their wildness. A never-ending thrill. But after *Oruro* the country below was not deserted. Rather there were occasional clusters of houses looking like geometric mazes from the air. And cultivated lands too. A checkerboard of browns in the *altiplano*. And walled fields on the hills, giving the impression of unfinished cloisonné. Our plane settled down on the level lands and *La Paz* was nowhere to be seen— only the brink beyond which it must surely be. Excitedly I started down with Panagra, hanging out the window of the car to better see what was to come. And there below was the city! A mass of buildings in the lap of the mountains. From the very beginning the people of this mountain city held me fascinated. They were moving along the road, and farther down they were selling their wares by the side of the road. Indians. Men wearing brilliant wool caps with earflaps; and women clad in brilliant skirts and shawls and wearing little derby-like hats perched high on their heads. A colorful array. What had seemed picturesque before was dulled by comparison. I had come to a new world here in Bolivia. As we entered the city, we rolled over cobblestones, and the buildings were tumble-down adobe huts. Glimpses of dark interiors and walled homes and life over flowing into the streets. Then down into the uninteresting respectability of the center of the city and here to the "only" hotel in *La Paz*. Almost immediately I was in the dining room, and after lunch, out into the streets which I couldn't resist. On foot about the center, but my enthusiasm waned almost at once. The will was strong but the legs were weak! High altitude. I wanted only to sleep! And slowly I walked back to my hotel and crashed into bed! After a couple of hours of rest, I was ready to go out again, and this time I walked down the canyon through the respectable residential section. But on the way back I climbed up on to the side of the canyon and followed cobbled streets that yielded a wealth of interesting sights. Steep, narrow ways following the contours of the hills at random. And dark little shops--were holes in the walls—opening off of the sidewalls. Indians, Indians, Indians. They sat like sparrows in rows along the curbs. They trotted along bent under heavy loads. They crouched behind little heaps of limas and popcorn. They lent bright dashes of color to crumbling adobe walls. What a confusion of life here in *La Paz*! And donkeys passed in the streets too—little beasts loaded with sheathes of barley. And once I caught a glimpse of *llamas*. When I finally returned home, my eyes were heavy with having looked so much, and I was quite ready for bed.

October 5, 1942—La Paz—Hotel Palace Sucre—10:00 PM

Yesterday, the 4th, a lazy Sunday spent in poking about *La Paz*. Closed offices confined my activity to aimless wandering, and I loved it! Up through town and along *Calle Mercado* to *Plaza San Francisco* with its old, old church. Inside, this church was mellow with its years. Massive round arches and solid square pillars with an elaborate altar painted in gold. And hosts of kneeling Indians. Passive faces that probably covered hopeful hearts. The whole aspect of the church and its congregation was one of weight, but this was relieved by the strings of paper flowers and fluffy papers strung across the nave. Back into the sunlight through a heavy, ancient door, I left those in the church to pray to their god while I went in search of new sights! A market caught my eye. Mobs of Indians thronging a narrow street lined with crude stalls and stolid saleswomen, and pouring into a building where men hacked at carcasses of meat and women sat amidst piles of fruits and vegetables. Crowds. Color. Confusion. Women pushed their way from stall to stall, filling their baskets with limas, carrots, tripe, chunks of meat, small tomatoes, lettuce, shiny fish—all tossed in together! And I followed the crowds, looking outside in the street, my only purchase was an Indian *bolsilla*. From the market I walked on around *La Paz*, past the station, and farther still trying to keep up on the hillside where life was interesting. A crowd in front of a church brought me to a halt; I would wait to see what went on. And my patience was repaid, for presently a band struck up some music, and out of the church came a figure of the Virgin born on the shoulders of a dozen men. She was clad in purple and gold and set amidst a froth of white and pink, and she was carried along streets decorated with flags. Flower girls in white dropped petals where she was to pass and priests in white directed her journey while behind followed a band of dignitaries and a group of Indian women dressed in high-heeled boots and silks and carrying incense burners. The band followed too, playing almost constantly, and the common rabble jammed the streets to pay homage to the image. Over the street were streamers in which the Virgin more than once caught her crown. And balconies were draped with fine shawls and crowded with folks who showered confetti and flower petals on the procession below. The thing seemed almost pagan with its blatant music and firecrackers. And I wondered what it meant to those Indians who filled the streets. Old wrinkled faces. Young laughing faces. Dark skin and dark eyes. High cheek bones and thick lips. Mouths stained with the brown of *cacao*. Rags. Dirt. And the priests shouted "*Viva la virgen*," "*Vive la religion catolica*." I followed the throng in a loop through the narrow steep streets, and when the *Virgen* had returned to her church, I went away with my hair full of confetti. As I returned home I passed *Plaza Murillo*, and here I stepped inside the cathedral and later paused a moment to listen to the band. Then back to the *Sucre*, past the monument "*Bolivia a Bolivar*." After dinner I rested a while and then went off for yet another *paseo*. Down the canyon this time. Down and down and down. Out of *La Paz* and down to [left blank]. The mountain was clear and sharp ahead. Snow-crowned. Impressive. But as I descended, it was lost to view, crowded out by the canyon walls. These, however, were truly beautiful. Some were eroded into columns and fingers, and ahead they stood up bare and sharp and colorful in the afternoon sun. I was so intrigued by that lovely jumble of hills that I followed a road heading down a canyon at their feet. Each curve drew me farther. *Lastima grande* that I had not the wings of my bicycle to follow farther still! And all the while I shared the road with Indians. Some carried burdens, some drove donkeys, and once a band of *llamas* passed. The latter were black and white and tawny beasts walking with dignity and carrying bags and ropes which looked to be woven of their self-same hair. When I felt I could go no farther, I returned to *Obrajes* and took a *colectivo* back to *San Jorge*. Thence I walked on toward the center, but looking back, I could see *Mt. Illimani* catching the evening sun, and I turned and climbed up the side hill in order to get a better view. Clear up out of the respectable section and in amongst the adobe huts and crumbling walls of the poor. Finally I came to more level ground where little patches of walled earth were cultivated, and from here I could see the mountain in all its snowy magnificence. I was content to just stand and look. *La Paz*, too, was lovely, lying in its hollow with each building a sharp entity in the late light. At dark I returned, and settled myself to write. But there were merry-makers in the hotel, folks who were trying to lead sophisticated lives here in this primitive city. And one, seeing I was alone, came to take paper from the desk, stopped to visit, and invited me to have a drink! Dekker, the crazy Frenchman! Over Martinis he showed me pictures of Libya where he had been in the Foreign Legion, told me of his plans to go to the *Amazonas*, asked me to go along, and warned me that he was going to try to seduce me! All in 15 minutes! Later I went to his room to look at a map, curious as to what his technique would be. But his only offense was an attempt to hold my hand and a banter of plain conversation which left nothing unsaid! Strange are the persons one meets in traveling!

October 6, 1942—Tiquina—"Alojamiento Incho"—Night

Yesterday, *Lunes*, was a day of business, for offices were open at last! But, like a good Richardson, I was out in the streets long before the hour of opening! To fill in time I explored, following lanes far up on the hillside. Narrow, cobbled lanes, leading upward at an amazing angle. Old buildings with heavy wooden doors, sagging tile roofs, overhanging balconies. And frequent dark cubbyholes where *comestibles* were for sale. Picturesque. Heavy with an atmosphere of age. But always most interesting was the human element. Those bright, billowing skirts which showed beneath the colors of other skirts which had gone before. Pink, green, blue, purple, red! And those mannish hats perched so high! Occasionally there was a very high, white one to be seen. The men were not so gaudy. Ear-flapped caps of red or magenta were their most extravagant note! Footwear, when there was footwear, was composed of rubber tires and leather thongs. And how simple their lives seemed to be. Sitting. Selling a few limas. Buying a bit of bread to eat. And they answered nature in the streets, the women simply squatting down within their bulky skirts, and leaving a damp spot in their wake! Babies were carried in shawls at their backs and when they cried, they were nursed in the streets. Life was devoid of all pretense. It was just lived as it came. When offices finally opened, I went first to the *Dept. of Extranjeria* to get my permission to leave Bolivia, and thence to the *oficina de tourismo* to find out what I could about places to go in Bolivia. Then I hunted for another place to stay, going first to the *Cruller pensión* and next to that of the Websters where I stayed for lunch. In the afternoon I bought enough *Bolivianos* to give me a sense of security and hunted out the traffic department where I got permission to cycle to *Copacabana*. And little by little my plans for the morrow took shape. I would attempt a cycling trip to *Lago Titicaca* in spite of warnings against the difficulties of high altitude. With this in mind I went out for a trial spin on Chester. Down the canyon to *Obrajes* again, again enjoying the afternoon light on those high barren hills. And I found I could climb back up the hill without difficulty. Good! A cop told me I couldn't ride in the streets, but he was neutralized by a friendly *Boliviano* who stepped up to answer my questions about roads in English. And I ended my day with a late excursion out to buy brakes. Thence to bed in anticipation of an early start.

October 7, 1942—Copacabana—Hotel Copacabana

What a day yesterday! Phew! Twelve hours of cycling! By 7:00 AM I had had my breakfast and was pushing off into the streets of *La Paz* already alive with Indians. Curious. Not Latin-like. Up to *El Alto* I trudged, pushing Chester most of the way. –right back to the airport from whence I had come. Part of the way I had a couple of Indian *trabajadores* for company—lads whose curiosity was roused at the sight of a woman cycling alone. And all of the way I had *Illimani* to add zest to my trip, but she was subtle and misty now with the sun coming from behind. At *El Alto* I was obliged to show my documents to the police, but they proved friendly, and I was soon pedaling on my way! The *altiplano*! Vast and level and rimmed to the east with high, snowy peaks of indescribable beauty. I was exhilarated. Barren lands yet abundant with life. Indian women in red skirts sat watching bands of sheep, and men drove little donkeys along the road. Piles of stone and scratched earth told of an effort to make the land produce. But bunch grass seemed to be the only product. Houses were of mud with grass thatch. And there were occasional bands of shaggy *llamas*. *Llamas* with bright wool tassels in their ears! At one point many Indians had gathered and they were making a social occasion of their plowing. Men were driving cattle hitched to crude wooden ploughs, and women were following with stones attached to sticks—crude tools with which to break the clods. Bands of *llamas* stood idly by as if such work were beneath their dignity. For lunch I sought out a pile of stone where I had an unimpeded view of those wild white peaks, and soon afterwards I lost them behind nearer hills. Hills showing red patches of cultivation. *Lago Titicaca* first appeared as a distant bit of blue, and as I approached its shores, houses and cultivated lands became more abundant. Here apparently was a land more yielding to the hand of man. Traffic on the road, too, became heavier. The high notes of flutes came from men who walked and played at the same time. Women passed with clay pitchers of water, and other women carried spindles and spun yarn as they walked. Hot sun made thirst a torment and in the little town of *Huarina* I stopped at the hotel to ask for water. Happy day! For here a *fiesta* was in progress. *El dia de San Francisco.* And I loved the cobbled courtyard of the hotel whirling with gaudy skirts as Indian women stepped and reeled with their dusty, tattered partners. Music was produced by drums and pipes, and the players made an amazing spectacle. Fancy hats with high feather plumes. Brilliant breeches in knicker style. And jackets gleaming with brilliant *adornos*. But most curious of all—there were wigs with long curls! And these men stepped around and around in a circle as they played. I was fascinated! But as I stood there watching, a dusty Indian stepped up to tell me that his blood was German (!) and that one *Boliviano* was worth 10 Germans and 50 English! Incongruous, this war talk in the midst of such a primitive display. Farther along the road I stopped to drink my water, but it tasted a bit like axle grease, and although I had reached the point where I would drink anything, I was a bit wary of what might be there in its murky depths. So I stopped at the church of which the official in *El Alto* had told me, and there I found Canadian missionaries and boiled water! After a sociable visit, I continued on my way—on around *Lago Titicaca* with its lovely blue waters and its purple hills and peninsulas. Past mud huts and mud walls. Walls occasionally lightened by openwork of bricks. Set on edge and in "v's". Past old settlements with extensive walls and great eucalyptus trees. Past pink flamingos on the lake—and reed boats. Past women endlessly spinning. On into higher hills where the road climbed above the lake and where farm lands were terraced with rock walls. Every cove in the lake seemed to hold a lacework pattern of rock walls. And on the road were workers from the fields, carrying their crude ploughs and clod-breakers. On and on I pedaled, delighted with the natural beauty and the picturesque civilization, and secure in the knowledge that in *Tiquina* I would find a comfortable hotel. But I had hitched my wagon to a star, for when I arrived at the *pueblo*, I found it divided by an expanse of water, and the hotel was on the far shore. Boats were lying by, but their owners refused to cross at such a late hour. I was stranded. But the *teniente* introduced me to an Indian *señora* who had rooms, and there I stayed the night, my dreams of comfort, merely dreams. Tired and hungry, I settled down to a cluttered room, a sheetless bed, and a cup of black coffee for sustenance! And I slept with my clothes on and my parka hood tied over my head to protect myself from whatever might be lurking in the ponchos on my bed! *Que vida*!

October 8, 1942—Tiquina—Hotel Tiquina—9:00 PM

And yesterday was another long and eventful day. Early in the morning I left my cheerless quarters, glad to be back in the open air even though it held a chill when there was no sun to make it burning hot. I crossed the lake in a native boat, a big clumsy thing with a mast and ropes of hide, but propelled by 4 oarsmen. And my *compañeros* were all Indians—women with their bright skirts, high hats and spindles and men with their tattered coats and ear flaps. On the far side I stopped at the hotel for a substantial breakfast before pedaling on my way, and here I not only found *café con leche y pan con manteca*, but also *3 Bolivianos* bound for *Copacabana* in a *camionetta*. And I was warned about the difficulties of the road ahead and was invited to ride. I accepted, and Chester was loaded behind, but my new *compañeros* must have a round of beer and *pisco* before starting, and it was late before we got underway. Glorious country between *Tiquina* and *Copacabana*. Magnificent panorama with the road winding through rose and tan and gray-green hills and with the lake lying in irregular splendor below. Several times we stopped, and the *"jefe de policia"* with whom I traveled drank more beer and cognac with fellow officials along the way. I began to wonder if we really would arrive! And meanwhile Chester jolted and slithered around in back. I was worried. But there were too many new sights along the way for me to think much of either myself or Chester. Hills terraced clear to their very tops. Droves of *burros* carrying sacks of potatoes. And finally a high point from which we could look down on *Copacabana*, a little village set at the foot of the hills beside the lake and dominated by an old and venerable church with domes and arches decorated in green tile. Down below we entered the *pueblo* on cobbled streets—narrow streets cobbled with little round stones and lined with plain mud fronts—nonchalant streets running this way and that. At *Hotel La Paz* we stopped and went into its low, cobbled interior to find more police officials and to drink more beer! And it was late when we finally reached *Hotel Copacabana* where we stopped for lunch. I immediately took a room, for I wanted to stay the night in this picturesque spot, and when my *compañeros* discovered that the blond *dueña* of *Tiquina* had come to *Copacabana*, they too decided to stay! In the afternoon they wanted to make a trip to *Yunguyo* on the Peruvian side, and, thinking to see yet a bit more of *Titicaca*, I went along as well as the blond *dueña*! Once more we rolled through terraced hills beside the lake, and once more I thrilled to this high country, so barren yet so full of life. At the *frontera* we were stopped by Bolivian officials who refused to let the *camionetta* pass, and the dignity of our *"jefe"* was ruffled when he had to leave his *coche* and continue on foot! We all walked together up past the arch which marked the boundary and down on the Peruvian soil. Peruvian officials proved more amiable, and they drank with the *"jefe"* from Bolivia. They even drove us on into town in their station wagon! In *Yunguyo* we looked up more officials and thence proceeded to the local dry goods grocery-bar for more drinks. Amazing, my Bolivian *compañeros*! But even they couldn't hold so much, and eyes became bleary and voices thick as the afternoon wore on. The *chofer* even told me confidentially that he was looking for a foreign wife, and that after he married he would never touch liquor again! But I wasn't interested in their drinking. Instead I watched the life in the *plaza*. In front of an old church a crowd had gathered, and a *fiesta* was in progress. Bulls made of wood and bright colored paper stood at the door, and every little while one was carried out into the *plaza* and ignited. There followed a great popping and cracking and the frame of the animal was left standing bare, but each time it was resolved into pieces by small boys who descended in droves. Later followed music and dancing such as I had seen before in *Huarina*. The whole *plaza* was cobbled, and there were a few trees and a fountain to distinguish it from the streets. All about it sat Indians behind little piles of wares. Business seemed a bit sluggish, but they didn't care. Over all was an atmosphere of age and indolence. It was dark when the *Bolivianos* started their unsteady way back towards the *camionetta*, and I was glad to leave the bar and walls through the narrow walled streets and out into the country where were the lake, the hills and the stars. Back at the hotel I had a bath and a late dinner and then immediately retired to my room to wash and write until the hour when the lights were turned off.

October 9, 1942—La Paz—Pensión Cruller

Yesterday morning was dark and ominous, and since I was without an impermeable, I decided to ride back to *La Paz* with the *Bolivianos* as they had suggested the night before. But I was up long before they, and so I spent the early hours exploring the *pueblo*! Up and around the narrow streets, all cobbled with the small round stones I have come to know so well. Blank mud walls. Closed doors. Simple, primitive structures, yet structure full of the picturesque quality of a different world. And the passageways left for the passers-by climbed up and around the hill and offered glimpses of the lake and the hills beyond. It was lovely in the peace of the morning. I wandered into the old church that harkens back to colonial times, and up in the *campin* where the Virgin is housed I found a mass in progress. Indian men and women in rags, some with babies in their arms, were kneeling on the floor while a priest in elegant robes officiated before the dazzling altar. What contrasts! Yet that elegant display gave hope to those poor souls with their poor faces, and they were unconscious of the fact that they had nothing while their church had much. Blessed ignorance. In the central part of the church, arches had the heavy massiveness of colonial Spain, but their weight was offset by an elaborate baroque altar of hammered silver and painted gold. And outside in the courtyard were disconnected arches in whose shadows had gathered Indians to sell candles and platters of hot food. Back at the hotel I found my Bolivian *compañeros* scarcely civil. The effects of their drink had worn off, and they wanted nothing to do with a girl who would not play their game. Better for me to go on alone. So I packed up Chester and pushed off, hoping fervently that rain would not come. Over the cobblestone of the *pueblo* and up the hill into the country. Relief. A new sense of life in the peace of the fields and the activity of my body. My mind cleansed of the memories of riotous companions. Re-creation in solitude. And I looked back on *Copacabana* with joy. Lovely primitive *pueblo* by the side of *Titicaca*, a *pueblo* set amidst dull gold and gray green. Dull gold in the bunch grass and gray green in the lichens of the rocks of the hills. I would never forget *Copacabana*. And my trip to *Tiquina* was beautiful beyond measure, with the road winding through the hills and the lake always in view, an iridescent mass with orchid hills rising from its waters. Nearer hills were populated with Indians who had built mud houses by the road and had terraced with stone their hilly fields. The landscape lost its gray-greenness and became rosy with turned earth. Soft warm colors of a land without trees, a land bathed in the intense sunlight of rarefied air. Everywhere Indians worked in the fields and guarded their flocks of small sheep, lean pigs, and nondescript cattle. Below on the lake were men in reed boats. Children gathered up their baby brothers and sister and ran away as I passed. Schoolboys ran along behind me. At one point, I stopped to talk to a man who spoke to me, and hoards of schoolboys gathered around, staring with unbelieving eyes. I was a curiosity in this land where bicycles were never seen. But I found the cycling ideal in spite of the altitude. Magnificent panoramas and picturesque life were all that anyone could ask for. At midday I wound down to *Tiquina*, and here I decided to stay, here on the brink of the lake where I could look across to cultivated lands and away to snow-capped peaks. And all afternoon I stayed and looked, reveling in the view from the dining room windows, talking with the young *dueños*, watching the boats plying back and forth between the two sections of *Tiquina*, listening to the music of pipes and drums. I was content to stay by *Titicaca*. But I was disturbed by the dark clouds and the high wind, and I accepted the invitation of a smiling Indian who came to ask me to ride to *La Paz* in his truck.

October 11, 1942—Chulumaine—Hotel Hamburgo

Friday, the 9th, was a long and weary day, though a happy one. The smiling Indian drove away without me, and so I was left to pedal to *La Paz*. No matter for the day was bright and cycling a privilege here by the side of the lake. With Chester I sailed across the lake in an Indian boat, and thence retraced my tracks to *Huarina*. Fast pedaling over a good road. Exhilaration in the breathless beauty of the lake and the wild, icy range of the mountains ahead. Bright skirts sat watching herds. The high notes of pipes came down the wind. I was glad to be pedaling, glad I had missed the truck. But storm clouds over the snowy tops grew ominous, and as I turned and pedaled across the *altiplano*, they pursued me in spite of a head wind. It was raining behind and off to the side and I hurried on, rolling toward *Illimani* which stood in sunlight ahead. Faster, I must pedal faster. And I turned and took the road to *Pucarani*, hoping for a better surface. But the wind was a mighty force against me, and I was losing the race, so I stopped in the shelter of a mud wall, one of those deserted shells so common in the *altiplano*. A few drops of rain fell and clouds of dust blew by. Nothing more. So again I took up the race. But, the road lead up hill now—forever up. The *altiplano* was not flat. And the wind was still strong. On and on and on until my legs were weak and I was merely crawling in low gear. I must get to *La Paz*. On and on. Ominous blackness over the hard, cold summits. A chill in the wind. On and on across the rocky planes. And finally *El Alto* where smiling officials took down the bars and let me pass. All down hill now. I could relax. Down, down to *La Paz* with its familiar confusion of Indians and urbanity. Hastily I pedaled to the *Sucre* and asked for a room. Nothing. Tired and dirty I was at a loss, and then I remembered that *Mrs. Cruellar* had a room vacant for the night. I would go there, so I pedaled to her door and begged like a tramp. And she and her *pensionistas* welcomed me in! *Qué suerte!* Hot tea and a bath and a sociable evening of English! I felt at home, contented.

And yesterday, the 10th, I left *La Paz* and came here to tropical Bolivia, a change so great that one day seems too short to encompass it. From high rugged crags to the tropics! From bare, rocky desolation to soft lush greenness! Incredible. Leaving my comfortable *pensión* before breakfast, I went to *Calle Yungas* and there waited for a truck, just any truck bound for *Chulumani*. Crowds of Indians waited too, for this was the poor man's method of travel but I had deliberately chosen it because I wanted to see everything as I went, wanted to be free of car tops which close exciting views. Finally I found a truck going to my chosen destination, and with 20 Indians I scrambled aboard, up on top of the cargo where nothing but Indians impeded the view. I settled myself amidst bundles and Indians and waited expectantly. The driver tried to talk me into riding in the cab but I wanted to ride on top and I would ride on top. I did ride on top! For 8 hours I sat with legs cramped under me and with Indians all about me, but they were not long hours for I was absorbed in the panorama which unfolded ahead. Glorious. Up out of La Paz we climbed, up through barren brown hills where we passed frequent bands of *llamas* with their tidy cargoes. Up and up and up. *Khantutas* were there, the red tubular flowers of the *altiplano*, Bolivia's own; and then they were gone, and only a wiry turf remained. We climbed still higher. The air was clear and bright, but very cold. Icicles hung from the turf by the side of the road; ice edged the streams. Ahead appeared the ragged snowy tops I had seen from the *altiplano*, but they were very close now. Up to 15,000 ft and higher, and then we reached the summit. Here we stopped, and as I looked at the surrounding mountains with a sense of awe, our Indian driver got out and knelt to pray at the cross by the side of the road. He ended his devotion by sprinkling a bottle of water or liquor all about the cross, and I too hoped that the gods might grant us a safe trip, for I had heard much of the narrow, precipitous road ahead. My Indian companions also prayed and crossed themselves devoutly. But I only looked at the mountains. I was the only heathen present. Starting again, our way led down. Down a winding road in the very shadows of those mighty peaks. At every turn a breathless view, and I gave thanks to Allah that I could see clear to the very tops of their majestic summits. Thrilling. Cramped legs meant nothing. Back and forth and down and down and down. Imperceptibly the black crags of the heights became clothed in green. A few bushes appeared by the side of the stream in our canyon. Down and down. There trees now and vegetation dotted the mountain sides. Down and down. Ferns and creepers and broad-leafed trees appeared. Lush growing things. A clear stream flowed far below, and canyon walls rose high above. Wisps of streams fell down abrupt slopes. Deep, mossy cuts held other streams. Creepers with orchid flowers. Bright red flowers. Large red star-like flowers hanging in the trees. Wild begonias. Rank luxuriance on every side. And houses lost the starkness of the heights and became smothered in tropical verdure. A confusion of bananas, coffee, oranges, limes, loquats, and unknown things. Down and down. There were cultivated lands now. Steep though the hillsides were, they had been cleared and planted in patchwork fashion. Bananas, coffee, oranges growing at amazing angles. And the air had become hot and lazy. Tropical. Fiery wild zinnias grew by the side of the road. And a great blue butterfly floated by. Little *pueblos* could be seen on the slopes across such precipitous lands. And finally *Chulumani* came into view, a collection of houses on the crest of a ridge. As I climbed out of the truck and walked to the hotel, I found my legs weak from a day without food. And tea was my goal! Tea, bread, and butter, bananas and limes revived me, and I was able to enjoy my new situation. High up on the hillside, I could look across to cultivated hillsides and blue mountains beyond. And here at the hotel I was surrounded with bright flowers and tropical plants. I didn't even mind having to live with a roommate in a crowded hotel.

October 13, 1942—La Paz—Sucre Palace Hotel 10:00 PM

The 11th was a lazy day passed pleasantly in *Chulumani*. A bountiful breakfast in the diningroom looking out across the canyon. Banana leaves swaying in the breeze. Tropical heat. I wandered out along the road and settled myself in the shade to write and to fasten in my memory the picture of those lovely Bolivian hills. Across the way, hillsides were cultivated in patches of green and brown, distinct from the green of the natural tropical growth. And near at hand were patches of coca and bananas. And mud walls and tiled roofs smothered in lush plants and flowers. Brilliant blue butterflies were my company. And down the road passed Indians. Women trotting barefooted. Men pushing burros. A lazy flow of life. And I, too, was lazy like the climate and people. After dinner I walked the other way into the *pueblo* of *Chulumani*. A hillside town with views down cobbled streets and off across blue canyons. Inexpressive mud walls. Rough stone passageways. Stolid women sitting behind their racks of dry goods and piles of comestibles displayed on the sidewalk. A market where had gathered a multitude of men and women and burros. Sacks and tables and stacks of all manner of things. Picturesque. Lazy. I walked on beyond the town where there were new vistas of canyons and hills and growing things, but the heat was enervating, and I didn't go far. Back home I washed and wrote and enjoyed the environs of the hotel. In the evening a Yankee introduced himself to me and asked if I'd like to go to a local dance. One Henry Schwellenback. Of course I'd like to go! Always, anywhere! So a crowd of us walked down the rough, dark road to *Chulumani* where a *fiesta* was being held in the *mercado*. Fireflies and soft air. And we sat about a table and drank and danced while a native orchestra played enthusiastic tunes, and *Bolivianos* danced with equal enthusiasm. The Bolivian clerk from the hotel spotted me and insisted on several dances, so for me, the Bolivian atmosphere was complete!

And yesterday, the 12th, was a day packed full of activity. At 6:00 I was up, and after packing I had an early breakfast and was ready for the trip back to *La Paz*, only this time I was to go in the hotel *colectivo*. Much more elegant. Seats! And no Indians! But there was a top which interfered with the magnificence of the view, and I wasn't any happier than I had been in my *camión*. However, we were a sociable crowd, and the ride was fun. Back up the long, long grade, leaving the tropical luxuriance of *Chulumani* and climbing up into the wild heights where black strata were tilted in confusion and clothed with ice masses. Gone the flowers and ferns. Gone the banana fronds. Only rock and a cold wind. Then over the top and down to *La Paz*. We had completed our trek from 1,100 meters to 4,600 meters. In the city once again, Henry was anxious to hurry off to a bullfight, and I decided to go along. We took a taxi to the *Sucre* and left our bags, and then went off again without even going to our rooms. We went covered with the dust of the *Yungus* and blown by winds of the summit! And we reached the bullring just as the band struck up its first notes! A small ring with an enthusiastic crowd, and down front were elegant *señoritas* dressed in the style of old Spain. A design in the sand paid tribute to the race of bullfighters. I waited with trepidation, wondering what my reaction would be to the killing of animals, and the butchery of the first confused little bull so sickened me that I scarcely knew what happened. The next 4, however, were much more savage, and once accustomed to the routine of the killing, I could see its more colorful side. There was excitement as the animals plunged into the ring, and there was artistry in the swirling of purple and gold capes as the *toreadores* dodged the charging animals. The *picadores* too were deft as they buried their pics in the necks of the beasts, but there was something inhuman about the nonchalance with which they opened red wounds with their bright instruments. And there was something unsportsmanlike in the way they dodged behind walls whenever there was real danger. The *matador* was the most deft of all. With a red cape draped over his saber he teased the bull and dodged his onslaughts. And then, almost too quickly to be seen, he buried that sharp steel in the heart of the bull. In a few minutes the beast was down and his dying convulsion was over. And he was dragged from the field amidst cheers. And so the fights passed. Bloody exciting things which appealed to the brute force in man. But the fighters were colorful in their pink stockings, tight breeches, and jackets with gold braid. And beyond the ring *Illimani* stood high and white and peaceful—a refuge for eyes weary of death in the ring. From the bullfights we returned to the *Sucre* anxious to clean up, and I prepared to spend a lonely evening, Happy, then, was I when Henry came to my door and suggested we dine out. We went across the way to the *Colón* and there we ate a long, long meal, punctuated with dancing. Later we returned to the *Sucre* and drank cokes and whiskies and danced some more. –And so far, far into the night. But I was content to have companionship, and I liked Henry. Perhaps too well, for another day would find me alone again, wondering why I had not been more matter-of-fact. A life of heights and depths seems to be my lot.

And today more arrangements. This morning I went to *Dirección de Tráfico* to get permission to take Chester out of Peru, and I was sent to *aduana*. Luckily there were no complications. And in the afternoon I went to buy soles and to arrange my ticket to *Cuzco*. Soles were scarce, and luckily I was directed to the *Banco Popular del Peru* before changing. Shopping for a flag was not so successful. *No hay en La Paz.* In the late afternoon I went to get Chester from *Cruellers* and I stayed for tea and a visit. Pushing the ole bike back up the street brought out a rear guard of street urchins. Fortunately I'm hardened now. For dinner I went back to *Cruellers* and spent another sociable interlude, and I needed sociability for today has been so lonely that it has almost brought me to tears. However, I have begun to feel at home in *La Paz*, for this day I have met in the streets a *Señor* from *Chulumani*, the missionary from Tiquina, and Mr. Webster!

October 16, 1942—Cuzco—Hotel Ferrocarril—7:00 PM

Another change. A long trek which has left in its wake a panorama of shadowy memories. Gone the familiar confusion of *La Paz*. Gone the high windy *altiplano* with its rim of wild peaks. Gone Bolivia—And now Peru. A new land with new sights and sounds and smells. New life. And in me the old thrill at seeing lifeless bits of map become living reality. October 14 I spent the morning tending to last minute details. –Bought my ticket to *Cuzco*, saw Chester delivered to the station, and had the date of exit on my passport changed. This last item caused considerable worry because I found the office of *Inmigración* packed with people, and I could not pass. Only by asking for special privilege and by allowing my way to the front was I able to make the necessary revision before the office closed at noon. Then everything ready, I spent my last hours in *La Paz* in carefree rambling. Stopped for *café*, bought a bit of silver jewelry, looked for the last time on the narrow, steep street with their amazing throngs of the ragged and the colorful. By 2:00 I had collected my poor little bag and had found my place on the *La Paz-Guaqui* train. And then I was on my way, slowly winding back and forth as the train climbed to *El Alto*. Past the poor, outlying mud huts with their walled plots. Indian houses where women could be seen washing and weaving. And up the mountainside where we could look down on the bright roofs of *La Paz* and away to

Illimani, always lovely. Upon the *altiplano* more peaks came into view, friends from my previous trip and the high plateau itself seemed familiar though I now followed a new route. Level lands where Indians worked the ground and where occasional mud villages had been raised. Burros, *llamas*, sheep, poor dark pigs. Bits of red where women sat in the fields. And than the plains were crumpled into hills, and we lost the sense of vastness of the *altiplano*. Brown hills bearing the scars of cultivation. Hills which became higher as we approached *Guaqui*. At *Tiahuanaco* we could see from the train the monoliths of an ancient civilization, but we had not time to explore them further. And then *Titicaca* again. At *Guaqui*, the train stopped, and we went through the formalities of customs, the same old baggage and passport examination which is almost as inevitable as the day and night. And thence we transferred to a boat, the *Ollanta*, a little steamer brought in pieces to *Titicaca* on the backs of mules. Up on deck I watched the loading of hides and of horses. And I looked away to the cold white summits of the *Cordillera Real* and out across the waters of *Titicaca* bounded by the usual sharp featured desert hills. And then the sun sank, and as we moved out into the lake, the shores became shadowy hills which harbored occasional lights. A cold wind reminded us that we were sailing the highest navigable lake in the world. At dinner time one of my companions was the heavily-made-up, not-too-young American I had seen in *La Paz*, and her conversation and attitude bespoke utter boredom. Later a young Scotchman joined us, one Alexander Fraser, and talk of the war became so heated that the New York blond walked off in anger! She couldn't tolerate the suggestion that America might lose the war. Up on deck I continued to talk to Fraser, and it was late when we finally had a drink and went to bed.

Yesterday morning, the 15th, I wakened very early to find the little *Ollanta* approaching *Puno*. The crests of surrounding hills were dusted with snow, for there had been a storm in the night, but cloudbanks were breaking now. An early breakfast. And visiting with the Scotsman and the plump nephew of the president of Peru who had been my train

companion of the day before. Then more customs procedures
for we were entering Peru. In the *aduana* they said I'd have to
pay duty on Chester, but I talked fast and they decided to let
my good bike in free. Relief! Then presently we were aboard
a train once more traveling into Peru. Along the shores of the
lake at first, where Indian urchins begged with open arms as
the train passed. Stony hills with stonewalled plots. And then
away from the lake up a broad valley. Dry hills. Withered
grass. But always life—Indians who worked those
inhospitable lands. In *Juliaca* I changed to the *Cuzco* train
and found myself with new traveling companions. A blond
lad looked at me twice and then ambled down and asked to sit
with me. *Como no!* And I had company for the rest of the
trip. Our way continued through the broad valley and the dry
hills. But as we traveled on, the hills became higher and the
valley narrower. And later we passed high, snowcapped
peaks. At noon we stopped at *Ayaviri* and I dined with *Sucre
Chehachi* in the local hotel. *Almuerzo* in 20 minutes! Then on
again. As we passed the summit and began to descend, there
was a gradual change in the character of the landscape. Green
fields came into being. And trees. And our deep canyon gave
birth to a river. Quantities of *llamas* and sheep. And women
wearing strange costumes; flat pancake hats and full navy-blue
skirts. Narrower and deeper became the canyon, broader the
river. And there were frequent villages of mud houses with
tile roofs. At the stations vendors of all sorts crowded about
the train, and *Sucre* bought several strings of bread that we
sampled at teatime. As the shadows grew long, the canyon
became lovely and the *vistas* more vibrant, and I longed to be
on my bike instead of in the train. An hour before reaching
Cuzco, *Sucre's* family joined him and I was surprised to see so
many nice looking girls and boys. Arabians. And just at dusk
we reached our destination, *Cuzco* at last! But I had no time
to ponder over the romance of the place. Instead I had to fight
to carry my own bag out of the train! But the hotel was a part
of the station, and in a few moments I was settled. A bath and
dinner, and then I waited for *Sucre* who had said he would
come. But like a good Latin, he didn't!

October 17, 1942—Cuzco, Peru—Hotel Ferrocarril

And yesterday, the 16th, I spent a delightful day browsing in *Cuzco*. No guides. No rushing to see this and that. Just browsing. In the morning I walked into town, full of anticipation, for I had heard much of *Cuzco*, and to see it I had had to struggle against the odds. But I was not disappointed. Here was a different kind of a city. A city full of life and color and antiquities. In the streets were throngs of Indians—ragged Indians, barefoot Indians, Indians with the familiar costumes of *La Paz*, and Indians with those queer flat hats. But *Cuzco* is not an Indian city of inexpressive, stark mud walls. It is instead a city of the ancient Incas and a city of old Spain. A city heavy with age and possessing the mellowness and beauty of things that have weathered the years. One is first conscious of its colonial facets. A lovely carved wooden balcony overhanging a narrow street, a doorway arched in carved stone, an ornamented church belfry silhouetted against the sky, a church façade of stone, its earthiness given a spiritual quality by some carver's hand. And through massive doors one glimpses cobbled courtyards and heavy round arches. Later one notes the Inca foundation of this strange city, unobtrusive stonewalls upon which the city has been built. Just walls. And yet walls so finely made that one wonders how they could have been raised by primitive hands. Stones cut and fit so perfectly that not even a pin can be introduced at the joints. Incredible! So perfect that the walls built upon them seem like the fumbling efforts of children. And past this awe-inspiring heritage of an ancient civilization flows the everyday life of the city, unmindful of the romance of the past. In *Plaza de Armas* I paused to feel the colonial atmosphere of the surrounding buildings, the churches and the low edifices with arcades and balconies. And thence I wandered into the cathedral. Cold stone floors and sturdy angular columns. Chapels guarded by gilded grate doors. And at the back an altar plated with silver. Rich beyond belief. In a side room I found interesting pieces of old furniture, stiff and heavy, yet beautifully carved. A mass was in progress and devout Catholics knelt on the floor. A ragged Indian with long hair and sharp, fine features knelt quietly at the front. As I walked out I caught glimpses of the fine wood carving of the choir. By this time I was beginning to feel ill. A touch of dysentery gave me a headache and weak knees, and I could go no further, so I walked home and crawled into bed. *Que turista!* But a couple of hours of rest and a dinner gave me new strength, and in the afternoon I went out again. This time I sought out the Temple of the Sun located within the convent of *Santo Domingo*. And here a young monk in cream and brown guided me along the arcades of the sunny garden patio. On the western side is the rock which supported the golden disk of the sun and here also is the temple of the moon. On the eastern side are small rooms for the worship of minor deities and outside is a curved wall of magnificent construction. I stood in awe before this stonework, in awe of the Inca past which it represented and in awe of the human skill by which it was wrought. And I tried to imagine the richness of the shrine before it became a ghost at the hands of the Spaniards. Wandering on from the temple, I passed the *San Pedro* district, and I stopped inside the church to admire its carved wooden pulpit. I also loitered in the market here, for markets always interest me. What a confusion of humanity, produce and dirt! Indians sat in the streets with ponchos spread before them, and on these ponchos they displayed their wares. Bananas, popcorn, cereals. Corn of all colors—black, yellow, red, white—tight little ears with immense grains. And potatoes of infinite variety—big and little, long and round, red and green. One gathered the impression that the market was an inseparable jumble of Indians and wares. Amongst the ponchos were ragged children and nursing mothers. And I saw one small boy with a conductor's hat and a shirt but devoid of pants and shoes! Again I returned to *Plaza de Armas* and sat reading until late. Then home to dinner and to bed.

October 19, 1942—Ollantaytambo—Hotel—8:00 AM

The 17th proved a hectic day, for when I went to collect Chester I discovered part of my gear missing. Unhappy day! A simple little gadget, but indispensable and irreplaceable. I had prepared for many contingencies but not for this one, and I was discouraged beyond measure. I was also angry with the railroad whose answer was *"No hay nada que hacer."* A brake cable was broken too, but this could be fixed. And I hunted out a shop in the *plaza* where the job was done. The balance of the morning was devoted to business. The bank and the *prefectura* where long waits made me nervous. There was so much to see in Cuzco! I also hunted out the Touring Club where a very pleasant woman helped me with plans for a trip to *Ollantaytambo*. And with this, the morning passed...After dinner I went off on Chester, an object of curiosity in the cobbled streets. Up the hill I pushed, up to *Sacsayhuaman,* the Inca fortress which overlooks the city of *Cuzco.* An amazing place! Stones laid with the same precision as the stones in the walls of the city, but tremendous stones. Parallel zigzag walls and on top a stone foundation of concentric circles. Water channels radiating from the center. A lovely pattern. Across the way, I found an English-speaking Peruvian who showed me the Inca throne and the Inca slide. And like a good tourist I sat and slid like the Incas before me! Then I pedaled on up the hill in search of *Khencco.* But I didn't find *Khencco.* Instead I found *Tampu Mackay* and the fortified hill which guards it. And I found a beautiful view of hills clothed in low gray-green and of snowy summits beyond. *Llamas* grazed by the side of the road. And there were Indians. My queries of *"Donde está Khencco?"* brought uncomprehending stares. These natives spoke only *Quechua.* In the evening I returned, winding back to *Cuzco,* looking away to blue and gray-green hills rising sharp and distinct and clearly stratified. And looking down on the mass of red tile roofs of the city. Those sagging, aged roofs which are such a characteristic part of *Cuzco.* In town I left Chester in the keeping of the *Guardia Civil* and went to see the

Saturday afternoon fair in San Francisco *plaza*.   Crowds of
people had gathered here and countless Indians were selling
all manner of things. Ponchos and temporary tables served as
counters, and business was active. Old books and locks and
shoestrings and combs. Sandals of rubber tires. Bread and
candy. Maize and tomatoes and strawberries and potatoes and
cereals. Dyes. Clothing of all sorts. Everything under the sun
but the white shoelaces I wanted to buy! Most interesting
were the Indians. Here there was a predominance of the flat-
hatted variety. Women who wore elaborate, shabby waists
and long navy-blue skirts trimmed in red. Flat, up turned hats
showed red also. And ponchos were woven with much more
elaborate design than I had seen in Bolivia. Red, red, red—
red in all the fabrics. From the fair, I went home for an early
dinner and to prepare for a trip the next day. I talked a little
with my fellow Americans at the hotel, but their conversation
about food leaves me cold, and I spend most of my time alone.
Rain and a fever inside of me made me skeptical of leaving
next day, but I went early to bed in hopes--.

October 20, 1942—Machu Picchu—Hotel arriba—Early

        The morning of the 18th I wakened with strength to
carry out my plans. And the day was fair. Good luck. At 5:30
I was on my way, pedaling down the *carretera* towards
Huambutio. Fun to pedal again in the early morning with the
sun bright on the sides of the canyon and with the early-
morning life streaming past me into town. The old thrill of the
pedals and the unknown road ahead. And I traveled easily
over a road which lead forever down—down through a
cultivated valley closed in by gray-green hills. The church
towers of *San Sebastian* formed a lovely pattern ahead. The
adobe houses, the rows of eucalyptus, the barefoot Indian were
picturesque. At *Huambutio* I turned down the *Rio Vilcanota*
and here the canyon became narrower, the hills higher and
there was little life. Broom, yellow and fragrant, grew by the
side of the road, and these were pepper trees. I ate my
breakfast of rolls as I pedaled and drank my boiled water, a

precaution which seemed rather futile in view of the fact that I
had been drinking everything! Below *San Salvador* I met a
strange troop in the road—Indians in bright costumes with
spangles and feathers, masks and animal skins. They were on
their way to a native *fiesta.* In *Pisac* I sought out the *plaza,*
and then I left Chester in the keeping of a *Peruano* while I
climbed up to the ruins. Up over a long series of terraces to
the towers guarding the hilltop and farther to what might once
have been an observatory. Here the stonework was of a finer
sort and there were the usual trapezoidal niches common to all
the Inca edifices. More of the incredibly firm joining of rocks,
which even in seeing one can scarcely believe. And what a
vantagepoint the Incas had chosen! From their hilltop they
could look up and down the valley of the *Vilcanota* as well as
down into one of its tributaries. A fine view. Up there on top
I met the American crowd from the hotel. They had come by
car and horse, but had arrived only shortly before me, and
probably had not seen half as much. After more than an hour
of rambling around, we all returned together. In the plaza of
Pisac a fair was in progress with the now familiar jumble of
Indians and wares. Gone the derby hats and in their place the
flat, red, upturned ones. Navy blue and red with intricate
patterns in the *tejidos.* And shading the *plaza* a great tree with
brilliant orange blossoms. By noon I was again on my way,
pedaling down the *Vilcanota.* Always down, thanks to Allah,
for my bike is no longer suitable for climbing. And all the
way a lovely panorama. Green fields in the valley by the
river. Hills of red earth and dark stone but softened by the
gray-green of lichens and the gray-green of low growth. Tall
cactus with white blossoms and small cactus, with red
blossoms. And beyond—occasional glimpses of high, icy
mountains. Spectacular summits. There was a feeling of the
desert in the clear air and the barren hills, an exhilarating
something that lent eagerness to pedaling. And on the road,
the always interesting Indians. They scampered away in
surprise as I passed on my bike and they giggled when they
realized I was nothing but a *gringa loca.* In *Urubamba* I
stopped at a little hole in the wall to escape from the midday

sun, and there I drank 2 "colas" while dirty children and cats eyed me curiously. *Al frente* Indians loitered under great trees with the same orange flowers I had seen in Pisac. And now energetic Indians walked deliberately down the cobbled streets. As the sun sank lower, I continued my way, but I was tired now, and the fever within me was burning again. Slower the pedaling. And a headwind rose to transform the *bajada* into *subida*. Great force was necessary to turn my high-geared pedals, a force which I no longer possessed. But the beauty of the canyon never dimmed nor the picturesque *poblaciones* with their mud walls and bright geraniums protruding from the doorways. At dusk I stopped to inquire where I was, and a ragged lad with only one good eye stepped up to tell me that *Ollantaytambo* was just ahead. He would serve me at the hotel! And sure enough, when I had bumped over the cobblestones of the narrow streets, across the unkempt *plaza*, and down to the station, with a crowd of small boys at my heels, there he was to greet me! Welcome refuge, my great room with its candle and wash basin. And delicious the *comida* of peppery meat and plain boiled potatoes. But best of all, the bed. And I turned in content with the thought the hills rose all about me, a river ran below, and down the canyon stood a great white mountain silvery in the moonlight.

October 21, 1942—Cuzco—Hotel Colón—7:00 PM

I woke with the sun on the 19th, and I felt much better. After café I walked alone up to the ruins for which *Ollantaytambo* is famous, and here I idled away the morning. More terraces and more of the fine rock work which one finds in all these ancient mysterious forts and cities. But at the center of the ruins there was a new form of workmanship. Here red granite had been used and the great rocks had been fitted together with narrow ones. Strange. Two urchins attached themselves to me in the capacity of guides, but their language was *Quechua*, and all they knew in Spanish was "*bonito, Señorita*" and "*propina*"! I couldn't shake 'em! With the Inca love of altitude I settled myself amidst the ruins and wrote, wrote, and enjoyed the view below. And not until the approach of train time did I wander down to join the crowd of Indians drifting toward the station with their baskets and bundles and jugs of food and drink to sell to the *pasajeros.* A short wait and once again I was on my way, this time *en tren, sin bicicleta.* And the ride to *Machu Picchu* seemed short because of the spectacular quality of the scenery. The canyon became narrower and more precipitous, and the mountains rose more abruptly. Below the river was a torrent. And little by little the hills lost their barrenness became more verdant. Then suddenly, we were in the tropics amongst creepers and ferns, begonias and strange flowering plants and trees. And there was damp heat and a languid atmosphere. At *Machu Picchu* station I met Bill Densel, another Yankee, and *Mr. Sato, dueño* of the hotel, and we decided to go *arriba* at once. A short way down the road we took the trail leading up, and for 4 kms we climbed through some of the most spectacular scenery I have ever known. For below wound the *Vilcanota.* And high above stood steep mountains dotted in tropical verdure. A precipitous world with a misty atmosphere. Beautiful beyond description. And beside the trail brilliant red flowers—all red—stems and all. At the hotel we stopped to rest and cool off before going out to see the ruins, and then we went with *Mr. Soto* as guide. Here on the mountain top, high above the river in an impregnable spot were the most extensive, the most perfect ruins I had seen. Awe inspiring in their perfection; awe inspiring in the mystery of their builders. A whole city with temples for worship, rooms for the dignitaries, tombs, fountains with water channels, stairways, jails, an amphitheater, a sundial. –All wrought in faultless stone, lovely in its absolute simplicity. The acme of functionalism. Not one bit of decoration. And one wondered who had lived there in this eagle's haunt—and why they had gone, leaving only their amazing handiwork. A mystery and romance hung over the ruins, inhabited now by begonias, maidenhair ferns, and wild strawberries. The reality of Inca life was only an echo. I was glad to go back to the hotel at the foot of the ruins where I could sit and watch daylight fade from the high green mountains all about. And when darkness confined sensation to the walls of the hotel, I found contentment in a cozy fire, a bouquet of dewy roses, and a long and interesting conversation with Bill Densel, whom I was just beginning to know.

The morning of the 20th we had hoped to climb a peak above the ruins, but rain in the night persisted through the dawn, so instead we ate a late breakfast and loitered, hoping for better weather. Once the clouds broke, and one could look across the high mountains which seemed even higher with their cloud effects. Unreal, rain-washed mountains rising there beyond the banana fronds, very near, very high, their feet planted far below beside the curling *Vilcanota*. Only for a moment could we see them. Then mists enveloped all. One of those fleeting moments so powerful in its beauty that it is forever remembered. Later from out of the dripping path came a German *señora* on seeing the ruins, and Bill and I joined her, for we wanted to see a little more before returning. Again we climbed the stairs and followed the walls and looked through the 3 windows. And bits of light revealed the canyon below. But time was short, and at 11:00 AM we rushed away, back the steep trail to the station. At noon we arrived, but the *autocarril* was late, so for a couple of hours we lunched and watched the life of the station. A ramshackle place in a beautiful setting. And the people, who didn't care, just sat at their front doors. No movement, no ambition, no enthusiasm. Just living. Waiting to sell a banana or a pineapple. Watching dirty babies playing in the dirt. Watching pigs and sheep mingle with the babies. Life so simple that it was almost no life at all. Finally, the autocarril arrived, and we started the trek back to *Cuzco*. Back up the canyon, out of the tropical indolence of *Machu Picchu*, back to the high barren hills. At *Ollantaytambo* I picked up Chester who became a respected passenger. While behind me Indian women pleaded that I recommend that they be permitted to ride all the way to *Cuzco* where a daughter was dying. From *Pachar* we climbed up a narrow, dry canyon and came out on a high plateau where cultivation was much more abundant.

The air took on a chill. And behind, the gold of the sunset mixed with the ethereal whiteness of snowy peaks. At dark we wound down to the warmth of the lights of *Cuzco*. And the whole trip had been interesting because of its glimpses of ruins along the way. Terraces along the river valley. Buildings on the hillsides above. A bridge. Bits of cobbled roadway. Here truly was the "archeological capital of South America." I tried to get a room at the Hotel *Colón* for a change, but all was filled, so I returned to the *Ferrocarril* where I felt quite at home. A hot bath, a meal, and a bed were all that interested me. I was sick, unable to read or write or brush my teeth.

October 22, 1942—Cuzco—Hotel Colón—7:00 PM

But yesterday morning, the 21st, I was again able to carry on, and I was up early to pack and move up to *Hotel Colón* where I had been promised a room. Not a fine room as in the Ferrocarril, but a room in an old building with a cobbled courtyard, balconies, thick walls, round arches, and a sagging roof! A place which feels like *Cuzco*. And it was still early when I went out to visit churches which open for mass only in the early hours of the morning. The inside of *La Compañia* proved rich in decoration with altar and chapels of carved and gilded wood, but I liked the outside better. Columns of reliefs of carved stone in conventionalized design. *La Merced*, on the contrary, seemed bare and colorless, but the convent was fine. A monk showed me to the first cloister, and, being a woman, I could penetrate no further into its sacred interior, but I was permitted to admire the architecture from the pleasant patio. Pillars and arches of carved stone with a ceiling of carved wood, unpainted. A simple, decorative fountain at the center, and paving stones bearing letters and numbers. A fine sample of colonial architecture, rich in decoration, yet strong in basic line. And standing in complete tranquillity secluded from the outside world. Later in the streets I met *Sucre Chehadi* and uniformed friend, and the 3 of us went for a *paseo* up into the *San Blas* district, up narrow, steep streets, and back by way of

Hatunrumiyoce St. with its fine wall of large, irregular stones, amongst them the famous *piedra de los doce angelos*. After lunch I went out with Bill Densel to look for picturesque corners, and we wandered also up *Hatunrumiyoce St.* Thence down to the Temple of the Sun and back *Loreto* Lane, lined on both sides with impressive Inca walls. Buying photographs and visiting the Club Touring completed my business, and the balance of the afternoon I devoted to a 2nd excursion in search of *Khencco*. This time I went on foot, climbing up through the *San Blas* district and following a worn trail to the top of the hill. Success! There was *Khencco*! An amphitheater of stone, subterranean passageways and a zigzag cut for the conveyance of *chicha*. A fine vantagepoint, I sat on the rocks to write and not until dusk did I wander back to the life and color of the city. Narrow streets with overhanging balconies framing the roofs and walls and church towers of the city below. Eternally picturesque. As I passed the adobe edifice of *San Blas*, I noted a man with keys, and so I asked to see the church. An unprepossessing adobe edifice, inside it contains an altar of hammered silver and a pulpit of intricately carved wood—the latter considered the best of all the finer pulpits in *Cuzco*. It seemed illogical to find such richness inside such a building, but this is *Cuzco*, where one sees humble houses with foundation of the finest Inca workmanship and where one meets Indians bundled up in rags yet possessing some bit of hand woven fabric of exquisite color and design. A city of contrasts. A city of surprises. No modern keenness of line and composition. No 20th century organization. Rather, a hodge podge of the centuries. A colorful jumble of the past and present, hoary with age, vibrating with life. Inimitable *Cuzco*. In the *plaza* I sat to feel the beauty of dusk in the city. Silhouetted church towers, the first lights, and the tolling of the bells of the Cathedral. Back at the *Colón, Sucre Chehadi* came to call, and we walked out to see the city by night. Thence up to a vantagepoint in the hills where we could look down on the lights of *Cuzco*. A nice boy, *Sucre* became romantic in the moonlight, (always to be expected in South America!) and suddenly passionately he tried to force a kiss.

Only by sheer force was I able to avoid it, and after a struggle, we walked soberly back to the city, had a drink, and parted company.

October 23, 1942—Cuzco—Hotel Colón—Afternoon

Yesterday morning early I went again to visit churches. –To *Jesus and Maria* beside the Cathedral, and thence to *Belen* in the western part of the city. The latter presents a rather different atmosphere from the other churches. Diffused light from above, combined with gilded, carved wood, lightens the weight of stone and dark paintings. And white, lends a feminine touch to this particular temple. The pulpit too is delicately carved, though not so ornate as many of the others, and above in the choir loft one catch glimpses of more fine wood carving. Wandering back to the *Colón*, I stopped in to see *San Francisco*, but found nothing of note inside. So I devoted the balance of the morning to shopping for Indian fabrics. What temptation! There are so many things I would like to have and so little that I can actually carry. In the afternoon I went to visit the Archeological Institute, and with the help of a very pleasant young man, I spent a couple of hours looking at exhibits of objects from the vicinity of *Cuzco*. Most interesting! Fine potteries intricately formed and decorated with good conventional design. Plates with decorative bands across the diameter. Shawl pins of bronze and silver. Small animals of gold. Great earthen jugs for *chicha*. Mummies, all in a sitting position. Exquisite fabrics wrought by Indians during the colonial period. And best of all—stone objects. For the people of *Cuzco* were masters of stone. Beautiful forms of stone. And some reserved decoration forming an integral part of the whole design. A modern conception of art. At the end of my tour, I gave my affable guide a tip, and then would have given anything to have had it back, for the gentleman looked so hurt that I was sure I had offended. Typical of Richardson— always doing the wrong thing at the right time! At dusk I chose again to climb one of the hillsides up to the top of the city. And I made my way up to the church of *San Cristobal* where is the wall of *Ccoluampata*, a long Inca construction with niches large enough to hold a man. From this vantagepoint I could look down on the darkening roofs of the city and the lights of the *plaza*, seemingly unnecessary beneath a brilliant moon. I loitered long up there, aloof from the sights and sounds of the city, and then made my way home down dim narrow passageways. After dinner I went to a movie with Bill D., a war propaganda picture, but a welcome excuse with which to miss *Sucre's* phone call!

October 25, 1942—Cuzco—Gran Hotel Colón—8:00 PM

Friday, the 23rd, I had expected to leave *Cuzco* and go by train to *Arequipa*, but I changed my plans because I just couldn't resist the temptation to make the trip through the mountains by way of *Ayacucho*. So I had arranged to take a truck Saturday, and hence I had yet another day to spend in *Cuzco*. But I didn't stay in *Cuzco*; instead I went off to the country on Chester—pedaling to satisfy the restlessness inside of me. Up the hill to the north, following the road to *Urubamba*, pushing up until I could look down on the sea of red tile which is *Cuzco*. Then across a summit and down the same valley which I had passed on my return from *Machu Picchu*. A lovely shallow valley with green patches and dry hills. Bits of old Inca road, cobbled with worn stones, were the preferred way of the Indians who drove their donkeys and llamas along these historic tracks. But I kept to the main road, which is infinitely more passable for wheels, and from its curves I could look across to high wild mountains exciting in their grandeur. Lines of trees by the side of the road—and adobe huts and then a lazy little village where Indians sat behind their piles of corn and potatoes. Here I turned off and followed the road up to *Lago Huaipu*. Rolling cultivated land—turned earth of rosy red and reddish brown, even purplish. And then the lake, a silvery sheet reflecting the great icy mountains behind it. Here I stopped to eat my *Cuzco* chocolate, to write, and to just be. The purple beyond and the

winding roads were a mighty force calling me on, but I had
cycled down hill for a very long way, and I had to return, so I
sat by the side of the lake until midday when the chill of the
puna stirred me again to activity. Back the same road to
Cuzco. Always lovely. And by mid afternoon I was again in
the city, tired from highgear cycling, but refreshed by the
peace of the country. Out in the streets I found a funeral
procession which I followed out of curiosity. Frames and
crosses bearing greenery and roses, school girls with veiled
heads, the casket born on the shoulders of 4 men, a group of
mourners dressed in black with long-tailed coats and feathery,
boat-like hats, and a crowd of idlers. At the *Arco de Santa
Clara*, the casket was lowered and priests offered some kind
of an oration before continuing up the hill. As the procession
passed the market, I branched off to buy oranges and bananas,
for my legs were a bit wobbly from hunger. And back home I
crawled into bed to rest a while before dinner. When I went
down to eat with Bill, a couple of others were waiting, *Sucre*
and a *Peruano* called *Velasquez*. But afterwards the party
dwindled to just *Sucre* and me, and so we went for another
paseo, carefully avoiding *el campo*! Down the *Prado* to the
station and back past *el Templo del Sol*. Through *Loreto
"Lani"* where I searched for the carved snake over one of the
doorways and thence up to *San Cristobal*. A beautiful night, it
was fun to walk and talk, but back home *Sucre* was slow to
leave, and I was so weary that I became truly angry. He
finally went with "*ciao*" which spelled fine.

  And yesterday the truck didn't leave! A good
Peruvian truck, it would go *mañana*! So another day was
passed in *Cuzco*. In the morning I went with Bill and
Valasquez to make arrangements to go by car to *Lima*, but I
was a bit skeptical of the new set up, and I held my truck
ticket—just in case--. Then, business done, I treated myself to
the luxury of a morning in my room, mending and setting
things in order. After lunch Bill wanted to go to
Sacsayhuaman, and I was glad to go along for the activity. Up
the canyon to the *fortaleza* and farther to *Pucara* and *Tambu
Machchai*. This latter I had not actually seen before, for I had

stopped a few yards before reaching it. And I found it one of the loveliest of the ruins with its fountain of water and its neat walls, stairs, and doorways. Not extensive but quite perfect. By now the hour was late and we had to hurry towards home, scarcely taking time to look at the saffron hills of *Cuzco*. The purple hills beyond, and the white mountains far beyond. Down an Indian trail through the hills. And I with bad shoes! Since *Machu Picchu* they had practically fallen apart and now they threatened to really do it! For a while I went barefoot, and then with the aid of God and a string I managed to complete the last lap through the city! –While the Indians smiled from their barefoot security! Happy the moment when I finally reached the haven of my room! And there I washed and changed in preparation for a *fiesta*, of all things. *Velasquez* came at 7:30, but Bill and I hadn't eaten, so he went on, and we followed later. A going-away party for a *señorita*—all very elegant with a long table continuously loaded with good things to eat and a bar continuously supplied with whisky and soft drinks. We danced to the tune of an orchestra and chattered about nothing and sampled the endless variety of olives and cookies and sweets on the table. It was fun and sociable, even though I drew no more than half a dozen partners, and when they played "*Hay Carramba*—" I could have wept for joy! At midnight the table was set for *cena* and thereafter the dancing continued, but Bill and I came home at 1:00 and I was content with the evening even though I danced it away in patched shoes and holy socks!

And today I'm still in *Cuzco*! –Seems as if going away is quite a problem, but I still have hopes for *mañana*! This morning I slept late for the first time in days. Luxurious. And the whole day I devoted to nothing. Also luxurious. When I finally ambled out, I went looking for special things. *El Cristo de los Tembores* in the Cathedral. The alleyway of the *Siete Culebras* where Inca snakes are carved in Inca stones. *San Borja*, an old colonial house where *Bolivar* once stayed. The *Calle de Marques* where is a fine old house with elegant entrance and exquisite balconies of carved wood. Odds and ends of *Cuzco*. Interspersed with sitting in the plaza to listen to the band and watch the people go by! Firecrackers also for this Sunday, *dia de fiesta*. After dinner I wrote and washed, and then went for a long walk, perhaps my last in *Cuzco*. Out of the city and down to the *pueblo* of *San Sabastian*, noting the bell towers of the churches, clear against the sky, and the picturesque streets, full of Sunday leisure. Never again, perhaps, would I have the privilege. And the country was lovely with roadside trees framing the towers of *San Sebastian* and the purple canyon ahead. In the *pueblo* I found the church open, and I went inside to find a rather dilapidated building with many paintings, a carved pulpit, and a silver altar. But the best part of the church of *San Sabastian* is its façade of delicately carved stones, more delicate than that of any of the *Cuzco* churches. Back in town, I changed, had dinner, and waited for someone who had called to say he was coming at 8:00. But he hasn't come. So I'm ready for bed, wondering who and why? –Such is South America--.

October 27, 1942—Cuzco—Gran Hotel Colón—Noon

Still in *Cuzco*! Yesterday, the 26th, I spent the day hoping to leave, but I had only my hope--. In the morning *Velasco Heraclio* came with an order for gasoline, and assured me the car of his uncle would leave before noon, so I waited, but no car came. And *Lima* Express confessed that their truck would not leave *tampoco*. *Que dificl viajar en el Peru. Siempre—mañana!* In the afternoon too I waited without success. And then discouraged, I went out to wander again in the streets of *Cuzco*. The old familiar streets with the bell towers against the sky, the delicate balconies overhanging narrow, cobbled streets, and the masses of colorful Indian life. Majesty and age and color and dirt! The beauty of carved stone in the façade of *La Compañia*; and the poverty of Indians in breeches and ponchos patched and repatched until the original is lost. Romance in the weight of a momentous past; pathos in the reality of a destitute present. *Cuzco!* And I, too, felt at home now, for in the streets I met 2 of the *Chehadi* girls and also the guide from the museum. As

always, evening in *Cuzco* had its charm. In spite of heavy
rains in the morning skies had cleared and down *Avenida del
Sol*, I caught a glimpse of saffron hills with purple shadows.
And as the light faded, the bells of the Cathedral and the
promenaders in the streets maintained in the dusk a sense of
life in the city. Before dinner, Bill and I looked at ponchos
brought to our rooms by an Indian, and afterwards we went to
see a show. But there was no show, so we wound up the
evening with a cup of chocolate!

October 28, 1942—Limatambo—Hotel—4:30 AM

And yesterday, *por suerte,* I found a truck and started
my long trek to Lima, but not until late. In the morning, Bill
called *Velasco* and the 3 of us went to look up the auto and
chofer, only to find that they had left the day before! All that
our trip yielded was a glimpse of the *Casa Comerical de
Calvo in Calle Santa Catalina*, an old colonial house with an
elaborately carved balcony. At Lima Express I was assured
that a truck would leave in the afternoon, but I was skeptical
after all the hollow assurances which had issued from that
office. Nothing to do but wait. At the Club Touring, Bill and
I obtained the address of the *Museo de Rosas*, and we trekked
off to see what was there, but it yielded nothing. All the good
things had, apparently been sold. On our way back, we
shopped at the little stores behind the arcades of the *plaza*, and
I came away with a couple of dolls. More junk to find a place
for! After dinner I sallied out to look for the truck which was
leaving for *Huancayo,* and I found it in the street above the
hotel. I would wait at Lima Express, I thought. But I decided
that waiting at the truck was *mas seguro*, so I stood by while a
cargo of coca was loaded. Then the *chofer* suggested that I get
my things and we leave directly without going to the office. It
would *"sale mas barrato"*! And he also would make
something out of the deal! Such are the ways of the Latins.
And I conformed. Not for love nor money would I leave that
truck; I would stay right with it until it left! And at 4:00 PM
we left *Cuzco* en route for the north. I was on my way at last,

praise be to Allah! Up over the hill we went, following the familiar road to *Urubamba*, and looking back, I saw the familiar tile of Cuzco, nestled in the hollow and guarded by purple hills and a great white peak. A lovely last view. Then down the *Izcuchaca* and across the *Pampa de Anta*. A mountain meadow full of sheep and cattle and brooded over by snowy mountains. High mountains which caught the last rays of the sun. Then up again through barren hills. And at dark, we plunged down a mighty canyon. High dark forms all about and the road winding down. Down, down, down to the light of *Limatambo*. Weird. At 8:00 we arrived, and a sharp, nervous little woman served us soup and stew, and fixed a bed for me. And for want of anything else to do, I closed my eyes to a dirty bed and retired early.

October 29, 1942—Talavera—Pensión Inca—5:00 AM

What a night last night turned out to be! No rest for the weary. A bed full of *chinchas* and the fear that the *chofer* would drive away and leave me kept me awake most of the night! Whenever I heard a motor I jumped up to make sure that the *"Papacito"* was still there! And as for the bugs— well, I disposed of all my blankets, killed the animals on the lower sheet, and slept restlessly under my coat! Welcome the first sign of dawn at 4:00 which I welcomed with one eye half closed! For breakfast a glass of *ponche*, hot and white with a red froth, and a cup of coffee. And shortly after 6:00 we were on the road again. Farther down the canyon, the narrow canyon of the *Apurena*. With broom and pepper trees and the great orange-flowering trees, once so startling but now familiar. At *Puente Aleman* we crossed the river and commenced to climb, and we climbed as if our only object was to regain all the altitude we had lost the day before. Up and up and up we ground, stopping only once at a little hill village, *Curahuassi*, for *"control"*—inspection of our tax-bearing load of coca. Then up again, up into the bare, dry hills, up where we caught glimpses of icy mountains rising into the clouds. And then the summit, and a long road coiling down into a purple valley far below, down to the *pueblo* of *Abancay.* Here the air was hot and the landscape was enlivened with fields of yellow-green sugar cane, a change from the browns and reds and purples of the turned earth. In a hotel in the lazy little town we stopped for *almuerzo,* and later at a *hacienda* we stopped for a very long time to rearrange the cargo and take on a couple of tanks of alcohol. I was conscious only of heat and of yellow-green cane and of brown and purple hills. It was late afternoon when we finally continued our way, leaving the valley of *Abancay* and again climbing to the heights on a road which coiled back and forth up the mountains. Below the valley with its brown and yellow-green patchwork. And all about, the wrinkled barren hills—tawny and chocolate-brown and purple. That these hills were high and that this was in truth the *Andes* was born out by the high wild peaks which forever looked down upon us. There were no forests, but there were great heights. At dusk we came out upon the *puna*—yellow and smooth and barren and then it was dark, and I could see no more of the wild hills through which we passed, could only guess at their form and color and the gashes in their sides. Alone in the night with a grinding truck, a load of coca, and 2 *Peruanos!* Shadowy *pampa* and *quebradas.* And then a lopsided moon behind the dark clouds, and the silhouettes of trees. Houses and a town— *Andahuaylas.* A few silent forms in the dark, silent streets. Narrow, cobbled streets and blank mud house fronts. There more trees. A garden amongst the barren hills. And then another silent town, *Talvera.* In the *plaza* where trees and church were now illuminated by more light we stopped and the *chofer* sought out a dark, ramshackeled *pensión.* It seemed deserted, but in the kitchen was a fire and the *dueño* at once set about preparing our comida. We waited in the kitchen. A most amazing kitchen! Dirt floors littered with corn husks and clay pitchers. A high ceiling where roosted pigeons. An Indian woman squatting on the floor. Chickens. An open fire where our potatoes and meat and eggs sizzled in grease. A shadowy scene, eerie in the flicker of the firelight. But the meal was good, and it put me in the proper mood for bed; but since there were no beds left, ten chairs and a mattress became my resting place.   And I retired in the *comedor* where the *dueño* came in with a pillow just as I was ready for bed and when latecomers dined and laughed.   One came over and roused me with a *"Francisco!"* and was startled to see a blond head rise out of the covers!   Such privacy!   But I can always put up with anything for one night.   And when the dirty bedding proved free of *chinchas*—well—there was something to be thankful for!

October 30, 1942—Ayacucho—Hotel Imperial—8:30 PM

And yesterday morning at 5:00 I roused from my bed of chairs, and went out to see if my truck still waited.   And there it was!   *Buena suerte!*   The chubby, jolly little *chofer* is nice, but I don't trust *Peruanos!*   Better to keep an eye on the truck!   Breakfast amidst a confusion of kitchen, café, people. And we had *caldo de pollo* in addition to *café*.   In the kitchen one sees how things are done, and it is no place for one with qualms.   Cups and plates dipped into a pail of cold water.   Dirt everywhere.   Murky water, perhaps dipped from the street as is the custom of the Indians.   But the food comes out tasty, if one is hungry, and fortified with a philosophy, one can eat it.   I have learned not to look too closely at spoons and cups, nor at the food *tampoco*.   The *yerba* in the *caldo* turned out to be feathers!   Once again we were on the road early, climbing to compensate for the descent of the night before.   And by daylight I could see that *Andahuaylas* and *Talvera* were truly gardens amidst the desert hills, green trees and fields amidst dry browns and yellows.   Up and up we climbed.   Up again to the *puna*.   And then down again with a feeling of futility in having climbed so high for nothing.   Down to the land of brown cultivated fields, each bit of tilled earth outlined in trees or rock.   A patchwork of browns reaching high up on the hillsides.   In *Chincheros* we stopped for "control", and when it was   discovered   that   the   *chofer*   had   not   stopped   in *Andahuaylas*, we were ordered to wait for the *teniente*.   And wait we did—for more than an hour.   Then the *teniente* was in favor of sending us back to *Andahuaylas*, but *"por consideracion de la señorita turista"* we were permitted to continue! I had passed the time pleasantly, talking with the natives, but I was anxious to be on my way, for I liked to travel by day rather than by night, so I left with a grateful *"gracias"* to the *teniente*. Farther down the canyon we traveled—down to cane and the stifling heat of the valleys. And across the *Rio Pampas* we stopped for *almuerzo* in *Ninabamba*. Soup and beans with rice and café in a swarm of flies. But there was lemonade to enliven the scene, and I drank it as if it had no relationship to the water dipped form the ditch! Then in *Ninabamba*, I asked for the bathroom, as is my want whenever I have the opportunity. But with grandiose lack of imagination, they brought out a washbasin! And I had to go in search of a bush! How I envy the Indians with their long skirts and their simple ways! I suffer from too much civilization. From *Ninabamba* we climbed again, up and up and up and up to the high, tawny *puna*—up to more than *4,000 metros de altura*—looping back and forth, back and forth, until we reached the open summits. Here we stopped to put in gas, and meanwhile the day ended with a last burst of beauty. Above, a dark, ominous cloud, with frothy orange edges, dropped hail on the *pampa*, while beyond the mountains were purple and sharp in clear air. As we continued our way across the *puna*, darkness came, and I knew only that I was riding across the top of the world. And when there was no longer anything to excite my senses and imagination, I dozed. Then suddenly we were riding down to the light of Ayacucho. At the "control" we were stopped, and I no longer served as a special reason for continuing, so with Chester and my luggage I pushed on to the town, my way lighted by an official who showed me the road with his flash. Beside the *plaza* I found a hotel with a private room and a clean bed, and I luxuriated in my quarters even though I was too late for dinner. A *vuelta* in the *plaza* yielded nothing interesting to eat, so I retired to my clean bed, which was such a precious thing. Complete contentment!

October 31, 1942—Huanta—Hotel Leuro—Tempranito

Yesterday, the 30th, I wakened refreshed and at 6:00 I went out to see the town before the *Papacito* continued her way towards Lima. Shops were closed at this early hour, but already Indians were in the streets moving towards the market with baskets of bread on their backs and baskets of bread on their heads. They were carrying lettuce too, and some had quarters of mutton with legs waving in the air above their backs! The same colorful array which I had first seen in Bolivia, but which was now common place. Other ragged Indians were busy sweeping up the streets with branches of broom, a thankless task in this land where all things are disposed of in the *calles*. But the beauty and not the dirt was impressive. Bright sun on an early morning haze formed a halo about the city and turned the surrounding hills to pastel shades. I walked aimlessly, noting the many church towers, solid and simple, and feeling the picturesqueness of this typical *Sierra pueblo* with its cobbled street, its stolid house fronts, and its inevitable activity in the streets. One *calle* led me to an arch dedicated to Peru's liberty and to an avenue lined with brilliant orange trees, and another took me past the *mercado* where I stopped, fascinated as always with the confusion of popcorn, Indians, cheap clothing, bananas, everything. Later I just sat in the *plaza* to speculate on the dashing form of *Sucre* preserved in bronze there, to look at the church towers and the arcades, to enjoy the purple *jacaranda*, and to watch the people go by. –Also to keep an eye on the *Papacito*! But we didn't leave at 9:00, so I went off with a lad from the hotel to visit a few of the churches, buildings rich in silver and carved wood, though not as fine as those of *Cuzco*. And I was sidetracked by horse trappings which I couldn't resist buying! The lazy morning had worn on to 11:00 before we finally left, and then we were detained at the control office. The *chofer* came back to say that he had been cross-questioned concerning me because the office had a telegram regarding a nazi spy called Helen Richardson. I was disturbed. Was my checkered past, left so far behind in

Uruguay, coming back to interfere with my happy wanderings? Was Mr. Wright really right? I crossed my fingers with fervent hope. And when I was told to go to *investigaciones*, the *chofer* winked, turned the corner, and drove off towards Lima. And I was left to wonder from whence the telegram had come and if it really concerned me--. Out of *Ayacucho* and across desert lands we drove. Cactus and thorn bush and white earth even whiter in the midday sun. Heat. But where that barren earth was watered by a river, it bloomed as a garden and furnished welcome shade. And in the shade of *Chajo* we stopped for *almuerzo*, one of those popular affairs where everyone gathered about the same open air table. After lunch our *chofer* returned jolly from too much drink, and we swang up the hill to *Huanta* devoid of our usual caution. Narrow roads and heavy load added nothing to the joy of the trip, nor did the competition furnished by other trucks and omnibuses. And I was glad to roll into the hill town of *Huanta* and to be relieved of the *chofer's* tipsy braggadocio. Here I secured a room opening directly on the street, and I felt as if I should set up a shop to be logical, but I did nothing more than wash and rest, And then I joined the town's loitering in the *cantina* where I made a pretense of writing but where I was all the while watching the world go by. The town's young bucks wandered in to drink and to talk with the *dueños*, and they eyed me curiously. Strange to find a lone *gringa* in *Huanta*--. One was very personable and I looked at him twice, smiled faintly. Guess South America has made a coquette out of me! Or perhaps the war and the uncertainty of tomorrow has made loneliness more intolerable than ever. Anyway, the gentleman, one *Javier Angulo*, responded. He smiled, bought colas for all including me, and finally sat down at my table! Another little man, who talked all the time, was there too, and I finally yielded to his invitation to go and eat some special dish peculiar to *Huanta*. "*Vamos pues!*" And we went, up the main street and along the edge of the town where we could look out across the jumble of *sierras* across the canyon. *Huanta* seemed to be perched on the edge of the world. In the mud house of an Indian we stopped, and the *señora*, who sat on the ground amidst her pots and braziers, served us a handful of *chicharrones*, a handful of maize, and a handful of lettuce! And we both ate with our hands out of the same plate! Back at the hotel I met *Javier* again, and he suggested we walk, but the little man with whom I had just eaten *chicharrones* came along too. He was something of a leach and more and more obnoxious. And when we walked, he always squeezed in between *Javier* and me! *Paciencia*! We went to the church and sat in the dim light as mass was said. And as we returned, we stopped at a dim bakery to look at the great earthen oven, the troughs of dough, and the hand-propelled sifter. Then *Javier* lead us to a *rinconcita* in a side street where we entered a little low room and where Indian women served us *chorrascos* with *huevos* and *papas*. The dim light, the crude room, the women tending their kettles and pots—all made me feel that I had come to another world. And indeed I had, for this was the real Peru. Back at the hotel I returned to writing as an excuse to shake the persistent small man, but later I met *Javier* again and we went off alone. Intrigue! But we didn't walk far—only to a bench in the *plaza* which fronted our hotel. A place where the air was cool and the night brilliant with stars. A place calculated to stir the romance in the soul of *cualquier latino pasionado*. And Javier ran true to form. He held my hands and made pretty speeches. *"Gringita linda,"* *"encantita,"* *" simpatica Elenita"*! And I liked his pretty lies, although I surely wasn't the *"flor debil"* for whom such words were meant. I was only the more conscious of the callous on my hands, the sunburn on my nose, and the muscles in my legs! *Javier's* arms about me felt good. They gave me a sense of protection and companionship and affection—a feeling that the world was no longer mine to battle alone. And I wished that this sense of dependency might endure, that it were not a hollow, fleeting thing snatched at hungrily because tomorrow would find it gone. At midnight we took tea in the corner shop. And then I went to bed for a snatch of sleep before the truck was ready to leave.

November 1, 1942—Huancayo—Hotel Ritz—7:00 PM

Yesterday morning, the 31ˢᵗ, I was up and dressed after only an hour's sleep. And *Javier*, who was still abroad, came to say good-bye as the *Papacito* rolled away at 2:00 AM. Out of sleeping *Huanta* and into a world of moonlight and hills. Feathery pepper trees and stiff century plants, black in the moonlight. And a feeling of goneness inside of me, because I always react deeply and each show of affection leaves its scar. Down into the valley of the *Rio Montero* and along the river for miles and miles. Dark hills high above, and water rushing below. And the road a narrow trail carved from the mountain side—sometimes so narrow that our cargo scraped the rock walls. Innumerable times we crossed deep and narrow gullies running down to the river as we continued our way up the canyon. Once the *chofer* stopped and rested. "*Mucho sueño.*" And I was glad that once again we were traveling cautiously. Dawn finally dimmed the moonlight and brought color to the hills. And dissipated the mystery of a dark world. We stopped for café in *Anco*, and there continued our way up the *Mantero*, always up through the barren, colorful hills beside the muddy stream. But finally we left the river and looped our way up to the *puna*, to the desolate yellow heights. And before long we were passing mud houses and mud walls and rows of eucalyptus trees. *Huancayo* at last! And the end of my journey in *carro*. Tired, dirty, stockingless. Covered with insect bites, I sought a hotel. But with Chester in one hand and my saddle bags in the other I didn't cut a very impressive figure. However, I was shown to a room and given a late dinner, and after I was able to clean up a bit, I felt more or less human. A few more days in that truck and I would have been no better than an Indian! How quickly one sinks to their level when deprived of ordinary conveniences! Put in the streets of *Huancayo* I found myself in a more modern city than I had seen before in Peru. Pavement in the one main street! And the Indians sitting on the curb instead of on the cobblestones! But the tone of life had not changed. As I passed the plaza, I met a couple of men who had been traveling along in the same caravan as I was since *Ayacucho*, and they invited me to join them for a drink. We had a couple of *piñas* and a *papaya*, but I drew the line before we reached *piscos* and whiskies. Then when the *"que lindas"* began to blossom, I insisted on going home. An early dinner and bed were all that interested me at that moment. And this morning at 7:00 I was ready for the day. But before *desayuno* I went out into the streets, for this was Sunday—fair day in *Huancayo*. Already the town was buzzing with activity. There were rows of stalls at the side and in the center of the main street, and where there were no stalls, ponchos and sacks were heaped with wares. Indians were busy buying and selling. And the women, as always, created a colorful picture. White straw hats, elaborate blouses, *mangos*, bright skirts, and mantas with a new design. After *desayuno* I found the fair at its best, and hours passed as I wandered fascinated, trying to resist the temptation to buy things which I could not carry. For blocks there was a hubbub of activity, and every conceivable thing was for sale. Stalls hung full of bright skirts and blouses. Rows of *botas* and shoes lay on the pavement. Gourds and spoons and kitchen utensils. Dyes. Bananas, papayas, avocados, oranges, pineapples. Maize of all colors— red, white, black, yellow. Potatoes. Grains. Peanuts. Coca. Sheepskins, *mantas*, rugs. Hauls of wool ready for spinning. Bread and cakes and taffy. And the inevitable hot food, ready to be dished out and eaten in the street—great jugs of soup and stew and coffee. I looked at *mantas*, but preferred the ones which the Indians were weaving and I looked at silver but found many of the things rather poorly made. Corn, on the other hand, intrigued me, and I could have bought a whole sack of the colorful ears! After dinner, rain kept me indoors, and I wrote as I have not written in weeks. But in the late afternoon, restlessness turned me to Chester, and I ventured out to find the station and to explore a bit of the road to Lima. Then I came home to walk the streets until darkness drove me indoors to write away the hours before supper. Tonight I am restless and lonesome--.

November 2, 1942—Casapalca—Hotel Central—7:00 PM

Ages ago, this morning, I wakened at 5:00, and made ready to leave, for I had decided to take the train. In cycling clothes and with saddlebags bulging beyond capacity, I pedaled to the station, and there I bought a first class ticket because of the prestige that it lends to cycling and because of the police inspection that it avoids. Since *Ayacucho* I have felt that it behooves me to be careful. At 6:30 we puffed away from *Huancayo*, across the *puna* with bare hills rising on either side, past eucalyptus trees and cultivated earth, past frequent *pueblos* of brown mud, always dominated by a church. Then we turned up a narrow river canyon, and thenceforth we followed the river, winding up and up and up. The mountains here seemed to be formed with careless abandon. Strata stood on end and at all manner of angles. And the *cerros* created by this up-thrusted strata were utterly devoid of vegetation—ragged peaks clothed only in the soft reds and browns and purples of the earth. Along the river were occasional *pueblos*, and in each the cemetery was the scene of great activity. People with wreaths of natural and artificial flowers were there paying tribute to the dead. Up and up and up we traveled, and the world became more and more desolate. But in *Oroya* there was life. Here was no Indian *pueblo*, but rather a mighty plant built by the "Colossus of the North." Steel and smoke and industry dedicated to extracting copper from the rich ores of the hills beyond. And a thrill went through me as I thought of the power inherent in my *paisanos*. In *Ticlio* I came to the end of my journey, and I hurriedly descended and went to collect Chester. If he had been disabled en route I would have to continue in the train. But a quick inspection showed that brake cables were still intact and that wheels still turned. I would stay, even though the day had become cold and gray and snow was falling. I was at the highest point on the line, up at an altitude of 4758 *metros* or 15, 610 feet. And I was left alone in the snow with nothing but a bleak station beside me. But *Ticlio* was not so desolate as it first appeared. Curious employees came out to talk with me. And from an Indian woman I bought 2 plates of hot *mondoqito*, a yellow concoction of potatoes and vegetables and meat. Then, as I waited for the weather to improve, I visited with the *jefe* and other curious employees. For a while we sat in the *autocarril*, a warmer spot than the station, and then we adjourned to the "*calentador*" which was even warmer. All the while snow fell and the mountains were veiled. A band of *llamas* drifted over the hill as disdainful of the snow as of all other things. But I was impatient for I must reach a hotel for the night. Late in the afternoon the weather cleared a bit and revealed the surrounding peaks, ragged and snow patched. Magnificent! And with hot coffee and *panqueque* from the *cantina* to fortify me against the cold, I started on my way. The jefe and 2 employees walked with me as far as the *carretera*, and thence I rolled on alone in that forbidding mountain pasture. But the way was down and the road paved—a cyclist's paradise—and I could almost forget the bitter cold which cut through my cotton clothing and numbed my hands. Ahead the road spiraled down into a bottomless canyon, and all about were wild peaks. An impressive *viaje*. But the cold became intolerable, and in *Casapalca* I stopped. A dingy, black mining town with a cheerless hotel—at least it was a place where I could get a meal and a bed. So I resigned myself to the "*Central*" where flowered wallpaper had been stripped from the mud walls, where the "*baño*" was hidden at the end of a dark and tortuous cobbled alley, and where my bed had 2 blankets but only one sheet! A welcome hot meal I ate with miners while a busy *mozo* shouted "*dos primeros,*" "*uno tercero,*" "*quatro segundos,*" to a hole in the wall through which one could see a fire and an Indian.

November 4, 1942—Lima—Hotel Maury—past midnight

And the night in *Casapalca* I passed shivering with cold. There were no *chinchas* in my two blankets. But there was little warmth *tampoco*! And yesterday morning. I crawled out into a cold gray world. Hot coffee helped, as did the eternal thrill of the open road. And I managed to keep my hands warm with a rag hung over one and an old bag over the other! Down again in the mighty gorge of the *Rimac*, a stream growing larger and larger as I followed it down. Sheer walls and precipices, and a narrow winding road. Color but no vegetation. And close by the phenomenal railroad of the Harmon Brothers whose building is a story of audacity and romance. Past *Casa Blanca* where both road and railroad loop and double back in an amazing manner. Forever down. Below *San Mateo* there was an almost imperceptible softening both of weather and terrain. Warmth in the air, and a valley that permitted some bit of cultivation. But still the road spiraled down, and I swung around the curves with joy and abandon. More warmth in the air and bananas and cane growing by the river. And then *Chosica*, and suddenly I was in another world. Gone the slow life and the other world atmosphere of the *Sierra*, and in their place a modern work-a-day feeling. Good roads and speeding cars. Wealthy homes. Opulent agriculture. I was approaching Lima. And shortly I arrived, a dazed cyclist in a throbbing city. *"Donde está la Plaza de Armas?"* I must pedal to the center in spite of the curiosity that I roused. And I gave thanks to Allah that this was *siesta* hour when a minimum of people were up and around. The *Maury* at last, and a welcome opportunity to escape from the streets, change my clothes, and eat a good square meal. And then out into the streets to accomplish what I could not in the late afternoon. A word at the consulate; a mended sock; window shopping; walking. And after dark, the luxury of a place where I could write and read. I felt settled, as if my ride down from almost 16,000 ft. marked the end of the trail for me, as if Lima were the final point of a glorious adventure. But nevertheless I turned over and over in my mind what I would say to the consul next day. I couldn't really hope for more time, but I did hope, for I wanted desperately to see more of South America. Even the thrill of going home could not eclipse this desire.

"Forget me not my dear friend" [signature unintelligible]

November 5, 1942—Lima—Hotel Maury—8:00 AM

And yesterday after coffee I walked down the *Jiron Union* to *Plaza San Martín* and the consulate wondering what they would do to me there. I wanted to speak with the consul, but the privilege is denied a mere person, and I was ushered in to see a Mr. Johnson. The moment I saw him I knew what his reply to me would be, and I was not surprised when, after a few short words, he asked me to leave his office. He couldn't be bothered. But my passport was taken for checking and shortly a Mr. Walsh came out to ask me to his office. Here was a man of more importance. Evidently there was something of more than usual interest about me. Settled in his office, he asked his secretary to leave and shuffled papers until we were alone in the room, and then he opened a paper marked "strictly confidential" and began to question me. But his approach was kindly, and I was relieved to talk. Who was I? Where had I been? Did I know various other persons? Was I of German stock? Just what happened in Uruguay?--. Had I ever been asked to carry messages? And more—all directed towards the same hypothesis. The specter of the spy had returned. And when I had answered to the best of my ability, I, too, asked questions. And what Mr. Welsh told me cast more light on what had happened to me than anything I had hitherto heard. All of South America was a hotbed of espionage and counter-espionage. All foreigners were watched, and everything out of the way was reported. Everyone was under suspicion. From the beginning, my movements had been watched. Perhaps a girl traveling on a bicycle was carrying messages that couldn't be sent by mail. And before my troubles had come to a head in Uruguay, my name had been reported by anti-Nazi Germans! I was listed as suspicious! I was aghast at this news. While I had been pedaling blithely across South America conscious of nothing but the gold of the poplars, the glory of the mountains, the goodness of the people, the breadth of the *pampa*—during all those joyous weeks the clouds were gathering above me. It seemed incredible. But the news made me feel that what had occurred in *Minas* was not merely a stroke of ill fortune, but rather an inevitable climax to my vagabonding. And that I had been sent home seemed logical under the circumstances, I was grateful to Mr. Walsh who had given me this new point of view and who had dealt with me as a person, but I was disturbed by the knowledge that I had been living in a world of suspicion. All the starch went out of me as I walked the streets after dinner and turned over in my mind all the things which had happened since I first arrived in Chile. Had the folks I had called friends had some particular interest in me? Had I said anything which I shouldn't have said? Had anyone ever done or asked anything which was a little strange? What of the lone horseman of *Octay*? What of the German woman in *Colonia Suiza* who had asked me to write to her brother? What of Bill Densel who had asked me to carry a message to Lima? And I hated myself for my suspicions, for I would rather trust and be occasionally betrayed than to never trust at all. Little by little, as a river eating out a canyon, the war is disintegrating my world. I walked and walked and walked— aimlessly. I had unknowingly become associated with this hateful thing, and it engulfed me as a flood. Words were useless—like the puny struggles of a drowning man. For innocent little acts became incriminating evidence in the imagination of others. All I could do was to go on living in an honest manner and rest content that nobody could prove anything against me. But I hated the thought that this or that act might be misinterpreted. Mechanically I went to Panagra and arranged to go home at an early date. Mechanically I walked about the heart of the city. I was not seeing Lima; I was seeing myself and my trip in a new light. And I felt terribly alone. Tears in the privacy of my own room. But café revived me, and in the evening my thoughts turned outward to the City of Kings. I saw the cathedral and the *portales*, *San Francisco* church, the *Rimac*, and *cerro San Cristobal* with the lighted cross at its crest. Life was brighter. And in the evening I forgot my troubles when the young *Chileno* who sat near me at dinner asked me to go to a show, a Chilean comedy.

November 6, 1942—Cali, Colombia—Hotel Alferez Real

Almost the whole of yesterday, the 5th, was devoted to business, with a little sightseeing tucked in the side. First to Panagra, and thence with their representatives to 3 Peruvian offices in each of which my passport received a new stamp. Then the *Ministerio de Hacienda* for permission to export steel—my inseparable Chester! After a hearty lunch of bananas and chocolate, I went out to see a little of *Lima* during the hours when offices are closed. And I was capable of real activity now that my sense of futility had passed. Along the *Plaza* in front of the cathedral and the archbishop's palace and past the spot where *Pizarro* painted his final cross in his own blood. Thence to *San Francisco* church, which has a horizontal feeling in its heavy façade, and beyond through old Lima where balconies and weighty arches hark back to a colonial past. Across the *Rimac* I asked a question of a policeman, and when he learned I was a tourist, he took it upon himself to show me about. We passed the ancient bull ring, climbed to the top of a dilapidated *torreon*, once used by *la gente noble* as a vantage point from which to view the bull fights, and thence we walked to the *Paso de Aguas* near which is a very old colonial balcony where *Pericholi* once dined. An old man with clean, strong features permitted us to climb to the balcony, apologizing all the while for the poverty of what was now his home and workshop. From him I took leave of my gracious guide and returned to the center to change my money and complete arrangements for my ticket. But 3:00 found me back again on the other side of the *Rimac*, this time at the *Cuartel de la Republicana* which was once the famous *Pericholi's* palace. Here was a fine airy building with great doors and windows simply barred and simply carved. Rich and elegant, yet lacking the profuse decoration of many colonial things. Secret mirror doors, great airy rooms, hand-made furniture, pictures of the-----and of *Pericholi*, a bathtub of a simple piece of marble. And in back, a fine garden with baths, a fishpond, and a huge grapevine remaining from colonial times. Everything here had the feel of a summer palace of a lovely lodge of long ago. From here I walked back again to the center and thence to the *Universidad de San Marcos,* oldest university in South America. I didn't enter for I had no business there, but I peered into the entrances with their gardens and heavy architecture. Thence I continued to *Avenida Wilson* where I looked up the Club Touring and asked for maps as is my wont. In spite of the difficulties which maps have brought me and in spite of the fact that I no longer cycle, I still love *planos*! Out in this section of the city streets are broad, parks are frequent, buildings are elegant—a tremendous contrast from the city across the *Rimac* and in the neighborhood of *San Francisco.* Back in the center I waited anxiously at the *Ministerio de Hacienda* for the document which would permit me to take Chester out of Peru, but not until the last minute was it given to me. Relief! I was afraid that their reply would be the eternal "*mañana*", and there was no tomorrow for me. Relief! And now all was ready, and I was free to use my time as I liked. No more official business. So I devoted my last hours to spending my remaining *soles* for silver. And when stores closed and I could shop no more, I went home to pack. At suppertime I went down to the *comedor* to look for my jolly Chilean friend, *Hector Enrique Alfredo Meirone*, and after visiting with him over coffee, he came to my room for a moment. But the "moment" lengthened out to hours as we talked about Chile and the states and the status of women. And he sucked a dozen cigarettes and thought of a dozen things to delay his going. And he held my hands and asked me not to forget him. And it was past midnight when he finally got around to ciao! But I didn't mind because I liked the snap in his eyes, and I found my Spanish flowered much more freely as the evening wore on. Besides he wasn't the aggressive sort. And what matter if I did have to get up at 5:00. I could sleep for a month when I returned to the States. And this was my last opportunity to talk with *Hector Enrique Alfredo*--.

November 7, 1942—Panama City—Hotel Colón—5 PM

But yesterday morning at 4:30 they roused me to say that Panagra was waiting! *Que cosa*! However, I needed only a few moments to dress and pack, and then I was riding away from Lima through the deserted, early morning streets. –Away from the City of Kings so steeped in the romance of the past. At *Limatambo* there was breakfast, and passport and baggage inspection, and waiting too. But at 6:30 all was ready, and once again I was flying through the air 180 miles per hour! Three days worth of cycling per hour! Ease and speed but not the intimate knowledge which comes of cycling. Only a superficial glimpse of the earth below. Leaving *Callao* we followed the coast northward. A desert coast. Bare earth and crescent sand dunes with desert hills rising in the east and the Pacific stretching away to the west. Sometimes beaches polkadotted the landscape. And sometimes river valleys converted the desert to garden. *Chicalayo*, where we stopped for a few moments was such a garden with trees and a patchwork of green fields. *Talara*, on the other hand, was desolate with yellow earth and oil wells and a small cluster of buildings below the bluff by the sea. Northward there was cloud and I drowsed, and when I again saw the earth, we were following the sluggish *Guayos* where it winds its way through patchy tropical vegetation. *Guayaquil* and heat and tropical enervation. Then north again over green cultivated earth and tropical verdure. Dinner was one of those amazing lap affairs, complete with avocado and lobster and chicken and apple pie! At about 2:00 we crossed the equator without knowing it, and again we were lost in the clouds. Again I drowsed, but I wakened with a start to find myself over Colombia where below was a paradise of green. Earth crumpled into mountains clothed in green fields and green plantations. Rivers lined with green vegetation. Houses amidst green banana trees. Green, green, green! Incredible that only a few hours ago we were flying over a desert! Looking back, the sunlight show on the water and revealed the fact that the green fields were

almost swamps so wet were they. This was the time of the
rainy season in Colombia. Further on the mountains flattened
out to form a valley, the valley of the *Cauca*, and in a moment
we were landing in *Cali*. Here we were destined to spend the
night, and as soon as we had passed through the formalities of
arriving in a new country and had been driven to our hotel, I
went out to see what Colombia might be like. And I found it
quite different from the countries to the south. Palms waved
in the air. Black people were numerous in the streets. Plants
grew luxuriantly. Trees with large orange flowers grew in the
park beside the river, and there was a delicate odor from some
flower I could not see. The town itself seemed ordinary, but
the greenness of its surroundings and the tropical *tempo* of its
life forever pressed in upon one's consciousness. Until dark I
walked the streets and then, lazy with the heat, I returned to
my comfortable room to bathe and rest before dinner. The
balance of the evening I spent in writing.

November 8, 1942—Guatemala City—Pensión Fernandez

Yesterday morning at 4:30 I was again roused from
the oblivion of a good bed, and by 6:00 we were at the airport
waiting for one of Panagra's silver ships to carry us speedily
on our way. But there were no bells of departure because a
persistent rain dimmed the skies and grayed the brilliance of
the green landscape. For hours we waited, but finally when
the weather lightened we took off, climbing up above the
clouds into the sunlight. Glimpses through the white puffs
below showed the greenness of the *Cauca* valley which we
followed for some time, flying over fields and neat towns. To
the north the earth became yellow, showing brilliantly in every
gash and scar and turning the muddy rivers to ribbons of
saffron. And then, little by little, hills crowded out the valley
and *selva* crowded over the hills. Up in the clouds my only
social diversion was a lesson in English delivered to a
Brazilian army officer! And I spent my time straining to see
the earth below. As we passed over Panama there was nothing
but jungle below—impenetrable, mysterious jungle.   A

veritable ocean of trees. But long before we reached the canal, our windows were curtained for military reasons, and even the jungle was left to our imagination. As I stepped out of the plane in *Balboa* there was a familiar something in the air. −A sluggish heat and a lackadaisical feel that made me know I was back in Panama. And passing customs made me realize I was in an important war zone. I had to dig out all my maps once again! And a man from the war dept. asked to interview me. He questioned me about Nazi activity in Chile and Argentina and I smiled to myself as I told him that he was asking confidential information of a person suspected of Nazi espionage! Panagra sent me immediately to the dept. of foreign relations to reclaim my $150 deposit, and then I made my way to *Hotel Colón* where I was lucky to get a room. But I was disappointed not to find *Moles* there. However, a mutual friend was in the diningroom, and he promised to carry my message to *Antonio*. Meanwhile I returned to Panagra to fix up my ticket north, and then I just wandered about the city indulging in *helados* and *piñas*! Panama hadn't changed a bit. The heat was still oppressive. The streets were still crowded with people of all colors. Laundries still hung from balconies. Harsh music still blared from open doors. Folks still moved with a don't-give-a-damn tempo. The lottery was still the principal business. The past year of my life suddenly became as nothing, and I felt as if I had never left Panama. And I was glad that my plane had been too late to make connections with the plane for Guatemala and that I had had to stay over, for I liked Panama just as I had liked it before. In the evening *Moles* called, and once again I went out with the professor. First we stopped for a *helado*, one of the tall elaborate kind which had become a tradition with us. And then we went to an "*acto*" commemorating the defense of Madrid. Here I met the rest of the crowd who had previously been at the *Colón*. And a long period of listening was broken only by the serving of whisky and sodas and cakes. Afterwards we went to *Balboa* for a drink and an interlude of conversation while we watched others dance. And still later we groped our way through the blackout to *Mole's* new home. He showed me all through what had once been the house of a wealthy man, now his quarters, and we stopped only when we reached the roof terrace and the freshness of the night and the solitude of the darkness. Romance in the darkness. Tender words. Pleas that I stay on in Panama. A proposal. And at 3:00 AM a snack in the kitchen—ginger ale, grapefruit, and *tamale*—before I returned to the *Colón* and a few hours of sleep before catching another plane.

November 9, 1942—Guatemala City—Pensión Fernandez

Yesterday morning, the 8th, I was up again at 6:00 getting ready to leave. Darns in my one and only pair of stockings, a handful of junk tossed into a red sock, breakfast, and I was ready. But Panagra's car didn't arrive, and I had to remind them to come and get me at the *Colón*. *Moles* waited for me at the airport, and after traveling so long alone, it was nice to have someone there to see me off. We both were wishing that the rain that delayed the takeoff would keep the plane another day in Panama. But shortly the clouds lightened, and we whirred away into the north. Again, blinds on the windows to keep us from seeing any of Panama's secrets. And when they were removed we were flying over the familiar woods and fields of the republic. For a while we followed the Atlantic side where mountains sent rivers down to the sea. And then the flatter Pacific side. Blinds on the windows marked the approach of another landing and when I stepped out of the plane I was in *David. David*! Memories of my first exciting days in the tropics when the year ahead was a mystery of unknown adventure. That mystery was reality now and again I was in *David*, living in the memory of the past rather than the anticipation of the future. Northward in Costa Rica we flew over *selva* again. And part of the time we followed the coast with its lovely green water and lines of white surf. Meandering streams, looping and curving as if reaching a destination were of no importance whatsoever. And farther north—large banana plantations carved out of the *bosque*. As we flew over the mountains – encircled valley that holds *San José*. The capital, the earth below became a magnificent patchwork of green fields. Lovely beyond measure. And then blinds again to take the joy out of life. From the airport in *San José* I could get some idea of the pretty countryside with its tropical plants and trees and some feeling of the blue mountains beyond. But this glimpse was not enough; I wanted to see ever so much more. Inside the station there was solace for my sorrow in the form of bananas, papaya, and orange juice, but I was still unhappy at the thought of flying away and leaving this new country unexplored. Northward we flew again over the beautiful cultivated valley. The hills with less and less agriculture. In Nicaragua there were vast be-jungled plains. And frequent volcanic cones, some of them quite perfect. From one a wisp of smoke rose upward to infer that all was not tranquil within. There we passed over a lake, an immense body of water lying close to the Pacific coast, and as we approached its northern end, blinds were put up to mark the approach to *Managua*. Damn the blinds! As we continued our way we passed over another lake, and then more hills and valleys carpeted with jungle. In Honduras there was a change in the character of the earth below. Hills were drier, vegetation sparser, and there were pine trees on the mountainsides. Bands of vertical rock showed where rivers had cut through ancient lava masses. As the plane set down in *Tegucigalpa*, the capital, we could see the red roofs of the city, but I was more intrigued by the roads running off into the beckoning distance. Yet another stop we made in San Salvador, and then on to Guatemala—with anticipation. Ice cream served on the plane! And at the station, 2 gardenias for every lady! Pan American's cars took us to our respective hotels, but mine was full, and the *dueño* sent me here to the *pensión*, a clean, quiet place with much tile and a patio full of plants and flowers. After dinner I hopped into bed, utterly weary from the previous day's dissipation. Knowing Guatemala could wait until the morrow.

November 10, 1942—Guatemala City—Pensión Fernandez (4 Calle, Poniente 1)—Midnight

And yesterday morning, after long hours of sleep had revived me, I was ready to go out and make the acquaintance of this nice land. Guatemala City—a clean active town with much of the feel of the towns at home in its substantial buildings. But with all of the picturesqueness of a far-away land in its Indian population. Good looking women walking barefooted and carrying great baskets on their heads—baskets of corn and cabbage and lettuce and loquats and chickens. Hand-woven skirts and bright belts wrapped around and around. Pretty blouses. Long braids of black hair plaited with bright ribbons! Fine, graceful women. Men, on the other hand, were more drab in their nondescript clothes and straw hats. And they wore shoes and never stooped to carry baskets on their heads, but they carried bales on their backs and drove loaded burros through the streets. Over all, both the city and the people, was an atmosphere of cleanliness that stood in vivid contrast to what I had known in Bolivia and Peru and Panama. But I was not free to just wander and speculate on Guatemala. There was business to be done. First to Pan American to talk about my ticket, thence to the police to register, and thence to the *Ministerio de Relaciones Exteriores* to leave my passport. Still more time I spent in *aduana* asking to bring my bike into the country, for I had discovered a *taller* who had said he could make for me the missing part of my Sturmey-Archer. And the balance of the morning I spent in looking at Indian things in shops too expensive to patronize but where I could get a fair idea of what was to be had. After lunch I went out to the airport to get Chester and I found to my dismay that my brake was bent, my chain was twisted, and my pump was missing. Great guns! –If this goes on I'll have no bike at all when I get home! But a kindly custom's official helped me straighten out the difficulties, and I delivered Chester into the keeping of the repairman, hoping with fingers crossed that he wouldn't muddle up my gears. From there my steps lead me to the *Mercado Central*, a building covering a whole block and devoted to the sale of everything under the sun. And the rest of the afternoon I spent shopping for *tejidos*, wandering fascinated from stall to stall. As I walked home along 6th Ave., I passed in front of the president's palace, and here they were making ready for a *fiesta* in honor of the president's birthday. What elaborate preparations! Streetlights were brilliant and ornate. Building fronts were decorated with many strings of various colored globes. The street was carpeted with pine needles. And chairs were set up in anticipation of after-dinner crowds. And I became one of 'em. With a couple of ladies from my *pensión* I went out to see the gaiety and listen to the music. Already the chairs were filled with eager folks, poor folks most of them, and the others were milling up and down the sidewalk, kept in constant motion by the police. We crowded along with the rest, but as we passed the orchestra, one of the ladies saw a friend there, and he managed to get 3 seats for me. *Buena suerte*! So we sat in state and listened to the music and watched the crowds and watched the various dignitaries who strode down to some official function within the president's house. But most impressive were the floral pieces that streamed in all evening. Elaborate plaques made of all kinds of flowers—hearts and stars and lyres and butterflies of roses and daisies and orchids and carnations. A magnificent tribute to a man who had really been a good president. We stayed for some time, and after we went home we could still hear the playing of music and the popping of fireworks until far, far into the night.

November 12, 1942—Mexico City—Hotel Ontario—9:00 PM

But that night's celebration was only a forerunner, for the 10th was the day of the president's birthday. And festivities commenced at 4:00 AM when the dawn was greeted with the playing of the national anthem. After breakfast I went immediately into the streets. Paused a moment to listen to the band and then walked on to 12th Ave. and the *cerrito del Carmen*. Here on the hilltop was an interesting old church, gray and stolid, and from its peaceful surroundings one could look out over the town and away to the mountains. Returning by another street, I discovered an open-air market that was a din of activity. Indian women and men sold from stalls and from heaps on the ground. Everything! Potatoes and onions and strange green vegetables. *Chiotes* and little red chilies. Tomatoes and peas. Bananas and melons and *chirimoyas*. Avocados. Black beans. Potted plants. Cheap clothing. Cheap drinks and snacks. Everything! And the place was jammed with salesmen and with people come to buy. From the market my steps lead me once again to the *Mercado Central*—that fascinating place where I always stop in to look at *tejidos* and leather articles and carved wood and from whence I always come away with something that I couldn't resist. In 6th Ave. I stopped again to listen to the band and I loitered with the crowds for so many people jammed the sidewalk that I felt sure something was going to happen. And sure enough. A ripple of applause ran down the crowd, and in came an Indian runner, carrying a smoking coal and panting for breath. He had come from the Mexican border. Others arrived later—lean brown men with knotty legs and stolid faces, all wearing red cloths over their heads, but some without shoes. They traveled with an easy trot, but there were other contestants who were walking, and speed had turned their gait into a painful forced thing. After dinner I was again in the streets, poking about, looking at the city. I walked through the two central parks that are lovely with trees and vines. I went into the cathedral too to see its plain white interior. Undecorated arches. But an angry lady in black invited me to leave because I had entered its holy portals with uncovered head. I left. And went around back to the market. But it was closed to the public while the *vendedores* held a *fiesta* within. Shops along the side were open, however, and once again I drifted from one to another looking at *tejidos*. Looking, looking, looking—but buying little because of limited space. In the street a crowd gathered about a drunken Indian woman who sat on the curb and shouted. The police came with a pushcart, lifted her in and rolled her unceremoniously away. One of the pathetic aspects of *fiesta* day. Back in the park I found it packed with people, common people, and little portable kitchens had been set up along one side. Fires burned, grease bubbled, grills kept food hot. There were *tamales* and doughnuts and *tortillas* for sale. And little counters were heaped with sweets, peanuts, and bright drinks. I, too, bought some of the strange foods just to be in Guatemalan style, for by now I'm quite convinced that my iron constitution can stand anything! I no sooner arrived back home than the Miss Thompson whom I had met the evening before suggested we go out and see the ceremony of taking the flag down. So out I went again back to 6th Ave and the president's house. Back to the crowding throngs and the band. And after the band had marched away I went with Miss Thompson to walk in the streets and to have ice cream down in 12th *Calle*. She, I learned, had come to Guatemala to write for a year. After supper in my *pensión*, I went out again to the festivities. Once again I was treated to a seat behind the orchestra, and until midnight I listened to the music, joked with the band members, watched the dignitaries pass in front, and marveled at the floral pieces that were still coming in. I even saw the brother of the president of Mexico arrive amidst great ovation! For these people love pomp and ceremony. And long after I returned home, I could still hear the music playing. A long *dia de fiesta*.

The 11th there was business to attend to. And in the morning I went out to see Panagra about my ticket, to collect my passport from the *Ministerio de Relaciones Exteriores*, and, best of all, to retrieve my bicycle. Gears again! I was delighted beyond measure to have the missing part replaced and to feel that once again I could travel anywhere. I bought a new pump too, cursing Pan American for the loss of the old one, and then I pedaled home in exhilaration. Once again, my Chester was whole! In the afternoon I couldn't rest from cycling. There was my bike, and the country was calling. So in spite of the fact that I was not supposed to use my bike in Guatemala, I found myself "back in the saddle again." Down to the *Hipodromo* first to see the large relief map of the country, and then around the town in a wide loop in search of a road out of the city. Just any road! For I must see what the country looked like. And I picked up the *carretera to Villa Nueva.* Satisfaction. Life was good out amongst the greenery of the country, out where tropical things were growing. But there was none of the lushness of Panama. Instead the landscape was relatively dry, perhaps because Guatemala had already entered her dry season. Moving along the road were numerous Indians, women in colorful costumes and carrying baskets and *ollas* on their heads and Indian men guiding their plodding oxen. And I found *Villa Nueva* to be a sleepy little town with mud walls and with a tremendous tree in the center of the *plaza.* Trees bore masses of yellow flowers. Women drew water from public wells. Banana fronds moved lazily in the hot air. It was charming. On the way back a truck driver asked me to ride, but I was too delighted with cycling to give it up. And even though I pedaled all the way, I reached town in time to bathe and change and reach the market before closing time. I just had to buy a few more things before leaving! But the evening brought a headache when I tried to squeeze my new purchases into already overstuffed saddlebags. It couldn't be done, but it had to be done. And I did it! Then I relaxed and visited with a Mrs. Crocker, mother of Pat who had done a whole series of Guatemalan Indians in watercolor. When I finally turned in it was late, too late for the early start that I must make in the morning.

November 13, 1942—Mexico City—Hotel Ontario—9:30 PM

And yesterday morning at 5:00 an alarm clock blasted me out of the peace of the night. Just time to dress and drink the thermos of coffee which the *señora* had left for me—and Pan American was calling at my door. But the *chofer* was taken aback to find a bicycle as part of my equipment! There was no room for such machines, and so I must pedal to the airport. And pedal I did—through the cold gray of the morning and a fine rain which wet me through and through. The first bad day I had had in Guatemala. Other passengers watched me curiously as I checked in, rain streaked and with bicycle pump in hand. But in spite of the fact that I carried most of my bicycle apparatus in my purse and in my hand, my bag had so increased in weight that I had to pay additional for it! Heck! As I flew away from Guatemala City, I looked down with regret on the green fields and hills which I knew only so slightly, and I vowed I'd return again one day on my bicycle. A fleeting panorama of wooded hills and cleared fields. Acres of the starry fronds of bananas. A crater lake. And then Guatemala was gone. At *Tapachula* we checked into Mexico—tropical southern Mexico where all was green and hot. And as we flew north the country below was still green. Then clouds shut out the earth and ours was a world of sunlight and puffy whiteness. Bumps in the clouds. And the passenger across the way ghostly white. Ahead a snow-crowned crater rose above the clouds into our world. *Orizaba*, highest of Mexico's volcanoes, rising in snowy splendor to 18,000 ft. Farther north the clouds thinned and we looked down on a different landscape. Gone the tropics. And below brown hills and fields. A sense of vastness in the land. Hills whose bare crowns seemed feather-stitched to the earth. Scant vegetation. A few *pueblos*. Northward *Popocatépetl* and *Ixtaccihuatl* came into view, high and white, the one a perfect cone, the other lovely and rugged. And we passed quite close. Then the mass of buildings which is Mexico City, and again we left the air for the more substantial earth. Customs, confusion, money exchange. Cars to the heart of the city. And I was relieved to have a room and solitude. A good meal to satiate the emptiness of the long hours since early morning, and I went out eagerly to see this new city of which I had heard so much. But I did no real sightseeing. Instead I wandered aimlessly which is the thing I like best to do. Just walked and looked—looked at the people, at the buildings, at the things for sale. And tried to get the spirit of the city, to feel its essence. I was surprised to find it so modern with fine buildings and busy streets. To be sure it is an old city. Carved facades and old doors testify to its antiquity. But these things are overshadowed by the power of the present day. And except for the straw hats and the sandals of the working classes, the people are prototypes of the people in the States. Skins are darker and eyes browner; all else is the same. Taken with a practical turn of mind, I shopped for footwear. Here amongst the Latins where the men look first at a woman's feet, I was more and more conscious of my shabby shoes and socks. So I decided to splurge, and I bought a pair of *huaraches* and 2 pairs of stockings! For supper I bought a collection of strange tropical fruits. And then I retired gratefully to a hot bath and bed.

November 14, 1942—Mexico City—Hotel Ontario—8 PM

Yesterday, the 13th, I set out in earnest to see *Mexico City*, and all day long I rambled from one point of interest to another. Through *Zocalo*, which is now very familiar because it is so near the hotel, and into the cathedral. Here the interior is confused with a choir occupying the center, and the edifice lacks the religious dignity which a long nave gives. Outside, the gray towers are more impressive and at the side, the carved stones of the façade of the *sagrado* is very lovely. The National Palace, a long official-looking building contains a maze of patios and corridors, and over the door hangs Mexico's liberty bell. But of primary interest are the frescoes of *Diego Rivera*. Done with smooth bright colors and with smooth, simplified figures, they depict Mexico's history—the conquest and the revolution. The degeneration of the church and the spread of communism are there too. Powerful figures. But one must study each group by itself in order to appreciate it. Otherwise the whole is nothing but a jumble. From the National Palace I went around the corner to the museums. From frescoes to monoliths in half a block! And the monoliths were truly fine. Exquisite carved stone. If the Incas were masters of masonry, the Aztecs were masters of decoration. Nature simplified in the imagination and adapted to stone. Beautiful tracery. Figures admirably suited to occupy their place in the design. Great blocks of stone and small ones, square ones and round ones—all decorated with great skill. And there were figures too—figures of gods and

figures of snakes. Heavy stone wrought into heavy idols—
heavy as stone should be. Upstairs in the museum were other
things—jade and pottery and carved wood, but these were
dwarfed by the monoliths, and I passed quickly for I have a
special distaste for endless rows of museum cases. At 2:00 I
realized I was hungry and I went in search of a Mexican
restaurant. At *Mittas*, I found it, and here in a room over-
decorated with "Mexican touches" I ate a Mexican meal in
solitary splendor. Costumed waitresses, a dull light, a guitar
and songs. And *puchero* with fried bananas! *Bien Mexican*!
In the afternoon I walked through the *Alameda* and down
Paseo de La Reforma. Past the large bronze of Charles IV and
past the statue of the *Aztec Cuanhtemacalong,* the broad tree-
lined drive that is Mexico City's best. A detour to the govt.
touring office yielded an armful of tourist propaganda, and
another to the home of *Mole's* friend *Rosa* netted a sociable
conversation with the vivacious *señora*. Then, as the sun set, I
continued down the *Paseo de la Reforma*—clear to its end in
the woods of *Chapultapec Park*. It was late now and almost
dark, but the *teniente* at the gate offered to walk to the top of
the hill with me if I wished. And I wished! So we climbed up
under the dark branches of many trees, and from the terrace of
the building at the top we looked out across the lights of the
city. A beautiful night with a young moon—too young to
penetrate the depth of the woods surrounding the hill. When
we came back down, the *teniente* put me on my streetcar, and
with a warm handshake sent his *saludos* to fellow *tenientes* in
the states. Just another bit of the innate Latin courtesy that
makes me so fond of these people of the south. From the
Alameda I walked back home, looking at the windows full of
silver and *serapes* and stopping for a supper of *helados*. Then
up to my room to wash and write and sleep. A long day
whose passing gave me the satisfaction of knowing a little of
Mexico City.

November 15, 1942—Mexico City—Hotel Ontario

The 14th I went early to the market of *La Merced*, and down there in the old section of the city. I found a confusion such as I had never seen before! For blocks the streets in all directions were lined with stalls and counters, and mobs of shoppers jammed the streets and sidewalks. Every imaginable sort of fruit and vegetable was for sale, a fresh and colorful display that revealed the versatility of the Mexican earth. Little brown men straining under bunches of bananas and crates of vegetables shouted "*golpe*" to clear a path through the crowds. For an hour I loitered and looked, and then as offices opened, I went back to the center, stopping at Sanbourn's House of Tile for café. Money had to be changed at the bank, and a package left at the post office and then I wandered at will, looking up special points of interest. The National Express Office, an old colonial building with a fine carved stone façade. The Aztec ruins, walls excavated near the cathedral. The university. And the Ministry of Education where I spent a very long time looking at the *Rivera* frescos decorating the walls of the two large patios. Indians working the fields. Indians fighting. And Indians exploited by the conquerors. To reassure myself in the matter of transportation to *Taxco*, I walked down to the office and as I returned, I passed the *Hospitál de Jesus*, oldest on the continent, and the *Palacio del Conde de Santiago* with its very large and ornate carved wood doors. Then I purchased some red bananas and bread for supper and breakfast, and this completed my business for the day! The rest of the time I just poked around. After a long Mexican dinner at *Tacuba Café*, I sat in the *Alameda* until a couple of fellows annoyed me and sent me on my way. I hunted out the *Quetzalcoatl Palace* to inquire about rooms of the talkative landlady. I window-shopped along *Av. Juarez*. I went into the elegant Palace of Fine Arts to see a special exhibition. And I looked up relatives of the Guatemalan consul of B.A. Then I went early to bed in anticipation of 2 days of no-stop living.

And this day, the 15th, was even longer than I had anticipated! At 5:00 I was wakened, and after a hurried breakfast of bread and bananas, I went off in the dark to catch my bus to *Taxco*. But all the seats on the early bus were taken, and I had to wait 2 hrs! I tried to improve my time by writing, but the people in the station kept me pretty well distracted. At 8:00 I finally got under way, and in a thick blanket of fog I rolled out of Mexico City. On the roads men were marching, hundreds of them. Civilians using their Sunday leisure to learn the art of war. Leaving the valley of Mexico, we wound out of the fog and up into wooded hills where we shared the sunshine with "Popo" and "Sleeping Woman." Pine woods. And hills with a feeling of home. Then down to *Cuernavaca*, village of red roofs and an intimate, shady plaza. Continuing on to *Taxco* we passed many, many flowering trees—trees with myriad of white, moon-like flowers, lovely beside the sky-blue of roadside morning glories. Many more hills, and then *Taxco*. Here I found myself in a hillside town with narrow, roughly cobbled streets, tall church towers, and a jumble of red tile roofs and white walls clamoring up the mountainside. All was brilliant and warm under cloudless skies. Aimless steps lead me almost unconsciously to the market where there were several levels of stalls of dry goods and heaps of fruits and vegetables. And later I poked about the silver and shoe shops and followed precipitous lanes up the hillsides. *Taxco* is picturesque, but it has learned the ways of the tourist, and its picturesqueness is now an expression of tourism instead of anything innate in the lives of the people. For dinner I found a hotel with a view across the red roofs of the *pueblo* and the canyon beyond. And then, lazy after my good meal, I joined the Sunday crowds in the shade of the *plaza*. Dark men in white suits. Straw hats with strings tied in back. Old men come out for a walk! Pretty girls come out to be looked at but always carefully guarded by their mothers. A dimpled Indian coquette holding hands with a farmer boy. All the life of *Cuzco* milling about the plaza. And because a new shoe had made a cripple out of me, I sat and watched most of the afternoon. At 5:00, I went to catch my bus, but the darn thing didn't come, and again I waited for 2 hrs.! Such is life in the Latin style! Riding back to the capitol I had a Swiss seatmate, and this time passed pleasantly. But I arrived very late, and then I had to pack for an early start next day. How to reorganize my baggage so as not to pay overweight, that was the problem! I would carry a box and my tools in my purse. I would carry my books and a wool blanket in my hands. And I would carry a red bandanna of extras in my hands also. Perhaps I'd get by!

December 7, 1942—Porterville—Home

In the early black of the morning of the 16th I was again wakened, and shortly, I heard the familiar sound of "*Panagra, la espera.*" My fingers were crossed as I weighed in, but all went smoothly. No charge for overweight! And in a moment I was soaring into the air on the last lap of my long, long journey. A last look at the white buildings of Mexico City and its neighboring shallow lake, and we headed northward. Northward over broad valleys and sharp hills and many bodies of water. In the neighborhood of *Guadalajara* we lost the valleys, and the scene below became a jumble of blue mountains. And then at *Mazatlan* there was heat and a carpet of vegetation which gave the feeling that this perhaps was the last outpost of the tropics. Farther northward the vegetation thinned to scattered bushes and then was gone, and below was only bare brown earth and bare brown hills. We could see the Gulf of California as we followed its coast northward. Armies of crescent dunes marched away to the east. And then we passed near the mouth of the Colorado where it empties its muddy waters into the Gulf. Near Mexicali there were green fields where the desert was irrigated and as we flew into Imperial Valley we caught a glimpse of the Salton Sea. Then the blinders were put up to keep us from seeing the war secrets of the States, and we continued on to Burbank in a total black out. At Burbank, I stepped again on U.S. territory for the first time in nearly a year, but there was none of the spirit of the "land of the free" in my return. All of us passengers were hustled into a waiting room where we were held as virtual prisoners until the authorities had satisfied themselves that it was safe to let us enter. Panagra employees served us cider and cookies, and were all solicitude and service as they tried to allay the passengers' irritation at being detained. One man could not go and greet his family who waited outside. I was not permitted to phone Mrs. King, but had to transmit my messages through an employee. Meanwhile we were given lengthy blanks to fill out. Who were we, who were all our family? What stock and bonds did we possess; what was our income? What schools had we attended; what were our special skills? –And, heaven forbid, had we ever been jailed in a foreign country! I was honest because I knew I was known here, and I was convinced of official suspicion when I was held until the very last in the thought that mine would be a long investigation. A stern, uniformed man checked my baggage, and he left no stone unturned! I had to bring out and open every thing I possessed! With a gleam of hope in his eye he looked into my bulging purse, and asked what was in the box inside--. Pills and pins, *no mas,* I showed him with exaltation! And then there was my tool kit with the suspicious tire repair box. And an ear of Peruvian corn! Together we emptied every thing out, and he felt around inside to be sure I hadn't forgotten anything. At last he was convinced. And my heart settled down to normal; for beneath the lining of that purse was $100 in cash— contraband! From amongst my shabby possessions he sorted out my 4 ears of corn, the pod of a *palobarracho* from *Tucuman,* and all of my diaries, books, maps, letters, photographs and scratch paper! These would be censored before I could have them! Then I waited for my turn at questioning. Through a small, soundproof window I could see the others go up, one at a time. But I must wait until last and I knew it without being told. Waiting, waiting, waiting. I finished the cookies. And I packed Chester ready for travel. And I waited. Finally I was called, "Miss Richardson, please," and I wondered what this last investigation would involve. Surrounded by 3 officials, I answered the same old questions—questions directed towards finding out if I had any totalitarian ancestors, if I was subsidized by Hitler or Hirohito, if I had ever been active in peace demonstrations, if I was really what I said I was--. At long last I was permitted to go, and I went back to Chester and pedaled away into the night.

And so ended my third great adventure—perhaps the best of them all because it was the longest. For a whole year I had lived a happy, irresponsible life, pedaling from one country to another and living with the constant joy of activity, the beauty of an ever-changing landscape, the warmth of a stranger's hospitality. And I loved it all! There was bitterness in my defeat in Montevideo, but I returned to the States satisfied to have added twelve months of vivid recollections to my life. The future is dull, disconsolate---Interminable war---. But few people have the beauty of a year such as mine to look back upon when spirits ebb low--.